A HISTORY OF IRAQ
THIRD EDITION

To understand Iraq, Charles Tripp's history is the book to read. Since its first appearance in 2000, it has become a classic in the field of Middle East studies, read and admired by students, soldiers, policy-makers, journalists and all those seeking to make sense of what has gone wrong in this troubled country. The book is now updated to include the events of the last few years: the American invasion, the fall and capture of Saddam Husain and the subsequent descent into civil strife. What is clear is that much that has happened since 2003 could have been predicted, and in fact was foreshadowed in the account found in the pages of this book. Tripp's thesis is that the history of Iraq throughout the twentieth century has made it what it is today, but also provides alternative futures. Unless this is properly understood, many of the themes explored in this book – patron–client relations, organised violence, sectarian, ethnic and tribal difference – will continue to exert a hold over the future of Iraq as they did over its past. There is much to learn here, and there can be few books which tell this sad story to such effect.

CHARLES TRIPP is Professor of Politics in the Middle East at the School of Oriental and African Studies, University of London. His publications include *Islam and the Moral Economy: The Challenge of Capitalism* (2006), *Iran–Saudi Arabia Relations and Regional Order* (with S. Chubin, 1996) and *Iran and Iraq at War* (1988).

A HISTORY OF IRAQ

Third Edition

CHARLES TRIPP

School of Oriental and African Studies, University of London

CAMBRIDGE
UNIVERSITY PRESS

CAMBRIDGE
UNIVERSITY PRESS

University Printing House, Cambridge CB2 8BS, United Kingdom

One Liberty Plaza, 20th Floor, New York, NY 10006, USA

477 Williamstown Road, Port Melbourne, VIC 3207, Australia

4843/24, 2nd Floor, Ansari Road, Daryaganj, Delhi - 110002, India

79 Anson Road, #06-04/06, Singapore 079906

Cambridge University Press is part of the University of Cambridge.

It furthers the University's mission by disseminating knowledge in the pursuit of education, learning and research at the highest international levels of excellence.

www.cambridge.org
Information on this title: www.cambridge.org/9780521702478

First edition published 2000
Second edition 2002
Third edition 2007
Third printing 2010

A catalogue record for this publication is available from the British Library

ISBN 978-0-521-70247-8 Paperback

Cambridge University Press has no responsibility for the persistence or accuracy of URLs for external or third-party internet websites referred to in this publication, and does not guarantee that any content on such websites is, or will remain, accurate or appropriate. Information regarding prices, travel timetables, and other factual information given in this work is correct at the time of first printing but Cambridge University Press does not guarantee the accuracy of such information thereafter.

For Venetia

Contents

List of illustrations   x
Chronology   xii
Glossary   xx
List of abbreviations   xxii
Map 1 Iraq: principal towns   xxiv
Map 2 Basra, Kuwait and the Shatt al-'Arab   xxv
Map 3 Iraq and the Middle East   xxvi
Map 4 Kurdish Iraq   xxvii

Introduction   1

1 The Ottoman provinces of Baghdad, Basra and Mosul   8
   Power in the three provinces   8
   The Ottoman 'reconquest' of the three provinces   13
   Sultan Abdulhamid II and the Young Turks   19
   The Committee of Union and Progress
   and its opponents   23

2 The British Mandate   30
   British occupation and reactions   31
   The Iraqi revolt of 1920   39
   The institutional definition of the state   44
   Mandate and treaty   51
   The Mosul question: territory and oil   57
   Different communities, different purposes, different histories   59
   Emerging trends in politics and the economy   63

3 The Hashemite monarchy 1932–41   75
   Communal identities and tribal unrest   77
   Social criticism and political conspiracy   82
   The coup d'état of 1936   86
   Military politics: pan-Arabism and army conspiracies   91

Iraq in the Second World War   97
The coup d'état of 1941 and the British military occupation   100

4 The Hashemite monarchy 1941–58   105
   Re-establishing the regime   107
   Thwarted liberalisation   111
   Foreign policies: Arab issues, Palestine and the Portsmouth Treaty   115
   Economic development and party politics   123
   Nuri al-Saʿid: the politics of reform and repression   127
   Nuri al-Saʿid: foreign initiatives and domestic challenges   134
   The coup d'état of 1958   139

5 The republic 1958–68   143
   ʿAbd al-Karim Qasim: dictatorship and disillusion   144
   Iraqi foreign policy under Qasim   157
   The politics of conspiracy and the coup d'état of February 1963   161
   Baʿthist control and loss of control in 1963   164
   ʿAbd al-Salam ʿArif: Nasserist aspirations and Iraqi realities   169
   Patrimonialism and the rule of the clan   175
   ʿAbd al-Rahman ʿArif: a weakening hold on power   178

6 The Baʿth and the rule of Saddam Husain 1968–2003   186
   Ahmad Hasan al-Bakr and the consolidation of power   187
   Kurdish and Shiʿi challenges and relations with Iran   192
   Economic patronage, political control and foreign policy alignments   197
   War in Kurdistan   203
   Oil revenues, foreign policies and the rise of Saddam Husain   206
   Saddam Husain's presidency and the war with Iran in 1980   215
   Defending the regime and Iraq after 1982   226
   A war of attrition 1984–8   230
   Resistance amongst the Kurds and the Shiʿa   234
   The aftermath of war and the invasion of Kuwait 1988–90   239
   The war for Kuwait and the uprisings of 1991   244
   Iraq under sanctions and the long aftermath of the Gulf war   250
   Kurdish autonomy and Kurdish politics   254
   The 'shadow state' in Iraq   259
   War and the fall of Saddam Husain   267

7 The American occupation and the parliamentary republic   277
   The rule of the Coalition Provisional Authority (CPA)   278
   New institutions and old politics   292
   Insurgency, sectarianism and the spectre of civil war   303

Conclusion   317

Notes   323
Bibliography   336
Further reading and research   344
Index   349

Illustrations

1. Sayyid Talib al-Naqib, c. 1912. A. T. Wilson, *Loyalties: Mesopotamia 1914–1917* (London, 1930)   25
2. Shaikh Mahmud, 1920. A. T. Wilson, *Mesopotamia 1917–1920: a clash of loyalties* (London, 1931)   35
3. Sir Percy Cox, c. 1918. A. T. Wilson, *Loyalties: Mesopotamia 1914–1917* (London, 1930)   37
4. Gertrude Bell, c. 1921. Lady Gertrude Bell (sel. and ed.), *The Letters of Gertrude Bell*, vol. II (London, 1927)   38
5. Sayyid ʿAbd al-Rahman al-Kailani, c. 1920. A. T. Wilson, *Mesopotamia 1917–1920: a clash of loyalties* (London, 1931)   46
6. King Faisal I, c. 1932. © Popperfoto   49
7. King Ghazi, c. 1933. © Popperfoto   79
8. Nuri al-Saʿid, 1956. © Popperfoto   121
9. Prince ʿAbd al-Ilah and King Faisal II, 1953. © Popperfoto   129
10. General ʿAbd al-Karim Qasim, 1961. © Popperfoto   145
11. President ʿAbd al-Salam ʿArif, c. 1964. © epa/Afp   170
12. President ʿAbd al-Rahman ʿArif, 1968. © Popperfoto   180
13. President Ahmad Hasan al-Bakr, c. 1970. © Rob Walls   188
14. Mustafa Barzani, c. 1973. © Chris Kutschera   192
15. Jalal Talabani, 1996. © Popperfoto   205
16. Ayatollah Sayyid Muhammad Baqir al-Sadr, c. 1978.   213
17. President Saddam Husain, 1995. © Popperfoto   215
18. Masoud Barzani, 1996. © Popperfoto   220
19. Ayatollah Sayyid Abu al-Qasim al-Khoʾi, c. 1985. Photo courtesy of the Imam al-Khoʾi Foundation   247
20. President Saddam Husain and family c. 1989. © Popperfoto   262
21. President Saddam Husain and family portrayed in 1996. © Popperfoto   263
22. L. Paul Bremer III, 2003 © AFP/Getty Images.   282

23. Ayatollah Sayyid ʿAli al-Sistani poster, 2005. © Wathiq
    Khuzaie/Getty Images   284
24. Sayyid Muqtada al-Sadr, 2005. © Mohamed Messara/
    epa/Corbis   294
25. Ibrahim al-Jaʿfari, Nuri al-Maliki and Sayyid ʿAbd al-ʿAziz
    al-Hakim, 2006. © Thaier Al-Sudani/Reuters   302
26. Saddam Husain on trial, 2005. © John Moore/POOL/
    epa/Corbis   313

Chronology

1831 Ottoman reconquest of Baghdad: capture of the last *mamluk* governor

1908 Young Turk revolution in Istanbul

1909 Sultan Abdulhamid II deposed

1914 November: British occupation of Basra

1917 March: British occupation of Baghdad

1918 November: British occupation of Mosul

1920 April: San Remo meeting assigns Mandate for Iraq to United Kingdom
July–October: Iraqi revolt
November: Sayyid 'Abd al-Rahman al-Kailani forms first Iraqi government

1921 March: Cairo Conference decides on Prince Faisal bin Husain al-Hashemi as king of Iraq
August: enthronement of King Faisal in Baghdad

1924 March: Constituent Assembly opens
June: Anglo-Iraqi Treaty passed

1925 March: Iraqi government signs Turkish Petroleum Company oil concession
December: League of Nations decides that Mosul should remain part of Iraq

1927 First major oil finds near Kirkuk

1930 June: new Anglo-Iraqi Treaty signed promising Iraqi independence

1932 October: League of Nations ends Mandate and grants independence to Iraq

1933 September: King Faisal dies; King Ghazi succeeds

1935 January: official opening of Kirkuk – Mediterranean pipeline

1936 October: military coup d'état, backed by General Bakr Sidqi; Hikmat Sulaiman forms a government

1937 August: Bakr Sidqi assassinated; Hikmat Sulaiman overthrown by army

1939   April: King Ghazi killed in car accident; succeeded by infant son, Faisal II, under regency of Prince ʿAbd al-Ilah

1941   April: military coup d'état: 'Government of National Defence' formed by Rashid ʿAli al-Kailani; regent flees Baghdad
May: British troops march on Baghdad; collapse and flight of Rashid ʿAli al-Kailani's government
June: regent returns to Baghdad

1948   January: new Anglo-Iraqi Treaty signed at Portsmouth; mass protests in Baghdad – known as *al-Wathba* (the leap); treaty abandoned
May: Iraq sends expeditionary force to Palestine

1949   February: Iraqi army withdraws from Palestine

1952   February: Iraqi agreement with Iraq Petroleum Company (IPC) on 50–50 share of profits
November–December: demonstrations erupt in Baghdad – known as *al-Intifada* (the uprising)

1953   May: King Faisal II enthroned; regency ends

1955   February: formation of Baghdad Pact

1956   October: Suez Crisis; riots in Baghdad, Mosul and Najaf

1958   February: formation of United Arab Republic (Egypt and Syria); Jordan and Iraq form Arab Union
July: military coup d'état in Baghdad; monarchy overthrown and republic established; Brigadier ʿAbd al-Karim Qasim becomes prime minister, minister of defence and commander in chief
September: Agrarian Reform Law

1959   October: Mustafa Barzani asserts his control of Kurdistan Democratic Party (KDP)
December: Iraq withdraws from Baghdad Pact

1961   June: Kuwaiti independence; Qasim demands its integration into Iraq; Great Britain sends troops to Kuwait, replaced by Arab League force in August
July: Barzani demands substantial autonomy for Kurdish region
September: fighting in Kurdistan between Barzani's forces and Iraqi army
December: Law 80 reclaims unexploited areas of IPC's concession

1963   February: military coup d'état by Baʿthist and Arab nationalist officers; Qasim and colleagues killed
October–November: splits and confusion in the Baʿth
November: President ʿAbd al-Salam ʿArif and military allies eject Baʿthists from power

1964   July: nationalisation of all banks, insurance companies and large
        industrial firms; further land reform
        October: Kurdish autonomy talks break down and fighting resumes
1965   April: full-scale war in Kurdistan
        September: ʿAbd al-Rahman al-Bazzaz appointed prime minister
1966   April: death of ʿAbd al-Salam ʿArif in helicopter crash; succeeded by
        his brother ʿAbd al-Rahman ʿArif
        July: Barzani accepts al-Bazzaz's twelve-point programme on
        Kurdish autonomy
        August: ʿArif dismisses al-Bazzaz
1967   June: war with Israel; Iraq sends token force to Jordan
1968   17 July: military coup d'état by Arab nationalist and Baʿthist army
        officers; ʿAbd al-Rahman ʿArif sent into exile; Ahmad Hasan al-
        Bakr becomes president
        30 July: Baʿthist military coup d'état organised by al-Bakr ousts
        non-Baʿthist allies
1969   June: major agreement between Iraq and USSR on Soviet assistance
        in exploiting Iraqi oil fields
        November: Saddam Husain appointed to ruling Revolutionary
        Command Council (RCC) and becomes its vice-chairman
1970   March: manifesto on Kurdistan, granting limited autonomy;
        Barzani calls cease-fire
        May: land reform measures
        July: new provisional constitution recognises Kurdish nationalism
1971   November: relations between Iraq and Iran severed
1972   April: Iraq and USSR sign fifteen-year Iraq–USSR Treaty of
        Friendship and Co-operation
        June: IPC nationalised
        November–December: fighting in northern Kurdistan
1973   July: failed coup attempt by Kazzar; al-Bakr and Saddam Husain
        reinforce their hold on the state
        October: limited Iraqi participation in war with Israel
1974   March: Autonomy Law for Kurdish areas announced despite con-
        tinuing disagreement between government and KDP; widespread
        fighting throughout Kurdistan
1975   March: Algiers Agreement between Saddam Husain and shah of
        Iran ends Iranian assistance to KDP; Kurdish revolt collapses
        June: Kurdish movement split; KDP–Provisional Leadership led by
        Masoud Barzani, and Patriotic Union of Kurdistan (PUK), led by
        Jalal Talabani

1977   February: 30,000 process from Najaf to Karbala; called the Safar *intifada*, it becomes a general anti-government protest

1978   October: expulsion of Ayatollah Khomaini from Iraq
        November: Baghdad Summit following Camp David accords marks Iraqi bid for Arab leadership

1979   Spring: success of Iranian revolution encourages Shi'i Islamist organisations to launch more active campaign in Iraq
        July: al-Bakr resigns; Saddam Husain immediately sworn in as president; purge of RCC and Ba'th Party
        November: KDP Congress elects Masoud Barzani as chairman and calls for continuing armed struggle inside Iraq

1980   March: law for election of National Assembly in Iraq
        April: Ayatollah al-Sadr and his sister, Bint al-Huda, executed in Baghdad; over 40,000 Shi'a expelled to Iran
        September: Iraqi forces invade Iran

1982   June–July: Iran's counteroffensive recaptures most of its territory; 9th Regional Congress of Ba'th Party reasserts Saddam Husain's absolute control
        Autumn: sudden death of former president Ahmad Hasan al-Bakr

1984   Escalation of war in the waters of the Gulf
        Iraq re-establishes diplomatic relations with United States

1986   Iran captures al-Faw peninsula

1987   Iraqi government campaign against KDP and PUK in Kurdistan

1988   February: beginning of *al-Anfal* in Kurdistan
        July: Iran accepts UN cease-fire resolution; war with Iraq ends

1990   August: Iraq invades and annexes Kuwait; UN imposes total trade embargo and sanctions on Iraq

1991   January: 'Desert Storm' begins: air bombardment of Iraq by US-led allied forces leading to liberation of Kuwait by allied forces in February
        March: eruption and crushing of *al-Intifada*, uprisings against Iraqi regime in Shi'i south and Kurdish north
        April: UN Security Council Resolution 687 – demands Iraqi recognition of Kuwait and destruction of all Iraq's non-conventional weapons, and affirms that economic sanctions would continue until full compliance; 'safe haven' established in northern Iraq, effectively placing most of Kurdistan under allied protection; Resolution 688 calls on Iraqi government to stop oppressing its own people
        May: first visit of United Nations Special Commission on Disarmament (UNSCOM) weapons inspection team
        October: Iraqi armed forces blockade Kurdistan

1992 May: elections in Kurdish zone: more or less equal balance between
      KDP and PUK
      July: Kurdish Regional Government formed by both parties, but in
      effect two parallel administrations created, running separate areas
1993 May: UN Security Council approves demarcation of Iraq–Kuwait
      border in Kuwait's favour
      June: United States launches missile strike on headquarters of Iraqi
      intelligence services in Baghdad in reprisal for Iraqi plot to kill
      President Bush during his visit to Kuwait
      October–November: Iraqi forces launch campaign against inhabi-
      tants of marshes in south of Iraq and finalise plans for draining of
      marshes
1994 May–August: open fighting between KDP and PUK
      October–November: Iraqi threats to Kuwait lead to crisis and even-
      tual Iraqi recognition of Kuwait as an independent state
1996 February: Iraq finally accepts UN Security Council Resolution
      986 allowing limited Iraqi oil sales for purchase of vital civilian
      supplies
      August: Iraqi government forces enter Kurdish region at invitation
      of KDP and help to capture Arbil from PUK; United States
      responds by launching missile attacks on southern Iraq and extend-
      ing southern no-fly zone north to 33rd parallel
      December: Iraqi oil flows again through pipeline to Turkey; Iraq
      returns to world oil market as a producer
1998 September: Washington Agreement ends fighting between KDP
      and PUK
      November: Iraq Liberation Act passed by US Congress
      December: 'Operation Desert Fox', air bombardment of Iraq by US
      Air Force and Royal Air Force in retaliation for Iraqi non-cooperation
      with weapons inspections; Iraq ceases all co-operation forthwith
1999 January–December: weekly attacks by American and British planes
      on Iraqi forces challenging their right to overfly Iraqi territory in
      southern and northern no-fly zones
      December: UN Security Council Resolution 1284 offering to
      suspend sanctions if Iraq cooperates with a new weapons inspection
      regime for 120 days; new weapons inspection agency set up –
      UNMOVIC. Iraq rejects the resolution and refuses to allow
      UNMOVIC into Iraq
2000 March: Iraq defies UN ban on civil air flights and organises flights
      of pilgrims to Mecca

September: Baghdad airport reopens. Much-publicised flights arrive from Russia, France, Syria and other countries

November: domestic civil flights resume within Iraq

2001   January: Masoud Barzani (KDP) and Jalal Talabani (PUK) meet for first time in three years

February: extensive American and British air strikes against air defence systems around Baghdad

May–July: UK and United States try and fail to persuade UN Security Council to adopt 'smart sanctions' resolution

August: extensive American and British air strikes against air defence systems in southern Iraq

October: KDP–PUK cooperation proceeds. PUK forces in armed combat with Kurdish Islamist group Jund al-Islam

November: UN Security Council Resolution 1382 renews six-month 'oil for food' arrangement and opens way for possible reform of sanctions regime and return of weapons inspectors

2002   January: US President Bush identifies Iraq as part of an 'axis of evil'

March: public Iraqi reconciliation with Saudi Arabia at Arab League Summit in Beirut

June: President Bush and staff finalise war plans against Iraq

October: US Congress passes resolution authorising use of military force against Iraq

November: UN Security Council Resolution 1441: requires Iraq to re-admit weapons inspectors of UNMOVIC. Iraq accepts

2003   January: General Garner appointed to head Office of Reconstruction and Humanitarian Assistance to rule Iraq after invasion

February–March: US and UK try and fail to obtain UN SC resolution explicitly authorising the use of force against Iraq

March: 'Operation Iraq Freedom' launched by US, UK and allied forces to overthrow Saddam Husain and occupy Iraq

April: Basra, Baghdad and Mosul fall to allied forces; Saddam Husain flees into hiding; widespread looting and destruction of government buildings

May: Paul Bremer replaces Garner as chief US authority in Iraq, heading the Coalition Provisional Authority (CPA): dissolution of Ba'th Party and of Iraqi armed forces; UN SC Resolution 1483 grants US and UK power to govern Iraq and ends thirteen-year sanctions regime

July: CPA sets up Iraqi Governing Council with limited powers; US military command admits it is facing 'guerrilla war' in Iraq

August: UN headquarters in Baghdad blown up; Ayatollah Baqir al-Hakim (head of SCIRI) assassinated

October: sectarian violence in Baghdad; inter-ethnic violence in Kirkuk

November: US creates timetable for handover of power to Iraqi government

December: capture of Saddam Husain

2004   March: IGC approves draft provisional constitution (Law of Administration for the State of Iraq for the Transitional Period [TAL])

April–May: fierce fighting between US forces and insurgents in Fallujah; US and Mahdi Army forces clash in Najaf

June: CPA and IGC dissolved and sovereignty handed to an interim government, headed by prime minister Ayad ʿAllawi

August: US forces fight Mahdi Army in Najaf

November: US and Iraqi forces attack insurgents in Fallujah – widespread destruction

2005   January: general elections for the transitional national assembly charged with drafting a new constitution, boycotted by Sunni Arabs: United Iraqi Alliance ('Shiʿi list') wins overall majority; elections for Kurdish Regional Assembly dominated by KDP and PUK

April: Ibrahim al-Jaʿfari of UIA becomes prime minister and forms government; Jalal Talabani elected president of Iraq

August: constitutional committee presents draft constitution to assembly which submits it to a plebiscite

October: constitutional plebiscite approves constitution by 78% to 22% – Shiʿi and Kurdish provinces vote in favour, Sunni Arab provinces against; trial of Saddam Husain and associates begins

December: general elections for national assembly: UIA largest single bloc, but no overall majority

2006   February: al-Askariyya mosque in Samarra blown up; sectarian conflict intensifies

April: Jalal Talabani sworn in as president of Iraq

May: Nuri al-Maliki of UIA forms new government

July: British authorities hand over Muthanna province to Iraqi control

September: Italian forces hand over Dhi Qar province to Iraqi control

October: national assembly passes law allowing groups of provinces to form federated states

November: Saddam Husain sentenced to death by Iraqi High Tribunal

December: Saddam Husain executed; death toll of US forces since 2003 reaches 3,000; UN estimates over 100 Iraqi civilians die violently every day

2007   January: draft law allowing foreign investment and participation in Iraqi oil industry put before national assembly

February: US sends 28,000 extra troops to Iraq to implement new security plan for Baghdad

Glossary

agha	Kurdish chieftain
amir	prince
al-Anfal	literally, 'the spoils of war', and the title of the eighth *sura* of the Qur'an; the codename given by the Iraqi authorities to their forces' operations in Kurdistan in 1988
ashraf (sing. *sharif*)	descendants of the Prophet Muhammad
naqib al-ashraf	senior descendant of the Prophet Muhammad in a community
'Ashura	tenth day of month of Muharram, held in special reverence by Shi'i Muslims since it commemorates the death of Imam Husain in 680 CE at Karbala
'atabat	literally, 'thresholds' or 'doorways'; denoting Holy Cities of Shi'ism in Iraq: Najaf, Karbala, al-Kazimiyya, Samarra
ayatollah	literally, 'sign from God'; an honorific title for senior Shi'i clerics
fatwa	a formal opinion or judgement delivered by an expert in the *Shari'a*
fiqh	Islamic jurisprudence
hajj	Muslims' annual pilgrimage to Mecca
hawza	short for *al-hawza al-'ilmiyya* – 'the seat of knowledge', meaning the Shi'i clerical establishment
iltizam	tax-farming or tax-gathering concession
jahsh	literally, 'little donkeys'; derisory term used about the National Defence Battalions, Kurdish tribal irregulars employed by the Ba'thist government
jihad	war against unbelievers according to the *shari'a*
mamluk	member of a military elite, originally a slave

xx

marja' al-taqlid	literally, 'source of emulation', the highest accolade of the most senior of Shi'i scholars
millet	a recognised autonomous religious community in the Ottoman Empire
mujtahid	a Shi'i cleric recognised as competent to deliver independent opinions on matters relating to the *shari'a*
peshmerga	literally, 'those who face death'; term referring to Kurdish guerrilla forces
qaimaqam	district governor, subordinate to governor of a province
salafi	term used to denote a believer in the need for Muslim reform with reference to the example of earliest Muslims (*al-salaf al-salih* – the pious forebears)
saniyya lands	land belonging to the Ottoman sultan
sarifa	literally, 'hut made of reed matting'; general term for shanty towns that grew up around Baghdad
sayyid	descendant of the Prophet Muhammad
shaikh	in Arab Iraq, either an Arab tribal chieftain or a religious scholar; in Kurdish Iraq, a man of saintly descent, usually head of a religious order
shari'a	the body of rules guiding the life of a Muslim
Sufi	member of an Islamic mystical (*sufi*) order
Thalweg	median line of deepest channel of a waterway
'ulama (sing. *'alim*)	those learned in Islamic law
vali	governor of a province (*vilayet* (Turkish))
waqf (pl. *awqaf*)	religious endowment, generally landed property

List of abbreviations

CPA	Coalition Provisional Authority
CUP	Committee of Union and Progress; Constitutional Union Party
DFI	Development Fund for Iraq
GFIW	General Federation of Iraqi Workers
IAEA	International Atomic Energy Agency
ICP	Iraqi Communist Party
IFTU	Iraqi Federation of Trade Unions
IGC	Iraqi Governing Council
IIP	Iraqi Islamic Party
IMF	International Monetary Fund
INA	Iraqi National Accord
INC	Iraqi National Congress
INOC	Iraqi National Oil Company
IPC	Iraq Petroleum Company
ISG	Iraq Survey Group
IWN	Iraqi Women's Network
KDP	Kurdistan Democratic Party
KDP-I	Kurdistan Democratic Party – Iran
KRG	Kurdish Regional Government
LUP	Liberal Unionist Party
MEF	Mesopotamian Expeditionary Force
NCRC	National Council of the Revolutionary Command
NDP	National Democratic Party
NGO	Nongovernmental organisation
OPEC	Organisation of Petroleum Exporting Countries
ORHA	Office of Reconstruction and Humanitarian Assistance
OWFI	Organisation of Women's Freedom in Iraq
PKK	Partiya Karkeren Kurdistan (Kurdistan Workers' Party)
PUK	Patriotic Union of Kurdistan

RAF	Royal Air Force
RCC	Revolutionary Command Council
SCIRI	Supreme Council for the Islamic Revolution in Iraq
TAL	Law of Administration for the State of Iraq for the Transitional Period
TPC	Turkish Petroleum Company
UAR	United Arab Republic
UIA	United Iraqi Alliance
UNMOVIC	United Nations Monitoring, Verification and Inspection Commission
UN SC	United Nations Security Council
UNSCOM	United Nations Special Commission on Disarmament
WAFDI	Women's Alliance for Democratic Iraq
WMD	Weapons of mass destruction

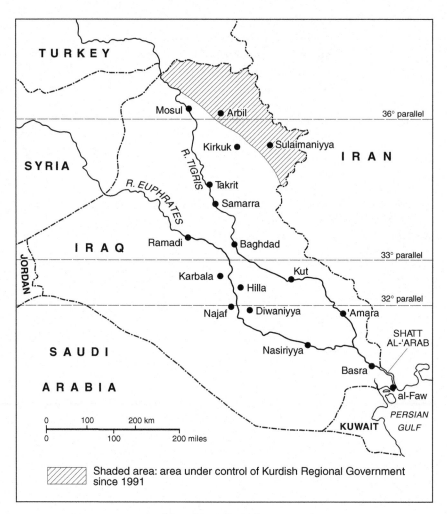

TURKEY

Mosul ●   ● Arbil   36° parallel

Kirkuk ●   ● Sulaimaniyya

SYRIA   IRAN

R. TIGRIS

R. EUPHRATES

● Takrit

● Samarra

IRAQ   Ramadi ●   ● Baghdad   33° parallel

JORDAN

Karbala ●   Kut ●   32° parallel

● Hilla

Najaf ● ● Diwaniyya   ● 'Amara

SAUDI   SHATT
                                   AL-'ARAB
                    Nasiriyya ●

ARABIA   Basra ●
                              ● al-Faw

0   100   200 km   PERSIAN
                            GULF
0   100   200 miles   KUWAIT

Shaded area: area under control of Kurdish Regional Government
since 1991

Map 1 Iraq: principal towns

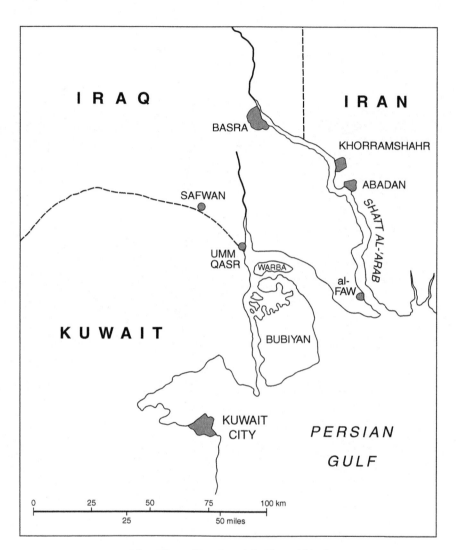

Map 2 Basra, Kuwait and the Shatt al-ʿArab

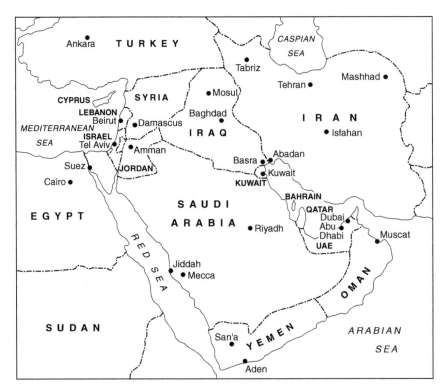

Map 3 Iraq and the Middle East

Map 4 Kurdish Iraq

Introduction

The modern history of Iraq is a history of the ways in which the people who found themselves living in the new Iraqi state were drawn into its orbit. The creation of a state centred on Baghdad in 1920–1, with its frontiers, its bureaucracy and its fiscal system, established a new framework for politics, embodying distinctive ideas about government. Controlled first by British and then by Iraqi officials, the state made new demands upon its inhabitants, causing people to rethink existing political identities, values and interests. Sometimes these were adapted to serve the state and its rulers; sometimes they were marginalised or suppressed. The history of the state, therefore, is in part a history of the strategies of co-operation, subversion and resistance adopted by various Iraqis trying to come to terms with the force the state represented. It has also been a history of the ways the state transformed those who tried to use it. These different forms of engagement over the years shaped the politics of Iraq and contributed to the composite narrative of Iraq's modern history.

Throughout this process, two important features emerge. The first is the power of the state to act as a centre of gravity, gradually drawing people into a field of distinctively *Iraqi* politics. This is connected to the second feature – the narratives used by Iraqis to understand and to justify their political engagement over time. 'Narratives' here mean the accounts people give of themselves and others in relation to the state, as well as to their efforts to make the history of that state conform to their self-image. It is both an imaginative construct and an organising principle, embodied in the way power is handled by those in a position of command. For them the goal has been to ensure that their account – and their account alone – of Iraq should triumph and become both the prism through which all Iraqis must see their country and the measure used to judge its rulers.

From the moment of the foundation of Iraq in the 1920s, it was clear that there were very different ideas about its future. Across the country as a whole, the boundaries between these ideas shifted as different groups, variously empowered, tried to assert control, to bring others in line with their own vision for Iraq. Over the course of Iraqi history, these visions have been contrasting and competing. The British mandatory authorities during the 1920s, tribal shaikhs under monarchy and republic, Arab nationalists since the 1930s, Shi'i *'ulama* throughout this period, the Iraqi Communist Party during its heyday in the 1950s and early 1960s, the Kurdish parties in their struggles with each other and with the central authorities, Saddam Husain and the Ba'th party into the twenty-first century and, most recently, the United States and the forces its brief occupation brought to the fore – all have left their imprint on the story of Iraq.

Marking all these eras of Iraq's history has been a powerful tendency for politics to be seen chiefly as a way of disciplining the population to ensure conformity with the rulers' visions of social order. Even those who challenged established order have been as authoritarian in their outlook. Of course, many Iraqis have tried to champion instead the idea of politics as civility, advocating a framework of laws and a shared space for political activity. A minority view in Iraq's political history, this tendency has appeared intermittently under particular circumstances, but has generally been overwhelmed by people organised according to very different notions of trust, where the community is not one of citizens, but of family and clan members, fellow tribesmen, co-sectarians or conspirators. They have seen the state as the guarantor of their own privileges, giving them advantages over the bulk of the Iraqi population.

It is here that the various narratives associated with Iraq's political history come into play. They tell us something about the ways in which different groups have identified themselves and highlight some of the main political struggles, as one version of the Iraqi state was asserted over another. In Iraq, as elsewhere, power can create its own pragmatic as well as normative grounds for acceptance, despite reservations about its legitimacy. This can be seen in Iraqi history as dominant narratives are eroded when a shift in power occurs.

One example has been the changing idea of the 'tribe' and the 'tribal shaikh' in Iraqi history. They have played various roles under different regimes, many of which have tried to use them to extend the power and reach of the centre. In these circumstances, they have been incorporated into the narrative of the regime in question, whether in Hashemite Iraq under the monarchy, the Iraq of Saddam Husain or the fragmented Iraq that emerged after 2003 under US auspices. Other regimes have tried to write the tribal leaders out of the story of Iraq. However, in all cases the very attention paid to the questions of lineage and status associated with tribal identity has helped to transform them, inscribing into the notion of 'tribal identity' different meanings for individual Iraqis at different moments of their history. Similarly, ethnic and sectarian categories such as 'Kurd', 'Shi'i' or 'Sunni' have not only meant different things politically over time, but have also been used in a variety of ways, by government and opposition alike.

Nowhere have these transformations, and the associated dilemmas and contradictions, been better captured than in the story of the majority Shi'i 'community' of Iraq. Iraqi history shows that the Shi'a may comprise the major part of the Iraqi population, but they are not a single political community. Yet for much of this time the political activities of many Shi'a could hardly be understood outside the context of a state that was dominated, since its inception, by small cliques drawn from the minority Sunni Arabs of Iraq. This led to the strategies of resistance marking the restive 'Shi'i politics' of the 1920s and the 1930s. It was then that the authority of the *mujtahids* of Najaf, Karbala and al-Kazimiyya was linked to powerful rural, tribal interests in southern Iraq and helped to mobilise large numbers of urban and rural Shi'a, working together.

However, since that time, changes in the condition of the state have brought out different, sometimes opposing, currents in 'Shi'i politics'. Some identified with Arab nationalism, in the belief that this could bridge the gap with the Sunni Arabs and finally grant the Shi'a equality of opportunity. Others believed this could best be achieved through a distinctively Iraqi nationalism. Many, of course, still revered their leading *mujtahids*, but the increasingly dominant narrative of ethnic Arab nationalism meant that large numbers of Shi'a were torn between their respect for their communal leaders – often Persian by origin – and their desire to play a full part in the life of the Iraqi state. If they moved too close to one side, they found themselves condemned by the other.

For some, this led to wholesale rejection of the authority of the *mujtahids*. They turned instead to secular, radical forms of politics, informed by their awareness of the miserable condition of the majority of Shi'a. For others, the conclusion was to adopt a modern, activist but Islamist political stance. This was equally radical in its implications for the established Shi'i *mujtahids*, but by the 1970s it was a distinct and powerful voice among the Shi'a of Iraq, coming to dominate Iraqi politics in the aftermath of the fall of the dictatorship of Saddam Husain. Many Shi'a who had pragmatically sought accommodation with the narrow clique that had controlled the state for nearly forty years discovered a political identity focusing on communal solidarities. This seemed to provide a reassuring and empowering narrative in the new world of representative politics after 2003.

The history of the state is but one history among many which help explain the politics of Iraq and of the Iraqis. In this study it is the principal focus. Other histories – of different individuals, families, groups, communities and political parties which make up the Iraqi population – are of course no less valid. However, for the purposes of this study they will be examined largely for the ways in which they may have become entangled in the narrative of those who have tried to dominate the state as an apparatus and to appropriate it as an idea.

Some of those who have ruled Iraq owed their existence to the formation of the state itself, such as the officers who had served under the sharif of Mecca during the First World War and who formed the backbone of the new Iraqi army in the 1920s. Others emerged from the economic changes that touched all sectors of Iraqi society during the twentieth century, such as the great landlords under the monarchy. Still others, such as the Kurdish or Shiʿi leaders, or the rural clans that came to dominate the Iraqi security forces under the Baʿth, are rooted in older communities, drawn into the field of Iraqi politics which has nevertheless changed them in various ways. Thus the state has often been captured by distinct groups of Iraqis, but it has also reconstituted social identities through the logic of state power. In neither case has the process been complete. Nor has it always been clear which logic has been the dominant one – that of state power, or that of the group which happens to be in the ascendant. It is this very ambiguity which is characteristic of the modern history of Iraq and has given rise to the 'shadow state' – the web of associates, patrons and power brokers which penetrates, underpins and has often undermined public state institutions. The resilience and adaptability of the networks and the often unspoken rules on which they have been based have defied and subverted various attempts at institutional reform, whether under monarchy, dictatorship or in the brief periods of parliamentary life.

Equally distinctive and possibly related to this feature has been the fact that neither the state nor those who have commanded it have managed to ensure that the multiple histories of the Iraqis are subsumed into a single narrative of state power. Despite the resources available to them and their sometimes ferocious methods, Iraq's rulers have had little success in forcing the histories of Iraq's various communities to conform with their own timetables and objectives. Indeed, the logic of political survival has often dictated otherwise. The exploitation of fracture lines within the population and restrictive understandings of political trust have kept hierarchies of status and privilege intact, subverting the very idea of a national community in whose name successive governments have claimed to act.

To some degree the same has also been true of class identities, the other social category most commonly associated with the modern state and influential in shaping the way any contemporary state is viewed. Whether class is defined as indicating a person's relationship to the ownership or to the control of the means of production, the complicating factor has always been to identify it either as a conscious or an underlying motive of political action. In Iraq, the definition of people's interests with regard to property or the lack thereof has certainly played an important part in politics. However, even where it has been important in understanding people's actions, it has not been comprehensive enough to justify the claim that a class exists as a political actor. The groups that could justifiably be said to act collectively in politics have been smaller and more particular, their boundaries determined not by their place in the division of labour in Iraq, but by their sense of where they stand in relation to the status map of Iraq's inhabitants, and to the dominant power within the state.

In this account of the troubled narrative of the state of Iraq, three interlinked factors stand out. The first is the resilience of patrimonialism, with all it has meant for the relationship between social formations and the organisation of state power. The networks of patrons and clients throughout Iraqi society have been decisive in the political history of the state, from the people who associated themselves with the Hashemite regime in the early years, through the groups that clustered around Saddam Husain to the various factions that have colonised the state machinery in the aftermath of his demise. This process has been associated with the rise and fall and rise again of 'tribal' politics, the demographic shift from countryside to city, the consequent 'ruralising' of the political universe and the resurgence of local and communal politics to contest the power of the centralised state after 2003. Communities of trust have formed and reformed, marked by wariness and often fear of other similar groups in a political arena the rules of which have been made by the strongest. In these circumstances, patrimonialism has been a way of guaranteeing narrative consistency, founded on the belief that those who share your identity or are heavily dependent on you must to some degree share your fate. This explains why such ruthless energy has gone into keeping these ties alive and in ensuring that other principles do not prevail. It also shows that identity politics are not based on some unchanging 'tradition', but are deeply implicated in material interests, reinforcing the pragmatic reasons for accepting one narrative over another.

These processes have been greatly enhanced by the second factor: the shifting basis of the political economy of Iraq as oil revenues became increasingly important, delivering massive and unprecedented financial power into the hands of those who had control of the state. It might be argued that this enhanced the autonomy of the state in Iraq, but it also reinforced particular conceptions of the state held by those in a position to direct its future, from Nuri al-Saʿid to the Shiʿi Islamist parties and the Kurdish nationalists more recently. The economic foundations of power in Iraq have shaped relationships between those who control the state revenues and various sectors of Iraq's population. They have also informed a number of ideological debates about the future of the country. Most importantly, whether the currency was land or oil rents, for much of Iraq's history they reinforced the patrimonial ties which have made the majority of Iraq's population dependent on those who have taken control of the centre.

The third factor is similarly connected with the other two: the part played by violence in the brief history of Iraq. Any state is to some extent an organisation that disciplines and coerces. In Iraq, the imposition of a political order that challenged existing values and interests, or that created and maintained systems of privilege, has meant a readiness to use coercion from the outset. Beginning with British ideas of order, the use of violence to suppress dissent, much of which took violent form itself, has been reproduced by central governments in Baghdad since the foundation of the state. Indeed, control of the means of coercion has been one of the lures for those who seized the state apparatus, resulting in the prominence of the armed forces which introduced a baneful logic to Iraq's political life. In the circumstances of insurgency and communal strife that pushed Iraq towards civil war after 2003, this was played out in a fractured political world where militias, rebels, foreign troops and proliferating security forces at the disposal of different factions of the government reinforced the grammar of violence, costing thousands of Iraqi lives.

Examination of these themes – patrimonialism, the political economy of oil and the use of violence – will form threads of argument throughout the book. However, for the sake of clarity, a chronological framework will be followed. Within this chronological framework, with its various implications for the narratives of different communities in Iraq, the three themes outlined above will be explored. More generally, it will trace the continuing tension between the efforts by ruling elites to organise various elements of Iraq's population according to their own ideas of political order and desirable social peace – and the forms of resistance, indifference or acceptance they found in the framework of the state that they were trying to impose. The attempt by successive Iraqi governments to dominate all three of these spheres of political life in the name of a single hegemonic principle has been a marked feature of the composite narratives of the Iraqi state. Furthermore, the lengths to which they will go in a political game with few rules may help to explain the depth and bitterness of the conflicts which have characterised the history of this state in often terrible ways.

CHAPTER I

The Ottoman provinces of Baghdad, Basra and Mosul

During the sixteenth and seventeenth centuries the lands that were to become the territories of the modern state of Iraq were gradually incorporated into the Ottoman Empire as three provinces, based on the towns of Mosul, Baghdad and Basra. The term *al-'Iraq* (meaning the shore of a great river along its length, as well as the grazing land surrounding it) had been used since at least the eighth century by Arab geographers to refer to the great alluvial plain of the Tigris and Euphrates Rivers, a region known in Europe as Mesopotamia. It was here that the Ottoman sultans were extending their own domains during these years and trying to check the ambitions of the Safavid shahs of Persia. Imperial and doctrinal rivalries between the Sunni Ottomans and the Shi'i Safavids touched the histories of the peoples of these frontier lands, requiring strategies of accommodation or evasion from their leaders and affecting them in a variety of ways. The political world that resulted was a complex and fragmented one. Centres of power existed in many cases autonomously, interacting under shifting circumstances that gave advantage now to one grouping, now to another, and in which the control of the central Ottoman government in Istanbul gradually diminished. Instead, initiative and power lay with those who could command the forces needed to defeat external and internal challengers alike.

POWER IN THE THREE PROVINCES

At the summit of the systems of power in the three provinces stood the military elite of *mamluk* pashas who acknowledged the sovereignty of the Ottoman sultan, but were increasingly beyond his control. From the beginning of the eighteenth century, a succession of powerful Georgian *mamluks* (taken as boys from Christian families in Georgia and converted to Islam) ruled Baghdad, often extending their rule to the province of Basra as well. In addition to managing the military forces at their disposal and defending their domains from Persians and others, they needed to maintain alliances with the powerful Arab tribal chieftaincies which pressed in upon Baghdad and Basra. Meanwhile, in the north, the local dynasty of the Jalili had entrenched itself as overlords of Mosul, and a number of semi-independent Kurdish principalities, most notably that of the powerful Baban dynasty of Sulaimaniyya, dominated the Kurdish mountains. In the centre and the south the shaikhs of the great Arab tribal confederations of the Muntafiq, the Khaza'il, the Zubaid and the Banu Lam, as well as of large and powerful tribes, such as the Shammar, the Fatlah and the al-Bu Muhammad, commanded forces that could often prove more than a match for those of the pashas of Baghdad or Basra. However, they could also be useful allies against the Persians or against other tribes reluctant to pay the tribute on which the patronage and thus much of the power of the *mamluk* pashas depended.

The *mamluk* pashas ruled over a tributary system. The main function of government was to maintain them and their entourage in an appropriate style by extracting the revenues which would enable them to service their clients and to defend the system against all challengers, internal or external. Thus, taxes were levied on rural communities within reach of the major towns and tribute was forthcoming from those tribal leaders who found it advisable to keep on good terms with the power that the most successful of these *mamluk* pashas could command. These funds were supplemented by the dues charged on goods in transit through Mesopotamia, increasing during the eighteenth century as trade developed with the British East India Company, in particular.

The attitude of these pashas to the Ottoman Empire was formally correct: the sovereignty of the Ottoman sultan was acknowledged in the coinage, in the Friday prayer and in other outward symbols of state. The pashas of the three provinces were also careful to obtain imperial confirmation of their position as *vali* (governor). However, they were less ready to accept material limitations on their rule. Appointees from Istanbul served on their staff, but only in subordinate positions. Imperial Janissary troops were stationed in Baghdad, but the pashas kept them under their direct command and ensured that their own elite force of *mamluks* could always subdue them. Tribute was sent to Istanbul, but irregularly.

In their dealings with the inhabitants of the three provinces the Georgian *mamluks* did not differ much from the ruling elites of the Ottoman Empire more generally. Their methods were those of contemporary Ottoman administration, whether in the realm of tax-farming (*iltizam*), customs charges, raising armed forces or enforcing the will of the governor and, by association, that of the Ottoman sultan. Doctrinally, there was no taint of heresy to challenge the authority of the Ottoman sultan-caliph. Nor was there any desire on the part of the *mamluks* to change the established hierarchies of the many communities and societies that comprised the social fabric of the empire. They simply wanted to dominate them.

Taken as a whole, the inhabitants of the three provinces of Mosul, Baghdad and Basra provided as broad a spectrum of social and communal structures as anywhere in the empire. In the Kurdish-speaking areas of the north and north-east of Mosul and Baghdad provinces, dynastic, parochial and tribal identities and loyalties shaped the lives of the inhabitants. Also important was the influence of the Sufi orders – most notably the Qadiri and increasingly the Naqshabandi – which lent to the observance of Islam in these regions a distinctive character, strongly shaped by Kurdish shaikhs and *sayyids*. Also prominent in this region were the communities of Yazidis (Kurdish-speaking adherents of the syncretic religion of Yazidism), of Christians and of Shi'a, some Kurdish and some Turkmen. These features, as well as broader linguistic differences and geographical isolation, had led to the emergence of a number of local lordships and small principalities which enjoyed complex and shifting relations with each other and with the Ottoman and Persian Empires, the borders of which they straddled.

In the Arabic-speaking districts of Mosul province, the rural population was divided among sedentary and nomadic tribal groups, engaged in agriculture or pastoralism, with some profiting from the opportunities offered by the transit trade. Here too, strong tribal and local attachments coloured everyday life and helped to create distinct communities with particular identities and practices, linked by real or imagined bonds of kinship. These determined the relationship of individuals to the land and shaped the hierarchies of clans and families in the various settlements. Leadership was decided on this basis, but the size and remoteness, as well as the economic and military capacities, of the community in question would determine the power of the leader relative to that of the local Ottoman governor and the degree of autonomy he could therefore enjoy. For the majority of the members of such communities, any contact with the Ottoman state would be mediated by the leading family, encouraging worlds of difference to emerge in the views that people held of the histories of which they formed a part.

By contrast, Mosul itself was a much more directly integrated part of the Ottoman imperial system. Powerful local families, such as the Jalili, as well as prominent families of *ashraf* such as the 'Ubaidi, dominated certain quarters of the town. Reflecting to some degree the composition of the surrounding countryside, the population was predominantly Sunni Arab, but there were also distinct communities of Turkmen and of Kurds, as well as of Jews and of Christians. The relative weight of these communities and their leading families was strongly influenced by the political hierarchies, the judicial system and the trading networks of the Ottoman Empire itself. Although families such as the Jalili tried to preserve a sphere of action free from the direct control of Istanbul, they, no less than the leaders of the *millet* communities in the city, owed their prominence to their successful and distinctive engagement with the powers of the Ottoman state. As the nineteenth century was to show, they were equally vulnerable when the priorities of that state began to change.[1]

Much the same could be said of the city of Baghdad. As a provincial capital, it had much in common with other great Ottoman cities. However, in several senses it was more remote from the controlling influence of Istanbul. The Georgian *mamluks* had introduced a distinctive and formidable military caste at the head of its social structure, dominating but separate from the respected hierarchies of the *ashraf*, led by the family of the al-Kailani. Furthermore, the proximity of Persia and the size of the Shiʿi community in nearby al-Kazimiyya added a distinctive character to the city, as did the size and prominence of the long-established Jewish community, which constituted nearly 20 per cent of the population. The frontier nature of the province also left its mark through the steady influx of people from various parts of the empire. Whether they were Ottoman officials who came, stayed and intermarried with one of the established Baghdad families, or formed part of the inevitable trickle of immigrants from Baghdad's rural hinterland, or were traders who settled in the city, bringing with them their connections to Persia, the Gulf or India, the population of Baghdad underwent various forms of renewal – vitally necessary if the city was to survive the devastating man-made and natural disasters that afflicted its inhabitants during the seventeenth, eighteenth and early nineteenth centuries.

Baghdad, like Mosul, ruled over a province that was only nominally under the control of the authorities in the capital. As in the north, the lives of most of the rural population were shaped by the practices and values of the sedentary, semi-sedentary and nomadic tribes and tribal confederations to which they belonged. Only in the regions closest to Baghdad, more easily subject to the direct control of the administrative and political elite of the city, did tribal identities have less obvious political consequences. However, the *mamluk* pashas could rarely impose their will on the more inaccessible, larger and more formidably armed tribes and tribal groupings, limiting their ability to extract tribute across the whole of the province of Baghdad.

A peculiarity of this province was the presence of the *'atabat* (thresholds or doorways) – the collective name given to Najaf, Karbala, al-Kazimiyya and Samarra, four of the most venerated towns of Shi'i Islam, long associated with the sacred history of the Caliph 'Ali bin Abi Talib and his descendants. These towns – particularly the more important centres of Najaf and Karbala – had always constituted a potential problem for the Ottoman authorities in Baghdad. They were centres of learning and scholarship of the Ja'fari school of law which the Ottoman state did not recognise. Consequently, the Shi'a generally ignored Ottoman institutions. They were inhabitants of the Ottoman state, but they scarcely engaged with it. Furthermore, the importance of these centres of Shi'i pilgrimage and learning for the Safavid and Qajar rulers of Persia meant not only a constant flow of pilgrims, traders and settlers from Persia itself, but also the close scrutiny of the Persian state, ever sensitive to real or imagined injustices by the Ottoman authorities against the shah's subjects who had settled there.

Finally, the influence of these towns and of the Shi'i *'ulama* on the tribesmen who gravitated to them and had begun to settle in the mid-Euphrates region was becoming ever more marked. The notorious Shi'i disdain for the pretensions of the Ottoman sultan-caliph and thus for the legitimacy of the Ottoman state accorded with tribal suspicion and dislike of central state authority. This may explain in part the growing appeal of Shi'ism to the tribesmen of the region, large numbers of whom adopted the precepts of Shi'i Islam during the eighteenth and nineteenth centuries. Thus an increasingly large proportion of the inhabitants of Baghdad province saw little reason to associate themselves with, let alone pay taxes to, a state which seemed not only alien, but even doctrinally repulsive. Some of the *mamluk* pashas of Baghdad handled this problem adroitly and maintained good relations with the notables of the holy cities. Others, whether under the threat of Persian invasion, or in order to ingratiate themselves with Istanbul, or indeed out of their own prejudices as new converts to Sunni Islam, succeeded in deepening the divide between the Sunni and the Shi'a under their rule.[2]

A similar set of tribal and doctrinal differences weakened the allegiance of most of the inhabitants of Basra province to the Ottoman state. In particular, the powerful tribal confederations of the Muntafiq and the Khaza'il and the substantial tribe of the al-Bu Muhammad dominated the lives of much of the population of the province, whether they were settled farmers, pastoralists or marsh-dwellers. The *mamluk* pashas in Basra had little or no influence in these regions, except on terms largely dictated by the tribal chieftains. Occasionally a pasha would emerge who through force or guile could get the better of one or all of the confederations. However, these were relatively short-lived episodes in a history that showed the balance of power favouring those who could dominate and mobilise the rural population. This was rarely the governor in Basra.

The society of Basra, as in Baghdad, was composed of a number of distinct groups, under the rule of the *mamluk* military caste. Overwhelmingly Arab and largely Shi'i in composition, its elite families were however predominantly Sunni. These were headed, in terms of status, by the family of the naqib al-ashraf, but they also included Ottoman officials and property owners and traders who had major interests in the local economy. This was based either upon the intensive cultivation of Basra's hinterland or on trading links with the Gulf and the Indian Ocean. The importance of the Indian trade, in particular, had been underlined by the opening of trading concessions by the British East India Company (as early as 1639), as well as by French and other European traders who were seeking to profit from and eventually to monopolise this trade during much of the period in question. This greater openness towards India, as well as towards the Gulf and eventually Egypt, with all that this implied in the eighteenth and nineteenth centuries, was to have a significant effect on Basra's society, as well as on the attitudes of its inhabitants towards the changes they were soon to experience.

THE OTTOMAN 'RECONQUEST' OF THE THREE PROVINCES

The significance of these differences among and within the three provinces became clearer with the Ottoman 'reconquest' in the early nineteenth century. The weaknesses of the empire vis-à-vis the European states and the worrying example of the growing power of the provincial governor of Egypt, Muhammad 'Ali Pasha, had set in train a reformist reaction in Istanbul. Under the rule of Sultan Mahmud II (1808–39) the central Ottoman government began to reassert its authority in outlying provinces, and reconstructed the military forces of the empire. The *Nizam-i Cedid* (New Order) implied the consolidation of power in the hands of the sultan and his government and left little room for semi-autonomous provincial governors. It was not long, therefore, before Istanbul turned its attention to Baghdad, Basra and Mosul. In 1831, when Da'ud Pasha, the *mamluk* governor of Baghdad, refused to comply with the sultan's edict that he relinquish his office, an army under the governor of Aleppo, 'Ali Rida Pasha, marched on Baghdad, capturing the city and Da'ud Pasha himself. With his capture the rule of the *mamluks* in Baghdad ceased abruptly.

'Ali Rida went on to occupy Basra, bringing *mamluk* rule in that city to an end, and in 1834 central Ottoman authority was restored in Mosul, ending the hold of the Jalili family on the governorship. As a result, by the beginning of the period of the *Tanzimat* (the reforms) of Sultan Abdulmecid, the three provinces were under direct rule from Istanbul, opening them up to successive reforms in landholding, administration, conscription, law and public education. However, these reforms were implemented at different rates, depending upon the initiative and energy – and length of tenure – of the Ottoman governors sent out by Istanbul. For much of the period that followed, the norms and methods of the *mamluk* era prevailed in government and administration, just as the great majority of the *mamluk* families retained their wealth and status, providing many of the key officials of the New Order. In addition, the reassertion of central Ottoman control over the major cities did not automatically bring about a greater degree of control over the semi-autonomous tribes and tribal confederations of the countryside. Nevertheless, the direct and indirect consequences of the reforms had the effect of creating new interests and groups, some with an explicit commitment to the reforms themselves, others seeking to find a role as the reforming measures began to erode their hitherto secure status.

Most notable from the point of view of the future of the political society of the three provinces were the gradual changes in the state itself as a distinctive regime of power. Ottoman reform had been prompted by the belief that the weakness of the empire was a structural weakness of the state when confronted by the phenomenon of European power. As a result, there was a growing determination to reconstruct the administrative, legislative, educational and resource bases of the state, in large part on the European model. This radical refoundation was piecemeal and many of its implications did not show themselves until much later, but aspects of it were soon felt in the three Mesopotamian provinces. However tentative or resisted at first, new ways of engaging with state power created new spheres of action and required imaginative departures from the established forms of thought about the nature of politics itself.

It is during this period, therefore, that the rules (and languages) of a new kind of politics emerge to regulate power and to define authority and administrative duty. This was no longer a matter of choice, of willed engagement or disengagement: the modern state, with all its techniques of persuasion and compulsion, its retinue of committed servants, its opportunistic camp followers and its overall ethos, had come to the land of the two rivers and was not to be easily dislodged. A distinct political society began to form in the three provinces, owing much to the Ottoman reforms, but drawing also upon existing hierarchies of wealth and status. The interplay of these forces helped to create new social positions for individuals and gave them an opportunity to play a part in the Ottoman state and the new social order.

The principal instruments in the Ottoman attempt to reintegrate its Mesopotamian provinces into the empire were the reforms stemming from the Land Law of 1858 and from the Vilayet Law of 1864. The former sought to bring some regularity into the land tenure system of the empire, creating security of tenure (whilst reasserting state ownership of land) in the hope that this would encourage a more productive and settled agriculture, attracting investment and generating revenues for the imperial treasury. The second measure was the beginning of the administrative reorganisation of the empire. It was intended not only to demarcate the various provinces, but also to define the nature and shape of the state's authority vis-à-vis the provincial population and to spell out the exact functions and responsibilities of the provincial officials from the governor downwards.

With the arrival in Baghdad of the forceful and energetic Midhat Pasha as governor in 1869, decisive steps were taken to implement both the Vilayet Law and the Land Law. The Vilayet Law mapped out the territorial boundaries of the three provinces and established a new structure of administration from provincial down to village level, intending to bring the central administration systematically down to people who had hitherto been little touched by the apparatus of the state. More radically, at least in theory, it was also intended to involve them in the workings of the state through administrative councils which included not simply Ottoman officials, but also influential representatives of the population at large, both Muslim and non-Muslim.

Midhat Pasha was able to introduce these reforms with little difficulty since the initiative lay at this stage with the Ottoman authorities. The practical consequences were less clear-cut and took time to emerge. They were to be shaped by the personalities and the authority of the individuals involved, as well as by the changing fortunes of the advocates of decentralisation in Istanbul itself, who gradually lost out during the latter half of the nineteenth century to those who wanted to reassert close central control. During the second half of the nineteenth century, these were the factors which determined the nature of the three provinces' links to the centre and to some degree shaped the balance of power within the political worlds of Baghdad, Mosul and Basra.

Midhat Pasha's implementation of the Land Law was far from complete by the time he was recalled to Istanbul in 1872. Nevertheless, he began a process whereby the land tenure system was to be thoroughly revised, with far-reaching consequences for the majority of the population, who depended on the land for their livelihood. One of the main pillars of the land reform was the granting of title deeds (*tapu sanad*) to anyone who was in possession or occupation of land. The land remained the property of the state, but the registered owner of the title deeds would enjoy virtually complete rights of ownership. Across great tracts of the three provinces the Land Law introduced an institution akin to private property in agricultural land, initiating profound changes in structures of social power, the consequences of which were to be felt long after the demise of the Ottoman administration itself.

In the first place, collective ownership of land was expressly prohibited and registration of the title deeds could only be in the name of an individual. In areas of largely tribal cultivation, it was often the name of the shaikh, as the most powerful or prestigious individual, that was placed on the title deed. Either through ignorance or suspicion, or through a misplaced trust in the altruism of the shaikhly families, the great majority of the tribal cultivators failed to register and were thus transformed into tenant farmers. In other areas – and under Sultan Abdulhamid II – specifically the *saniyya* lands (the tracts belonging to the sultan himself), the practice of *iltizam* or tax-farming continued, leading to periodic auctions of the tax-farming rights and denying the peasants the possibility of establishing the kinds of stable tenancies that would allow successful application for title to the land. Attempts to enforce the new law were often fiercely resisted by the cultivators themselves, since the new principles conflicted with the rights recognised for years under various forms of customary practice. Hostility was sharpened in many cases by the fact that those who registered as owners of the title deeds were wholly unconnected with the cultivators of the land. Rather, they had used their influence or the capital they had accumulated within the urban administrative and trading worlds, as state servants, merchants or otherwise well-connected individuals, to secure for themselves rights over the land and over those who worked it.[3]

The consequences for the new political order associated with the refounding of the state were significant. As the potential for social conflict increased, based on different rights to the land, so the attitudes of new groups of landowners to the state began to change. For those in possession of title deeds, the state had become more than simply an exacting, tax-extracting agency. It was now something in which they had a material stake, since it guaranteed a certain kind of order and promised to enforce that order – and with it the rights of the principal beneficiaries. In this way, new groups of individuals in all three provinces became complicit in the state project. It was now in their interest that the writ of the central state should be enforced in the lands from which they stood to profit.

Among the shaikhly families who had registered as individual owners of tribal lands, there was also a growing realisation of the need for state assistance in extracting that which they felt was their due. This encouraged changing attitudes among some towards the mechanisms of state extraction. Rather than avoid taxation through violent resistance, they came to see that it was more fruitful to engage with the administrative personnel and offices of the state to ensure reduced tax demands or indeed exemptions. They would thereby also hope to enlist the force of the state to help them extract revenues from their tenants.

Consequently, even in this sector of society, traditionally wary of the state and disdainful of engagement with it, there was a growing number for whom the advantages of participation in some effective form began to outweigh the advantages of keeping their distance. However, it was to be a participation largely on terms set by the state. Hitherto the shaikhs had been powerful not because they owned land, but because of their authority over their tribesmen. In their new role as landowners, however, it was the state which conferred power upon them by granting them land rights – rights which could be withheld or withdrawn with equal facility. This did not break the relationship with their tribesmen, but it significantly transformed it and thereby helped to change the very meaning of tribal identity.

These transformations were, of course, gradual and drew different people into the state-directed reforms at varying rates. For certain families of urban notables and of Ottoman officials, the reform process satisfied both their material interests and their feelings of political propriety. For certain tribal chiefs, whether Arab or Kurdish, their welcome for the state's conferral of title deeds was unmatched by any sense of reciprocal obligation. Reluctance to pay taxes remained a constant irritant in relations between the state, based in the provincial capitals, and the countryside. Sometimes this was due to the inability of the title-holder, even though from a shaikhly family, to extract the revenues from his tribesmen who had now, in the eyes of the law, become his tenants; sometimes, however, it was due to the delayed acceptance of any sense of obligation to the state that went beyond symbolic fealty to the sultan.

From the time of Midhat Pasha, these were the processes which helped to shape political society in the three provinces. They were supplemented by further innovations and transformations such as the founding of a printing press and the publication of the first newspaper (the official paper

Al-Zawra', in 1869), the initiation of irrigation projects, the establishment of new factories around Baghdad and the setting up of a number of educational institutions. In addition, communications were improved, linking the provinces more effectively with each other and with the outside world. In some areas Midhat Pasha was building on the work of equally energetic predecessors, such as Mehmed Namik Pasha; in other areas, he instituted innovations which would be consolidated or neglected, depending upon the quality of his successors.

Inevitably, the growing intrusion of the Ottoman state into the lives of the inhabitants of the three provinces provoked resentment of new and unwelcome demands upon people's time and resources. In some cases this worked to the advantage of the Ottoman authorities. For instance, the late nineteenth century saw the decline of the great tribal confederation of the Muntafiq of Basra province, undermined in part by the changing relationship between the ruling family of *sayyids*, the al-Sa'dun, and their tribal followers. Regardless of other factors, the changes in land tenure and the tensions this had caused within the al-Sa'dun family and between them and the tribesmen had eroded their authority. Thus, by 1900, although the Ottoman governors could not afford to ignore the activities of the al-Sa'dun and the tribes of the Muntafiq confederation, the latter no longer wielded the kind of power that had once kept the Ottoman state itself in check.

In other cases, however, the very contested nature of authority, the unsettled feelings of the tribesmen, when combined with resentment and fear of the depredations of central government and augmented by local disputes over land rights, led to a series of revolts. On occasion these were crushed by the Ottoman forces stationed in one of the three provinces. However, in a number of instances, especially in the Kurdish areas and in Basra province, coerced compliance was often beyond the capacities of the Ottoman governor's forces. As a result, a wary relationship developed between the provincial capital and the tribal lands. It was in these areas that the Ottoman authorities fell back on a traditional strategy of encouraging dissent and factionalism within the tribes and their leading families. This weakened the capacity of any one of them to challenge the Ottoman state. At the same time it implicitly limited the degree to which the Ottoman state could undermine the tribal system, even while helping to transform it.

Senior officials in Istanbul and even in the provinces may have wished to weaken tribalism as such. For many it affronted the vision of modernity which they had mapped out for the empire. However, for officials of lower rank who were concerned with local order, tribal hierarchies and internecine tribal rivalries were too important a factor to be ignored and potentially too valuable an asset to lose in the task of maintaining control. By selecting allies within such a system and giving them the backing of the Ottoman state, the administration was inevitably complicit in a game which effectively reinforced a certain kind of tribal ethos, understood as the exploitation of networks of obligation deriving from real or imagined kinship. These networks supplied the channels through which the resources of the state could be distributed to chosen clients, giving the latter the means to sustain their own followings. In providing people with a material incentive to participate in such a system, the Ottoman state ensured that it acquired new meaning for some, whilst retaining it for many – a meaning appropriate to the demands of the new state order. This strategy undermined particular leaders at various times, just as other strategies were eroding the structures that had made certain tribes and tribal confederations formidable adversaries of central government in previous generations. However, it did nothing to undermine the importance of tribal affiliation or hierarchy. On the contrary, these were to remain crucial instruments of power, helping to sustain two languages and two worlds of political discourse.

In the province of Baghdad, this process was most advanced, in part because of the military strength of the Ottoman administration (Baghdad became the headquarters for the 6th Army Corps), but also because it was here that many of the tribal shaikhs had been drawn into a political game in which it was very much to their advantage to participate. The most prominent amongst them maintained agents and establishments in the city, supplying them with key intelligence and acting on their behalf to secure their interests at the court of the governor. It was in Baghdad that the centre of land registration lay, that decisions on changes of tenancy of *saniyya* lands were made and that public works central to the productivity of the lands in question – such as irrigation schemes or transport plans – were initiated. In exchange for this involvement by the shaikhs, which ensured a remarkable absence of rural disturbances in Baghdad province during the latter half of the nineteenth century, the Ottoman state honoured them, confirmed them in their positions and did little to undermine the principle of shaikhly domination in the countryside.[4]

SULTAN ABDULHAMID II AND THE YOUNG TURKS

The value of the shaikhs' involvement for the Ottoman authorities was all too apparent in the last quarter of the nineteenth century. It was then that the fiscal crisis of the empire manifested itself, indicating a chronic short-age of funds to back up many of the reform measures that had once been planned. It also meant that the revenues from the provinces were that much more vital to the well-being of the empire since, quite apart from other demands, there was the Public Debt Administration to service. This coincided with the accession to the throne of Sultan Abdulhamid II (1876–1909) and the suspension of the constitution, as well as the ending of the liberal reforms associated with the Young Ottomans. For the abso-lutist sultan, mistrustful of many of his officials because of their connec-tion with the constitutional movement and their Young Ottoman sympathies, it was important to establish direct ties with the chief notables in the provinces of the empire.

In the case of Mesopotamia, this led Sultan Abdulhamid to cultivate ties with prominent tribal leaders, with leading families of the *ashraf* and with the principal figures of the various Sufi orders. Connections of this kind were not only tactically useful, but, in the case of the *ashraf* and the Sufi shaikhs, also accorded with his pan-Islamic world view. The effect was to deepen the engagement of the prominent tribal and religious hierarchs with the Ottoman state, since they could now look to Istanbul for support against threats from provincial governors. However, the policy also ensured that frustrated Ottoman officials and social critics would make common cause, angered by the sultan's use of traditional hierarchies to bypass the administration and to reinforce his own absolutism.

These resentments eventually gave rise to the Young Turk movement throughout the empire, including the three Mesopotamian provinces. As the opportunities increased for young men from the provinces to undergo a modern education and to be trained either as officials or military officers, so were they influenced by the currents of thought both in Istanbul and in the provinces, among the growing circles of educated officials and profes-sional people. In Baghdad a number of state educational establishments had been opened since 1869, most notably the civil and military Rashidiyya schools, and increasing numbers of young men attended the Law School or the War College in Istanbul.

These developments indicated a growing critical engagement with the politics of the Ottoman state by increasing numbers of people in the three provinces. That engagement took various forms. It reflected both their positions within established society, but also the transformations of the pre-ceding couple of generations. The fact that different avenues and forms of involvement were open to people was testimony to the hybrid nature of the Ottoman state under Abdulhamid, filled with contradictions perhaps, but also seeking to accommodate existing structures of power and legitimation with new principles of order and new mechanisms of power. Increasingly, Ottoman officials, military officers, merchants, professionals, absentee landlords and tribal leaders encountered one another, as competitors or collaborators, on broadly similar terrain. The language and the proper sphere of political activity were becoming more generally recognised, but also more widely contested.

As a result, a variety of groups emerged in the three provinces, aimed at securing political advantage or reform, but their concerns were still those of subjects of the empire and the boundary of their political world was still effectively the boundary of the Ottoman Empire itself. In the process, however, they established close contacts with like-minded individuals from neighbouring provinces, often in the educational institutions of Istanbul where similar backgrounds and languages formed bonds between the growing numbers of young provincials. This made some realise how much certain provinces had in common with one another and for others it underlined the strategic value of co-operation in political activity.

Whilst these necessarily covert and scarcely organised forms of activity were beginning to shape the lives, the political concerns and imaginations of some of the younger officials and army officers from the three provinces, there were others who pursued a more traditional form of political activity within the framework of the empire. Focused on securing immediate advantage, although no doubt underpinned by a larger sense of political propriety and desirable social order, this otherwise diverse group is best represented by figures such as the naqib al-ashraf in Baghdad, ʿAbd al-Rahman al-Kailani, or the naqib al-ashraf of Basra and his son, Sayyid Talib, as well as by Kurdish chieftains, such as Shaikh Saʿid Barzinji, scion of a shaikhly family of the Qadiriyya order. They cultivated their links with the sultan in Istanbul in part to outmanoeuvre the transitory parade of Ottoman provincial officials and thereby to secure their own positions.

The same could be said of the shaikhly families of the great tribal confederations which sometimes needed the power of Istanbul to help them assert their own rights to land, or which were rent by intra-family disputes requiring mediation or recognition by the sultan. Furthermore, the advantages of engagement had become so apparent that it was not uncommon to find in many prominent families, such as the al-Saʿdun, both Ottoman officials and 'tribal shaikhs'. On a lower level, similar preoccupations drove lesser shaikhs to petition the relevant provincial governor and to maintain a presence in the main towns in order to take care of their interests at the governor's palace. Even on this level, of course, such access was still the prerogative of a very few. Nevertheless, it was drawing them into a world which was not simply the preserve of the governor or, behind him, the sultan. A different and larger kind of politics was taking shape throughout the empire and these apparently 'traditional' figures could not help but be affected by it, often adapting their public behaviour accordingly.

The Young Turk revolution of 1908, which forced the sultan to reintroduce the Ottoman constitution and saw the emergence into the open of the Committee of Union and Progress (CUP), allowed many of the hitherto suppressed currents of political opinion within the three Mesopotamian provinces to find public expression, as they did elsewhere in the empire. The proliferation of clubs, groups and societies after 1908, as well as the explosion of journals and newspapers (an estimated sixty titles were published at various times in the three provinces in the years following the revolution of 1908), is testimony to the political engagement of growing numbers in Mosul, Baghdad and Basra. At the same time, of course, other forms of political activity by no means disappeared, indicating varying political trajectories and contrasting narratives, playing themselves out at different rates in the three provinces.

The sultan himself was deposed as a result of the failed counter-revolution of 1909, but Istanbul remained as much the central hub of the empire as ever. However, the game of provincial politics became more complicated than before because of uncertainties about the political convictions and connections of any given official or officer. This made it all the more necessary for those keen to preserve and advance their interests to engage directly with a political world now swept by currents that could not easily be predicted or controlled. In the years that followed the 1908 revolution, some found new ways of organising and others found new reasons to organise. Young men from the Mesopotamian provinces, such as Tawfiq al-Suwaidi, Naji Shawkat, Hamdi al-Pachachi and Hikmat Sulaiman, took part in the debates raging in Istanbul about constitutionalism, liberalism, decentralisation and secularism. Equally, the common currency of Ottoman reform – strengthening the state through modern administrative techniques and the development of military and economic capacity – featured largely in their thoughts.

At the same time, among the Shi'a of the 'atabat, the revolutionary example of Persia was causing ferment. Debates about constitutionalism flourished here too, but in a very different setting from that of Ottoman officialdom. In Najaf, Karbala and elsewhere, the role of the clerics and, through them, of distinctively Shi'i sensibilities in the Persian constitutional revolution of 1906 had caused great interest. Although decried by some of the more conservative *ʿulama* of the *ʿatabat*, these new ideas and the visible success of clerical involvement in the political process had generated excitement among many. It had set them thinking about their own situation and the polity that dominated their lives, but that largely denied them a role.

With ideas of a politics of participation came the growing realisation that in the new political order some might find themselves better positioned to participate effectively than others. Initially, these concerns fuelled the ongoing debate about the relative merits of decentralisation versus central control. The restoration of the constitution and the elections to the Ottoman Parliament in 1908 had raised expectations about the commitment of the new regime to the representation of truly empire-wide interests and the possibility of meeting the varying claims of the provinces through some form of decentralisation. These hopes were dashed by the strong centralising policies of the CUP, and it was not long before groups began to form which called for equality of all Ottomans, for the Arabic language to be given equal status to Turkish and for greater power to be devolved to the provinces.

THE COMMITTEE OF UNION AND PROGRESS AND ITS OPPONENTS

As increasingly authoritarian CUP governments proceeded to entrench themselves in power in Istanbul, in the Arab provinces of the empire the frustrated calls for provincial autonomy fed into and reinforced emerging sentiments of Arab nationalism. In the Mesopotamian provinces, it was in Basra that this call was heard most loudly. In part, this was because of the proximity of the semi-independent Arab rulers of the Persian Gulf and the Arabian Peninsula, such as Shaikh Mubarak al-Sabah in Kuwait, Shaikh Khazaʿil of Muhammara and the emerging power of ʿAbd al-ʿAziz Ibn Saʿud in the Najd. The more cosmopolitan society of Basra was also in touch with Egypt, where many of the Arab critics of the Ottoman state had established themselves and where a lively and relatively free press gave voice to new ideas concerning both reform of the empire and questions of national identity. However, the phenomenon also owed much to the forcefulness and energy of Sayyid Talib al-Naqib, who was intent on carving out for himself a virtually unassailable position in Basra.

Having initially enjoyed the patronage of Sultan Abdulhamid, Sayyid Talib was elected to the Ottoman Parliament in 1908 and soon became associated with the opposition to the ruling CUP. In 1913 he set up the

Reform Society of Basra, demanding virtual provincial autonomy. This followed a meeting organised by him and attended by the shaikhs of Muhammara and of Kuwait at which, reportedly, a resolution was agreed calling for the autonomy – even independence – of Iraq (understood as the provinces of Baghdad and Basra). When Sayyid Talib proceeded openly to attack the 'Turkification' policies of the Ottoman government and called on Arab soldiers in the imperial army to rebel, the CUP government tried to arrange for his murder. The attempt failed and thereafter both Sayyid Talib and the CUP government called a truce. Indeed, in recognition of his power base, Talib was asked by the government to mediate with Ibn Sa'ud to secure his acknowledgement of Ottoman suzerainty; for his part Talib asked the government to grant a number of the Reform Society's requests. Surprisingly, they agreed to do so, but avoided committing themselves to a timetable. This seems to have satisfied Talib, who then declared that he was joining forces with the government and managed to secure the required pledge of allegiance from Ibn Sa'ud.

In recognition of this service, there was a plan to make Talib the governor of Basra province. This was perhaps Sayyid Talib's principal ambition and the main reason for his volte-face towards the Ottoman government. However, the plan was abandoned when the strength of local opposition became clear. Instead, in a curious reversal of policy, orders were sent to the governor of Baghdad to arrest Sayyid Talib in October 1914. Since this coincided with the British landing near Basra, following the outbreak of war, Talib lost no time in approaching the British (with whom he had long been in contact), and asked them to make him shaikh or *amir* of Basra under their protection. Although certain British officials were at the time toying with the idea of making Basra a British protectorate, they also knew of his chequered history and thought it safest to despatch him to India, where he remained until 1920.

In Baghdad, the emerging politics of the city and the province were not dominated by a single figure as they were in Basra. There was a greater variety of opinions and a number of powerful figures and families, many of whom had mixed feelings about the forced abdication of Sultan Abdulhamid in 1909. Those who had welcomed the sultan's fall were well represented in the CUP which brought together officials, landowners and merchants, encouraging political debate and disseminating the distinctive mixture of authoritarian and liberal reformist ideas characteristic of the CUP at this stage. Because of the composition of the CUP in Baghdad, where Arabic-speaking provincials predominated, there was little evidence of the Turkish nationalism that was later to become associated with the

1 Sayyid Talib al-Naqib (naqib al-ashraf of Basra), c. 1912

party. Instead, debate focused either on questions of political and social reform similar to those mooted elsewhere in the empire or on matters of parochial concern to the inhabitants of Baghdad province.

Disagreements in both these areas led to the emergence of a lively and varied press in Baghdad, as in the other two provinces. Sometimes political disagreements led to the establishment of branches of rival political parties, such as the Liberal Unionist Party (LUP), which also had a metropolitan origin. Attracting those who were concerned about the secularising and centralising tendencies of the CUP, as well as about the implications of some of its reform proposals for the privileges and wealth of established hierarchies, the LUP brought together individuals of a more religious, conservative and landed social background. Nevertheless, debate was still about issues that were empire-wide in their implication, even if they concerned the application of the general measures to the particular conditions of Baghdad province. As in the other provinces of the empire, those who were becoming involved in the widening political world still focused primarily on the limits and nature of state power, rather than on the legitimacy of the Ottoman state itself.

This was to change, particularly after the CUP coup d'état of 1913. In Baghdad province, as in Basra, young Ottomans of Arab origin and culture began to feel exasperation and frustration at the CUP's dictatorship, which not only seemed to bring with it a contempt for the concerns and interests of the provinces, but was also seen by some as tolerant of, or even impelled by, a decided 'Turkification' of the empire. Some feared the implications of this policy for the language and culture of the Arabs; others resented the centralisation which accompanied the policy, giving provincial officials and institutions less autonomy to deal with the particular concerns of the provinces in question; others, in the Ottoman officer corps or the corps of administrative officials, were angered by the effect of these policies on their own careers, since – rightly or wrongly – they believed themselves to be routinely passed over in favour of less qualified Turkish candidates. For many, of course, all of these forms of resentment were linked.

Increasingly, protest found expression in organisations or publications which emphasised the importance of Arab identity and Arab culture. The two most significant organisations that emerged at this time in Baghdad itself were the National Scientific Club and the Baghdad branch of al-ʿAhd (the Covenant). The National Scientific Club was founded in Baghdad in 1912 by a group of young Arab intellectuals, some of whom had been studying in Istanbul. It was led by Muzahim al-Pachachi from the School of Law in Baghdad and enjoyed the patronage of the prominent al-Suwaidi family of *ashraf* in Baghdad and of Sayyid Talib in Basra. This allowed its members to pursue the club's aims of promoting general knowledge, focusing particularly on Arab culture and literature. It also brought together Sunni and Shiʿi intellectuals. The latter were generally modernist reformers, but they also included representatives of a growing movement in the Shiʿi cities which sought to revive interest in Arab traditions and culture. Inevitably the club acted as a forum for political debate and took a role in organising opposition to the CUP's centralising measures. As the authoritarian side of the CUP showed itself ever more strongly, the club came under threat. By the end of 1913 its newspaper had been closed down, Muzahim al-Pachachi and others had fled to Basra, where they were protected by Sayyid Talib, and the remainder had been arrested by the Ottoman authorities.

Suppression of open opposition encouraged the growth of secret societies, the most significant of which in the case of the three Mesopotamian provinces was al-ʿAhd, founded in Istanbul by Arab officers from various provinces of the empire. Branches were soon established in Mosul and in Baghdad by Taha al-Hashimi, himself of Baghdadi origin. In Mosul his brother, Yasin al-Hashimi, became the leader of a branch which included a number of army officers who, like him, were to become prominent in the future Iraqi state – men such as Mawlud Mukhlis, ʿAli Jawdat al-ʿAyyubi and Jamil al-Midfaʿi. In Baghdad, Hamdi al-Pachachi (a cousin of Muzahim al-Pachachi) became head of the branch and was joined by Nuri al-Saʿid, Jaʿfar al-ʿAskari and others who were also to play prominent roles in Iraqi politics. Both of these branches established contacts with the Reform Society of Basra, and Muzahim al-Pachachi became the leader of the smaller branch of al-ʿAhd in that city.

The members of al-ʿAhd shared many ideas about the nature and direction of reform with the dominant CUP, but they differed sharply on the question of decentralisation and on the identity of the state itself. Al-ʿAhd had initially concerned itself with the rights of the Arabs within the empire, but came to question the raison d'être of the empire itself. The young Arab officers became convinced that the Ottoman Empire had become a vehicle for an increasingly strident Turkish nationalism and began to think about the possibility of independence for the Arab provinces. Their plans for action were neither coordinated nor well thought through. However, they showed that this group of Arab officers and officials was losing faith in the Ottoman state itself and was now dreaming of an independent state, ill defined territorially and of uncertain structure, but nevertheless with a distinct Arab identity.[5]

The Ottoman authorities, however, were already beginning to suspect the existence of al-ʿAhd and in 1914 began to move against it. Most of its members in the three Mesopotamian provinces avoided arrest, but some, realising that they were under suspicion, fled to Egypt or Arabia. By this stage, however, events elsewhere were taking a course that would have a lasting impact on the three provinces, paving the way for their eventual incorporation into the new state of Iraq. The CUP government's increasingly close alliance with Germany and its conflicts with Russia in the years preceding 1914 made it difficult for the Ottoman Empire to remain neutral when war was declared between Germany and Russia in the summer of 1914. In October 1914 the Ottoman Empire entered the war on the side of the Central Powers. This fateful move set in motion a train of events that was to end in the empire's destruction. Appropriately enough in this context, the first indication of how things might end came in Mesopotamia with the British occupation of Basra in November 1914.

It would be fanciful to assume that in the years leading up to the British occupation of Mesopotamia the future state of Iraq was somehow prefigured in the common experiences of these provinces. In many respects, the central political relationship with the Ottoman state was broadly similar to that of other Arab provinces where the forces of Ottoman reform and the unforeseen consequences of the interplay of those forces had been at work for over half a century. From the perspective of the government in Istanbul, the three Mesopotamian provinces were neither treated administratively as a unit, nor accorded any form of collective representation that set them apart from other regions of the empire. Meanwhile, those inhabitants who were beginning to rethink their identities as political actors tended to think in categories that linked them to like-minded people in other provinces. In some cases, their thoughts coincided with those of their compatriots elsewhere in Mesopotamia, but they also established organisational and imaginative links far beyond these provincial boundaries. Even Sayyid Talib's apparent reference to the autonomy of an entity called 'Iraq' cannot easily be separated from his view that the smaller stage of Basra was inappropriate for his personal ambition and that he needed to control Baghdad as well.

Nevertheless, some features of emerging political society in the three provinces had helped to create a basis for distinctive ties, if scarcely for unity of purpose or action. Baghdad, as the seat of the major governorate and the headquarters of an Ottoman army corps, did exert a certain gravitational pull on the other two provinces, stronger in the case of Basra than Mosul, but nevertheless visible even in the latter. Equally, as the emerging political organisations indicated, personal links were being forged between members of these groupings – links which were often reinforced by family connections through trade or through membership of the Ottoman administration or of the officer corps. The secrecy of associations like al-'Ahd placed a premium on personal trust and close acquaintance. This served to bring similarly situated young men in the three provinces together. Interconnections and interrelationships did exist therefore among certain sectors of society in the three provinces. Under the aegis of the Ottoman state, these were insufficient to create internal momentum for the establishment of a separate state. However, once that state was created by the intervention of the British, the interplay of these groups and the similar experiences they had undergone in the last decades of Ottoman rule inevitably influenced the positions and attitudes of those who were to find themselves inhabiting the new state of Iraq.

CHAPTER 2

The British Mandate

The British invasion and occupation of the three Ottoman provinces of Basra, Baghdad and Mosul and their subsequent consolidation into the new state of Iraq under a League of Nations Mandate administered by Great Britain radically changed the political worlds of the inhabitants of these territories. The history of Iraq begins here, not simply as the history of the state's formal institutions, but as the histories of all those who found themselves drawn into the new regime of power. It demanded new forms of identity and new strategies to exploit the opportunities that presented themselves. Narratives that had made sense of people's lives in one setting were being overtaken by changed circumstances as the emerging state became the vehicle for distinctive ideas and forms of order, prefigured by, but not necessarily identical to, those of the late Ottoman state. The Iraqi state became a new centre of gravity, setting up or reinforcing the structures that would shape a distinctively Iraqi politics.

In this project, the commanding visions of the British authorities were clearly decisive, but they varied, being contested both by British officials themselves and by the Iraqis. The British needed and found subjects to constitute the order which they believed best suited the idea of the Mandate and the protection of British interests. In some cases, they invented those subjects, encouraging particular individuals and groups to emerge as their chief interlocutors in shaping the narrative of Iraq's political history. Although there were differences among British officials about the best means of achieving this, their overriding concern was to ensure the establishment of a recognisable state and the development of a social order appropriate to it. Despite the ideas of nationalism and of participatory politics associated with the notion of the League of Nations Mandates, the prevailing visions of order were still unmistakably hierarchical and authoritarian.

Consequently, the British authorities looked to two groups in particular to carry their vision through: firstly, the sharifian and ex-Ottoman administrative elites for whom the new state of Iraq was the guarantee of their centrality and status; secondly, the notables of a society increasingly defined by property ownership, whose value lay in their dependence on a state which provided them with the means of ensuring social order. For others, such as the Shiʿi *mujtahids*, the Kurdish leaders or indeed the recently arrived Assyrians who aspired to different kinds of order, the British authorities and many of their Iraqi clients had little tolerance. As the pattern of politics under the Mandate demonstrated, these dissenting voices would not be allowed to deflect the state from the course allotted to it by those who commanded coercive and propertied power. Of the three million or so inhabitants of Iraq at the beginning of the Mandate, more than half were Shiʿi and roughly 20 per cent were Kurdish, with another 8 per cent or so composed of the Jewish, Christian, Yazidi, Sabaean and Turkmen minorities. Yet the government ministers, the senior state officials and the officer corps of the armed forces were drawn almost exclusively from the Sunni Arabs, who constituted less than 20 per cent of the population. Given their minority position, in economic and sectarian terms, as well as their authoritarian inclinations, this was not a promising basis for the national integration that was in theory intended to accompany the construction of the modern state.

BRITISH OCCUPATION AND REACTIONS

Soon after the outbreak of war in October 1914 between the Ottoman Empire and Great Britain, the British landed a Mesopotamian Expeditionary Force (MEF) at the head of the Persian Gulf near Basra, and by the end of November the city was in British hands. Initially planned by the British government of India as a pre-emptive move to protect British interests in the Persian Gulf, the capture of Basra began a process which ended in the British occupation of the three provinces of Basra, Baghdad and Mosul by the end of 1918. These actions laid the foundations for the establishment of the state of Iraq and it is from this period that the history of that state begins. Henceforth the inhabitants of each of these provinces had to contend with the reality of British power and with British plans for their future.

However, in 1914 there was no clear idea either in London or in India about the political future of Mesopotamia. The MEF had limited military objectives, but territorial gains came to be seen, perhaps inevitably, as a political asset in themselves. This mixture of motives led to the occupation of all of Basra province after the defeat of the Ottoman forces at Shuʿaiba in April 1915 and encouraged the rapid advance of a British force to within fifty miles of Baghdad by November. However, a powerful Ottoman counter-attack drove this force back to Kut, where it was besieged for the next four months, eventually surrendering in April 1916. The set-back led to a more cautious strategy. Only in March 1917 did Baghdad fall to British forces, and it was not until the late summer of 1918 that they occupied Kirkuk and effectively destroyed the Ottoman 6th Army. The simultaneous exhaustion of the Central Powers and successive defeats throughout the Middle East led the Ottoman government to sue for peace, paving the way for the Armistice of Mudros in October 1918. Under its terms, all Ottoman garrisons in Mesopotamia were to surrender to the British. This impelled the British commander to move on Mosul, demanding its surrender and ordering the evacuation of all Ottoman forces from the province. The Ottoman governor protested that Mosul was not part of Mesopotamia, but was nevertheless forced to comply, and the Ottoman forces withdrew in November 1918, establishing the armistice line at the northern border of Mosul province.

The inhabitants of the three provinces reacted in a variety of ways to the events which engulfed them. In Basra, the leading figures of the city came to a rapid accommodation with the British authorities, with whom, as merchants in the Persian Gulf, they had long been in contact. During the previous fifty or so years, British naval and commercial power had been predominant in the region and many of the principal traders of Basra had bowed to the inevitable, becoming linked to British trading houses, rather than trying to compete against them. This reinforced British commercial interests in Mesopotamia to such an extent that on the eve of the First World War these interests controlled over two-thirds of the growing volume of imports and roughly half of the exports that passed through Basra. It was scarcely surprising, therefore, that amongst the merchants of Basra the transition to British rule should have been met with relative equanimity, once certain disputes over army requisitioning practices had been settled.[1]

Amongst the Shi'a of the middle and lower Euphrates, in the *'atabat* and in the countryside, the Ottoman declaration of a *jihad* against the infidel British met with a mixed response. Some Shi'i *mujtahids* endorsed the call, but the most senior of them, Ayatollah Kazim Yazdi, refused to do so. Large numbers of tribesmen did join the Ottoman forces as auxiliaries, but many deserted after the defeat at Shu'aiba, sometimes turning on their erstwhile allies. In Najaf and Karbala in the months following Shu'aiba, uprisings against the Ottoman authorities broke out. These uprisings were anti-Ottoman in a broad sense, often sparked by particular local resentments, but they were not in support of the British war effort. Instead, the rebels seized upon the weakness of the Ottoman state to compel the authorities to grant both cities a large degree of administrative autonomy.

In Baghdad, as British forces approached in 1915, the possibility of an uprising against the Ottoman authorities was discussed by notables of the city and by members of al-ʿAhd. However, there were doubts about the propriety of such a rebellion among the leading families, and the Ottoman forces were, in any case, still too strong to be challenged openly. Some members of the Arab nationalist secret society al-ʿAhd in the Ottoman army took the opportunity to desert. Others, taken prisoner by the British, declared their desire to advance the 'Arab cause', but this had little definition until the outbreak of the Arab Revolt in the Hijaz led by the Hashemite Sharif Husain of Mecca and his sons in mid-1916. Thereafter, increasing numbers of Ottoman officers of Mesopotamian origin joined the army of the sharif, becoming the largest single grouping in the officer corps and occupying most of the senior command posts. Thus it was that when the Hashemite Amir Faisal (son of the sharif and future king of Iraq) entered Damascus in 1918 as part of the victorious Allied forces, he commanded an army largely officered by men from the provinces that would constitute the future state of Iraq. These were the men who would be instrumental in helping him to establish the short-lived Arab Kingdom, based on Damascus.

The great majority of the population of Mesopotamia was more concerned about surviving the fighting between the British and the Ottoman forces. Many welcomed the removal of Ottoman control, but were apprehensive about British military occupation. In some areas, it did not take long for resistance to appear. Thus, in early 1918, a few months after the British had established their control over Najaf and Karbala, the Society of Islamic Revival (Jamʿiyya al-Nahda al-Islamiyya) was founded in Najaf, bringing together notables, clerics and tribal shaikhs. Its ostensible purpose was the defence of Islam against the British, but its members were also reacting against tighter British administrative control of the city, as well as against British disbursement of the funds of the substantial Oudh Bequest. These feelings culminated in the assassination of a British official – an act which brought swift retaliation in the form of a British blockade of Najaf and the reassertion of British control.[2]

In the Kurdish areas the British forces were given an initial welcome when they captured Kirkuk briefly in May 1918. Indeed, a meeting of Kurdish tribal leaders in Sulaimaniyya that month offered the rule of their country to Great Britain. The British had already established contact with one of them, Shaikh Mahmud Barzinji, and, believing that his authority was acknowledged in much of the area, made him governor of Lower Kurdistan in December 1918 as part of a plan for indirect rule. Acting partly in his own interest and in that of his closest associates and tribal kin, Shaikh Mahmud soon fell out with some of the other Kurdish chiefs. It was also clear that he had larger ambitions for the Kurds in the region more generally than the British authorities were willing to countenance. The British, harassed at the time by sporadic rebellion elsewhere in Kurdistan, and divided amongst themselves about the wisdom of indirect rule, moved to restrain him, but met with resistance and with his defiant proclamation of an independent Kurdistan in May 1919. This strengthened the hand of those British officials in Baghdad who had been arguing for a return to direct rule in Kurdistan. A British military expedition was despatched, leading to the capture of Shaikh Mahmud and to the re-establishment of a British administration in Sulaimaniyya. However, this did not end the outbursts of revolt and defiance in Kurdistan.

Often local in nature, these could be aimed against neighbours as much as against the British authorities, but they stemmed from a similar desire, even compulsion, on the part of the Kurdish tribal chieftains to exploit any perceived weakness of central power to assert their own autonomy. They resented any attempt by outside powers to curb their own freedom of action, but across the large area that constituted the homeland of the Kurdish peoples – which extended far beyond the portion of Mosul province that had been incorporated into the emerging territory of Iraq – there was considerable uncertainty and some turmoil, given the collapse of the Ottoman state and the enfeeblement of the Qajar state in Persia.

These developments encouraged some Kurds to make a case for Kurdish self-determination, based on a Kurdish linguistic nationalism. Given the varieties of the Kurdish language, as well as the other social divisions within the Kurdish territories, this idea was not always well understood or well received. However, even for those Kurds whose primary sense of identity lay with their clan or their religious order, the disintegration of former power centres and the intrusion of Great Britain as the dominant power obliged them to make new calculations about how best to secure the future of their localities. Sometimes this led to defiance, but it could also lead to a pragmatic accommodation in which Kurdish leaders sought to enlist the power of Great Britain to their own advantage.[3]

In Baghdad and in the central regions of the three provinces, a wary attitude to the British military occupation developed. The Sykes–Picot agreement, with its plan for British and French division of the former Ottoman provinces, had become generally known and the fears it aroused were only

2 Shaikh Mahmud (Kurdish leader), 1920

partially counteracted by the Anglo-French declaration of November 1918 which seemed to promise self-government to these same provinces. Self-government, however, was the goal of the officers in al-ʿAhd. Many were now part of the military establishment in the sharifian administration in Damascus under Amir Faisal, but they did not lose sight of their home provinces. Indeed, their constant preoccupation led to the founding of al-ʿAhd al-ʿIraqi in 1918. For these men, the goal was the independence of Iraq, understood broadly as the three Ottoman provinces of Basra, Baghdad and Mosul, within a framework of Arab unity provided by the authority of Sharif Husain himself.

Many in al-ʿAhd al-ʿIraqi believed that the British would help them to achieve their goals and advocated strong ties with Great Britain. In this they differed from their colleagues in Iraq itself. Here the experience of British rule had not been encouraging, since former officers and government officials found themselves out of work or marginalised by the imposition of direct rule through British officials. Soon a rift in al-ʿAhd al-ʿIraqi reflected this difference of opinion. Yasin al-Hashimi, its effective leader, was wary of British intentions towards Iraq and, although he was Amir Faisal's chief of staff, had little affection for him. The other faction, led by Nuri al-Saʿid and Jaʿfar al-ʿAskari, was more attached to the idea of a Hashemite ruler and recognised the importance of Great Britain in deciding the future of Iraq.

The British themselves were undecided about its future – notoriously so, as the Iraqis found to their bewilderment. During the war, British civil administration had grown, reflecting the immediate desire for order and incorporating a distinctive set of ideas and practices, shaped largely by the experience of administration in India. This brought with it the structures and the ideas associated with direct British rule and was represented in British officialdom by those who came to be known as the 'imperial school'. British political officers were stationed throughout the provinces, backed by British-staffed departments in Baghdad which already treated the three provinces as a single administrative unit. Nominally under the British military commander in chief, the central administration was headed by the civil commissioner (Sir Percy Cox until May 1918; thereafter Sir Arnold Wilson as acting civil commissioner). The dominance of this trend in the early years of British rule left little scope for those who advocated a more indirect approach, on the model of the British occupation of Egypt. It also left little room for the former senior officials of the Ottoman state who were nevertheless aware that they had potential allies within the circles of British officialdom.

3 Sir Percy Cox (British civil commissioner in Iraq and first high commissioner
under the British Mandate), c. 1918

4 Gertrude Bell (oriental secretary to the British
civil commissioner, Baghdad), c. 1921

Extending the scope of direct rule, the British abolished institutions such as the Ottoman elected municipal councils, and depended instead on the political officers who worked directly through local notables on whom they relied to maintain order. In large areas of the countryside this created a form of indirect rule, but of a more recognisably imperial kind. The British officials remained in control and, in many cases, British policy was instrumental in shaping the very tribal hierarchies and units that, it was claimed, constituted the 'natural' order of the society. This tendency was reinforced by the introduction of the Tribal Civil and Criminal Disputes Regulation (based on the Government of India Act of the same name and later, in 1924, to be encoded into Iraqi law). It gave tribal shaikhs, designated by the British authorities, the power to settle all disputes with and between the members of their tribe and also charged them with collecting taxes on behalf of the government. It seemed to many therefore that Great Britain was preparing the way for the incorporation of Iraq directly into the British Empire.

This impression was reinforced when Arnold Wilson organised a survey (misleadingly labelled a 'plebiscite') of the opinions of notables in the three provinces in early 1919. When asked about the future shape and constitution of the state, they returned a variety of answers. There seemed to be some agreement, outside the Kurdish areas, that the state should comprise all three of the Ottoman provinces under an Arab government. However, there was little agreement about the form of that government, or the identity of its future ruler. Furthermore, Arnold Wilson greatly exaggerated the degree to which there existed general acquiescence to continued British control. At the time, the British government was preoccupied with the Peace Conference at Versailles and, in the absence of a decision on the future of Iraq, the civil administration continued to entrench itself.

This development was met with growing misgivings on the part of the military authorities and of Gertrude Bell, Wilson's oriental secretary. Having initially believed in the virtues of direct rule, Bell had become a strong advocate for Iraqi self-government under British tutelage. She had thus drawn closer to those British officials in London and elsewhere who favoured sharifian rule of Iraq, even if her reasons for doing so tended to differ from theirs. In London, the chief concern was the cost to the British Treasury of direct rule. Bell, on the other hand, had become convinced that Arab nationalism was developing an unstoppable momentum. For her, this meant that the British should work with the largely urban and Sunni nationalists to modernise the country and to end what she regarded as the reactionary and obscurantist influence of the Shi'i clerics and their tribal followings. This change of attitude caused a major rift with Arnold Wilson, but gave heart to the sharifian officers and others who were well aware of the split in British ranks. However, as contemporary accounts indicate, the Iraqis were often rather perplexed by the variety of opinions they encountered in the small world of British officialdom in Baghdad – and uncertain about its implications for their future and about how best to exploit these divisions.[4]

THE IRAQI REVOLT OF 1920

Inevitably, opposition to direct British rule began to form. Al-'Ahd al-'Iraqi held a congress in Damascus in March 1920 which declared the independence of Iraq under the kingship of Amir 'Abdallah, brother of Amir Faisal and one of the sons of Sharif Husain. Few recognised the authority of this congress and 'Abdallah himself was distinctly cool towards it. Nevertheless, it signalled a shift of al-'Ahd's activities towards Iraq. A number of officers moved to Dair al-Zur in eastern Syria, hoping to use it as a base of operations. Accordingly, in May 1920 Jamil al-Midfa'i, leading a mixed force of regular soldiers and tribal allies, captured the town of Tall 'Afar and then marched on Mosul, intending to time his arrival with a planned revolt in the city. However, the British dispersed the force before it could reach

Mosul and the revolt never took place. Thereafter, individual members of al-ʿAhd remained active, infiltrating into Iraq from Syria, but the organised activities of al-ʿAhd al-ʿIraqi came to an end. Within a few weeks the French, having been granted the Mandate by the League of Nations, had occupied all of Syria and the centre of events had switched to Iraq itself.

It was here that resentment of the British military occupation was at its strongest. The British authorities had prevented a delegation from going to the Versailles Peace Conference in 1919. In reaction, a secret society – the Independence Guard (Haras al-Istiqlal) – was formed. Like al-ʿAhd al-ʿIraqi, it called for the independence of Iraq (understood as the three Ottoman provinces) under one of the sons of Sharif Husain. It differed from al-ʿAhd, however, since it included more civilians than military officers and had a more diverse social composition. Al-ʿAhd drew almost exclusively upon the ranks of the Sunni Arab officers and officials who had been the mainstay of the Ottoman state, but the majority of the members of the Independence Guard were Shiʿi. It was led by Muhammad al-Sadr, a son of one of the most eminent Shiʿi *mujtahids*, Ayatollah Hasan al-Sadr of al-Kazimiyya, and had close links with another eminent *mujtahid*, Ayatollah Muhammad Taqi al-Shirazi, through his son Mirza Muhammad Rida.

The Independence Guard acted as a link, therefore, between those sections of the Sunni and Shiʿi Arab communities which were beginning to think about the future of the three provinces as the British authorities proceeded with their own plans for Iraq. These began to take shape following the development of the idea of League of Nations Mandates for the territories of the defeated Central Powers in the aftermath of the Peace Treaty of Versailles in 1919. This idea was based on the principle that the territories concerned should eventually become independent, self-governing nation-states, but under the tutelage of one or other of the Allies, accountable, in theory, to the League of Nations.

For educated and official circles in the territories of the Ottoman provinces, this was both ominous and patronising. It seemed to suggest European imperial rule by another name. Even at its most benign it seemed to many of the former officials of the Ottoman Empire, as well as to a number of notable families, that the idea was deeply contemptuous of their own administrative and political experience, belittling their own roles as leaders of their societies. These fears were reinforced when the Mandate for Iraq was awarded to Great Britain at the San Remo Conference in April 1920, apparently clearing the way for the British to set up a ruling Council of State, composed largely of British officials, with Iraqis in strictly subordinate positions.

It was at this point that a coalition began to form amongst those who were most concerned about incorporation into the British Empire. In the Shi'i city of Karbala, Ayatollah al-Shirazi issued a *fatwa* declaring that service in the British administration was unlawful. Meetings followed between Shi'i *ulama* and tribal shaikhs of the mid-Euphrates, as well as with members of the Independence Guard which set up branches in a number of provincial towns. These contacts produced a strategy for co-ordinated action which initially favoured peaceful demonstrations of protest, principally in Baghdad, the seat of British power. However, it left the way open for more violent forms of resistance should these protests fail to produce results.

Accordingly, beginning in May 1920, a series of mass meetings took place in Baghdad to denounce the Mandate. Gathering by turn at Sunni and Shi'i mosques, increasing numbers of Baghdadis attended, providing vivid symbolic proof of co-operation between members of the two sects in the cause of Iraqi independence. The numbers who came to listen to speeches and nationalist poems also indicated that a new form of politics was emerging in the intended capital of the new state. In order to give it focus and to capture the moment of apparent unity of purpose, one of the larger meetings in May nominated fifteen representatives to present the case for Iraqi independence to the British authorities. Arnold Wilson agreed to see them in early June, but only in the company of twenty-five Baghdadi notables whom he had himself selected. He was well aware that the new style of politics was deeply disturbing for many of the Sunni notables. Apparent reconciliation between Shi'a and Sunnis threatened to enhance the power of the Shi'i *mujtahids*, extending it into areas from which it had been excluded for centuries. In addition, the innovatory idea that numbers should now count in politics and the mobilisation of large crowds of people in mosques and on the streets seemed to many of the Sunni *ulama* and notable families both perverse and dangerous.

After a fruitless meeting between Wilson and the *mandubin* (delegates), the British continued to pursue their policy of limited self-rule for Iraq, impelled more by suggestions from London – encouraged by Bell in Baghdad – than by Wilson himself. In June 1920 it was announced that elections would be held for a Constituent Assembly, and a committee of former Ottoman deputies, headed by Sayyid Talib al-Naqib, was appointed to devise the electoral machinery. Sayyid Talib, having returned from exile, clearly hoped to profit from the many opportunities which seemed likely to arise as the new state took shape. In this he was not alone. Amongst the sharifian officers a significant number saw little point in engaging in a futile struggle with the British occupying forces. Instead, they tried to insert themselves into the new structures of the emerging state to ensure that it would be tailored to suit their purposes.

Similar motives appear to have worked on a number of the notables of the three provinces who looked to the British to secure their existing privileges and the social order which underpinned them. This applied both to Sunni Arab notables and to a number of Shi'i tribal shaikhs, insofar as British officials left them a degree of autonomy, and seemed willing to allow them to profit from the privileges which they had enjoyed through their engagement with the Ottoman state. In the case of the tribal shaikhs their attitude to the British authorities depended upon a variety of factors, ranging from their relations with their own tribesmen, especially over land ownership questions, through the vexed questions of taxation and water rights, to the nature of their personal encounters with the representatives of the new British power.

The evolving British idea of the state and the gradual implementation of the measures which gave it definition were thus provoking distinct and often opposing responses from different sections of the population. Nevertheless, in all cases the emerging state of Iraq, however dimly or variously perceived, was becoming the main focus of action, a centre of gravity that was exerting a new and distinctive force on the many communities and groupings which inhabited the territories of the state. It was towards this developing structure that people began to adjust their behaviour, insofar as engagement with it could not be avoided and might be turned to advantage. Consequently, it was scarcely surprising that as the British began to give the new state greater definition they found that the numbers of collaborators grew, but also that their critics became more vehement.

Faced by demonstrations in the streets of Baghdad, the British authorities reacted forcefully. By August 1920 organised public opposition in the city had become virtually impossible, given the weight of the British security forces and the activities of the intelligence services. However, the rebellion was developing its own momentum outside Baghdad. As early as May 1920 the shaikhs of some of the major tribes of the mid-Euphrates had discussed the possibility of acting against the British occupying forces. Their motives were various. Some had been in touch with opposition circles in Najaf and Karbala and they shared with many in Iraq a foreboding about British rule, whether as Muslims or as shaikhs who had hitherto enjoyed considerable autonomy. In some cases, they were also responding to the anxieties of their tribesmen about land tenure, taxation and the ways in which intrusive British administration might affect their economic situation. Very local motives were also at work in many cases. At the same time, it was obvious that the British forces were spread thinly and an echo of continuing misgivings in London about the wisdom of British occupation had reached Iraq, giving rise to the thought that armed rebellion might not drive the British from Iraq but might at least accelerate their departure.

At the end of June 1920 armed revolt broke out, triggered by a number of incidents. Following the arrest of his son, Ayatollah al-Shirazi (who had become the leading Shiʿi *mujtahid* in Iraq on the death of Ayatollah Yazdi in 1919) issued a *fatwa*, seeming to encourage armed revolt. Hoping to pre-empt any rebellion, the British authorities arrested a number of tribal chiefs in the mid-Euphrates region, but the arrests had exactly the opposite effect. The revolt gained momentum, deriving its strength from the weakness of the British garrisons in the area, as well as from the strong links between the spiritual centres of Shiʿism in Najaf and Karbala and the powerful armed tribes deployed against the British. By late July much of the mid-Euphrates region was in the hands of the rebels. This set-back for British control gave heart to others and the revolt spread to the tribes of the lower Euphrates, as well as to districts to the north, east and west of Baghdad. Seizing their opportunity, Kurdish chiefs in southern Kurdistan rose up and captured a number of towns near the Persian border, but this activity was largely opportunistic. There was no co-ordination with the Arab tribes and even in the Kurdish region the further the rebels moved from their home areas, the less support they found.

However, within a month the revolt generally was beginning to flag, to the evident relief not only of the British authorities, but also of many of the Sunni notables of Baghdad, apprehensive at this apparent manifestation of tribal and Shiʿi power. The spread of the revolt was largely determined by the view taken by local leaders about the ways in which British rule might affect their own situation. Thus, the tribal shaikhs of the regions of Kut and ʿAmara not only refused to join the revolt, but also worked against it. They and their extensive landholdings had been recognised by the British authorities and they were clearly unwilling to place these gains in jeopardy. These geographical limits to the revolt allowed the British forces to regroup and to counter-attack with a formidable modern arsenal at their disposal. They succeeded in regaining control of all areas by the end of October 1920 and, with the surrender of Najaf and Karbala, the rebellion was over.

The Iraqi revolt had cost the lives of an estimated 6,000 Iraqis and roughly 500 British and Indian soldiers. Politically, it had a number of important consequences. For the Iraqis it became part of the founding myth of Iraqi nationalism, however remote this idea may have been from the minds of most of the participants. As such, it was to be claimed by different groups of Iraqis and used to assert their own roles in the foundation of the state, privileging their particular ideas about the meaning, identity and interests of the new Iraqi political community. The events in Baghdad prior to the revolt showed unprecedented co-operation in the face of British rule and helped to bridge a powerful status divide between significant numbers of Sunnis and Shiʿa in the capital at least, but the lasting effects were less harmonious than these images suggest.

The Iraqi revolt of 1920 began as a general protest against British rule, but ended as a revolt of the mid-Euphrates. As such, it was a product of the specific conditions of that region which combined religious dissent, socio-economic insecurity and armed might. The British occupation helped to focus these forces and the debates over the future of Iraq provided an opportunity for the Shiʿa – through their *mujtahids*, tribal shaikhs and lay leaders – to stake their own claims in the emerging political order. They were defeated militarily and, although their power was not broken, they had to watch others benefit from the political opportunities that their sacrifices had helped to create. This left a legacy of resentment against the emerging political establishment in Baghdad which few members of that establishment saw fit to address and which was to have troubling consequences for the politics of the new state in the first decades of its existence.[5]

THE INSTITUTIONAL DEFINITION OF THE STATE

In London, the revolt and the cost of its suppression intensified the search for a more acceptable form of government in Iraq. Insistence on direct rule was seen as having contributed to the rebellion and was clearly going to cost Great Britain dear. Consequently, when Sir Percy Cox arrived in Baghdad in early October to take up his post as first high commissioner under the Mandate, he persuaded the elderly naqib al-ashraf of Baghdad, Sayyid ʿAbd al-Rahman al-Kailani, to accept the presidency of an appointed council of ministers working under British supervision. In November 1920, the government was formed, headed by the naqib and including twenty-one eminent Iraqis from all three of the old Ottoman provinces. Sunni Arabs predominated and held the most important posts, but the council of ministers also included a few Shiʿa and Christians, as well as a prominent member of the Jewish community. Within a short time the Ottoman administrative units were restored, as were the municipal councils, and Iraqi officials began to replace British political officers in the provinces (except in the Kurdish district of Sulaimaniyya). However, they were assisted in each case by a British adviser and British advisers were similarly attached to each of the new ministries.

One feature of the new state structures which became immediately apparent was the absence of any Shi'i appointees to senior administrative positions, save in the 'atabat. The old Sunni-dominated order of Ottoman times was apparently being re-established. Indeed, it could hardly have been otherwise. The Shi'a had largely been excluded from the Ottoman administration and consequently there were few amongst them with any administrative experience. Furthermore, the attitude of the naqib and other Baghdadi notables to the Shi'a in general and the wariness of the British towards the Shi'a following the recent revolt gave them common ground for looking elsewhere for the officials of the new state. They did not have far to look. Large numbers of predominantly Sunni Arab ex-Ottoman officials, hitherto excluded by the British, were now looking to the new government to restore them to the place that they regarded as rightfully theirs.

Nowhere was this more apparent than in the formation of the Iraqi army, one of the first steps taken by the new government in 1921. Ja'far al-'Askari, a former Ottoman officer from Baghdad who had joined the forces of the sharif of Mecca during the Arab Revolt, became minister of defence. He organised the return of roughly 600 former Ottoman officers of Iraqi origin, and from these men, drawn almost exclusively from the Sunni Arab families of the three provinces, the officer corps of the new Iraqi army was formed. Chief amongst them, and in some ways typifying this section of Iraqi society, was Ja'far al-'Askari's brother-in-law, Nuri al-Sa'id, who became chief of the general staff of the Iraqi army in February 1921. Generally, these men were products of the Ottoman educational and administrative reforms of the nineteenth century and, as such, they tended to come from relatively modest families of urban Sunni Arab or Arabised Kurds and Turks, connected to the Ottoman administration. The creation of the new Iraqi state, therefore, opened up a route to power and influence which many were quick to seize, hoping to find there the wealth and status they otherwise lacked in the existing hierarchies of the Sunni Arab community.[6]

Administratively the state began to take shape, but the question of its final constitutional form had yet to be resolved. These considerations in the Iraqi case, and equally important questions in other spheres of British interest in the Middle East, led to the convening of the Cairo Conference in March 1921 by Winston Churchill, the newly appointed colonial secretary now entrusted with Iraq's affairs. A large delegation from Iraq attended,

5 Sayyid ʿAbd al-Rahman al-Kailani (naqib al-ashraf of Baghdad and first prime minister of Iraq), c. 1920

comprising for the most part senior British officials and military officers, but also including two Iraqi ministers, Jaʿfar al-ʿAskari and Sasun Hasqail.

At the Cairo Conference the decision was taken to establish a kingdom of Iraq and to offer the throne to the Hashemite Amir Faisal. He had been forced to flee from Syria after the French occupation in 1920 and thereafter came under the protection of the British with whom he enjoyed generally good relations, based on the experience of the Arab Revolt and on close relationships with a number of well-placed British officials. As a public figure he was regarded as having a natural authority in the Arab world, but, equally importantly, he was believed to be amenable to British advice and well aware of the limitations that the reality of British power in the Middle East would place upon his ambitions.

Faisal accepted the offer of the throne of Iraq with some reservations. At the age of thirty-six he had few illusions about the power of empires to make and break his fortunes. He was also aware that authority was not given, but had to be striven for, and that here coercive power was necessary but not sufficient. Having been brought up in Istanbul, he had first-hand knowledge of his father's successful intrigues to be installed as sharif of Mecca. Equally, as a leader of the Arab Revolt during the First World War, he knew the difficulty of mobilising the Arabs of the Hijaz to fight for a unified cause and also knew that British material assistance had been vital in contributing to his success. Furthermore, his expulsion from Damascus, despite British patronage, reminded him that friendship had no currency when imperial interests were at stake. These experiences had made him an astute and realistic politician, aware of his own limitations, of the weakness of his position and of the struggle necessary to create a basis for his authority. This sensitivity, combined with considerable personal charm, served him well in helping to establish his authority in Iraq. However, it may also have contributed to the despair he felt when, shortly before his death in 1933, he contemplated the fractious and divided society that formed the precarious underpinning of the state which he had helped to found.[7]

In 1921, he was well aware that most of the inhabitants of Iraq either knew nothing of his existence, or saw little reason why he should be installed as ruler of the country. However, he also knew that he had a nucleus of local support among those who had been under his command during the Arab Revolt and in the short-lived sharifian administration in Damascus. They now occupied various posts in the Iraqi state and together with the British authorities they ensured that Faisal received a friendly, if unenthusiastic, welcome when he landed in Iraq in June. Within a few weeks the council of ministers passed a resolution declaring Faisal king of Iraq, a bogus 'referendum' was held in which it was claimed that 96 per cent of the population of Iraq accepted the new king and on 23 August 1921 Faisal was ceremoniously enthroned.

Despite the relative lack of enthusiasm for Faisal, there was little organised opposition, in part because there were no obvious alternatives. The

British had taken the precaution of deporting Sayyid Talib al-Naqib, who harboured his own ambitions to rule Iraq. In contrast to Sayyid Talib, Faisal had the advantage, as an outsider, of not being associated with any particular faction or region of the country. However, as an Arab, he did not have much support amongst the Kurds and, as a Sunni, he found little favour among the Shi'a, although some respected him as a *sayyid*. For their part, the established Sunni *sayyid* families in Iraq tended to regard him as an interloper, although his identity was reassuringly familiar and suggested no radical departures from the old order.

Faisal had few illusions about the precariousness of his position or about the problems of trying to give some semblance of coherence to the state over which he now ruled. His reign, which was to last twelve years, was marked by his attempt to give some strength to an office characterised chiefly by its weakness. He was sovereign of a state that was itself not sovereign. He was regarded with suspicion by most of the leading sectors of Iraq's heterogeneous society, for what he was, for his association with the British and for his patronage of the small circles of ex-sharifian officers. At the same time, he was aware that the same forces which could easily bring him down also wanted to use him for their different purposes. This gave him a certain room for manoeuvre which he used to the full, both to carve out for himself a position of personal authority unforeseen at the outset and to advance his own ideas of the kind of state Iraq should be.

These ideas revolved around two themes: the gradual achievement of real independence from British control and the integration of the existing communities of Iraq into a unitary structure in which they could feel that their identities and interests were fully respected. As far as the former was concerned, Faisal and his governments had considerable success, within the limits of the possible. For the latter, however, his aspirations were thwarted by the flawed nature of the enterprise. His was not an egalitarian vision, nor was it a disinterested one. On the contrary, it was marked by a strong sense of privilege. Furthermore, it depended for its execution on men, such as the ex-sharifian officers, who were themselves trying to advance particular interests and who believed confidently in the need for coercion to achieve the discipline and unity required.

With the installation of Faisal as king, not only did the state take on greater definition, but the distinctive patterns of its politics began to emerge. The intensity of the struggles that ensued can partly be explained by the feeling on all sides that there was everything to play for. The Electoral Law and the constitution would decide the formal allocation of power in the state, thereby affecting the relative strengths of those who

6 King Faisal I (King of Iraq 1921–33), c. 1932

could rely on significant societal support and those who would look to the state machinery for their strength. Equally, the vehemence of the debates over the nature of the relationship with Great Britain was due in part to the continuing rejection by many of any form of British domination, but also to the conviction by some that they still needed British support. Also important was the restricted scope of the political world, in the sense of those who took effective decisions or could hope to influence the policies of the government and thus the nature of the state. Much depended upon the personalities of the players themselves, their relationships and ambitions translating into positions of political principle. Much also depended upon the networks of clients and associates which they maintained, relying in the final analysis on these links to sustain their onward momentum in search of power and the goals which made the attainment of power desirable. This had a number of important consequences.

On the one hand, Baghdad became the centre of gravity for all aspirants to power. Exclusion from this world, for reasons of socio-economic status or provincial location, meant political marginalisation. Other worlds of great meaning and power, of course, still existed in the territories of Iraq, fostering resentment at exclusion or discrimination. This could produce direct action of varying kinds, whether among the Shi'i *mujtahids* of the *'atabat*, the tribal shaikhs of the middle and lower Euphrates or the Kurds of the northern hills. On the other hand, the state centred on Baghdad clearly had the power to attract. At one end of the social scale, the influx of peasants began, drawn to the city by rural destitution and hopes of employment. Politically, the consequences of this movement would become apparent only much later. More immediately relevant was Baghdad's gravitational pull on those at the upper end of the social scale who wished to end their splendid isolation and consequent marginalisation. Tribal shaikhs, Kurdish chieftains, notables of the other major cities of Iraq and representatives of diverse communities from the south to the north either congregated in Baghdad or ensured that they had agents in place to look after their interests when major decisions were taken.

In this way, a form of co-option developed, drawing these individuals into the reward system of the Iraqi state with its various sources of patronage. For those who were already well placed in the capital to shape the state and the disposition of its resources, clients in the provinces were useful. They extended personal power and were expected to reciprocate by acting in the interests of their patron. One effect of such a patronage system was that local interests were subtly transformed, becoming less inimical to the state as such and seeking fulfilment through closer association with the state and its hierarchies. This gradual engagement of social forces and diverse communities with the state continued a process begun in Ottoman times, albeit within a different framework.

The principal currency of this patronage system was land. In the newly emerging state, land was the reward for influence and power. It also conferred influence and power on its possessors. For the authorities, therefore, it was a way of purchasing social order. For individuals who found themselves well placed in the state it constituted not only a route to self-enrichment, but also a potent means of creating the following needed to establish a man's weight and credibility in the narrow circles of the political world. This had been evident under the Ottoman regime. It had also been a feature since the earliest years of the British occupation when Henry Dobbs (revenue commissioner during the military occupation and later high commissioner under the Mandate, 1923–9) saw the confirmation and grant of title to land and the distribution of leases as the most effective means of ensuring order in the countryside.

Strongly influenced by his belief in the 'natural' authority of shaikhs over tribesmen, Dobbs used land to reinforce – sometimes to create – the powers of tribal shaikhs over their tribesmen who now also became their tenants. Given the wide variety of prescriptive and other rights attached to land in different regions of Iraq, this policy sometimes had the opposite effect, provoking resistance and rebellion among those who suddenly found themselves dispossessed or beholden to shaikhs to whom they felt no special attachment. In these cases, more locally appropriate arrangements were sometimes entered into. Nevertheless, this did not lessen the degree to which particular and often very immediate political considerations shaped the patterns of landholding in much of Iraq, creating over time a profound interconnection between the political order and landed interests of various kinds.[8]

MANDATE AND TREATY

During this period, as the new state gained definition, a major preoccupation of those Iraqis who had been placed at the summit of power was the question of the relationship with Great Britain. Because of general Iraqi opposition to the idea of a Mandate, the British decided to organise their relations with Iraq by means of a treaty, giving the appearance of a normal relationship between two sovereign states. The facts that one of the parties was overwhelmingly powerful, was effectively in military occupation of the other and held the Mandate of the League of Nations to rule the other pending true self-government could scarcely be disguised by this fiction. For this reason, the council of ministers, when agreeing to the terms of the treaty in June 1922, insisted that they be ratified by the Constituent Assembly once it came into being. This decision had the effect of linking the treaty with equally controversial debates about the constitutional framework of the new state. Protest meetings were organised in the southern Shi'i cities and disturbances erupted in the mid-Euphrates region. These rallied anti-treaty opinion, but also highlighted the particular concern of the Shi'a that the treaty and the institutional arrangements needed for its ratification would consolidate a state over which they had no control and which might habitually ignore their interests.

These concerns gave rise to a style of political organisation suited to the new rules outlined by the Electoral Law of May 1922. Two political parties – the Watani (Patriotic) Party and the Nahda (Awakening) Party – were formed in the summer of that year by a number of prominent lay Shi'a, including Ja'far Abu al-Timman, who had been a member of the council of ministers until his resignation in protest over the treaty. Based principally in Baghdad and making the most of this new, concentrated site of political action, the parties organised demonstrations and published newspapers as part of a campaign against both the treaty and the forthcoming elections. These parties were hybrid organisations. In many respects, they represented the personal followings of the prominent individuals who led them and were thus confined to the limited number of people who saw some advantage, personal as much as communal, in attaching themselves to powerful figures in society. However, they also embodied the realisation that, in the emerging politics of the new state, with its ostensible commitment to the idea of popular sovereignty and its apparent attempt to represent the will of the people through elected representatives, the voice of the majority might count in a way that it had never done before. From the perspective of the leaders of these parties – and confirmed by the British population estimates of 1920 – the natural majority in Iraq was Shi'i. Consequently, they needed to organise to take advantage of the new situation in which this social fact would carry political weight.

These parties were not alone in opposing the treaty. King Faisal also resented its restrictive terms and was aware of the danger of being used as a cipher to validate British domination of Iraq. Consequently, he encouraged the anti-treaty opposition, thereby undermining the naqib, who promptly resigned the premiership. The king and the British were now in direct confrontation. This might have cost the king his throne, had he not been struck down fortuitously by appendicitis. Cox seized the moment to impose direct rule, suppressing the most radical parties and newspapers, banishing a number of opposition politicians and ordering the bombing of tribal insurgents in the mid-Euphrates. For the king and for others, there could be no clearer expression of British determination to see the treaty and their plans for the Iraqi state carried through. Thus, when King Faisal resumed his duties in September 1922, he reinstated the naqib as prime minister and affirmed his support for the treaty which was signed in October.

The terms of the treaty embodied the principles of the Mandate. It proclaimed that it was to be carried out 'without prejudice' to Iraq's national sovereignty. However, the decisive role assigned to the British authorities in financial matters and in international and security affairs, as well as in certain judicial questions, clearly indicated the limits on Iraqi sovereignty. Iraq had to prove itself ready and able to exercise its sovereignty in a way acceptable to the great powers that dominated the League of Nations. In the meantime, it was to be tutored in this role through 'such advice and assistance as may be required' from Great Britain through its network of resident advisers in the Iraqi administration. As British actions had recently demonstrated, this was not advice that the Iraqis themselves were at liberty to refuse.

In the light of this fact, and faced by continuing opposition in the Shi'i areas, as well as by demonstrations in Baghdad that gave substance to the new forms of politics which were so alien to him, the elderly and exhausted naqib resigned the premiership in November 1922. He was succeeded by 'Abd al-Muhsin al-Sa'dun, another Sunni notable and landowner who was a member of the family of *sayyids* which had ruled the great Muntafiq confederation of tribes on the lower Euphrates. He was regarded warily by the king, but the British saw him as someone with sufficient personal authority and social standing to carry through the treaty and the other measures required for the constitutional foundation of the Iraqi state.

However, the territorial limits of that state were now thrown into question. Turkey, under the leadership of Mustafa Kemal, had emerged victorious from its war with Greece and laid claim to the former province of Mosul. This complicated an already complex situation in the north of Iraq. Earlier in 1922 Turkish forces had penetrated into the Kurdish areas of the province, a number of northern Kurdish tribal leaders had risen in revolt and the British had evacuated Sulaimaniyya, leaving it in the charge of a council headed by a brother of Shaikh Mahmud. In an effort to re-establish some kind of authority in the region which would act as a bulwark against further Turkish encroachment, Cox decided to release Shaikh Mahmud from detention and install him once more as governor in Sulaimaniyya. Given Shaikh Mahmud's past record and troubled relations with the British, this was a surprising move, but at the time he appeared to Cox to be the only figure who had sufficient authority to check the spread of disaffection in the Kurdish region.

Cox was well aware that one of the main reasons for the unrest in the Kurdish region was the growing perception that the earlier promises of autonomy would be abandoned and, as the state of Iraq took on greater definition, it would bring the Kurds under the direct rule of the Arab government which the British had established in Baghdad. In an attempt to allay these fears – and to keep Shaikh Mahmud satisfied – a joint Anglo-Iraqi declaration was issued in December 1922, promising the Kurds the right to set up a Kurdish government within the boundaries of Iraq, if the Kurds themselves could agree on its constitution and on the territories it would cover. This seemed to water down assurances given to King Faisal that the Kurds would be fully incorporated within the Iraqi state. However, this commitment was also made dependent upon a degree of consensus amongst the Kurds which the British knew well would be virtually impossible to achieve. Indeed, when this promise was officially abandoned some four years later, the inability of the Kurds to come to an agreement amongst themselves was cited as the major reason.

However, the end of Shaikh Mahmud's administration in Sulaimaniyya came sooner than that. By February 1923, the British were aware that Shaikh Mahmud had begun to lay the groundwork for a truly autonomous Kurdistan, with himself as its king, if necessary under Turkish protection. In March they used the Royal Air Force against him and against the Turkish forces and rebellious Kurdish chieftains in the north. Exploiting local resentments of Shaikh Mahmud, the British reoccupied Sulaimaniyya in May although, when British forces withdrew in July, Shaikh Mahmud made a triumphant return. However, for the next twelve months an uneasy situation persisted, with repeated attacks by the RAF on Sulaimaniyya and the eventual occupation of the town by British and Iraqi forces in July 1924, obliging Shaikh Mahmud to flee over the Persian frontier. He made for the hills and led a guerrilla force which was to plague both the British and the Iraqi authorities until his capture in 1931.

The question of Mosul and the future of northern Iraq placed many of those who were calling for Iraq's complete and immediate independence in a difficult position. They recognised that Iraq needed British support and protection if Mosul was to be retained, but they resented the price Great Britain wanted to exact in exchange. The king and those who looked to him for advancement were doubly aware of the need for British help in sustaining their own positions and the integrity of the state. Furthermore, it was clear to them that, should the province of Mosul be lost, or even if substantial sections of it be separated from the Iraqi state, the existing Shi'i majority would become overwhelming, making even more precarious political domination by members of the Sunni minority. The British recognised this dilemma and exploited it to the full by agreeing with the prime minister in April 1923 that the proposed treaty would remain in force not for the twenty years originally specified, but for a mere four years after the signature of a peace treaty with Turkey.

It was significant, therefore, that during this period, with the complicating issues of the future of Mosul and of the Turkish threat looming large, opposition appeared once more in the Shi'i areas. In June 1923, as a prelude to the long-drawn-out process of indirect elections devised for Iraq, the Shi'i *mujtahids* renewed their *fatwas* against participation. Foremost amongst the critics of the Iraqi state was Ayatollah Mahdi al-Khalisi, but he was supported by other eminent *mujtahids*, such as Ayatollahs al-Na'ini and al-Isfahani. To many in Baghdad the Shi'i *mujtahids* appeared to be using the pretext of the generally unpopular treaty to organise opposition to the emerging Iraqi state, dominated as it was by a Sunni elite. King Faisal had now accepted that the treaty was unavoidable if he wished to retain his throne and also if Iraq were to retain Mosul, and the continued opposition of the *mujtahids* seemed intended to undermine the very order to which he himself was committed. Consequently, he authorised the arrest of Ayatollah al-Khalisi, who was taken to Basra and sent on the pilgrimage to Mecca, returning eventually not to Iraq, but to Persia. Once there, he was joined by a number of Shi'i *'ulama* in protest at his treatment and at the attitude of the authorities towards the Shi'i hierarchy (and by implication community) more generally.

However, this self-imposed exile evoked little response in Iraq. Amongst those Shi'i tribes whose leaders had been so close to the *mujtahids*, a different point of view was beginning to emerge. Although many shaikhs remained hostile to the British and to the Sunni establishment in Baghdad, they found themselves courted by both: the British had ensured special representation for the tribal shaikhs in the Constituent Assembly, giving them roughly 40 per cent of the seats; the king, for his part, had been using his patronage to grant them tax exemptions. It could no longer be assumed, therefore, that the attitudes of the Shi'i tribal shaikhs and of the *mujtahids* would coincide. The powerful seduction of the state, with its positions, patronage and resources, was beginning to exert its force on the tribal shaikhs, leaving the *mujtahids*, with their ideological and communal critique, bereft of the coercive social support which had hitherto made them so powerful an influence in southern Iraq.

Nor was the action of the *mujtahids* particularly welcomed by Shi'i lay political activists. They were discovering new forms of political action based on the power of numbers and seemed determined to make the most of the electoral system, seeing this ultimately as the best recourse against domination by unrepresentative Sunni elites. Elections, however flawed in practice, at least held out the possibility that numbers would count and that the long-neglected Shi'i majority would make its voice heard in Iraq. In addition to these considerations, the flight of al-Khalisi and some of the other *mujtahids* to Persia, where they sought the protection of the shah, caused dismay since identification of the leadership of the Shi'a with Persia served only to deepen the prejudices of other Iraqis and threatened to marginalise the Shi'a once again.

The dissident *mujtahids* were forced to recognise that their public gesture of defiance had not only failed to produce the desired effect, but had been counterproductive. Indeed, the decline of the political role of the *mujtahids* in Iraq dates from this period. They remained influential in many ways, but even movements which voiced specifically Shi'i grievances would now be led by lay figures, more concerned with the well-being of the Shi'a within the framework of the Iraqi state than hostile to the very idea of that state. This set-back also strengthened the determination of a number of the *mujtahids* to eschew involvement in the world of politics, turning back to the more abstract, but also more pristine world of Islamic jurisprudence and moral exhortation.

For his part, the king tried to repair the damage caused by al-Khalisi's detention. Ironically, this contributed to al-Sa'dun's decision to resign as prime minister in November 1923, but it was the prelude to the return of many of the Shi'i *'ulama* to Iraq and to an ostentatious state visit by the king to Najaf and Karbala later in the year. The king, although honouring the Shi'i clerical establishment with his visit, was also obliging the distinguished *mujtahids* who had remained in Iraq to demonstrate their respect for him as head of state. In the meantime, he had appointed his old associate Ja'far al-'Askari as prime minister to oversee the final stages of the electoral process and to ensure that someone who was unequivocally a 'king's man' was in office when the Constituent Assembly opened.

The Constituent Assembly began its session in March 1924 and immediately criticism of the treaty dominated the proceedings. Fearing its rejection, Sir Henry Dobbs (who had succeeded Sir Percy Cox as high commissioner in May 1923) issued an ultimatum stating that, if the treaty were not ratified by 10 June, Great Britain would seek other means of fulfilling its Mandate in Iraq. This threat led to the ratification of the treaty at the last moment and by the narrowest of margins, clearing the way for the passage of the Organic Law (embodying the constitution) and the Electoral Law soon afterwards. The Constituent Assembly was thereupon dissolved and Ja'far al-'Askari handed in his resignation as prime minister.

In this way much of the formal machinery of the Iraqi state was set in place. The constitution was the outcome of a compromise between the British desire for effective executive power, exercised by the king, and their recognition of the need to give powerful sections of the emerging Iraqi political society some stake in the new order. Thus the king was granted, through the exercise of the *Irada* (royal will), the powers to prorogue and to dissolve parliament, to select the prime minister and to appoint the other ministers on the latter's recommendation. In addition, his assent was necessary to confirm all laws and, although he was required to explain any refusal to do so, there was no mechanism for obliging him to assent to any given draft law. Furthermore, he had wide powers to issue ordinances when parliament was not sitting, relating to issues of security, finance and execution of the terms of the treaty. For its part, the parliament was composed of a senate, appointed by the king, and an elected chamber of deputies. The latter were elected indirectly, with every 250 primary electors voting for one secondary elector who would then elect a deputy. The cabinet was responsible to the chamber of deputies and the chamber could force the government's resignation by a simple majority vote on a motion of no confidence. Any deputy could propose legislation, provided he had the support of ten others and provided that the legislation did not concern financial matters, which were still reserved to British control under the terms of the treaty.[9]

THE MOSUL QUESTION: TERRITORY AND OIL

With the constitutional framework of the state apparently settled, there remained the question of Mosul. It was at this point that the king appointed Yasin al-Hashimi to the premiership, largely because of his past record of hostility to the Turks. The Turkish government had finally agreed to a League of Nations commission both to determine the validity of Turkish claims to Mosul province in the light of the views of its inhabitants and also to make recommendations about its final status and territorial boundaries. In July 1925 the commission recommended that the province remain attached to the state of Iraq, with its northern boundary corresponding more or less to the old northern border of the province. However, two specific conditions were laid down. The first was that Iraq should remain under a Mandate for twenty-five years. The second stipulated that the Iraqi state should recognise the distinctive nature of the Kurdish areas by allowing the Kurds to administer themselves and to develop their cultural identity through their own institutions. These recommendations were agreed by the League Council. In December 1925 Great Britain was required by the League to submit a new Anglo-Iraqi Treaty which would be in force for twenty-five years (unless Iraq were to be admitted to the League as a fully independent state in the interim) and at the same time to ensure that proposals for a special Kurdish administration were forthcoming. The Turkish government was deeply displeased, but had to accept the outcome.

In Iraq, the League's decision was met with mixed feelings. Many Kurds were encouraged by the fact that the commission had listened to their fears about domination both by the Turkish and Iraqi governments. They had avoided reoccupation by Turkey, but were apprehensive about what they could expect from an Arab government in Baghdad. Equally, the reassuring thought that the League would supervise the actions of the Iraqi government for a generation was qualified by concern that this could be terminated whenever Great Britain decided to recommend Iraq for membership of the League. Given the intimacy between the British authorities and the Arab elites at the summit of the Iraqi state, there was a justified fear that the notoriously disparate and often contradictory voices of Kurdistan would count for little in Great Britain's calculation of its strategic interests.

In Baghdad, the possibility that Great Britain might recommend Iraq for membership of the League tended to overshadow the prospect of a twenty-five-year duration for the treaty. Tellingly enough, this possibility, viewed by the Kurds with consternation, was seized upon by members of the Baghdad political elite as the unexpected ray of hope that would allow them to achieve true self-government within a fairly short space of time. This allowed for the relatively smooth passage through parliament of a new Anglo-Iraqi Treaty in January 1926. It incorporated the recommendations of the League and provided for 'active consideration' by Great Britain in 1928 – and at four-year intervals thereafter – of support for Iraq's admission to the League of Nations.

This process was presided over by 'Abd al-Muhsin al-Sa'dun who had replaced Yasin al-Hashimi as prime minister in June 1925. He also presided over the first general elections which returned a parliament – heavily weighted in favour of the tribal landed interest – which began to deal with the mass of legislation needed to regulate various aspects of the new state. In addition, this parliament ratified the oil concession agreement of March 1925 between the Iraqi government and the Turkish Petroleum Company (TPC) (after 1929, the Iraq Petroleum Company (IPC)).

TPC originated in a consortium of oil companies set up prior to the First World War which had won the agreement of the Ottoman government to prospect for oil in Mesopotamia. As part of the postwar peace settlements, the German and Ottoman shares in the company had been forfeited to Allied interests and by the late 1920s, once American interests had been accommodated, it was owned jointly by the Anglo-Persian Oil Company (23.75 per cent), Royal Dutch Shell (23.75 per cent), Compagnie Française des Pétroles (23.75 per cent), a US-based consortium, later shared equally between Standard Oil of New Jersey and Mobil (23.75 per cent), and Gulbenkian (5 per cent). British interests thus predominated in TPC, with a substantial stake belonging to the British government itself, given its holdings in the Anglo-Persian Oil Company.

Under the shadow of the Mosul crisis and the perennially impoverished state of the Iraqi government, the British oil companies, backed by the British authorities, saw the opportunity of establishing an extensive and exclusive concession for TPC and of removing the possibility of Iraqi part-ownership. This had been promised in 1920 when the future of TPC was being agreed and a 20 per cent share had been allocated to the 'native government'. Despite the strong objections of some of its members (two of whom resigned over the issue), the Iraqi government agreed to relinquish its rights to a share in TPC. In exchange, Iraq was to receive enhanced royalty payments and won a number of other points, such as on the construction of a refinery and a pipeline.

In addition to securing immediate revenues, the Iraqi government also believed that it had avoided the possibility of Great Britain making substantial concessions to Turkey over Mosul. In retrospect, this was unlikely, but it was alluded to by the British authorities during the negotiations over the TPC concession. Under the terms of this concession, TPC remained a British-registered company and was granted exclusive rights of exploration in all of Iraq, excluding the old province of Basra. It was given a fixed period in which to select a number of plots and to commit itself to begin drilling for oil within a few years thereafter, paying the Iraqi government an agreed sum for each metric ton of oil it produced. This also opened the way for the Iraqi parliament to ratify the tripartite Anglo-Turkish-Iraqi Treaty, finally settling the Mosul question in July 1926.[10]

DIFFERENT COMMUNITIES, DIFFERENT PURPOSES, DIFFERENT HISTORIES

For all its apparent docility, the parliament failed to support al-Sa'dun's candidate as speaker of the Assembly in November 1926, provoking his resignation and allowing the king to call upon his trusted associate Ja'far al-'Askari once more. It was during his premiership that two issues came to the fore which typified the nature of the emerging Iraqi state and its relationship with different sections of the Iraqi population. One was the issue of conscription as a basis for recruitment to the Iraqi army. The other was the related issue of Shi'i discontent.

Conscription was an article of faith for the sharifian officers and for those who believed that the strength of the Iraqi state lay in its armed forces. It was of particular relevance at this time since, under the Military

Agreements of 1924, Iraq was to take charge of its own defence by 1928, though the size and strength of the Iraqi army made it clearly unequal to the task. Those who demanded conscription generally shared certain beliefs about the nature of the Iraqi state and the role of its armed forces. The value of air power was being amply demonstrated by the British RAF (since 1922 the main instrument of British military force in the country), but for many of the ex-Ottoman officers the only guarantee of independent statehood was a large land army, based on universal conscription. Despite the limited financial means at the disposal of the government, it also seemed to them to be the most easily affordable option for Iraq if it was to demonstrate that it was capable of defending itself.

However, given the experiences of the Iraqi army in the Kurdish areas and in the tribal territories, a strong army was also seen as vital for a strong central state. In a country in which the rifles in the hands of the rural tribesmen far outnumbered those in the hands of government forces, the determination of the centre to dominate the provinces needed to be backed up at least by the threat of superior force. Strategies of co-option were being deployed by the state centralisers in Baghdad, but these were uncertain and would take time to produce an effect. By contrast, the events of 1920 had shown how easily concerted tribal action could wrest control of large areas of the country from a well-armed but outnumbered military force.

Finally, there were those who believed that universal military service would erode the particular loyalties of the inhabitants of Iraq, putting in place a sense of collective service and obligation to the new Iraqi state. Continuing the late Ottoman ideal of military education as the token and engine of modernity, Iraqi officers – products of just such an education – saw conscription as the key to the disciplined creation of a new social order to meet the needs of the state, as they themselves defined those needs. These modernising and nation-building rationales were to become increasingly current among the officials of the Iraqi state and would eventually provide the background and justification for the militarism that became so much a part of Iraqi public life in the 1930s.

By contrast, for many others in Iraq, particularly in the Kurdish and the Shi'i tribal areas which still comprised the bulk of the Iraqi population, conscription was deeply repugnant. It recalled some of the worst features of the Ottoman state and seemed to many of the shaikhs and *aghas* to be espoused by the governing elites in Baghdad for much the same reason: it would be used as an instrument for imposing central control and limiting tribal autonomy. In this, their fears were shared by the ordinary tribesmen, many of whom saw conscription as disruptive of their lives, threatening their livelihoods and implicating them in a world of violence far removed from the use of force sanctioned by tribal values. Understandably, therefore, it was a matter over which they were prepared to take up arms, and their leaders made no secret of this, particularly in their conversations with British officials.

For their part, the British, who anyway regarded conscription as beyond the meagre financial resources of the Iraqi government, saw it as a deeply disruptive issue. They were apprehensive about the likely resistance to conscription and feared that the RAF would be called upon to suppress provincial rebellions. Consequently, Ja'far al-'Askari and others were told that Great Britain would help neither to set up such a scheme nor to deal with the violent reactions it might provoke. This was held up as yet another example of Great Britain's desire to keep Iraq subservient and the issue resurfaced periodically until the end of the Mandate, poisoning both Anglo-Iraqi relations and relations between successive Iraqi governments and powerful sections of Iraqi provincial society.

In 1927 it formed a menacing background to the equally threatening issue of sectarian conflict. The publication of a book critical of Shi'ism by a Sunni government employee sparked off widespread protests and, increasing the tension, in July 1927 shots were fired by a unit of the Iraqi army during the Shi'i Muharram procession in al-Kazimiyya. A number of people were killed and, to the outrage of the Shi'a, the officer of the unit responsible was not only acquitted of any wrongdoing, but was even promoted. The protests which followed no longer emanated only from the *mujtahids*, but came also from the lay sections of the Shi'a, represented by the reconstituted Nahda Party. In response, Yasin al-Hashimi, the acting prime minister, tried to suppress the party, but this provoked such an outcry that he himself was forced to resign, further weakening al-'Askari's government.

This government was already in crisis due to the perennial question of the relationship with Great Britain. In July 1927, the British government had informed Iraq that it would consider recommending Iraq for membership of the League of Nations in 1932, but not in 1928. However, it was willing to negotiate a new treaty which was eventually signed in December 1927. The only concession to Iraq was the promise that the British government would support Iraq's membership of the League of Nations in 1932, thus setting a date to the end of the Mandate. For many Iraqis this was heavily qualified by the British assertion that their support would be forthcoming 'provided the present rate of progress in Iraq is maintained and all goes well in the interval'. This seemed like a threat.

The muted reception of the draft treaty in Iraq and the failure of the government to get its conscription bill through parliament, as well as continuing Shi'i unrest and the resignation of a number of powerful figures from his government, led to al-'Askari's resignation in January 1928. He was succeeded by 'Abd al-Muhsin al-Sa'dun who called for general elections in the belief that a new parliament would allow him to renegotiate the troubling Military and Financial Agreements with Great Britain and thus ensure the passage of the draft treaty of 1927. During the protracted electoral process from January to May 1928, government intervention produced both a supportive parliament and one which contained substantial Shi'i representation, helping al-Sa'dun's efforts at reconciliation with the Shi'a. He was less successful in renegotiating the Military Agreements. Great Britain refused to make any concessions and rejected al-Sa'dun's proposals of January 1929, forcing him to resign. He stayed on for some months as a caretaker prime minister, largely because few politicians were willing to take on a job that circumstances made almost impossible to hold successfully.

Perhaps encouraged by the departure of the intransigent Dobbs as high commissioner and his replacement in early 1929 by Gilbert Clayton, who had a reputation for sympathy with Iraq, Tawfiq al-Suwaidi was eventually persuaded to accept the premiership in April. Parliament supported him, but the king and Nuri al-Sa'id, who was now emerging as the leader of a formidable court faction, undermined him, causing him to resign in August and to give way to 'Abd al-Muhsin al-Sa'dun, who assumed the premiership once more. Meanwhile, everything depended on a British initiative. This came in September 1929, following the election of a Labour government in Great Britain and the announcement that it would be recommending Iraq's membership of the League in 1932, recognising Iraq's responsibility for its own defence.

The prospect of full Iraqi independence in 1932 led a section of Kurdish society to give voice to their collective demands as Kurds. Hitherto, public affairs in Kurdistan had been dominated by such figures as Shaikh Mahmud, or Shaikh Ahmad of Barzan, whose actions had been responsible for disturbances in the northern Kurdish areas in 1927. These leaders had sometimes referred to the independence of Kurdistan, but their objectives were generally parochial, depending on local tribal support, or on networks of Sufi brotherhoods. In the wake of the Mosul settlement of 1926, however, groups of urban Kurdish intellectuals began to develop ideas of how best to secure specifically Kurdish identity and interests within the given framework of the Iraqi state. Some had already entered into close relations with powerful figures in Baghdad, for reasons of individual advancement. Others, however, tried to use such patronage to achieve positions of authority within the Iraqi state, for example, by becoming deputies in parliament, which would allow them to give voice to distinctively Kurdish concerns.

In the summer of 1929, a number of Kurdish deputies submitted a petition asking for increased expenditure in the Kurdish areas as a whole and the formation of an all-Kurdish province composed of Dohuk and other districts of Mosul province, as well as the districts of Arbil, Sulaimaniyya and Kirkuk in which nearly all of the Kurds of Iraq resided. A specifically Kurdish set of demands was emerging, different in origin and intent from the demands habitually made of central government by the tribal leaders and enjoying a different kind of social support. The strategy was aimed at fuller engagement with the Iraqi state, based on the deputies' familiarity with this world. However, it also expressed a determination that their own concerns should not be excluded or marginalised by those who dominated the new state and hinted that, should this be the case, the Kurdish 'party' would request that the Mandate stay in force for the full twenty-five years stipulated by the League of Nations. As the pace towards independence accelerated, these demands were repeated with some force.

Although initially encouraged by the British initiative in 1929, al-Sa'dun had little success in either advancing the cause of a revised treaty or in winning the confidence of the king. Clayton's sudden death in September 1929 deprived al-Sa'dun of an important ally and his sense of political helplessness, compounded by personal problems, led to his suicide in November 1929. He was succeeded as prime minister by Naji al-Suwaidi (brother of Tawfiq), but he too proved unable to deal with the mounting pressures for a treaty to pave the way to independence. Street demonstrations, indicating more systematic use of the new style of urban politics, attacks in the press which he was unable to confront and the undermining of his position within the elite by the king and Nuri al-Sa'id led al-Suwaidi to resign in despair in March 1930.

EMERGING TRENDS IN POLITICS AND THE ECONOMY

The 1920s had been marked by an increasingly lively and sometimes scurrilous press in Iraq, as well as by the flowering of poetry that engaged with the politics of the day. Poets such as Ahmad al-Safi al-Najafi, Ma'ruf al-Rusafi and Muhammad Mahdi al-Jawahiri gave voice to an often romantic view of Iraq. In doing so, they helped to establish the landscape and the contours of this newly imagined entity, imbuing it with features that began to gain wide currency. A recurring theme was the natural bounty of a land which lay unrealised or was going to waste because of the oppression of foreign occupation and the great inequalities of wealth amongst its inhabitants. These were not reassuring messages either for the British or for the king and the ruling elites, who often came in for direct and trenchant criticism. However, as Ahmad al-Safi's verses made clear, romanticising Iraq did not necessarily mean adulation of the new political category of the 'Iraqi people', even if the plight of the country's poor increasingly stirred many of the poets' sympathies.

In this emerging debate, both journalistic and literary circles demonstrated a deepening involvement in distinctively Iraqi political issues. Among the still restricted groups of Iraqis actively engaged in national political debate this was influential in a number of ways. It presented an articulate opposition to British control, characterised by telling criticisms both of British policies and of their prejudices in dealing with the Iraqis. Furthermore, it tried to encourage a sense of a distinctively Iraqi national community that would bridge the many particular identities of Iraq's inhabitants. To some extent there was a conscious effort on the part of certain writers to construct a secular identity that would minimise sectarian differences between Sunnis and Shi'a. It was clear, however, that this was primarily an Arab identity which excluded the Kurdish, let alone the Turkmen, population from consideration – vividly illustrated in writings about the Mosul question which made much of its inclusion within Iraq, but said little about its largely Kurdish inhabitants.[11]

Whilst much of the literary production and some of the press dwelt on lofty themes such as nationalism and freedom, another side of the press reflected more exactly the deeply personal rivalries and antagonisms that formed the stuff of everyday politics. Denunciations, character assassinations and charges of betrayal were levelled against the limited number of individuals who formed the core of the political elite, fuelled not simply by a general delight in the irreverence involved in attacking such notables, but also by the active sponsorship of their rivals. These attacks were largely personal and it was only at the end of the decade that a more considered social critique of the structured inequalities of Iraqi society as a whole began to appear.

It was for Nuri al-Sa'id to deal with the first organised manifestations of these trends in Iraq's political history. Seizing the opportunity created by al-Suwaidi's resignation, Nuri al-Sa'id, by now the most trusted of the king's confidants, became prime minister. Leading the court faction, he gathered around him a circle of intimates, many of whom had been colleagues in al-ʿAhd and in the sharifian forces of the Arab Revolt. With the strong backing of the king and of the British, who were now eager to reach an agreement, Nuri al-Saʿid demonstrated the power which such a position gave him in Iraqi politics. He rapidly negotiated a new Anglo-Iraqi Treaty which was signed in June 1930.

This treaty formed the basis of Iraq's relations with Great Britain after Iraq's independence in 1932. It placed all responsibility for internal order in Iraq on the king and made Iraq responsible for its own defence, in theory giving the Iraqi government control over the last part of the state structure still in British hands. However, in return, Iraq agreed to give Great Britain the use of all the facilities in its power in the event of war, including the right to move British troops through Iraq if necessary. In addition, the Iraqi army's equipment and military advisers would be supplied by Great Britain, and the RAF would keep two major bases on Iraqi soil, one at Habbaniyya near Baghdad and the other at Shuʿaiba near Basra. The treaty itself was to remain in force for twenty-five years from the date of Iraq's entry into the League of Nations, but could be renegotiated after twenty years.

The treaty was not received with much enthusiasm in Iraq, but those who objected to its endorsement of the continued military relationship with Great Britain were too disorganised to mount effective opposition. In part, the promise of imminent independence defused much of the criticism. This may have been helped by the very feature of the treaty which so outraged the Kurds – the absence of any reference to their special position. It reassured the central elites in Baghdad that the British would not use the Kurdish question as a pretext for intervention. However, this made many Kurds increasingly apprehensive and they were not much reassured by Nuri al-Saʿid's promises to institute special administrative, educational, cultural and linguistic measures in the Kurdish region prior to 1932.

Nuri al-Saʿid did not take any risks with the passage of the treaty. He called a general election which ensured that his supporters won an overwhelming victory, allowing the ratification of the treaty in November 1930 by a parliament dominated by his clients and associates. The only disruptive element was the continuing unrest in the Kurdish areas where riots and demonstrations in the autumn led to the reappearance of Shaikh Mahmud, now openly linked to the urban Kurdish leaders. Going further than his urban counterparts, however, Shaikh Mahmud called for the separation of Kurdistan from Iraq and its transformation into a British protectorate. To back this up he began once more to rally the tribes which had traditionally supported him.

The fighting which then erupted pinned down a large proportion of the Iraqi army and made it clear that the Iraqi government both was unable to maintain order and had failed to fulfil its obligations towards the Kurds. This was an embarrassing development in the light of Iraqi (and British) attempts to convince the League of Nations that their conditions had been fulfilled and that the Mandate could come to an end nineteen years before the date set in the agreement of 1926. Consequently, after a formal request from the Iraqi government, the British sent units of the RAF to help suppress the revolt. After a month or so of fighting, Shaikh Mahmud sued for peace and in May 1931 he was sent into internal exile in Nasiriyya in southern Iraq.

Simultaneously, the Iraqi government made a gesture towards Kurdish cultural identity by promulgating the Local Languages Law. Intended to show the Kurds and the League of Nations that the Iraqi government took seriously its pledge to recognise the distinctive nature and interests of Iraq's Kurdish citizens, the watered-down version of the law which eventually appeared did little to allay Kurdish fears. With its half-hearted commitment to the official use of Kurdish and its failure to make provision for the appointment of Kurdish officials, it fell short of the guarantees that were expected to be a prelude to Iraqi independence. Consequently, using methods different to those of Shaikh Mahmud, Kurdish leaders in Sulaimaniyya and elsewhere petitioned the League of Nations, as well as the British and Iraqi governments, hoping that the minimum Kurdish demands for cultural autonomy and self-rule would be met. This had little impact. For Nuri al-Sa'id, if the security threat could be dealt with by military means, then political opposition in Kurdistan was not of great concern, given the forces ranged against it in the rest of Iraq. Neither the king, nor the British, nor the various opposition parties of central and southern Iraq put serious pressure on his government to fulfil the pledges made at various times to the Kurdish leaders. On the contrary, all of them seemed to agree that any tendency towards Kurdish separatism should be crushed, even if symbolic concessions to a specific Kurdish identity might be made.[12]

More preoccupying for Nuri al-Sa'id and for the political forces of the capital and the centre was the economic predicament of the country in the early 1930s. Hit by the consequences of the world depression in trade, Iraq's economy, especially insofar as it concerned government finances, was in a precarious situation. The Iraqi economy during the 1920s was predominantly agricultural in nature, with dates and grain representing the major exports. Cash crops, such as cotton, had been tried, but with only limited success. As the British Cotton Growers' Association's experiments in the 1920s had demonstrated, the climate and soil of lower Iraq were well suited to the cultivation of cotton and a number of Iraqi entrepreneurs had been tempted to invest considerable funds in cotton-growing ventures, with a marked effect on the volume of cotton exports. However, neither the landowning shaikhs nor the share-cropping peasants had shown much inclination to take up cotton cultivation. Their reluctance to do so appeared to be vindicated by the slump in world cotton prices in the late 1920s, intensified by the world depression that set in after 1929.

Also sensitive to the problems of government finance were the emerging industries of Iraq. Manufacturing was still largely based on small work-shops and traditional technologies and was geared to specialised domestic demand. However, in a few sectors modern industrial methods were being employed, fuelled by private capital, but heavily dependent on government finance to purchase their products. The textile and the construction indus-tries in particular had developed largely to supply the demands of the state as it took on definition in the 1920s, expanding its activities through public works and the proliferation of government agencies. With a reduction in government expenditure, these sectors found themselves having to reduce their activities and lay off staff. Those industrial sectors directly run by state agencies, such as the Iraq railways and their workshops, found themselves in a similar situation as the Iraqi government's financial plight worsened.

In 1930 Sir Hilton Young was engaged to investigate the causes of the economic and fiscal crises and to recommend possible remedies. Quite apart from the externally provoked collapse in agricultural prices, he iden-tified a number of internal causes for the fall in land revenues, the shortage of agricultural labour and the growing salinity of pump-irrigated agricul-tural land. However, radical changes in this area would have touched on fundamental interests of the governing elites of Iraq and would thus have interfered in the close relationship between political power and land own-ership that had been so much a feature of the emerging Iraqi state and the systems of patronage that it fostered.

During the 1920s land had played a major role in cementing relations of power. For some the state had come to mean a set of instruments for acquir-ing title to land whilst simultaneously avoiding possible fiscal obligations. Although this had sometimes encountered the opposition of those officials and state organisations responsible for enhancing revenue from taxation, the political gains for the British authorities and for many of the most prominent political figures had been too great to sacrifice in the name of fiscal orthodoxy. Thus, the king, successive prime ministers, ministers and well-placed officials had acquired extensive landholdings for themselves and for their networks of family and political clients. The task was made easier by the fact that the parliament and most of the organs of the state were dominated by men whose prime interest was in increasing the yield of their landholdings, more often by extending them than by intensifying capital investment in their productivity. The 1926 law encouraging the installation of mechanical pumps, ostensibly to increase the area under cultivation in Iraq, allowed townsmen with capital to invest to expand their interests into the countryside. Increasing numbers of peasants fell into their debt, as declining agricultural prices were accompanied by the falling productivity of land irrigated without due attention to the problems of soil salinity.

Problems of productivity, as well as the fall in agricultural prices, hit state revenues. So too did the many tax exemptions granted to numerous landowners and the feeble attempts to collect taxes when individuals of some social weight or with powerful connections were concerned. Political favours and patronage of this kind served the interests of both the landowners and the political elite. As far as the latter were concerned, there was the advantage that technically three-fifths of the cultivable land of Iraq remained in the legal possession of the state, and control of state domains was a powerful instrument of patronage. Equally, in theory at least, the impressive array of outstanding tax demands could be enforced. This was sometimes used selectively to threaten those who fell foul of well-placed figures in Baghdad and reinforced the power of the system as a whole, but did little to enhance the revenues of the state.[13]

Concern about these revenues in the light of the growing world economic depression had led to the Young visit. Related concerns about agricultural productivity, the condition of the agricultural economy and land questions also led to a commission of inquiry headed by Sir Ernest Dowson in 1929, leading to his report on land tenure in 1932. He criticised the emerging vast landholdings of southern Iraq and reiterated his belief (contrary to that of Dobbs and others) that the government should not rely on powerful intermediaries in its dealings with the countryside, but should establish direct contacts with all landowners, regardless of the size of their holdings. Equally, he recommended that, in the growing number of disputes between pump-owners and the indebted cultivators, the rights of both should be respected. This would be achieved, he believed, through specially constituted land courts, independent of the powerful local landed interests.[14]

The implications of his findings and recommendations were too radical for the landed interests which dominated the institutions of the state.

Instead, a number of technical committees took up some of his administrative recommendations, but the Land Settlement Law of 1932, claimed to have been based on his findings, strengthened the powers of the landlords in virtually all spheres, opening the way for extensive land acquisition by those who had invested in irrigation pumps during the preceding ten years. For his part, Sir Hilton Young avoided recommending radical changes in areas which would have touched on the fundamental interests of the governing elites of Iraq and advocated instead cuts in public expenditure and the raising of taxes in other sectors. This opened the way for the introduction of the consumption tax of 1931 whereby the landed elites nimbly avoided bearing the major tax burden themselves, passing a disproportionate share of it on to their tenant farmers and to the small landowners. Indeed, so adept were large landowners at avoiding taxation that by the time of independence less than 10 per cent of government revenues were derived from land taxes (by comparison with over 25 per cent in 1921).

Young's report also advocated government borrowing on the security of future oil revenues. Oil had been discovered in large quantities close to Kirkuk in 1927, but would not be exported until 1934. The Iraq Petroleum Company (IPC) was eager to renegotiate the 1925 agreement in order to open up a much larger area of northern Iraq for its exclusive exploration. As an inducement, IPC held out the prospect of substantial advances in the present against future royalties. Given the financial crisis facing the Iraqi government, this was a powerful draw. In March 1931, an agreement was signed, granting IPC an exclusive concession over the whole of northeastern Iraq, as well as tax exemptions, in exchange for annual payments of substantial sums in gold until exports began, some of which would later be recovered from royalty payments. So dramatic was the effect of this that in 1931–2 oil revenues constituted nearly 20 per cent of government revenues, having contributed virtually nothing in the previous year. Furthermore, the timely arrival of this income easily wiped out the threatened government budget deficit of that year.[15]

Nuri al-Sa'id's domination of parliament ensured the ratification of this controversial agreement. However, the economic crisis and transformations in the political world of Iraq faced Nuri with an unprecedented challenge in another sphere during 1931. This found expression in March 1931 when Yasin al-Hashimi (leader of the Al-Sha'b (People's) Party) and Ja'far Abu al-Timman (leader of the Watani Party) joined forces to form Hizb al-Ikha al-Watani (the Patriotic Brotherhood Party). This represented an alliance of two disparate personalities and linked two parties which drew on different sections of Iraqi society for their support. Yasin al-Hashimi's grouping was associated with those Sunni Arabs who, like its leader (or indeed like Nuri al-Saʿid himself), had long been active in the political and administrative worlds of the Ottoman state as well as the state of Iraq. Jaʿfar Abu al-Timman's party, on the other hand, although it included a number of Sunni figures, drew chiefly upon the educated, lay Shiʿi population of the cities who were becoming increasingly engaged in Iraqi politics. In addition, through its leader Abu al-Timman, the party enjoyed close relations with the Nahda Party (which was more explicitly based on the Shiʿi community and its concerns) with its links to the ʿatabat and to the Shiʿi tribal shaikhs of the mid-Euphrates.

Equally important in the context of 1931, Abu al-Timman and the Ikha Party had close links with the Artisans' Society (Jamʿiyya Ashab al-Sanʿa), a trade union founded, like a number of others, in 1929 partly in response to the effects of the economic recession in Iraq. Its members included employees of the railway workshops of Baghdad, but largely comprised artisans and small traders who were now the targets of new taxation proposals. As the new party began its campaign against the government in the streets of Baghdad and in the provinces, the Artisans' Society, under Muhammad Salih al-Qazzaz, played an increasingly prominent role. He had his own, union-based agenda, but he was willing to lend his support to Hizb al-Ikha's criticisms of Nuri al-Saʿid's government. These focused on its increasingly repressive style and on its apparent willingness to make concessions both to Great Britain and to the foreign-owned oil companies.

However, the specifics of the campaign were less important than its capacity to draw in opponents and critics of the government from all quarters. Some, like certain tribal shaikhs of the mid-Euphrates, were angered by the government's refusal to grant them their customary tax remissions, especially at a time of depressed agricultural prices. Others, like the ʿulama of the Shiʿi cities, were inclined to criticise the government as representative of a regime in which they had little stake and which they saw as antithetical to the interests of the Shiʿa in general. For many other Iraqis, however, there was widespread dissatisfaction and anxiety caused by the country's economic predicament and government inaction, as well as mistrust of the link between the government and Great Britain. This combination of factors, working in different ways upon diverse sections of the Iraqi population, made them receptive to the calls of the Ikha Party.

The forms of political activity, however, were limited. The security forces made it increasingly difficult to hold mass meetings or to stage demonstrations. Consequently, a campaign was launched to refuse to pay taxes, and petitions were sent to the king, calling upon him to dismiss the cabinet.

Preparations were also made for direct action, both in the mid-Euphrates, where certain tribal shaikhs were willing to call out their tribesmen at the appropriate moment, and in Baghdad and other cities where a general strike was planned. The government had exacerbated the situation by bringing in a Municipal Fees Law which had raised the taxes payable by all tradesmen. In July 1931, the day after the king left for Europe, a general strike was declared which started in Baghdad and spread to most of the towns of southern Iraq, including Basra. Transport ceased to run, shops were shut and ministries were brought to a standstill, whilst the opposition forces seized this moment to organise demonstrations in the streets. The specific complaints which had sparked off the demonstrations soon became more general slogans against the whole system of government in Iraq, including the monarchy. In some cases, violence ensued when the security forces intervened.

Meanwhile, in the mid-Euphrates region tribal disturbances broke out. They were serious enough for the Iraqi government to ask for RAF assistance in suppressing them, but they were not as widespread as the leaders of the opposition movement had expected. Many of the tribesmen were wary of lending themselves to a cause which did not seem to them to be fundamentally concerned with their own interests and in which they might suffer simply to bring about a change of cabinet in Baghdad. In addition, a number of the tribal shaikhs were disconcerted by the strikes, since they showed that ordinary people could act forcefully outside the framework of traditional systems and leaders.

In the event, the strike faltered in its second week. The government took steps to meet the complaints about the Municipal Fees Law, removing one very potent cause of grievance. In addition, the security forces had been deployed in strength throughout the towns, detaining a number of the organisers, including al-Qazzaz. This left people in no doubt about the cost of further defiance. When, in late July, there was an attempt to start the strike once more, it failed, and in August the government disbanded the Artisans' Society. The opposition became increasingly demoralised and Nuri al-Sa'id emerged triumphant, confident in the continuing support of the king, the court faction and the British.

The mixture of a new style of politics, in the shape of the general strike and the public demonstrations in Baghdad, with the more traditional outbreaks of unrest and sabotage in the tribal regions of the mid-Euphrates, had alarmed many who were not necessarily supporters of Nuri al-Sa'id. The threat of disorder was as disturbing to them as the prospect of a Shi'i–Sunni alliance dominated by the former, or the sight of urban and

rural elites collaborating with workers' organisations in the towns. As a
result, many rallied to the support of the government, seeing in these developments ominous pointers to a very different kind of politics in Iraq,
embodying a radical threat to their own positions. In some senses, they
were right to see that these developments introduced a new narrative or tra-
jectory into Iraqi political history. It showed that processes had been set in
motion which were inextricably linked with the growth of that state and
with the fate of the elites who appeared to have captured it.[16]

For the time being, however, Nuri had the upper hand. He successfully
separated the component parts of the disintegrating opposition coalition
and ensured that the main thrust of Iraqi politics during the following year
was the achievement of independence in 1932. To this end, he ignored the
controversial question of conscription. The situation in the northern
Kurdish areas had been volatile enough since the summer of 1931 when disturbances linked to Shaikh Ahmad of Barzan erupted once more. The violence which followed was in part due to very particular local circumstances,
but it owed something to growing unease across Kurdistan as the date for
Iraqi independence approached. The effectiveness of Shaikh Ahmad's guerrilla fighters pinned down the Iraqi army and led Nuri al-Saʿid to request
RAF assistance once again in late 1931. As in previous cases, this turned the
tide of battle and allowed the Iraqi army to occupy Barzan itself in the
spring of 1932, leading to Shaikh Ahmad's flight to Turkey where he was
promptly detained by the Turkish authorities.

By this stage the admission of Iraq to the League was proceeding apace.
In June 1931, the League Mandates Commission had agreed that the conditions for Iraq's admission as an independent sovereign state seemed to
have been fulfilled. However, it also recommended that Iraq should be
required to give certain guarantees concerning the rights of minorities
within its borders. As the date of independence approached, Kurdish
groups, but also others, such as the Assyrians and, to a lesser extent, the
Turkmen and the Yazidis, had been petitioning the League of Nations and
the British in the hope of securing some form of international protection.
However, the Kurdish activists were divided on this issue. Some advocated
foreign (British or international) supervision after 1932 to ensure that the
measures recognising the special character of Kurdistan would be put
into effect. Others believed that this was futile, since it depended wholly
on the goodwill of external powers. This would always be vulnerable to
their other interests, as indeed the conduct of the British government
showed. In seeking to ensure Iraq's admission to the League of Nations,
Great Britain continued to maintain the fiction that the Iraqi government

had conscientiously fulfilled the pledges it had made to the Kurds at the time of the Mosul settlement.

Heightened fears for the future circulated in the much smaller and less secure Christian Assyrian community. The Assyrians, who had arrived in the territories of the future Iraqi state as refugees from Anatolia during the First World War, saw the British administration as their main protector. They had supplied most of the troops for the British-officered Iraq Levies and had a troubled relationship with the surrounding Kurdish and Arab villagers of northern Iraq where the British had settled them. Understandably, therefore, the community felt particularly vulnerable as Iraqi independence approached. These fears led to a general conference of the Assyrians at Mosul in October 1931 and a request to the League of Nations for special consideration and indeed for permission to migrate en masse either to Syria or out of the Middle East entirely. The League's discouraging response led to talk of direct action. This was deflected by the British authorities, who promised to maintain a link of sorts by assigning the Levies to the two British air bases as guard units. However, this connection proved to be a liability for the Assyrians after 1932: it maintained the community's reputation as allies of the British at a time when Great Britain felt no obligation to protect the community as a whole from the consequences of such a reputation.[17]

At any event, the League demanded and received from the Iraqi government in the summer of 1932 a formal declaration promising to guarantee the rights of foreigners and minorities, as well as to allow freedom of conscience and religion. In return, those states which had hitherto enjoyed capitulatory privileges in the Ottoman Empire, and thus in Iraq, agreed to renounce them. In October 1932 Iraq's membership of the League of Nations was approved by a unanimous vote of the League's Assembly. Iraq thus became the first of the League of Nations Mandates to achieve full independence as a sovereign state. However, British influence continued, whether formally through the 1930 treaty, or informally through the many unspoken rules that governed British relations with much of the Iraqi elite. Nor had Iraq's achievement of independence meant a radical shift in the pattern of its politics.

On the contrary, the period of the Mandate had been a defining period in many ways. It had not only laid the institutional foundations of the Iraqi state and demarcated its territorial boundaries, but had also made the state the principal arena for the multiple struggles that were to constitute a distinctively Iraqi politics. On one level, it had unmistakably made of Iraq a British imperial project, corresponding in its shape and in its constitution to ideas current in Great Britain about the proper organisation of power and about the specific conditions that would enhance its own interests in the Middle East. This was a troubling legacy which the grant of formal independence did little to remove.

On another level, it had delivered into the hands of those who staffed the state machinery and who commanded its resources a powerful instrument for the acquisition of land, the preservation of privilege and the maintenance of a landscape ordered to suit particular networks of favour and interest. For those excluded from these circles, or whose vision could not be easily reconciled with the rationales of power, there seemed little obvious recourse. However, neither the site of conflict nor the conflicts themselves could remain static. Processes had been set in motion during this period, the unforeseen consequences of which were to show themselves at varying rates and at different moments in the history of Iraq. Narratives once thought suppressed or hopelessly marginalised could re-emerge to exact their revenge on those who thought they commanded not only the state, but also the story of Iraq.

CHAPTER 3

The Hashemite monarchy 1932–41

Iraq began its existence as a formally independent state in an ambiguous way. The British presence was as visible as before, with most of the British advisers and officials staying at their posts for the time being, a British military mission training the Iraqi army and the RAF retaining control of the bases at Habbaniyya and Shuʿaiba. British-owned companies were as conspicuous as ever in all the major sectors of the economy and British influence on the king and his ministers remained strong. Nevertheless, Iraqi politics were increasingly shaped by distinctively Iraqi forces which had emerged in the preceding decade as the state had begun to take on greater definition. Against a background of communal and rural unrest and disputes about the nature of Iraq itself as a community, intense rivalry for patronage and fierce competition between client networks for influence characterised this regime of power.

These processes drew in different political worlds and histories, obliging their protagonists to cohabit a world of Iraqi state politics, defined by those who controlled the centre, sometimes creating commonalities, but also exacerbating differences. It was a world that was increasingly secular in nature, revolving around questions of economic privilege and around calls for redistribution of wealth and the assertion of fundamental rights, as well as around varying interpretations of national identity and duty. Sectarian and communal identities were often important in shaping people's responses to these various issues and could surface at moments of crisis, but they by no means determined those responses. In certain settings and organisations, Iraqis from different backgrounds were discovering common concerns. However, such is the nature of politics that this could create new forms of antagonism, as much as it allowed new forms of co-operation to emerge.

Key state institutions became instruments in the hands of powerful individuals and their followings, encouraging factionalism among officials and throwing into question the nature of their loyalties. Nowhere was this phenomenon more apparent than in the officer corps of the Iraqi army (the strength of which grew from 12,000 to 43,000 during the period 1932–41). Army officers emerged as significant political players, attracting patrons and clients and helping to shape the rules of the political world. This was possible in part because of a shared centralising, authoritarian vision of political order among much of the political elite, notables and senior state servants alike, which assigned to the armed forces a leading role in the disciplining and definition of Iraqi society. Rebellions in the provinces rejecting this vision provided the background against which the men at the centre of the state developed their ideas of social order and national discipline, as well as the means of imposing it through strategies of co-option and coercion. The distinction between the 'rural' and the 'urban' was breaking down at a certain level of society. Common interests arose among those who now saw the countryside not as the basis of a distinctive moral order, but rather as an area of human and material resources to be pressed into service for the benefit of those who controlled the state.

Independence also encouraged substantive debate about the character of Iraq, as state and community. In particular, tension developed between the advocates of Iraq's Arab identity and those who advanced the idea of a distinctive Iraqi national community. This led to differences over domestic as over foreign policies. With the achievement of independence, Iraq was formally a sovereign state which could determine its own relations with other sovereign states. This opened up considerable scope for the making of a distinctively Iraqi foreign policy. However, it also meant that the direction of that policy became a matter of contestation, often expressing in vivid symbolic form the opposing ideas held by different factions in Iraq about the country's national identity and thus its national interests. In addition, although formally sovereign, Iraq could not easily escape British influence. Given Great Britain's position in the Middle East at the time, this restricted the scope of Iraqi foreign policies in its immediate region. As Rashid 'Ali al-Kailani was to discover to his cost during the Second World War, Iraq's foreign policies would not be allowed to run counter to perceived British interests. These limitations were frustrating and posed acute problems for the authority of successive Iraqi governments.

On the domestic front, the partisans of the varying ideas of Iraq had little difficulty in agreeing on the fundamentally authoritarian role of the state: for nationalists – whether Iraqi or Arab – the task of forming the nation was too important to allow the 'divisiveness' of democratic processes to intervene; for the radical critics of the social order, the entrenched power of the landed elites and others could be broken only by forceful government action. In both cases, therefore, there was convergence on the need for a strengthening of the state: the first to protect the established order and to inculcate the virtues of national identity on a notoriously recalcitrant society, reforming it where necessary in accordance with their views of desirable social discipline; the second to act as the agent for the reconstruction of that society and the dispossession of the privileged elites who had hitherto obstructed the route to progress.

COMMUNAL IDENTITIES AND TRIBAL UNREST

To begin the new era, King Faisal sought a more consensual form of government and consequently asked for Nuri al-Saʿid's resignation, appointing the relatively neutral Naji Shawkat prime minister in his stead. In February 1933 a new parliament was elected, comprising a large majority of nominal government supporters (many of whom had been Nuri's clients), but also containing a substantial number of supporters of the Ikha Party. Within a month their attacks on Shawkat had forced him to resign. The king thereupon called on Rashid ʿAli al-Kailani (head of the Royal Diwan, but also a leading figure in the Ikha) to form a government in which the Ikha Party was well represented, but which also included others, such as Nuri al-Saʿid, identified with the 1930 treaty. By holding out the fruits of office to the leaders of the Ikha Party, the king had tempted them in effect to accept the treaty, despite their earlier rejection of it. This caused a rift with Jaʿfar Abu al-Timman and provoked dissent in the ranks of the Ikha Party itself, contributing to its eventual disintegration a few years later.

The alienation of Abu al-Timman, with his more diverse following and particularly with his Shiʿi connections, reinforced the impression of a Sunni-dominated state, as members of the Sunni Arab elite accepted office at the expense of their erstwhile allies. The king was sensitive to this, but had no intention of overturning a system of patronage that privileged his own position as well as that of the almost exclusively Sunni Arab ex-sharifian officers. Thus, when in early 1933 a government employee published a book attacking the Shiʿa for being potentially disloyal to the state and demonstrations of protest erupted throughout the predominantly Shiʿi areas, the king made some gestures to placate communal feeling, but the structural imbalance remained. Nor would it be seriously altered by those in control of the Iraqi state. Few were bold enough to advocate a policy that might have placed their own positions in jeopardy.

These rumblings in the Shiʿi areas were an ominous prelude to the future cohesion and direction of Iraq. So too were the events of the summer of

1933 involving the Assyrian community. The Assyrians had failed to persuade the League of Nations in 1932 to recognise their right to autonomy,
and their fears for the future had led them to think about establishing an
autonomous enclave in the north of the country, if necessary by force. In
May 1933, the leader of the Assyrians, the Mar Shimun, went to Baghdad
for discussions, but when the talks broke down the Iraqi authorities
detained him. This caused alarm among the Assyrians and a large number
of armed men tried to cross into Syria in July, hoping that the community
as a whole could find sanctuary there. When the French authorities turned
the Assyrians back, detachments of the Iraqi army tried to disarm them on
their return. Arguments erupted and in the ensuing fight dozens of Iraqi
soldiers and Assyrians were killed.

This incident galvanised both the political world in Baghdad and the
Iraqi forces on the spot under Colonel Bakr Sidqi, commander of the
northern region. The Assyrians, despite the small size of the community,
were represented in the Iraqi press as a threat to the national integrity of
Iraq and, it was hinted, as part of a sinister design by Great Britain to re-
establish its control over the northern part of the country. However remote
this was from the truth, the Assyrians' long association with Great Britain
in the Iraq Levies and their continuing role in guarding the British air bases
helped to reinforce this impression. Bakr Sidqi was authorised to deal with
them as ruthlessly as he wished. In August 1933 this led to the massacre of
hundreds of Assyrian villagers by the Iraqi armed forces, joined by Kurdish
tribesmen who took the opportunity to loot dozens of Assyrian villages at
the same time.

The crushing of the Assyrian 'threat' was treated as a great victory for the
Iraqi army and for Bakr Sidqi personally, who was promoted and given a
victory parade in Baghdad. For some, this was a dismal beginning to Iraq's
independent existence. For others, however, it represented the triumph of
the new state over those who threatened the unity of the country, whilst at
the same time it crushed a community associated with service to Great
Britain. In addition, it was taken to vindicate the resources devoted to the
Iraqi army and greatly raised its status as 'saviour' of the country. The adulation set Bakr Sidqi thinking about the future role of the army not simply
in defending the state from external enemies, but also from internal dissent.
As commander of the southern region during the next couple of years, this
was a role which he helped to define when faced by successive tribal revolts
in the mid-Euphrates.[1]

In the wake of these events, King Faisal's health deteriorated and he left
Iraq in September 1933 for medical treatment in Switzerland, dying within

7 King Ghazi (King of Iraq 1933–9), c. 1933

a week of his arrival. He was succeeded by his son, Ghazi, a young man of 21 who had little interest in the political world, but whose general sympathies were broadly pan-Arab. Like many in Iraq, he also resented British domination. These sentiments drew him closer to the members of the Ikha Party initially, although he eventually formed his own circles of favourites, based on personal likes and dislikes and not much influenced by his late father's choices. However, he showed neither his father's sensitivity to the forces at work in Iraqi society nor his acumen in drawing them into the circles of royal patronage.

Ghazi was the product of a system which exacerbated Shi'i resentment of the Sunni-dominated state during the next few years. This took a number of forms. In the ruling circles it was exemplified by the resignation of two Shi'i ministers in late 1933 when the cabinet decided to divert funds

allocated for the Gharraf dam to the army. For them this indicated that the
government was less concerned about the largely Shi'i communities which
would have benefited from the dam than about the expansion of the armed
forces through conscription – another move which met with much protest
in the Shi'i areas of southern Iraq.

Jamil al-Midfa'i (who had succeeded al-Kailani as prime minister in the
autumn of 1933) introduced the National Defence Bill to parliament. This
was passed in February 1934, setting up the machinery for conscription and
for the rapid expansion of the armed forces – a project dear to the hearts of
most of the Sunni Arab elite and other state centralisers, but regarded with
suspicion and resentment by many Shi'a and Kurds. In August, al-Midfa'i
gave way to 'Ali Jawdat who persuaded the king to dissolve parliament. So
successful was 'Ali Jawdat in rigging the elections that in the new parliament the Ikha Party held only twelve seats. Also excluded were some of the
most important Shi'i tribal shaikhs of the mid-Euphrates, laying the foundation for a dangerous tactical alliance with the Ikha Party.

In January 1935 unrest erupted in the mid-Euphrates region. It had been
preceded by a meeting of some of the most prominent Shi'i tribal shaikhs
in Najaf with the chief *mujtahid,* Ayatollah Muhammad Kashif al-Ghita.
Tribal grievances had been discussed, often focusing on specific complaints
connected with the land and irrigation rights of particular tribes. However,
some of the issues related to the grievances of the Shi'a as a whole and were
embodied in Mithaq al-Sha'b (the People's Charter) presented to the government in March 1935. The charter represented the concerns of a large
section of the population which felt ignored by the government of 'Ali
Jawdat and excluded from the kind of state which governments such as his
seemed determined to fashion in their own image. It accepted the Iraqi
state, but focused on the lack of proportional representation for the Shi'a
in parliament and the judiciary, and called for free elections, freedom of the
press and tax reductions.

More immediately, the shaikhs also drew up a petition asking the king
to dismiss 'Ali Jawdat and to dissolve parliament. When this produced no
result, direct action followed. It was at this point that Hikmat Sulaiman,
an opponent of the prime minister and a leading member of the Ikha Party,
urged his old friend Bakr Sidqi (commanding officer of the southern
region) to refuse to suppress the tribal unrest. Faced by this and by dissent
within his cabinet, 'Ali Jawdat resigned. His successor Jamil al-Midfa'i was
then confronted by a spreading tribal rebellion in the Diwaniyya region,
led by two powerful tribal shaikhs who had been in close touch with Yasin
al-Hashimi of the Ikha Party. When Taha al-Hashimi, the chief of staff of

the Iraqi army and brother of Yasin, refused to crush the revolt, al-Midfaʿiʾs suspicions of a plot were confirmed and he too resigned. Yasin al-Hashimi, portrayed as the only man who could 'save' the situation (because he had largely instigated it), was then asked by the king to form a government in March 1935, having effectively carried out a coup d'état against his rivals.

Within a week the tribal rebellion was over – or, at least, that part of it led by the allies of Yasin al-Hashimi. It was followed by the spectacular entry of the two chief rebel shaikhs into Baghdad, accompanied by large armed retinues, determined to present a petition to the king and to remind al-Hashimi of their power. This curious month of the tribal 'invasion' of Baghdad in April 1935 can be seen as a tribal swansong, reproducing as theatre that which had once been a real threat: the depredation of the city by rural tribesmen. It convinced many in Baghdad that this was a manifestation of the 'old Iraq' which needed to be eliminated by the march of progress. For the Sunni ruling elites it also presented an opportunity to portray the Shiʿi tribesmen, clerics and shaikhs as obstacles to the needs of a modern state.

Considerations such as these helped to colour the government's attitude to the threat of further tribal unrest on the mid-Euphrates, among tribes which had no connection with al-Ikha, but which had been in touch with some of the younger *ulama* of Najaf. The latter were suspicious of the ease with which al-Hashimi's tribal allies could be bought off, despite their earlier claim to be standing up for 'Shiʿi rights'. Fearing the repercussions, the government arrested one of the more prominent clerical followers of Kashif al-Ghita in May, thereby provoking uprisings which spread rapidly in the lower and mid-Euphrates. However, the government had no compunction about using force to suppress the rebellions. Bakr Sidqi declared martial law in the province of Diwaniyya and used the full power of the newly formed Iraqi air force and the army against the tribesmen. He scattered them with relative ease and by the end of May 1935 the revolt was over. It was clear that the tribes were no longer a threat to the power of the central state.

This was not the end of tribal unrest. It would erupt from time to time, sometimes for very local reasons and sometimes due to more general causes, such as resentment at conscription. However, the tribes, as such, were not a direct threat to the state or to the elites commanding the state. Apart from anything else, they were too fragmented. The events of 1935 did not constitute a rising of 'the tribes' or 'the Shiʿa' against the government, although distinctly tribal and Shiʿi communal sentiments were at work. Very particular motives were also influential – motives relating to the security of specific shaikhs in their tribal world, or to their fears about tax assessments or land settlements that might disadvantage them in relation to their neighbours. Furthermore, for every Shi'i tribe or tribal section which revolted against the government, there were several which either helped the government or which remained neutral, waiting to see the outcome of the encounter between government and tribal forces before risking their own villages by taking up arms.

The voicing of distinctively Shi'i grievances, although heard frequently enough in the countryside, where it was generally reduced to a rousing sectarian call for an end to Sunni tyranny, was largely the work of the urban Shi'i intellectuals, both clerical and lay. These complaints derived from the confessional imbalance at the heart of the Iraqi state. The realisation that the Shi'a not only outnumbered the Sunni Arabs, but also constituted an overall majority in Iraq encouraged Shi'i activists. The clerics tended to press for greater communal representation, proportionate to the size of the Shi'i community, whereas many laymen believed that this could be achieved only by more thorough application of democratic principles in Iraq. For the urban secular Shi'a this had the advantage of allowing them to escape from the communal dominance of the clerical hierarchy, but also brought many into conflict with the tribal shaikhs who still controlled the lives of the great majority of the Shi'a in Iraq.[2]

SOCIAL CRITICISM AND POLITICAL CONSPIRACY

Meanwhile, another kind of solidarity was beginning to emerge in Baghdad, represented by the group of intellectuals and professionals who had been associated with the newspaper *Al-Ahali* since its appearance in 1932. These men came from a variety of backgrounds, but they were all of the younger generation (in their mid-twenties in 1932) and all were critical of the cliques and factions which had risen to prominence in the Iraqi state. They deprecated the way in which the ruling elites manipulated elections to their advantage, relied upon informal networks to cement an 'establishment' which successfully excluded most other aspirants to power and used their state offices to entrench their positions as major landowners in Iraqi society.

The Ahali group, as it came to be known, saw in particular that many of Iraq's financial difficulties and profound social and economic problems could be laid at the door of its principal landowners. Determined to extend and reinforce their landholdings and revenues, the large landowners, whether rural shaikhs, state officials or urban merchants, had ensured that the state gave priority to their own interests, even when this was apparently at the expense of the state itself. Thus, in 1931 they had strongly backed the introduction of a consumption tax which effectively reduced the taxes payable by them to the state, but had done nothing to relieve the burden of rent due from their tenants. In 1932, their influence had ensured that the Land Settlement Law incorporated none of Dowson's recommendations concerning short state leases and the distribution of lands to small peasant farmers. Instead, it became the chief instrument for the government to bestow and to confirm proprietorial rights on individuals – most of whom were already powerful and well connected. In 1933, the dominant influence of the landowners was again apparent in the Law Governing the Rights and Duties of the Cultivators. This gave landowners wide powers over their tenants, holding the latter responsible for crop failures, making them vulnerable to eviction at short notice on the one hand, and tying them to the land until all their debts to the landowner were discharged on the other. Given the condition of peasant indebtedness in certain areas, this caused many to flee the land for a life of destitution in the *sarifas* (reed and mud hut slums) around Baghdad. In these circumstances, it was not surprising that trenchant social criticism of the status quo should have emerged.

At the time it was given voice by ʿAbd al-Fattah Ibrahim, a Marxist, and Muhammad Hadid, who was more of a social democrat by inclination. The Ahali group's adoption of the vague term *al-Shaʿbiyya* (literally, 'populism') as its first principle allowed it to disguise significant differences among its members. Some advocated collectivisation, others held out for land reform within a strengthened parliamentary system, whilst others believed the prime task should be moral renewal. The founding of the Baghdad Club in late 1933 encouraged debate and drew in people from widely varying backgrounds. Some were associated with Muhammad Salih al-Qazzaz's Workers' Federation of Iraq which organised a strike at the British-owned electric power company in Baghdad in late 1933. The federation was suppressed by the government as a result, but many of those generally sympathetic to the idea of organised labour gravitated to the circles of *Al-Ahali*. Equally drawn to the group was Jaʿfar Abu al-Timman, whose own party was disintegrating. Sympathetic to the idea of social reform, he was also attracted by the emphasis the group placed on patriotism (*wataniyya* – suggesting specifically Iraqi loyalties) over nationalism (*qawmiyya* – suggesting loyalty to the ideal of an Arab nation). Former members of the Ikha Party, such as Kamil al-Chadirchi and Hikmat Sulaiman, also saw in the group a sympathetic audience for their own criticisms of the status quo, diverse as these were.

Advocacy of social and economic reform roused the suspicions of many who saw the group as a front for the spread of communism. In fact, the communists of Iraq were taking a different road. In May 1935 the first central committee of the Iraqi Communist Party was formed, but by the end of the year many of its members had been arrested and its newspaper closed down. This did not prevent the charge of communism being levelled at the Ahali group, suggesting a threat both to the existing social order and to Islam, whether Sunni or Shi'i. These fears allowed Arab nationalists to take over the Baghdad Club in 1935, playing also upon the Ahali group's apparent indifference to Arab nationalism and to the various Arab causes, such as Palestine, which were receiving growing attention in Iraq.

In these circumstances, the group began to organise itself more systematically, forming a central committee that included Ja'far Abu al-Timman, Kamil al-Chadirchi and Hikmat Sulaiman. However, there was no attempt to create a mass movement and its sympathisers came largely from the political and administrative elites, including the officer corps. Here the links between Hikmat Sulaiman and General Bakr Sidqi were to be decisive in shaping the political role of the group, leading to the coup d'état of October 1936 and the overthrow of the government of Yasin al-Hashimi.[3]

Al-Hashimi had suppressed the Shi'i tribal unrest with armed force, but he also recognised that behind many of the disturbances lay the resentment of particular tribal shaikhs at their exclusion from the spoils of office. Consequently, in the general elections of August 1935 he ensured that many of them entered parliament. Having been drawn into the networks of government patronage (much strengthened by al-Hashimi's introduction of a law which effectively licensed the spoils system), they seemed more supportive of al-Hashimi. However, this could not prevent opposition to conscription (often a convenient rallying point for other grievances) from appearing in the provinces.

In August 1935, in the northern Kurdish region, a revolt broke out to trouble the Iraqi authorities. Its origins lay in feuds and mutual mistrust among the Kurdish tribes, but the fear of conscription also played a part. It was not finally crushed by the Iraqi armed forces until March 1936. More obviously due to fears of conscription was the rebellion of the Yazidi Kurdish community of the Jebel Sinjar. The government refused to allow the Yazidis collective exemption from conscription and they showed their defiance by refusing to enrol. This led to the declaration of martial law in the area and to an outbreak of fighting in October 1935 which ended in the victory of the government forces. Some hundreds of Yazidis were killed and imprisoned and a dozen or so villages were destroyed. However, the government victory was a hollow one. Yazidis continued to evade conscription and, when pressed by government security forces in the coming years, either resisted with force or simply migrated across the border into Syria. In southern Iraq some of the Shi'i tribes of the lower Euphrates also rose in rebellion against the conscription law. As in the other cases, deep-seated grievances against central government and local factors contributed to the rebellion. However, al-Hashimi had no compunction about ordering in the armed forces to crush the rebellions with a now characteristic ruthlessness.[4]

Although intended to serve as an example to other tribes, the harsh reaction of the government towards provincial rebellions could not prevent them from breaking out, given their many underlying causes. The tribesmen may not have counted on success in any strategic sense, but there were numerous grounds for provocation and in each case they may have hoped that the government would listen to their particular grievances. Thus, in early 1936 an uprising broke out in the Gharraf region. It was crushed, but was followed within a relatively short space of time by a more serious uprising near Rumaitha and, in June, by an uprising near Diwaniyya. As ever, a mixture of motives came into play. Particular shaikhs were either disappointed with the treatment they had received from the government, or their authority within their tribe was in question, possibly because of previous government attempts to interfere in the selection of the shaikh. Equally, land and irrigation problems both of a long-standing and an immediate nature provided a broad base for grievance. These discontents were heightened by the government's apparent disrespect for distinctively Shi'i customs and by the threat of conscription. Once more, Bakr Sidqi was ordered to suppress the uprisings – a task which he accomplished with little difficulty and with few scruples about the severity of his methods.

In Baghdad, Yasin al-Hashimi's authoritarian instincts became ever more apparent during 1936. He legislated by decree, developed the police and intelligence services and came down hard on any criticism of his government, whether in Baghdad or in the provinces. Under the influence of Arab nationalist disciplinarians in the Ministry of Education, he introduced compulsory military training into schools, echoing ideas about the virtues of military discipline fashionable in some European and Middle Eastern states at the time. Convinced that his opponents in the capital were colluding with the tribes (as he himself had done when in opposition), he not only crushed all signs of provincial revolt with great severity, but also closed down critical newspapers, such as *Al-Ahali*, and tried to prevent public protests in Baghdad itself.

In appearing to set himself up as dictator, al-Hashimi alienated many, including the king, who became increasingly nervous of al-Hashimi's ambitions. More dangerously, he also alienated General Bakr Sidqi, who was well aware of the key role he himself played in suppressing provincial dissent and who suspected that the prime minister's brother, Taha al-Hashimi, chief of the general staff, was blocking his own promotion. Personal frustration and resentment at this lack of recognition led Sidqi to listen sympathetically to Hikmat Sulaiman's plans for the toppling of Yasin al-Hashimi's government.

THE COUP D'ÉTAT OF 1936

In October 1936, Taha al-Hashimi left Iraq on a visit to Turkey, appointing Bakr Sidqi acting chief of the general staff in his place. In collusion with Hikmat Sulaiman and the forewarned leaders of the Ahali group, Bakr Sidqi ordered units under his command to march on Baghdad, heading the 'National Reform Force'. At the same time, leaflets were dropped on the capital, announcing that the army had asked the king to dismiss Yasin al-Hashimi and to appoint Hikmat Sulaiman as prime minister. Simultaneously, a message to that effect was delivered to the king who probably had foreknowledge of the coup and forbade any attempt at resistance. The air force heightened the drama by dropping a number of bombs near the prime minister's office, hastening Yasin al-Hashimi's decision to resign (he left the country and was to die in exile in 1937). The king then called on Hikmat Sulaiman to form a government. Ja'far al-'Askari, al-Hashimi's minister of defence, tried to take a message from the king to Sidqi, requesting that the army stop its march on Baghdad, but Sidqi believed this was part of a ploy to crush the coup and ordered his officers to intercept and kill al-'Askari. The murder was promptly carried out, thereby earning Sidqi the enmity not only of al-'Askari's political associates, but also of a large number of officers who had entered the armed forces under al-'Askari's patronage.

Hikmat Sulaiman formed his new administration principally from his associates in the Ahali group, leading to a cabinet that included a higher proportion of Shi'i ministers than had any previous administration. Bakr Sidqi, now chief of the general staff, busied himself consolidating his personal power base in the armed forces. His influence on the policies of the new government lay chiefly in the realm of foreign affairs. Like Sulaiman himself, he wanted to encourage closer links with Iran and, in particular, with Turkey since he shared with Sulaiman a strong affinity with all things Turkish.

Iraqi independence had allowed for some scope in the development of an Iraqi foreign policy, at least as far as regional states were concerned. This was to be an important symbol of Iraqi sovereignty which no government could afford to ignore. In addition, King Ghazi came to see this as the political field in which he could best make his mark, leading occasionally to friction with his ministers, but also used by them sometimes to divert the censure of the British. In terms of the sympathies and interests of much of the ruling Sunni Arab elite, the Arab world attracted most of their attention, especially the territories of Syria, Lebanon, Palestine and Transjordan. As the first of the League of Nations Mandates to achieve independence, Iraq could be presented as the vanguard of these emerging states, increasing the obligation for Iraq to assist them in their own independence struggles and holding out the possibility of an Iraqi leadership role among the states of the Fertile Crescent. However, the difficulty was that any independent foreign policy in that area would bring Iraq up against the controlling interests of Great Britain in particular, facing any Iraqi government with the choice between subservience and defiance which had so vexed Iraqi leaders under the Mandate.

For politicians such as Hikmat Sulaiman who had little sympathy with the pan-Arab sentiments and ambitions of most of the ruling elite, there were also other reasons for looking elsewhere in shaping a distinctively Iraqi foreign policy. The emergence of Iraq as a territorial state demanded that attention be paid to its boundaries and to its powerful neighbours. Two pressing questions in particular faced any Iraqi government seeking to secure Iraqi state interests. The first concerned Iraq's only access to the sea via the Shatt al-ʿArab, a waterway which constituted the frontier between Iran and Iraq and which therefore raised Iraqi fears about its vulnerability. The second question revolved around the attitude of Turkey and Iran, respectively, towards the Kurdish question, with Iraq's permeable frontiers and the recently discovered oil fields of the region heightening the Iraqi sense of vulnerability in this area as well.

As far as the Shatt al-ʿArab issue was concerned, the Treaty of Erzerum of 1847, the Constantinople Protocol of 1913 and the Delimitation Commission of 1914 had established Ottoman control over the whole of the waterway up to the Persian shore. This was the frontier which Iraq had inherited. In 1932 Iran challenged this delimitation and demanded a revision of the Iran–Iraq boundary to the *Thalweg* (median line of the deepest channel). Iraq rejected this demand. Tension between the two countries rose, marked by claims and counter-claims that each side was assisting or giving refuge to rebels, or that the other was interfering in the flow of water for irrigation. Occasionally, armed clashes erupted on the border between police or gendarmerie units.

During 1934 Iraq felt so pressed on the issue that it took its case to the League of Nations, although without success. This led in turn to direct negotiations between Iraq and Iran in 1935, but the compromise worked out by Nuri al-Saʿid (minister of foreign affairs at the time) and the shah of Iran was rejected by the Iraqi cabinet since it involved ceding some control over the Shatt al-ʿArab to Iran. The government of Hikmat Sulaiman, backed by Bakr Sidqi, had other priorities. For them it had become crucially important that Iraq should be assured of tranquil relations with its powerful eastern neighbour, even if it meant making concessions. This resulted in the Iran–Iraq Frontier Treaty of July 1937, which settled the border question by establishing the frontier at the *Thalweg* for four miles in the vicinity of the Iranian port of Abadan, but otherwise recognised Iraqi sovereignty across the waterway up to the Iranian shore.

Despite opposition to this treaty in Iraq, it cleared the way for the establishment of the Saadabad Pact, bringing together Iraq, Iran, Turkey and Afghanistan in an alliance aimed ostensibly at countering Soviet penetration of the area. There may have been some concern about this rather remote possibility in Baghdad. More importantly, it expressed the Iraqi government's desire to ensure stable and regular relations not only with Iran, but also with Turkey. The frontier between Turkey and Iraq had been recognised in the 1926 Mosul settlement. However, there could be no disguising the Turkish government's unhappiness at the loss of Mosul. For the newly independent Iraqi government, therefore, it was important to ensure good relations with Turkey. The earlier promise of massive oil reserves in the Mosul region had been realised, thereby increasing its value. Equally, it was clear that the Kurds had by no means been reconciled to the subordinate role allotted to them by Baghdad.[5]

Demonstrations in Baghdad and Basra against the treaty of 1937 accused the government of ceding Iraqi territory and of betraying the Arabs of Arabistan/Khuzestan. This set the tone for a more general criticism, emanating particularly from members of the Sunni Arab political elite, that the direction in Iraqi foreign policy was implicitly downgrading the importance of Iraq's ties with the Arab world. Under this interpretation, any emphasis on Iraq's identity as a country with significant links to its Turkish and Iranian neighbours was called the 'Iraq first' policy. It was associated with the attempt to create a sense of Iraqi national identity, free from the hegemony of the predominantly Sunni Arab nationalists, and struck a chord among many Iraqis, Arab and non-Arab. By the same token it also generated considerable hostility among the Arab nationalists who felt that Iraq was being cheated of the role it should be playing in the wider Arab world. This was particularly the case at a time when the Arab revolt in Palestine was a burning issue for the Arab nationalists in Iraq and elsewhere.

An inclination towards an 'Iraq first' policy was shared by most of those associated with the new regime. For many, however, it meant primarily concentrating on social reform. Accordingly, the formation of the new government was greeted by demonstrations of support in towns throughout Iraq, arranged by various radical discussion groups, by the informal and underground labour associations and by the embryonic Iraqi Communist Party (ICP), all expecting that their various goals could now be achieved. Hoping to build on these sentiments, the Ahali group sponsored the formation of the Popular Reform Association (Jam'iyya al-Islah al-Sha'bi). Its executive committee included four of the most reform-minded ministers, Kamil al-Chadirchi, Yusuf 'Izz al-Din Ibrahim, Ja'far Abu al-Timman and Naji al-'Asil, as well as 'Abd al-Qadir Isma'il (editor of *Al-Ahali* and later a prominent figure in Iraq's communist movement) and the labour leader Salih al-Qazzaz. It called for greater democracy, land reform and the legalisation of trade unions. Specifically it demanded the repeal of the Law Governing the Rights and Duties of the Cultivators and the introduction of progressive income tax and inheritance tax, as well as a minimum wage and a maximum working day. The association brought together all those who wanted some of the fundamental injustices of Iraqi society to be addressed and promised a radical programme of legislation for the new parliament.

However, this prospect alarmed many. Faced by mounting opposition, Sulaiman suppressed hostile newspapers and intensified purges of officials suspected of disloyalty, but alarm at the reformists' intentions was spreading to Sidqi's supporters in the officer corps. Their vision of an authoritarian regime ruling over a disciplined society was deeply antithetical to many of the reformists' ideas. As the latter discovered, the balance of established power was tilted firmly against them, despite their influence in the cabinet. The general elections of February 1937 produced a parliament in which they were greatly outnumbered by Bakr Sidqi's nominees and by the combination of conservatives, nationalists and tribal shaikhs who saw the spectre of communism behind the Popular Reform Association. Sulaiman made some concessions to the reformists in the ambitious government programme unveiled at the opening of parliament, but little was achieved. Even the modest proposal to distribute a limited amount of government land to individual peasant proprietors was represented as the beginning of radical land reform and was blocked through the vehement opposition of a wide range of disparate allies in the chamber.

For Sulaiman the support of the reformists counted for less than the continuing alliance with Bakr Sidqi. In March 1937, Sidqi publicly attacked the reformists for being secret communists and for advocating the dissolution of all the fixed points of Iraqi social and political life, confident that reform sympathisers amongst the army officers were in a minority. A series of strikes in March and April over questions of pay and conditions of work were taken up by those reformists who wanted to put on a show of defiance against their growing exclusion. However, this only hardened the lines of conflict. Hikmat Sulaiman showed his own authoritarian preferences by using police to end the strikes, arresting some of the organisers and sending others into internal exile.[6]

Similar tactics were employed by the government in its dealings with the tribal shaikhs of the mid-Euphrates. Alarm at the implications of land distribution proposals had been compounded by the familiar complaint by some tribal shaikhs that they had been unjustly excluded from the 1937 parliament. Sulaiman had tried to reassure the shaikhs that the government intended them no harm and had done much to settle the tribal disturbances which had marked the last year of al-Hashimi's premiership. However, when it seemed that certain shaikhs were preparing for open rebellion, Sulaiman agreed with Bakr Sidqi that pre-emptive action should be taken. In May 1937 the armed forces moved into the mid-Euphrates and arrested the leading shaikhs, provoking the very rebellion which the government had tried to prevent. It simmered on for much of the summer, but the government forces showed that they were able to contain it, while Hikmat Sulaiman tried conciliation of the shaikhs once again.

More significant than the rebellion itself was the cabinet crisis which followed, since Sulaiman and Sidqi had sent troops to suppress the impending revolt without consulting their colleagues. For the reformists, this was the last straw and in June 1937 four ministers resigned – Abu al-Timman, Kamil al-Chadirchi, Salih Jabr and Yusuf 'Izz al-Din Ibrahim. They criticised the government for its lack of commitment to genuine reform and condemned Sulaiman for his secrecy and for the nepotism and favouritism which he condoned. The resignation of four of his seven ministers weakened Sulaiman, but also gave him the opportunity to make a final break with the reformists. In their place, he appointed men more acceptable to Bakr Sidqi and his following in the officer corps. The conservative, authoritarian direction became clear with the subsequent suppression of the

Popular Reform Association and the exile of some of its most prominent leaders.

However, by this stage, the centre of gravity had shifted to the officer corps itself and away from the cabinet. Within the armed forces, resentment at Bakr Sidqi's favouritism combined with more general concern about the leadership's seeming neglect of pan-Arabism and the 'duties' which an Arab nationalist creed was assumed to bring with it. These sentiments led to a plot in the officer corps to assassinate Bakr Sidqi. The opportunity presented itself in August 1937 when Bakr Sidqi paused in Mosul on his way to visit Turkey. He was shot, together with his close associate Muhammad 'Ali Jawad, the commander of the Iraqi air force, at Mosul airfield.

By killing Sidqi, his opponents within the army severely weakened the loyalty of the armed forces to the government, as Hikmat Sulaiman discovered when he ordered the arrest of some of the conspirators and their transfer to stand trial in Baghdad. The commander of the Mosul garrison, Amin al-'Umari, refused to comply and instead sounded out the sympathies of the army commanders in the north. Having gained their agreement, he declared that the northern army command would no longer obey the orders of the government, implicitly threatening the country with civil war. When the army commander of one of the major military bases near Baghdad also declared himself in support of al-'Umari, Hikmat Sulaiman found himself caught between opposing army factions. Growing numbers of officers declared themselves in support of the rebellion and the hitherto dominant supporters of the late Bakr Sidqi found themselves isolated and outnumbered, forcing Sulaiman to resign in the middle of August 1937.

MILITARY POLITICS: PAN-ARABISM AND ARMY CONSPIRACIES

The emergence of the seven senior officers (Husain Fawzi, Amin al-'Umari, Salah al-Din al-Sabbagh, Mahmud Salman, Kamil Shabib, 'Aziz Yamulki and Fahmi Sa'id) who had conspired to kill Baqr Sidki and had caused the collapse of Hikmat Sulaiman's government introduced an era in Iraqi politics during which civilian politicians held office only with the consent of these men. They were not much concerned about the details of day-to-day government, but they would intervene periodically when two issues came to the fore. The first was the question of the attitude of the government towards pan-Arabism. This was not simply a question of foreign policy, even though it often came to a head over specific foreign policy issues. It was more a question of their vision of Iraq's identity which they felt it was the duty of any government to preserve.

These officers, all Sunni Arab by origin, tended to share a predominantly pan-Arab view of Iraq's identity and destiny, giving them an ambivalent attitude towards the state of Iraq itself. On the one hand, it could be seen as a temporary edifice, due to disappear once the Arabs as a whole had won their independence from the European imperial powers, when, in theory, a single state should be constructed to encompass all the Arabs. On the other hand, they were officers in the armed forces of the Iraqi state which, even if still tied to Great Britain in various resented ways, was formally independent. It was thus a regime of power capable both of shaping and disciplining its own society and of playing a leading role on the larger stage of the Arab world.

These views and to some extent their ambivalence had been in evidence since the ending of the Ottoman occupation and, in many of their particulars, resembled late Ottoman thinking on national identity and the importance of authoritarian command and military discipline in the creation of an ordered society. Most current and most plausible initially among the former Ottoman officials and officers who formed the administrative elite of the new state, they had been reinforced during the 1920s by the appointment of Sati῾ al-Husri as director-general at the Ministry of Education. A former Ottoman official whose family came from Aleppo, al-Husri had come to Iraq after the fall of the sharifian administration in Damascus, and was well connected to the sharifian elite of the new state. In this position, he was able to lay the foundations for a highly centralised, tightly disciplined and elitist education system in Iraq and to determine a curriculum (and the context of textbooks) based on a secular understanding of Arab nationalism.

Deeply insensitive to the specific character of the communities which he found in Iraq, al-Husri was regarded with suspicion by Kurds and by Shi῾i traditionalists. Both groups saw him as typical of the centralising, hegemonic Sunni Arab-dominated state – which in most respects he was. For that very reason he was able to retain his influence for the first two decades of Iraq's existence. However, within the Ministry of Education itself, al-Husri was displaced by Fadhil al-Jamali. A Shi῾i from al-Kazimiyya, he shared many of al-Husri's views on Arab nationalism and on the virtues of military discipline in the formation of a modern society. However, he differed significantly from al-Husri in advocating a more decentralised, less elitist educational system and ensured that resources were distributed more equitably in the provinces. This provided opportunities in particular for the Shi῾i majority, hitherto largely excluded by al-Husri, and led to the training of a new generation of Iraqi teachers to replace the Syrians and

Palestinians favoured by al-Husri. Al-Jamali's educational system, although promoting Arab nationalist ideas, was sensitive to a distinctively Iraqi context. Even the Kurds who naturally rejected the system's Arab nationalist bias made the most of the opportunities offered by decentralisation.

At the same time, however, the educational system became increasingly militarised as politicians tried to inculcate the virtues of discipline and obedience in the hope of creating an ordered, submissive society out of Iraq's fractious population. This project was inextricably linked to certain ideas about the social functions of an Iraqi and a larger Arab identity. As such, there was a contradiction at its core. By introducing military training to schools and teachers' training colleges in 1935–6, or by establishing the paramilitary Futuwa (youth) movement in 1939, state officials were trying to ensure disciplined acceptance of the status quo in the name of some variety of nationalism. Yet the complex of relationships and power that constituted the status quo was far removed from any such national, collective ideal. It was founded instead on economic privilege, status hierarchies and multiple forms of discrimination – tribal, familial, sectarian and ethnic – that vitiated any practical form of either Iraqi or Arab nationalism. It is therefore not surprising that the debates at the Baghdad Club (after 1935) and above all at the Muthanna Club in the 1930s should have exhibited so many contradictory tendencies and aspirations. As participants in these debates and as players and beneficiaries of these networks of discrimination, the pan-Arab officers showed many of the symptoms of a confusion only partially masked by their rhetoric.[7]

The second set of motives which maintained these officers' interest in the political process was connected quite simply to concern for their own positions, relative to the politicians of the day, but also relative to rivals amongst their fellow officers. Although overlaid by the myths of later nationalist historiography, there can be no disguising the fact that all of these officers tried to maintain personal networks of patronage which gave them positions and influence in Iraqi politics far beyond their rank. This was a struggle for power which provided its own rationale. It was fuelled neither by the ideals which some have tried to attribute to these men, nor by the baser motives of self-enrichment which others have alleged. Rather, the lure was power itself and the knowledge that the price of defeat was political oblivion. As the game progressed, the stakes became higher, eventually costing the losers their lives.

These were the themes dominating the years during which this group of army officers was in the ascendant. In some ways it was the logical conclusion of a process whereby the political world had become equated ever more narrowly with the restricted circles of officials (and officers) who dominated the state from the capital. The rest of Iraq's population, its communities, hierarchies and social formations, recognised the power of these men, their command of coercive force and their capacity to dispense favours. They formed the necessary background for the officers' exercise of power, but the latter had little interest in and no incentive to reform or reconstruct the status quo. Preoccupied with their immediate factional concerns or with the larger questions of Iraq's place in the world, the condition of Iraqi society, as long as it remained more or less passive, failed to engage them. When set against a background in which the dominant economic interests – landed or commercial, Iraqi or British – were satisfied with their acquired privileges, it is not surprising that no significant structural changes occurred during this period. Instead, state consolidation through conscription and other methods continued and the extension and entrenchment of a landowning interest proceeded undisturbed.

When Hikmat Sulaiman resigned, Jamil al-Midfaʿi was asked by the king to form a government, but consented only once he knew that he had the approval of the rebellious officers. Al-Midfaʿi thereafter tried to pursue a policy of letting bygones be bygones, largely in order to survive. Elections were held and in December 1937 a new parliament assembled, but its general composition had changed little, save for the disappearance of Bakr Sidqi's nominees and of the reformists associated with the radical wing of the Ahali group. However, decisive power now lay with the officer corps. Al-Midfaʿi initially tried to placate the seven most influential army officers by giving them senior posts. Yet they did not trust him and there were always plenty of politicians eager to exploit that mistrust. In December 1938 forces were concentrated at Rashid camp near Baghdad, and al-Midfaʿi was informed that a coup d'état was in the offing, whereupon he immediately resigned. The chief of the general staff then told the king that the army had lost confidence in the government and that either Nuri al-Saʿid or Taha al-Hashimi (both had been busy cultivating the officers in question) should be asked to form a new administration.

When Nuri al-Saʿid was asked by the king to form a government, he too found that his power depended largely on his ability to placate the 'circle of seven'. To some degree he was able to do so because of the views they shared on the importance of the question of Palestine. During the previous few years, Nuri al-Saʿid had made considerable efforts to establish a role for Iraq – and thus for himself – in Palestine. In 1936, with the outbreak of the general strike organised by the Arab Higher Committee in Palestine, Nuri had made several unsuccessful attempts to mediate first between the Arabs and the Jewish Agency and then between the Higher Committee and the British authorities. His professed hope was to bring all sides together in agreeing to a solution to the Palestine problem within the framework of a larger Arab federation of the Fertile Crescent, led by the Hashemite dynasty. This was an idea that he repeatedly sought to promote, making much-publicised visits to various Arab capitals and suggesting that he held the key to a reconciliation between the British and the Palestinian leader Hajj Amin al-Husaini. This proved not to be the case, but it served to create the impression in Iraq that Nuri al-Saʿid, more than any other of the established politicians, was determined to work on behalf of the cause of Palestine. This stood him in good stead with the pan-Arab officers of the Iraqi army. Consequently, when he became prime minister he was careful to pursue these initiatives, personally heading the Iraqi delegation to the London Round Table Conference on Palestine in January 1939, where he tried to bring about agreement between the Palestinian and British sides. He failed, but his commitment won the approval of the 'circle of seven' in the armed forces.[8]

Nuri's next move was to have parliament dissolved and to set in motion plans for general elections. Against this background, in March 1939, he claimed to have discovered a plot to assassinate King Ghazi and a number of senior political figures. He indicted Hikmat Sulaiman and his associates, had martial law declared at the Rashid military camp and brought the accused before military courts. Sulaiman and the others were found guilty and sentenced to death, but the sentences were commuted to terms of imprisonment. The evidence was so flimsy and the plot so fantastic that the whole episode seems to have been concocted by Nuri to avenge the death of his friend and brother-in-law, Jaʿfar al-ʿAskari, and possibly to reassure the 'circle of seven' that there could be no come-back of the Sulaiman–Sidqi regime.

It was at this point that the sudden death of King Ghazi in a car crash in April 1939 seemed to strengthen Nuri's hand still further. King Ghazi had not been a very consistent political player and the nature of Iraqi politics during his reign had been such that the initiative lay with others. In general, the king's political sympathies linked him to his generation among the Sunni Arab elite of Iraq. He resented the continued British influence, but in a rather unfocused way, since the question of that influence was not the burning issue of Iraqi domestic politics by the time he came to the throne. However, these sentiments, together with his sympathies for pan-Arab causes and his pride as sovereign of Iraq, led him to be increasingly critical of British policy elsewhere in the Middle East, particularly in Palestine and in the Persian Gulf. He was associated with the first serious public airing of the Iraqi claim to sovereignty over Kuwait and on this question, as in the other regional issues, the king made his voice heard through broadcasts from a radio station which he had established in the palace in 1937. This also allowed him to be linked to more radical views than he could otherwise express as king.

The immediate political consequence of his death was the need to appoint a regent since his son, who was proclaimed King Faisal II, was only 3 years old. The choice fell on Prince ʿAbd al-Ilah, the 26-year-old son of ex-king ʿAli of the Hijaz and brother of Queen ʿAliyya, mother of Faisal II. As events were to prove, ʿAbd al-Ilah's appointment changed the delicate balance between the Palace, the officer corps, the civilian political elite and the British. ʿAbd al-Ilah differed from his late brother-in-law in that he was more tolerant of the continued British presence in Iraq. Indeed, he was in some respects positively enthusiastic about the link with Great Britain, seeing it as one of the principal guarantors of the Hashemite dynasty. This meant that he had little in common with the Arab nationalist army officers whom he tended to regard as social upstarts, unworthy of his cultivation.

The regent's attitude was to be a complicating factor since Iraqi politics were increasingly overshadowed by the approach and outbreak of war in Europe. The relationship with Great Britain came to the fore once again, partly because the growing number of British demands reminded the officers and others of the more controversial aspects of the 1930 treaty. At a time when the British were increasingly intolerant of dissent or reluctant compliance by Iraq, many of the Arab nationalist officers were wary of being drawn into the British orbit. Strongly influenced by the example of National Socialist Germany, the image of which had been assiduously promoted by the German ambassador to Iraq during these years, Fritz Grobba, the officers resented Great Britain's demands and were, in any case, convinced that the Axis Powers would win the war. Many of the civilian politicians and the regent found themselves caught between two opposing forces and relatively helpless as a consequence.

Before this pattern of events became clear, Nuri organised general elections in May which returned a parliament predictably dominated by men selected by him. However, Nuri knew that parliamentary support was no match for the kind of power represented by the army. Prudently, he ensured that he stayed on good terms with the 'circle of seven', particularly with its four leading members, Salah al-Din al-Sabbagh, Fahmi Saʿid, Mahmud Salman and Kamil Shabib. These four colonels formed the picturesquely named 'Golden Square' that had become the effective arbiter of power in Iraq.

With the outbreak of war in Europe in September 1939, Great Britain asked Iraq to sever diplomatic relations with Germany, to intern all Germans and to give whatever assistance Great Britain would require under the terms of the treaty. Nuri al-Saʿid was quick to comply and assured Great Britain of Iraq's full support. Additionally, he introduced censorship, curfews, rationing, requisitioning and all the regulations needed to place Iraq virtually on a war footing. His government now had the power to rule by decree and by administrative regulation, causing great concern among Nuri al-Saʿid's political opponents, since they rightly feared that these powers would be used against them.

At this stage the 'circle of seven' in the officer corps saw no reason why Iraq should not comply with Great Britain's requests. Nor were they perturbed by the strengthening of Nuri's position since they knew that he was aware of the terms on which he occupied the office of premier. For his part, Nuri still believed that he could maintain the balance between their brand of Arab nationalism and the demands made upon his government by the British. He therefore made no objection – whatever misgivings he may have felt privately – when the officers invited the defeated leader of the Palestine revolt, the mufti of Jerusalem, Hajj Amin al-Husaini, to Baghdad in October 1939. The mufti was to become an influential figure during the following two years, keeping alive both the cause of Palestine and the hostility towards Great Britain which that cause evoked. Nevertheless, Nuri tried to exploit the opportunity to mediate once again on the Palestine issue by seeking to persuade the mufti of the virtues of the British White Paper on Palestine of May 1939. Although obliged to be critical of the White Paper in public, Nuri approved of its abandonment of partition, of its limitation on Jewish immigration and of its promise of eventual independence for a unified Palestine. However, he was unable to bring the mufti round to his point of view and the differences between the two men became ever sharper, contributing to the growing polarisation of Iraqi politics.

For Nuri al-Saʿid's political opponents, the only hope of removing him lay in cultivating rival officer factions. When Nuri al-Saʿid's close associate, Rustum Haidar, the minister of finance, was assassinated in January 1940, some of these tensions erupted. The assassination was the work of a

disgruntled civil servant who had moved in the circles of anti-British and
pro-Axis Iraqis. Consequently, Nuri chose to see this as part of a more
general plot organised by his enemies and seemed ready to use the Haidar
case as he had done the alleged 'plot' of March 1939 to ensnare and to eliminate his political rivals. Their unease communicated itself to the officer
corps. Here a rift was developing between some of the older members of
the 'circle of seven', particularly General Husain Fawzi, the chief of the
general staff, and the younger Golden Square with whom Nuri enjoyed
closer relations. This led to the crisis of February 1940 when Nuri resigned
as prime minister and his military allies promptly demanded his reinstatement, mobilising their forces at Rashid camp and apparently preparing to
march on the capital. General Fawzi mobilised his forces at Washshash
camp and the scene seemed set for a military confrontation to decide on
the future government of Iraq. At this point, the regent, seeing where the
balance of power lay and being sympathetic himself to Nuri, called on him
to form a government. Nuri did so and promptly retired General Fawzi and
his two colleagues, thereby satisfying al-Sabbagh.

However, Nuri's subservience to the Golden Square undermined his
authority, exemplified in his failure to get his way in the trials associated
with Haidar's murder and in the inability of his minister of defence, Taha
al-Hashimi, to break up the Golden Square itself. The latter saw this
attempt as the first move in a plan to re-establish civilian control over the
officer corps, particularly in the light of a meeting of senior politicians summoned by the regent in March 1940 to discuss the problem of army intervention in politics. Faced by rifts within his cabinet, by increasing criticism
of his policy of close co-operation with Great Britain and aware of the shifts
within the officer corps, Nuri resigned as prime minister in March 1940.
The regent thereupon turned to the head of the Royal Diwan, Rashid 'Ali
al-Kailani, to form a 'national coalition' which included Nuri al-Sa'id as
minister of foreign affairs. By bringing most of the senior politicians into a
single government which implicitly accepted the 1930 treaty and the assistance which Great Britain might ask of Iraq under its terms, Nuri and the
regent believed that they could deprive the increasingly vociferous
members of the Golden Square of significant political allies.

As the war in Europe unfolded, bringing with it a succession of German
victories, the entry of Italy into the war and the fall of France, opinion
within the cabinet and in Iraq became more clearly divided between those
who believed that Iraq should do what it could to assist the Allied cause
and those who believed that this would be fatal for Iraq's interests. In
general terms, Nuri al-Sa'id and the regent were seen as advocates of a

strongly pro-British policy, whilst the Golden Square, Naji Shawkat in the cabinet and the circles of Arab nationalists surrounding the mufti believed that the Axis Powers were likely to be victorious and that therefore Iraq should do nothing to provoke them.

The prime minister, Rashid ʿAli al-Kailani, was more aware of the immediate balancing act that he needed to perform. The British were still a power to be reckoned with in Iraq, whatever set-backs they were experiencing elsewhere. Consequently he advocated a studied neutrality, although his justifications for this position meant that he became increasingly associated with the more openly pro-Axis sentiments of the Golden Square. Given the nature of his backing in the army and elsewhere, it was also increasingly difficult for Rashid ʿAli to comply with the growing number of British requests with the alacrity expected by the British government in wartime. In July 1940 a dispute arose concerning British requests to transfer troops through Iraq. The Iraqi government eventually agreed, but the prolonged argument over the exact section of the treaty which authorised this gave the British the impression that the prime minister was more concerned to placate pro-Axis sentiment in Iraq and indeed the Axis Powers themselves than to fulfil Iraq's obligations to Great Britain under the treaty.

The same impression arose over the question of Iraq's relations with Italy in the summer of 1940. Nuri al-Saʿid proposed that Iraq should sever relations, but this was rejected in the cabinet and Rashid ʿAli failed to give Nuri his full support. Consequently, by the autumn of 1940 British officials were making it known that Rashid ʿAli would have to go. For Rashid ʿAli, general knowledge of the British attitude made his survival as prime minister a matter of principle. To resign would look like an act of abject surrender. Quite apart from the question of the war and the attitudes of the Axis Powers, this evoked powerful feelings of resentment in Iraq about British intervention. Rashid ʿAli successfully tapped into these sentiments, which he undoubtedly shared, but in doing so he became ever more closely identified as the figurehead or symbol of the anti-British (and in the context of the war pro-Axis) movement in Iraq. As events were to show, this was a dangerous position to hold.

Despite his set-backs in cabinet, Nuri al-Saʿid was also reluctant to resign. Nor was the whole of the cabinet against him. At this point, in January 1941, the regent decided to intervene. He took the unprecedented step of letting it be known that the government should resign. Rashid ʿAli, secure in the knowledge that he now enjoyed the support of the Golden Square, and aware that the regent had no constitutional power to dismiss him, refused the regent's request. When the regent insisted, Rashid ʿAli persisted in his refusal, but found to his dismay that most of his ministers were prepared to hand in their resignations.

Rashid ʿAli promptly enlisted the help of al-Sabbagh, who threatened the regent with direct military action if he insisted on Rashid ʿAli's resignation. The regent was forced to comply. Nuri (now out of the cabinet) mobilised his parliamentary following, leading Rashid ʿAli to demand that the regent dissolve parliament. The regent did not sign the dissolution order and left Baghdad for Diwaniyya where he knew that he could rely on loyal army units. This put a new complexion on events and obliged Rashid ʿAli finally to resign at the end of January 1941, since the officers of the Golden Square had made it clear that they were not prepared to risk civil war simply to keep him in office.

The regent then asked Taha al-Hashimi to form a government. He had the initial support of the officers of the Golden Square, since they regarded him as an Arab nationalist and he too had his own networks of influence in the armed forces. However, when he once again tried to break up the Golden Square, they, together with General Amin Zaki (acting chief of the general staff) and Rashid ʿAli, decided to move against both the regent and al-Hashimi in April 1941. They forced al-Hashimi to write a letter of resignation, but the regent, realising that the palace was being surrounded by troops, managed to escape, making his way to Basra and eventually to Transjordan. As the armed forces took over Baghdad, he was joined in exile by Nuri al-Saʿid, Jamil al-Midfaʿi and ʿAli Jawdat, all opponents of Rashid ʿAli.[9]

THE COUP D'ÉTAT OF 1941 AND THE BRITISH MILITARY OCCUPATION

The coup d'état of 1 April 1941 was significantly different from previous ones. It was no longer simply aimed at replacing one prime minister with another. Instead, it was directed against the monarch – in the shape of the regent ʿAbd al-Ilah – whose authority was constitutionally necessary to legitimise the actions of the armed forces and their civilian allies. The regent's refusal to play the game obliged the conspirators to find new ways of sanctioning their behaviour. These proved to be a curious mix of the old and the new. The first move was the establishment of a Government of National Defence, presided over by Rashid ʿAli al-Kailani and justified by the need 'to safeguard the country's integrity and safety'. At the same time the regent was indicted for trying to undermine the army, for harming national unity and for flouting the constitution. This mixture of national salvationism and constitutionalism marked the rhetoric and the actions of the new regime. Rashid ʿAli put a motion before parliament deposing ʿAbd al-Ilah and replacing him as regent with a cousin of the king, Sharif Sharaf. Surprisingly, given the fact that the parliament contained a large number of people who were by no means sympathetic to Rashid ʿAli, the motion was passed unanimously. Thenceforth, matters could proceed with a semblance of constitutional propriety since the new regent, Sharif Sharaf, promptly signed the order approving Taha al-Hashimi's resignation, and authorised Rashid ʿAli to form a government.

In seeking to abide by forms of legality, Rashid ʿAli was concerned to carry with him much of the Iraqi political elite who were disconcerted by the flight of the regent and wary of the power of the Golden Square. Regardless of constitutional niceties, these men were upstarts. Their undisguised appearance in politics seemed to presage a more radical dispensation of power, not because of their ill-defined political programmes, but because they were 'unknowns'. Through their power in the army, they brought with them a self-sufficiency or at least an independence of the old networks of family patronage. It was this which implicitly threatened the influence of the established families and personalities, contributing to the unease of much of the elite once the army officers began to act in their own interest, no longer as the clients of others. The events of April 1941 seemed to many to exemplify the dangers of such a development and Rashid ʿAli's desire to give a veneer of constitutional propriety to these proceedings was intended to reassure them that their world was not on the verge of collapse.

However, Rashid ʿAli was also aware of the need to persuade the British that no fundamental change had occurred. Thus, he hastened to reassure Great Britain that Iraq would respect all its obligations under the treaty. For their part, the British were deeply alarmed by the return of Rashid ʿAli to power and by the strongly nationalist colour of his new cabinet. They were also aware of the fact that a 'shadow government' existed, composed of Rashid ʿAli and a few members of his cabinet, together with the four officers of the Golden Square and Hajj Amin al-Husaini. Consequently, Great Britain withheld recognition of the new government, belying Rashid ʿAli's claims to constitutionality, and took the decision to test the intentions of the government by requesting permission to land troops in Iraq under the terms of the treaty.

Rashid ʿAli agreed to the British request, but soon found himself under intense pressure from the Golden Square and from his cabinet colleagues to impose conditions which would effectively limit the capacity of Great Britain to land any more troops in Iraq. The British saw this as confirmation of their worst suspicions and rejected all limiting conditions outright. Instead, they pressed ahead with troop landings at Basra. This was met by an official protest from the Iraqi government which then authorised units of the Iraqi army to take up positions overlooking the British air base at Habbaniyya. The British commander was informed that all air activity must cease forthwith and that any plane trying to take off would be fired on. The British rejected this demand and in turn demanded that the forces overlooking the air base should be withdrawn – and that failure to do so would be regarded as an act of war.

The Iraqi forces refused to comply and, consequently, the British commander at Habbaniyya ordered his forces to attack on 2 May. Fighting lasted for some days, but eventually the Iraqi troops were forced to fall back towards Baghdad and took up position at Falluja. By this stage, however, the British were sending more troops from India and a British force was being prepared in Transjordan to cross the desert to Iraq. In this situation, Rashid ʿAli, backed by those in the army and in his government who saw this as an opportunity for a more general assault against British influence in Iraq, sought the help of the Axis Powers. Naji Shawkat was sent to Turkey to impress upon the German authorities Iraq's urgent need for military assistance. Both Germany and Italy naturally favoured any attempt to undermine British power in the Middle East and enlisted the support of Vichy France to this end, but the timing was such that the Axis Powers could do little to tilt the balance of forces in Iraq against Great Britain. In the event, Germany and Italy sent some shipments of small arms and about thirty warplanes to Mosul, but they played a negligible part in the campaign.

Meanwhile, British forces built up in Iraq, occupying Basra and cutting Baghdad off from the north. Although numerically superior, the Iraqi units could not withstand the military power which Great Britain brought to bear and it was not long before the British forces reached the outskirts of Baghdad. The government of Rashid ʿAli and the Golden Square disintegrated, demoralised by the relentless advance of the British forces on the capital. Nor did the great majority of Iraqis seem particularly involved in the plight of the government. Despite calls for *jihad* by a number of clerics and despite the best endeavours of the government media, those sections of the Iraqi population which might have made a difference to the military outcome – the Shiʿi tribes of the south and the Kurdish population of the north – failed to respond to the government's rallying cry. On the contrary, in many cases Kurdish and Shiʿi tribal leaders assisted the British forces.[10]

By the end of May Rashid ʿAli and the members of his government, as well as Hajj Amin al-Husaini and the officers most deeply implicated in his regime, had fled Baghdad, leaving the mayor of the city, Arshad al-ʿUmari, to negotiate an armistice with the British forces. The collapse of the government also gave sections of the population and of the security forces the opportunity to wreak a violent and vicarious revenge upon the Jewish community of Baghdad. The *Farhud* (the term signifies pursuing things to excess and violent dispossession), as it was known, claimed the lives of nearly 200 Jewish Iraqis and was accompanied by the looting and destruction of Jewish businesses in the city. Already targeted by anti-Zionist Arab nationalists in the 1930s, many of the Jews of Iraq saw these events as a turning point in their relations with their Iraqi compatriots. After two days, when the looting threatened to become more widespread, the Iraqi and British authorities finally decided to intervene and forcefully restored order to the city. This allowed the regent ʿAbd al-Ilah to enter Baghdad, accompanied by Nuri al-Saʿid and the others who had fled in the wake of Rashid ʿAli's coup in April.[11]

In this way, the immediate crisis came to an end. The activities of the army officers and of Rashid ʿAli's government had threatened the interests of the regent, Nuri al-Saʿid and others, as well as the British in a number of ways. They had no difficulty, therefore, in agreeing on a common strategy for dealing with the problem. The fact that this strategy was based on military action and *force majeure* was due in part to the underlying nature of continuing British power in Iraq, as well as to the conditions and exigencies of wartime. However, it had also been due in part to the developing patterns of Iraqi politics, whereby armed force or the threat of it had become the means of deciding in whose hands command of the state should lie.

The Iraqi state itself was thus becoming not simply the arena of significant political action, but also an array of procedures, attitudes and practices. These grew out of the actions and visions of those who were able, for a variety of reasons, to wield significant power over the greater part of the Iraqi population and constituted the field of distinctively Iraqi politics. Although contested by those who felt excluded or disadvantaged by this regime of power, it nevertheless had come to represent an increasingly well-defined set of preoccupations, articulated by the people who had succeeded in mastering it. Regardless of personal or factional differences, or even of significant ideological divergence, certain features were becoming apparent. Principally, these comprised the importance of personal trust, the determination to preserve inequality, whether materially or status-based, and the prominence of the disciplinary impulse, expressed primarily through the use of coercion. These features made any construction of an Iraqi identity ambiguous, since it was obvious that any such identity would be determined largely by individuals who had an overdeveloped sense of Iraq as an apparatus of power and an underdeveloped sense of Iraq as a community. The emergence of army officers during the 1930s as the supreme arbiters merely made these features crudely apparent. The restoration of the regent and the return of Nuri al-Saʿid and his allies gave the semblance of a restoration of civility, but the same rules and the same logic applied. They would merely take on different forms.

CHAPTER 4

The Hashemite monarchy 1941–58

British military intervention in 1941 abruptly ended the cycle of military coups d'état which had marked Iraqi politics during the preceding few years. It allowed the regent and those politicians who had found themselves increasingly at the beck and call of ambitious army officers to take stock and to reassert the kind of control with which they felt more comfortable. In the restricted circles of Iraqi elite politics, this did not alter the highly personalised relations which determined political alliances and antagonisms. Nor did it have any noticeable effect on the hierarchies which determined the flow of power and favour between the ruling elite and Iraqi society in all its variety. The structures of political power and of economic reward were much as they had ever been and were simply reinforced in the interests of the principal figures of the period, the most prominent of whom was Nuri al-Saʿid.

Nuri dominated the world of postwar Iraqi politics, both in its domestic and in its foreign policies, despite problems with the regent and challenges from within the elite and from the widening political circles of an engaged Iraqi political public. For Nuri, the political world seemed to exist on two levels. The first, deeply personalised world of politics required constant attention and manipulation. It was dominated by the immediate need to cement alliances, to co-opt and cajole potential adversaries and, if necessary, to deter and destroy intransigent opponents by the ruthless use of force. Success at this level opened up the possibilities of acting on the larger stages of the region and of Iraqi history. These were the fields which encouraged Nuri's ambitious visions of a Hashemite-dominated federation of Arab states, and of an Iraq in which social friction would give way to common acknowledgement of the benefits of a patrimonial state founded on oil revenues.

The different kinds of activity associated with these contrasting views of politics created the impression of energy, curiosity and attention to detail for which Nuri was famous. However, it also meant that he was easily and often diverted by immediate, short-term considerations, sometimes losing sight of the need to sustain his initiatives systematically. Equally, his tendency to see day-to-day politics in highly personal terms meant that he was prone to neglect or underplay the need for the kind of institutional solidity that could be created only through a degree of institutional autonomy – something which might, in any case, have run counter to his own, largely authoritarian view of power.

On the surface at least, during this period Nuri had all the instruments of state power at his disposal and could thus be confident of determining the narrative of the Iraqi state during these years. However, it was a narrative which was gradually escaping his control, partly because of the growing capacity of Iraqis to organise around distributive issues that he found hard to address. The perennial questions of sectarian and ethnic representation resurfaced, but these could be dealt with by the traditional means of co-option, concession and deterrence. Less amenable to such strategies were the growing demands for greater social and economic justice. These seemed to require a radical overhaul of the whole system of privilege on which were founded not only the structures of the kingdom, but also the vision of the proper ordering of Iraqi society shared by Nuri and most of the elite. Nuri's belief that the hard choices suggested by this logic of the modern state could be avoided through major economic development funded by oil revenues was flawed in two important respects.

In the first place, he would be developing a fundamentally inegalitarian society in which the major beneficiaries of public expenditure would be the very families who stood at the core of the system that was provoking increasing unrest. Consequently, he risked creating a coalition between the traditionally disadvantaged who were slowly becoming better organised and the emerging entrepreneurs and professionals – military and civilian – who resented the hold of the old, restricted elites on the resources and positions of power in the state. Nuri believed that these contradictions could all be dealt with in the short term through the development of the state's security apparatus. From this perspective, the security forces would protect the regime and prevent deflection from the chosen course until such time as the public came to acknowledge the merits of the system itself. However, this strategy could work only if the loyalty of the security forces was absolute or at least if there were mechanisms in place that could successfully pre-empt any attempt by members of the security forces to seize the initiative themselves. As events were to show, this was to be the key weakness in Nuri's plan. He underestimated the vulnerability of a regime such as his to a conspiracy of a relatively small number of officers acting

ruthlessly and decisively against an equally small number of leading personalities, concentrated in Baghdad, who formed the apex of the pyramid
of patronage and power that sustained the Iraqi monarchy.

RE-ESTABLISHING THE REGIME

With the return of the regent to Baghdad in June 1941, accompanied by the
politicians who had fled the country in the wake of the coup d'état of April,
the political life of Iraq resumed much as before. It was true that Great
Britain had entered the equation more directly and more forcefully than
had been the case for some years, but for many this simply made obvious
that which had hitherto been partially concealed. At the instigation of the
British Embassy, as well as of the regent, the new government of Jamil
al-Midfa'i began a purge of Rashid 'Ali's supporters, but the task of cutting
through the complex web of patrons and clients in Iraq's small political
world overwhelmed the prime minister and he resigned in October.

Nuri al-Sa'id succeeded him and presided over a government intent on
retribution. In early 1942, courts martial sentenced to death in absentia
three of the four officers who had constituted the Golden Square, as well
as Rashid 'Ali al-Kailani. (Only Rashid 'Ali escaped execution since he
eventually found a safe haven in Saudi Arabia and did not return to Iraq
until after the overthrow of the monarchy in 1958.) In addition, long prison
sentences were handed down and several hundred people were sent to the
internment camp at al-Faw. Purges in the armed forces removed many
officers prominent in the factionalised politics of the 1930s, and similar
purges in various branches of the civil administration, particularly in the
Ministry of Education, removed others whom Nuri al-Sa'id regarded as
potentially hostile.

Nuri al-Sa'id had no difficulty in brushing aside the protests these moves
provoked, even from cabinet colleagues who tried to intercede on behalf of
members of their client networks. In this he was assisted by his protégé,
Salih Jabr, the first Shi'i minister of the interior. Jabr attracted much of the
criticism, both from Sunni Arab politicians unused to seeing a Shi'i in such
a position of power, as well as from Shi'a who thought he should have done
more to promote the interests of the Shi'i community. The purges created
vacancies and opportunities for exceptional promotions, opening up the
scope for the exercise of patronage. Inevitably, this raised once again an
issue which was to become increasingly prominent: the relative under-
representation of the Shi'a in the state administration, particularly at senior
levels and in the officer corps. It was a widely voiced complaint against

successive governments and was eventually taken up by Salih Jabr himself and the party he was to form.

Of no less importance was the continuing concern in the Kurdish areas of Iraq about the place of the Kurds in the Iraqi state. In 1939 this had led to the formation of Kurdish nationalist organisations, such as Hiwa (Hope), among a younger generation of Kurdish professionals and towns-men apprehensive of the pan-Arabism which then informed political debates in Baghdad. After 1941, with the eclipse of the pan-Arab faction in Iraq, Hiwa and the Kurds generally were more concerned about Baghdad's domination and the insensitivity of Baghdad's elite to the deteriorating eco-nomic conditions in the Kurdish areas. This combination of factors led to the re-emergence of Mulla Mustafa Barzani (brother of Shaikh Ahmad) as a leader of Kurdish insurrection. He escaped from detention and re-established himself in his local power base of Barzan in 1943, entering into negotiations with the government through the intermediary of a Kurdish member of Nuri's cabinet, Majid Mustafa. Barzani's demands were largely local in nature, concerning amnesties for himself and members of his family, as well as the alleviation of the devastating famine affecting many of the villages under his protection. However, they also included more general pan-Kurdish demands, such as the separation of the Kurdish dis-tricts from the governorate of Mosul and the formation of a distinctive Kurdish governorate. Despite opposition from some of his associates, Nuri al-Saʿid agreed in principle to this demand, allowing Mulla Mustafa to come to Baghdad in 1944 to make his peace with the central authorities.

As far as the exercise of power at the centre was concerned, Nuri al-Saʿid and the regent initiated a series of constitutional amendments in October 1943 that strengthened the powers of the monarch. Nuri believed it would give him an advantage over the rest of the political elite because of his close relationship with the regent. However, ʿAbd al-Ilah, who was both regent and heir presumptive, saw this as an opportunity to become a political player in his own right, independent of the politicians whom he was empowered to appoint and to dismiss. His emergence as a political figure with distinct, if inconsistent ideas about domestic and foreign policy inevitably led him into conflict with Nuri al-Saʿid who expected the Palace merely to give him the authority to do as he wished.

This was not the view of the regent. ʿAbd al-Ilah wanted to carve out a role for himself, but his notorious indecisiveness and impressionability meant that his strategies were not consistently pursued. Nor was it always clear whether he intended to continue in public life, since he was a shy and somewhat retiring man, happiest when amongst his circle of private friends. In some respects, the public world of Iraqi politics, with its fractious personalities and its increasingly restive forces, appeared to alarm him – an alarm that became more marked during the 1950s. A noticeable feature of his regency was his tendency to take up causes with apparent enthusiasm, only to drop them a few months later, having either lost interest or having been discouraged by others more forceful than he. This applied both to his initiatives concerning the internal condition of Iraq, as well as to his periodic interventions in the field of foreign policy. As far as the latter were concerned, they appeared to be motivated by a mixture of Hashemite dynastic ambitions and by a personal desire to find a leading position for himself in the Arab world. However, here too he seemed to have little grasp of what the Arab world was becoming in the 1950s and to have retained a rather anachronistic and politically unhelpful faith in the power of Great Britain.[1]

By early 1944 the relationship between the regent and Nuri al-Saʿid, hitherto so close, was coming under strain, leading Nuri to resign the premiership in June. The break was not a dramatic one. His successor, Hamdi al-Pachachi, included several of Nuri's allies in his government, but also brought in favourites of the regent who had become uneasy about Nuri's capacity to rule autocratically and to eclipse not only all the other politicians, but also the monarch himself. Nuri's apparent lack of concern at the dire effects of wartime inflation and shortages on most of his fellow countrymen had caused even some of his former allies to distance themselves from him. Martial law allowed him to censor the press and to control all forms of organised political activity, so Nuri's critics tried to work through the regent. For his part, ʿAbd al-Ilah began to voice his own concerns about the lack of social and economic reform and of political freedoms. Although not publicly broadcast, the regent's views were known to the political elite and at the British Embassy, where there was growing apprehension about the explosive political consequences of Nuri's repressive and conservative regime.

There was some expectation of change, therefore, when al-Pachachi became prime minister in June 1944. In fact, al-Pachachi was able to achieve little, but he released a number of those who had been detained in 1941 and relaxed strict press censorship. With the regent's encouragement he also introduced the 1945 Miri Sirf Law. Initially applied to Dujaila, an area near Kut, the intention was to distribute state lands to landless peasants, as well as to small landowners and retired government officials. In this and in other schemes, a limited amount of land was involved and, in practice, much of it fell into the hands of absentee landlords who sublet their plots to peasant cultivators. Nevertheless, it alarmed the newly formed 'Parliamentary Bloc' of tribal shaikhs, who agreed to the measure only once they were convinced that it was not the thin end of the wedge of more radical land reform and once they saw that they too could become substantial beneficiaries.

However, al-Pachachi was faced by growing rebellion in the Kurdish region. Mulla Mustafa, angered by the failure of Nuri's successor to uphold the terms apparently agreed in early 1944, began to organise resistance in northern Kurdistan. He formed alliances with various tribes concerned about the mixture of government interference and neglect which had caused resentment throughout the Kurdish region. This led him to make increasing demands of the government, aimed at enhancing his own power, but also at securing advantages for the Kurds more generally in the balance of power in the Iraqi state. Al-Pachachi's rejection of his terms resulted in the outbreak of full-scale armed revolt in mid-1945.

Although Barzani's forces were initially successful, the weight of the Iraqi army and the fragility of the alliances he had constructed led to Mulla Mustafa's defeat, forcing him to flee with his men across the Iranian border in October 1945. Once in Iran, he became an influential player in the short-lived autonomous Kurdish Mahabad Republic under Qadhi Muhammad. However, when the shah's forces routed the Kurds and reoccupied Mahabad in December 1946, he was forced to flee once more. In April 1947 he and his men were driven over the border back into Iraq. They avoided major confrontations with Iraqi forces, but came under increasing pressure. Barzani decided to seek refuge elsewhere and in May–June 1947 he led his men on an epic journey through the mountains to Soviet territory. Barzani was granted asylum by the USSR and lived there in exile until his return to Iraq after the fall of the monarchy in 1958.[2]

Military success against Barzani had gained al-Pachachi considerable kudos, but seemed to annoy the regent. He continued to urge 'reform' of a rather general kind, but felt ignored by most of the established politicians. This led to his speech of December 1945 in which he called publicly for greater political freedom, the formation of political parties and the holding of free elections, as well as the implementation of reforms that would lead to greater social justice and to a system of social security. For many, the regent's speech came as a distinct encouragement. Restive at the continuation of martial law in Iraq and scenting a weakening of the bond between the prime minister and the regent, critics of the government stepped up their attacks. Knowing that he no longer had the support of the regent, al-Pachachi resigned, giving way to Tawfiq al-Suwaidi in February 1946.

THWARTED LIBERALISATION

During his brief tenure of office al-Suwaidi ended martial law, closed the al-Faw detention camp, lifted press censorship and introduced a new Electoral Law which retained the system of two-stage elections, but which divided the country into 100 electoral districts (rather than the 3 which had existed before). In principle, this allowed greater representation to the urban areas of Iraq where the population was expanding rapidly. Al-Suwaidi also permitted political parties to form once again. The two principal ones, Al-Hizb al-Watani al-Dimuqrati (National Democratic Party (NDP)) and Hizb al-Istiqlal (Independence Party), corresponded to two main currents of thought in evidence since the 1930s.

The NDP, led by Kamil al-Chadirchi and Muhammad Hadid, brought together many of those who had been associated with the Ahali group. They advocated social democracy and political reform by parliamentary means. The party tended to concentrate on the condition of Iraq itself and displayed an interest in foreign affairs only insofar as these affected the political situation within Iraq. Thus, it was a determined critic of the continued British military presence and of British influence in Iraq's affairs. However, it was considerably less interested in the affairs of the Arab world in general, especially when these were set in the context of pan-Arabism. This, however, was the major preoccupation of the Istiqlal Party. Led by Muhammad Mahdi Kubba, Fa'iq al-Samarrai and Siddiq Shanshal, the party brought together those who had been attracted to Arab nationalism and to pan-Arabism in the 1930s. The party had little to say about domestic reform beyond criticism of the parliamentary system which, it believed, denied it proper representation. However, it was vociferous in denouncing any form of British influence in Iraq and in the Middle East, since it saw this as bound to work against the aspirations of pan-Arabism.

A couple of small socialist parties were also licensed. They did not last long, nor did they gain large followings, but their emergence indicated a growing trend in criticism of social and economic inequalities in Iraq, at least among the urban intelligentsia. At the same time, the Iraqi Communist Party (ICP) unsuccessfully applied for permission to form Hizb al-Taharrur al-Watani (National Liberation Party). The activities of the ICP had intensified since October 1941 when Yusuf Salman Yusuf (Comrade Fahd) had become secretary-general of the party. He had made a determined effort to expand the party's membership beyond the circles of the urban intelligentsia into the small provincial towns and among the workers in a number of sectors such as the port at Basra, the Iraqi national railways and the oil industry. In addition, cells were established in the educational sector and, on a much smaller scale, in the armed forces.

After the German invasion of the Soviet Union in June 1941, the ICP had adopted a position of grudging support for the British military presence in the country, insofar as it was part of the Allied war effort. This eased the party's relations with successive Iraqi governments and, although it still operated under restrictions, it was able to publicise its views and to expand its organisation to an unparalleled degree. With the growing tension between the USSR and the Western Allies after 1945, the ICP reverted to the more congenial – and popular – position of vehement denunciation of the British military presence and of the monarchical regime. However, the ICP's 'National Charter' of 1945 outlined a programme of progressive social democracy, rather than of rigorous Marxism-Leninism, allowing the party to appeal to a wider audience and to co-operate with other organisations and individuals whose critique of the status quo was broadly similar, despite the fact that it remained an illegal organisation.[3]

In one area in particular, the ICP had had considerable success. In the Kurdish towns of the north, where a distinctive Kurdish nationalism was developing, a powerful critique of the inequalities and injustices of Kurdish society was also emerging. As in the Arab regions of Iraq, there was much to criticise in terms of the distribution of wealth and the power which unequal land ownership gave a small minority over the lives of the vast majority of Kurds. Hitherto, the leaders of Kurdish insurrection had been landowners seeking individual or tribal advantage, however much they may have used appeals to pan-Kurdish sentiment to rally support. The recent Barzani revolt had followed this pattern. In reaction, a distinctively radical form of urban Kurdish nationalism emerged, expressed in such organisations as the Kurdish Communist Party or Shurish (Revolution) which in turn was a leading force in forming Rizgari Kurd (Kurdish Liberation), bringing together Kurdish nationalists and socialists. Other Kurds joined the ICP, seeing it as the most effective critic of the status quo, as well as a link to possible Soviet patronage for the project of national liberation.

With the lifting of press censorship and the ending of martial law, the activities of the small opposition parties became more visible in the major towns of Iraq and particularly in Baghdad. A lively press and publishing sector re-emerged after years of forced silence, giving voice to trenchant criticism of political and economic conditions and outlining ideas for the future of Iraq which were radical in their implications. Against a background of mounting social and economic grievances, some born out of the long-term structural inequalities of Iraqi society and many out of the immediate concerns of people who had seen the cost of living outstrip their wages, the activities of the opposition parties and of the newly recognised trade unions seemed to promise a period of escalating social protest. Strikes were organised at Basra port and unrest continued among the workers of the Iraqi railways whose union had been banned the previous year following the strikes of April 1945.

The economic condition of many ordinary Iraqis had deteriorated markedly during the previous five years. Wartime shortages, bad harvests and the increased purchasing powers of the British forces stationed in Iraq had dramatically forced up the prices of most commodities, affecting foodstuffs and clothing most of all. There had, consequently, been a five-fold increase in the cost of living, hitting salaried employees, whether government officials or industrial workers, hardest, especially since this had not been matched by any corresponding increase in their wages. The spiralling prices of cereals (by this stage Iraq's main export), not simply in Iraq but throughout the region, had encouraged landlords and merchants to profit from the export opportunities this offered. This not only added to the inflationary pressures within Iraq by creating scarcity, but, in some parts of the country, particularly in the Kurdish regions, created real hardship, amounting to starvation.[4]

The strikes organised during these months of relative freedom were almost all aimed at securing wage increases and better conditions for the workers concerned. The involvement of the ICP was partly due to the fact that the party was already clandestinely present in the workforce of these industries. In other cases, ICP involvement was due to the desire of the party to establish its credentials among the workers. Nevertheless, although tied to the immediate concerns of the workers, the strikes inevitably assumed wider political significance. For the British, who had a strategic interest in the major industrial sectors of transport and oil, strikes of this kind and the unions that promoted them seemed to be part of a more general assault on British interests. For many in the ruling elite, direct action by organised labour and the involvement of the ICP were seen as a prelude to more widespread revolutionary activity. When this was combined with the proliferation of the opposition press, it created a feeling that al-Suwaidi, by licensing opposition activity, had lost control.

Caught between the growing expectations of the opposition parties and the fears of those who dreaded radical upheaval, al-Suwaidi resigned in May 1946. The regent, having enthused only six months before about the need for social reform and greater freedoms, was also affected by the alarm of the Iraqi political elite and appointed Arshad al-'Umari to the premiership in the hope that he would curb the opposition. Al-ʿUmari thereupon embarked on a repressive policy with such enthusiasm that he succeeded in alienating virtually all sectors of opinion. In doing so, he caused the regent and others to doubt his ability to contain the developing social unrest. Most notoriously, in July 1946 a strike of some 5,000 workers at the Iraq Petroleum Company's Kirkuk oil fields over pay and conditions ended with the police firing on a crowd of oil workers, killing a number of them. These events caused a more general uproar, to which al-ʿUmari responded with arrests and the closure of newspapers.

It was significant, however, that during this period the Iraqi Kurdish Democratic Party (KDP) was able to hold its founding congress in Baghdad – in August 1946. Developing from Rizgari Kurd and from the KDP in Mahabad, the Iraqi KDP at this stage was organised largely by Barzani's allies. The party adopted a nationalist programme and elected Barzani as its president. It accepted the sovereignty of the Iraqi state and was conspicuously silent on questions of social or economic reform. Barzani was still in exile in the Mahabad Republic in Iran (where he was to remain until forced over the border into Iraq by the Iranian army in April 1947). However, he had been in contact with the Iraqi government and had suggested that the formation of the KDP would bring together all the Kurdish organisations under his control, implying that he could thereby rein in the more radical factions. In view of the strike at Kirkuk and the known activities of the ICP in the Kurdish areas, the prospect of an organisation that would bring the Kurdish national movement under the control of a leader who had no interest in provoking radical change was welcomed by al-ʿUmari. However, further strikes among railway and printing workers in response to al-ʿUmari's repression and the loss of confidence in al-ʿUmari by both the regent and the British, particularly when he requested the declaration of martial law prior to the imminent elections, led eventually to his resignation in November 1946.

In these circumstances, the regent turned once more to Nuri al-Saʿid, seeing him as someone who could maintain the same authoritarian stance, but with considerably more skill. Nuri proceeded to demonstrate these skills. He threw much of the party-based opposition into confusion by persuading some of their members to accept ministerial posts. Fahd and other leaders of the ICP were arrested, leading to a temporary suspension of much of the party's activity. General elections were held in March 1947, returning a predictable majority in support of the status quo. Nuri then declined the regent's invitation to form a government, suggesting instead his associate, Salih Jabr, who became Iraq's first Shiʿi prime minister. This allowed Nuri greater freedom of manoeuvre: he could be influential behind the scenes without necessarily attracting either the opprobrium of the opposition parties or the antagonism of the regent in the year ahead.[5]

FOREIGN POLICIES: ARAB ISSUES, PALESTINE AND THE PORTSMOUTH TREATY

Nuri al-Saʿid's decision to stay in the background seems to have been due to two problems looming on the horizon. The first involved Arab issues in general and specifically the question of Palestine. These issues had re-emerged in a number of ways after the end of the Second World War. Nuri had tenaciously pursued his idea of a federation of the Arab states of the Fertile Crescent, despite the widespread suspicion and opposition it had evoked from other Arab leaders, particularly those of Egypt and Saudi Arabia. Nor was Abdallah of Transjordan keen on a plan which seemed designed to thwart his own schemes for 'Greater Syria' and to carve out a leading role for Iraq – and the Iraqi branch of the Hashemite family – in Palestine and the Levant. This was indeed very much part of Nuri's longer-term strategy. However, he was realistic enough to see that it could not be pursued by Iraq unilaterally in the face of such widespread opposition.

Consequently, he became closely involved on Iraq's behalf in the foundation of the Arab League in 1944–5, seeing it as providing a forum for bringing together the Arab states, leaving the door open for a possible future federation. At the same time, he was determined that the Arab League should not give encouragement – and external support – to the ideologically driven Iraqi pan-Arabists whom he had been trying to hold in check since at least the late 1930s. The charter of the League which emerged was therefore very much to Nuri's liking, since it enshrined the principle of the independent sovereignty of the member states and made only rhetorical reference to pan-Arabism. He was less pleased, however, with the first secretary-general of the Arab League, the Egyptian ʿAbd al-Rahman ʿAzzam, whom he regarded as mesmerised by the romantic visions of Arab unity with which he himself had little patience.[6]

Nuri was well aware of the importance of the Arab world for Iraq, but his understanding of Iraq's interests meant that its foreign policies should pay as much attention to the cultivation of its northern and eastern neighbours as to the Arab world. However, as he discovered in 1946 when he negotiated treaties of friendship with both Turkey and Transjordan, this was a view which was shared neither by many in the Iraqi political elite nor by the regent. Continued suspicion of Turkey's territorial ambitions in northern Iraq and the question of Alexandretta coloured much of the Iraqi political elite's views of Turkey. This was sharpened by the final withdrawal of French troops from Syria in 1946 which awakened in the regent – and in others – hopes of an eventual union between Iraq and Syria, whether driven by dynastic or nationalist aspirations. The case of Transjordan was more unambiguously a question of dynastic union. However, the picture was complicated by the apparent enthusiasm of King 'Abdallah (paternal uncle of the regent 'Abd al-Ilah and some thirty years his senior) of Transjordan, raising the question of which branch of the Hashemite family was seeking to dominate the other. Nuri had little difficulty in persuading the regent that anything more than a fairly anodyne treaty of friendship might have dangerous consequences.

In 1947, it was clear both that the regent's and others' ambitions in the Arab world would only increase. Nowhere was this likely to be more contentious than on the question of Palestine. In February 1947 Great Britain had referred the problem to the United Nations. Effectively this meant that Great Britain would surrender the Mandate and with it the 1939 White Paper, a variant of which Nuri had been seeking to promote in the attempt to maintain a unified Palestine with an Arab majority. British withdrawal raised the possibility of an outcome much less favourable to the Palestinian Arabs, exciting pan-Arab feeling in Iraq, as elsewhere, and forcing governments to make choices which they would rather have avoided. Given these troubling issues in the Arab world, and given the disputes which they would cause within Iraq itself, it was scarcely surprising that Nuri should have preferred to stay in the background during these months.

He had another reason for doing so. No less troublesome and considerably more provocative of ill-feeling in Iraq was the re-emergence of the issue of the Anglo-Iraqi Treaty. As Nuri suspected and as events were to prove, the renegotiation of the treaty awakened all the old resentments. Partly for these reasons, Great Britain was reluctant to open up the question of the 1930 treaty: it stood for much that Iraqis disliked about their country's relationship with Great Britain, but it was not a burning issue. However, any Iraqi government renegotiating the terms of the 1930 treaty would have to demand the final evacuation of British troops and the surrender of the two major air bases to Iraqi control. For that very reason, Salih Jabr opened the subject of renegotiation soon after he took office in March 1947, hoping thereby to gain the kudos of achieving final British withdrawal.

Talks with Great Britain began in secret due to fear on both sides that public negotiations would provoke agitation on the streets in Iraq and would mobilise the many political factions which wanted to see an end to all forms of British influence. By December 1947 agreement was finally reached and it was only in early January 1948 that most Iraqis learned, to their surprise, that negotiations had been taking place. With the signing of the treaty at Portsmouth on 15 January 1948 its terms became generally known. Although the treaty promised the final withdrawal of all British forces and the handing over of the RAF's two air bases to Iraqi control, it set up a joint defence board, composed of British and Iraqi officials, to oversee Iraq's military planning. In addition, Great Britain would be permitted to take over the air bases again in time of war and Iraq would still be tied to Great Britain for military supplies and training. As many had feared, the treaty was to last for twenty-five years, formally sanctioning British influence in Iraq until 1973, fifteen years beyond the expiry date of the 1930 treaty.

The outrage this caused, added to the way in which the negotiations had been conducted, led to protest marches in Baghdad, as all the opposition parties sought to mobilise the public against the treaty. The fact that much of the cabinet was in Britain for the signing ceremony gave the impression of a leaderless government, which the opposition on the streets and among the political elite quickly exploited in their different spheres. Such was the extent and vehemence of this opposition that the regent took fright and announced that he would refuse to ratify the treaty. This was ominous for Salih Jabr who returned to Baghdad while the marches and demonstrations continued. The day after he returned, the largest of these processional marches took place and was fired on by the police, resulting in a large number of casualties.

Twenty or so members of parliament resigned in protest, as did two of Jabr's ministers. The regent then insisted that Salih Jabr himself should resign and called on Muhammad al-Sadr, the veteran Shi'i politician, to form a government, composed largely of the rivals of Nuri al-Sa'id and Salih Jabr. Al-Sadr's appointment showed that the regent was sensitive to the sectarian question which had been hovering in the background and had occasionally found a voice in the demonstrations. Salih Jabr had been the first Shi'i prime minister of Iraq and this break with the tradition of Sunni dominance had disconcerted some and stirred the prejudices of others. Whilst all was peaceful, the jibes to which this gave rise were largely muted. However, the eruption of anti-government demonstrations had led to sectarian barbs being directed at Salih Jabr, interspersed with denunciations of him as a traitor and servant of Great Britain.

For their part, the opposition parties responsible for organising the demonstrations were discovering a new, immediate form of power, denied them both by their small numbers and by the rigging of the parliamentary system. Initial anger at the Portsmouth Treaty had allowed them to focus attention on a number of grievances. These included a general indictment of the government, denunciation of the monarchy itself and the many discontents arising from the miserable economic conditions of most of the inhabitants of Baghdad. The public's economic grievances had been sharpened by the financial crisis of late 1947 when a shortage of hard currency, a poor harvest and the hoarding and continued export of grain had led to food shortages even in the capital where the staple food for the great majority was bread. Jabr's government's response had been wholly inadequate, giving his critics the chance to address a wide public audience, angry and fearful of what the future might hold. When brought together on the streets of the capital for a few days in January 1948, it suggested both the coherence and mass support which the opposition parties notoriously lacked and which few of them tried to cultivate in any systematic way. Furthermore, it generated an atmosphere which clearly had an effect on the regent and thus helped to decide the fate of the government.

The incoming prime minister, al-Sadr, discovered that, despite abandoning the Portsmouth Treaty, he was faced by continuing demonstrations. They were not as large as before, nor were they met with police violence. Nevertheless, they maintained a relentless pressure which al-Sadr tried to diffuse by promising general elections. This had only a limited effect. The NDP agreed to end its protests, but then found that they were no longer as much in control of the streets as they had thought. Instead, the marches continued as other organisations, many affiliated to the ICP, were able to call out significant numbers of people onto the streets. This disconcerted the NDP leadership and led them to rethink the utility of mass demonstrations as an instrument to advance their own cause.

In fact, the momentum could not be sustained. Some marches and demonstrations did take place in the following months, but they were generally small, localised affairs involving diminishing numbers. They came to an end abruptly in May 1948 when the government proclaimed martial law due to the outbreak of war in Palestine, concluding the series of events characterised in Iraq as *al-Wathba* (the leap). The term suggests a dramatic break with the past in the forms of political activity and in the involvement of the urban masses and has been interpreted retrospectively as paving the way for the overthrow of the monarchy in 1958. This aspect should not be exaggerated, but these events did allow some of the parties in Iraq to rediscover the power of 'the street' in Iraqi politics. It was a powerful stimulus to action, but it may have prevented them from seeing that key factors in enhancing this power were the tensions, rivalry and vacillations within the ruling elite, some of whom were happy to engineer the fall of their rivals against a theatrical background of street demonstrations.[7]

In the elections which took place in June under martial law, the three opposition parties won a mere 7 seats (of 138) between them, graphically illustrating the difficulty they faced in trying to work through the formal institutions of the state. As always, these were dominated by men who already enjoyed a certain position and status, whether in the countryside or in the towns, because of their independent sources of wealth or because they were clients of the regent or of other powerful individuals in the established hierarchy. The fact that Nuri al-Saʿid and Salih Jabr were able to ensure that a large number of their own clients and supporters won seats, despite the best endeavours of the government, merely demonstrated their informal power and did not, of course, help the opposition parties.

Following the elections, Muhammad al-Sadr resigned the premiership and the regent asked Muzahim al-Pachachi to form a government which had much in common with the preceding one. Plagued by internal division, the cabinet was insufficiently strong to withstand the backlash from the unfolding series of disasters in the Palestine war. Iraq had dispatched 3,000 troops to the front in May and in the months that followed a further 15,000 troops were sent, making them the largest single Arab force in Palestine. They successfully defended the triangle of Jenin–Nablus–Tulkaram, but their failure to launch an offensive and the strong suspicion that they were being used by King ʿAbdallah of Jordan simply to reinforce his annexation of Arab Palestine had led to a barrage of criticism in Iraq. This was redoubled when the military reverses of the Arab armies led them to agree to the cease-fires of June and July 1948, clearly negating the government's claim of Arab victories and giving the Israeli forces the opportunity to go on the offensive in Galilee, Lydda/Ramleh and finally the Negev.[8]

The minister of defence, Sadiq al-Bassam, denied much say in the conduct of the war, used the opportunity to initiate systematic harassment of the Iraqi Jewish community, whose loyalties were now more suspect than ever. Their movements were restricted, Jews were barred from certain government posts, courts martial were used extensively to imprison and intimidate Jews and a prominent member of the community was executed for allegedly assisting the new state of Israel. The international outcry that ensued gave the prime minister and al-Bassam's political rivals the opportunity to oust him from the cabinet. However, this could not diminish the increasing sense of threat within the Jewish community as the Arab armies in Palestine suffered a succession of defeats.

These events were the prelude to the eventual disappearance of the large and long-established Jewish community in Iraq (in 1947 they numbered 117,000, or 2.6 per cent of the Iraqi population). The establishment of the British Mandate for Palestine simultaneously with the British Mandate for Iraq had made the position of the Jewish community in the new Iraqi state peculiarly invidious. It was not long before the Jews in Iraq were being accused of serving both the British authorities in Iraq and the Zionist project in Palestine which the British Mandate had facilitated. During the 1930s, with the outbreak of the Arab revolt in Palestine and the heightening of pan-Arab and anti-Zionist agitation in Iraq, press attacks on the Jews became ever more vehement. Soon Jews in Baghdad were being physically assaulted, causing the leaders of the Jewish community to protest publicly to the Iraqi government.

Public attempts by the leadership of the Jewish community to impress upon their fellow countrymen that they were by no means supporters of the Zionist enterprise in Palestine carried little weight when contrasted with the accusations emanating from the Arab nationalist circles of the Muthanna Club. With official encouragement from the army officers who dominated Iraqi politics in the late 1930s, the charges levelled against the Jewish community in Iraq made no distinction between Zionist and Jewish identities, vilifying both in terms of an imported anti-semitism that also exploited local sectarian prejudices. This was a potent mixture, the violent results of which were seen in the *Farhud* of 1941. For many Jewish Iraqis it was an ominous indication not only of their vulnerability in Iraq, but also of the apparent indifference of the authorities, both Iraqi and British, to their fate.

Eventually, Iraqi reaction to the defeats in Palestine brought down the government of al-Pachachi in January 1949. The defeat and encirclement of the Egyptian army in southern Palestine in November 1948 led the Egyptian government to shift the blame onto the alleged inaction of the Iraqi forces. This theme was taken up by a growing number of demonstrators – as well as by al-Pachachi's political opponents. Faced by a developing crisis on the streets of Baghdad, the regent called on Nuri al-Sa'id once again to form a government. By now cast in the role of authoritarian 'strong man' of Iraqi politics, Nuri turned his attention to the problems of disorder with his characteristic ruthlessness and despatch.

Courts martial were used to try those accused of instigating public disorder, consigning hundreds to prison. The campaign against the ICP and its perceived sympathisers was stepped up. Most notoriously this involved not simply the arrest of large numbers of communists, but also

8 Nuri al-Sa'id (prime minister of Iraq) at a meeting of the Baghdad pact, 1956

the execution of Comrade Fahd and two of his colleagues. They had been in prison since their arrest late in 1946 and had been tried and sentenced to death in June 1947, but this had been commuted to a term of imprisonment. In February 1949, however, they were brought before a court martial, charged with organising subversive activity from within prison, sentenced to death and publicly executed within the space of a few days.

Having dealt this series of blows to the domestic opposition, Nuri turned his attention to the question of Palestine. He initiated a parliamentary inquiry into the conduct of the war and the diplomacy which had preceded it. Whilst not wholly exonerating all the Iraqis involved, the commission's report tended to portray successive Iraqi politicians as making the best of a bad job, laying the blame for the disaster largely at the feet of the other Arab states and of the Palestinian leadership.[9] At the same time, Nuri added to the Iraqi Jewish community's sense of insecurity by threatening to expel the entire community if the Palestinian refugees were not allowed to return to their homes. This was later turned into an offer of population exchange – the Jews of Iraq would be exchanged for an equivalent number of Arab refugees from Palestine – with the threat that the Jews' property in Iraq would be used to compensate the Palestinians for what they had lost in Palestine.

It was at this juncture that the Iraqi security services uncovered a Zionist network in Iraq which was helping Iraqi Jews emigrate to Israel. This led in turn to extensive arrests in the Jewish community and to increased suspicion, effectively barring young Jewish Iraqis from employment by the state or in the professions. For many in the Iraqi Jewish community it appeared that there was indeed no future in Iraq itself since neither their community leaders nor any international body was willing or able to defend their rights as Iraqi citizens. Encouraged both by successive Iraqi governments and by the Israeli authorities, the vast majority of the community of over 100,000 took advantage of a 1950 law allowing them to renounce their Iraqi citizenship and to leave Iraq forever. By 1952 the community had virtually ceased to exist, much of its property had been expropriated by the Iraqi government and only a few thousand Jews remained in Iraq.[10]

Whilst taking these initiatives, Nuri al-Saʿid also put forward his solution to the Palestine question. This would have deprived Israel of many of the territorial gains it had made in the war, but nevertheless would have acknowledged the partition of Palestine as a fact and would thereby have implied recognition of Israel. Whether seriously meant or not, the proposal was unsurprisingly rejected by all parties to the conflict and by the great powers. This gave Nuri the pretext he needed. He ordered the immediate withdrawal of all Iraqi forces from their positions on the front line, abruptly disengaging Iraq from a conflict which had brought its governments so little credit, but which had excited dangerous political passions in Baghdad.

The Palestine debacle was meanwhile having its effect on Syria where the coup d'état by Husni Zaʿim in March 1949 began a period of coups and counter-coups. Fuelled by certain factions in Syria, ideas of union with Iraq began to emerge. Nuri was markedly unenthusiastic about such projects, in part because he feared that any agreement would be prey to the vicissitudes of Syrian politics. Consequently, Nuri discouraged Zaʿim's early talk of union between the two countries. This helped to drive Zaʿim into the opposing camp of Egypt and Saudi Arabia – both of which were determined to check Hashemite influence. However, in Iraq, the regent seized on the idea of Syrian–Iraqi union, seeing in it a vehicle for his own ambitions. Consequently, when Zaʿim was overthrown in August 1949 by Colonel Hinnawi, backed by the Iraq-oriented People's Party, the regent believed union could be achieved. He resented Nuri's lack of enthusiasm, leading to a certain amount of friction, and, when compounded by disputes within his cabinet, this led to Nuri's offer of resignation in November. ʿAli Jawdat formed a government in early December 1949, but, ironically, a coup d'état in Damascus a few days later brought 'Adib al-Shishakli to power intent on forestalling any possibility of union with Iraq.

The issue of Syrian–Iraqi union seemed to be dead. However, as 'Ali Jawdat discovered, it was not forgotten. When his minister of foreign affairs, Muzahim al-Pachachi, tried to repair Iraqi–Egyptian relations by coming to an agreement with the Egyptian government which effectively promised that Iraq would not seek union with Syria for at least five years, he outraged many in Iraq. Whatever they felt about the question of union with Syria, they saw the move as an abject submission of Iraqi foreign policy to the will of Egypt. The regent shared these views and in February 1950 Jawdat resigned, having realised that he had lost the regent's confidence. The regent then asked Tawfiq al-Suwaidi to form a government, but in many respects this signalled the return of Nuri al-Sa'id. He did not himself hold a cabinet post, but played an influential role from his chosen position in the wings, helped by the power which he now openly wielded in parliament.

ECONOMIC DEVELOPMENT AND PARTY POLITICS

During his premiership in 1949 Nuri had published the 'National Pact', a manifesto in which he spoke of the desirability of setting up a one-party state in Iraq. The single party would constitute the only legitimate political organisation in the country and all politicians would be obliged to participate. On the basis of the solidarity allegedly created by this unified position, the party would devote itself to the 'real' tasks of politics, understood by Nuri as the promotion of economic development and the countering of subversion. A belief in the virtues of a single party dedicated to the task of national guidance and progress and aimed at overcoming factionalism was familiar from Ataturk's Turkey and would become even more familiar throughout much of the Middle East in the years to come. In 1949, however, it was met in Iraq with little enthusiasm. Most people saw it as a transparent expression of Nuri's desire to subject the political world to his own overall control.

Nevertheless, Nuri pursued the idea of forming a political party and in November 1949, prior to relinquishing the premiership, he had established Hizb al-Ittihad al-Dusturi (the Constitutional Union Party (CUP)). This organisation incorporated not simply the clients and following of Nuri al-Sa'id himself, but also those of Salih Jabr whom he persuaded to join the party, as well as most of the tribal shaikhs in the Parliamentary Bloc who had hitherto been attached to the regent. Thus Nuri managed to cement his support in parliament and extended his already wide network of patronage into areas previously dominated by his political allies. Consequently, when Tawfiq al-Suwaidi was appointed prime minister in February 1950, Nuri was in a good position to offer him his support and that of his party in parliament – as well as to replace him should the occasion arise.

This came sooner than even Nuri had anticipated. The cause was chiefly cabinet disunity. Personality clashes played a part in this, but it also owed something to mistrust of Salih Jabr's communal affiliations now that he was minister of the interior once more. As in previous years, he was suspected of being indifferent to corruption charges levelled at members of the Shi'i community, just as he was accused of showing favouritism in appointments and promotions. Regardless of the truth of these accusations, it was noticeable that they regularly surfaced whenever a Shi'i held a senior ministerial post and were much less prominently or consistently raised when Sunni Arabs held the same posts. This apparent sectarian solidarity among the Sunni Arab political elite, even those who claimed to be close colleagues of Salih Jabr, was increasingly irksome and led him to found his own political organisation, eventually breaking with Nuri and the CUP.

By September 1950, Salih Jabr's problems and other cabinet disputes led al-Suwaidi to resign. The regent was in London and Nuri seized the moment to ask for authority to form a government himself, believing that indecision at the top encouraged open dissent to take the form witnessed in 1948. The regent, obliged to acknowledge that Nuri had successfully managed to take over many of his own networks in Iraq, entrusted Nuri with the formation of a new government. Nuri al-Sa'id could now begin to implement his vision for Iraq. He did not try to bring in the single-party system that he had once advocated, but in many ways his domination of Iraqi politics made this unnecessary. It was against this background that he pressed ahead with his ideas for the economic development of the country. Bypassing or avoiding the contentious questions of land reform and the restructuring of the rural economy amongst whose notables and shaikhs lay much of his support, Nuri looked to Iraq's growing oil revenues to supply the motor for development.

In 1950 he persuaded IPC to increase the royalties paid to the Iraqi government, but this was criticised by many for not going far enough. In 1951 the Aramco agreement with Saudi Arabia which introduced the '50–50' profit-sharing formula, as well as the oil nationalisation in Iran, prompted Nuri al-Sa'id to reopen negotiations with IPC. These talks resulted in the 1952 agreement whereby IPC and the Iraqi government agreed to share profits on a '50–50' basis. In addition, IPC guaranteed a minimum revenue for the Iraqi government, agreed that Iraq could receive up to 12.5 per cent of net production as part of its share, to sell on the world market, and agreed to the appointment of Iraqi directors to the board when the question of oil prices came up for discussion. This agreement was the framework for a dramatic development of the oil industry and for a fourfold increase in Iraqi oil production between 1951 and 1958 (with a sixfold increase in government revenues), due in large part to the growing world demand for oil.[11]

From the outset, Nuri al-Saʿid determined that 70 per cent of the oil income was to be set aside for infrastructure development, to be administered by a Development Board, established originally under the premiership of Tawfiq al-Suwaidi in compliance with the conditions for a substantial World Bank loan. The board was intended to disburse funds and to oversee development projects in an atmosphere relatively free of partisan and personalised politics. Consequently, three of its six members were technical experts, one of whom was British and one American. Inevitably, this foreign presence as well as the IPC agreement were roundly attacked by Nuri's critics. They called instead for the nationalisation of all Iraq's oil resources, partly inspired by events in Iran. Nevertheless, given Nuri's hold on the state apparatus, there was little they could do to make their voice heard. When they tried to organise a day of national protest in November 1951, there was little to show for it, given the overwhelming police presence and the preventative measures taken by the minister of the interior. This was impressive testimony to the power of Nuri's regime since both Nuri and the regent were out of the country at the time – usually a signal that the government would lack the firmness to respond to organised public protest.

By this stage, Salih Jabr had broken with Nuri and had formed his own party, Hizb al-Umma al-Ishtiraki (the Socialist People's Party), and Taha al-Hashimi had emerged as leader of the United Popular Front, which constituted a gathering of the enemies and rivals of Nuri al-Saʿid among the political elite. Jabr, however, sought to appeal to the younger intelligentsia and professional urban classes, especially among the Shiʿa, although this was not an explicit intention of his party. He combined this element with the following he had always enjoyed among the more traditional Shiʿi rural notables of the middle and lower Euphrates who had their own reasons to be unhappy with the status quo. In large measure, this discontent was not caused by collective or communal grievances, but by their sense of exclusion from the rewards and privileges that were being distributed to Nuri's followers in the CUP, many of whom were their local rivals.

The formation of these new parties, together with Nuri's hold on parliament and the suggestion that he was going to alter the Electoral Law but retain the two-stage electoral process (thought to give the government an inbuilt advantage in rigging the elections), began to dominate political life in Baghdad. Repeating his tactic of directing events from the wings, Nuri resigned the premiership in July 1952. A government to oversee the elections was formed by Mustafa al-ʿUmari, with Nuri's approval. Meanwhile his former colleague Jabr became more closely identified with the rest of the opposition which was focusing not only on the iniquities of Nuri al-Saʿid, but also on the issue of electoral reform, calling for direct elections to parliament. This call became more strident as the election date approached. Some believed that cutting out the layer of secondary electors would make it harder for the government to intervene. As events were to prove, this was a naive hope. For the elections to allow anything like a fair representation of political opinion a number of other – very rarely achieved – conditions needed to exist as well. Nevertheless, electoral reform became a slogan around which much of the opposition could rally and, in doing so, could attract others who had more fundamental objections to the status quo.

In particular, the ICP became involved once again in organising workers and in setting up a front organisation – the Peace Partisans. This association appeared in 1950, ostensibly in response to the growing tensions of the Cold War, and became a focus for all those in Iraq who wanted the country to adopt a neutral position, in opposition to Nuri al-Saʿid in particular, with his open and vociferous support for the Western powers in the developing global struggle. However, 'neutralism' in Iraq did not primarily imply taking a stance in the Cold War – a remote subject for most Iraqis. Rather, it meant calling for an immediate end to the alliance with Great Britain, thereby tapping into a much richer vein of political sentiment in the country. This allowed the Peace Partisans not only to gather widespread support, but also to form links with other political parties, despite concerns about the organisation's communist inspiration.

By the autumn of 1952 these forces were coming together, encouraged by the government's decision to postpone the elections. The impression was that al-ʿUmari feared the strength of the opposition on the streets, despite enjoying the support of Nuri and the regent. In fact, once the regent returned to Iraq in October, it was clear that his faith in al-ʿUmari was being undermined and he began to plan for a successor. When the prime minister heard of these plans he realised that he himself was caught between three forces over which he had no control: the regent, Nuri al-Saʿid and the opposition. The latter had formed a 'Contact Committee', setting up an improbable – and temporary – alliance between the Peace Partisans, the

NDP, Taha al-Hashimi's United Popular Front and the Istiqlal Party, tacitly supported by Salih Jabr's Socialist People's Party. Faced by this combination of circumstances, al-ʿUmari resigned in late November. He did so on the very day that opposition demonstrations erupted in the streets of Baghdad, convincing the 'Contact Committee' that it was their action alone which had precipitated his downfall.

As with *al-Wathba* of 1948, it was an intoxicating moment and gave heart to all those who were frustrated with the status quo. Demonstrations continued in the streets of Baghdad and spread to other towns, voicing grievances similar to those of 1948 since many of the fundamental discontents remained the same. Although the scale of the demonstrations did not match those of 1948, the army came to the assistance of the police, leading to scores of deaths among the demonstrators. The episode has been remembered as *al-Intifada* (the upheaval), suggesting once again that 'the people' of Iraq had risen up to express their displeasure at their rulers. It has also become part of the revolutionary myth elaborated after the overthrow of the monarchy in 1958, which suggested that this was a necessary step in the revolutionary development of Iraqi society – and in establishing the revolutionary credentials of those who claimed to have led the movement.

Ostensibly, the regent's appointment of the chief of staff of the Iraqi army, General Nur al-Din Mahmud, as prime minister was a desperate attempt to head off a revolutionary situation. Martial law was declared in the province of Baghdad and electoral reform was promised. However, this development may not have been as desperate a measure as has been claimed by those who depict *al-Intifada* as heralding a revolution. On the contrary, the regent's choice seems to have been dictated only in part by the need for an authoritarian figure to restore order in the capital. His other main concern was to avoid becoming beholden to Nuri al-Saʿid once again. This had been the thrust of his policies since his return to Iraq in the autumn, contributing to the crisis which had presented the opposition forces with such an encouraging opportunity. In the chief of staff he found someone who could restore order, but who had no political following and could be expected to oversee the elections with no ulterior motives. The regent hoped that this would allow the Palace to play a decisive role in determining the composition of the chamber once again.[12]

NURI AL-SAʿID: THE POLITICS OF REFORM AND REPRESSION

Ironically, however, it was Nuri al-Saʿid's party which emerged the indisputable winner in the general elections held under the new system of direct elections, placing Nuri in a strong position to influence the government formed by Jamil al-Midfaʿi in January 1953. As minister of defence in the new government, Nuri ensured that the armed forces returned to their previous state of unconditional obedience. He succeeded among the most senior officers, but the reaction amongst a number of the junior and middling officers was quite different. It was here, not on the streets of Baghdad or among the general public, that the seeds of the downfall of the monarchy were sown. These younger officers reflected much of the social and political discontent of the larger political world and still smarted from the humiliation of defeat in Palestine. It was not surprising, therefore, that the Free Officers' coup d'état in Egypt in July 1952 had led some of them to think about organising a similar group in Iraq.

In particular, Rifʿat al-Hajj Sirri had begun to sound out acquaintances about their willingness to join such an organisation. These men took heart from the appointment of the chief of staff to the premiership, since it suggested that the army was the only force standing between the regime and the forces of opposition. A number of the younger officers sympathised with the goals of the various opposition parties and consequently redoubled their efforts to recruit others in the officer corps, preparing for the day when the government's reliance on the armed forces would expose its vulnerability to decisive action by a small group of officers. For the time being, however, the nucleus of the group that was to become the Iraqi Free Officers was small, and it did indeed seem to many that Nuri had preempted the threat of a return to military intervention in politics.

Public opposition activity continued, on a restricted scale, mobilising in particular against martial law in the Baghdad area and the censorship and control that came with it, but it was unable to shake the hold of a government that included Nuri al-Saʿid, ʿAli Jawdat and Tawfiq al-Suwaidi and which continued to enjoy the confidence of the regent. The latter remained as influential as ever, pursuing intermittently his initiatives in foreign and domestic politics, despite the fact that King Faisal II came of age and assumed his full constitutional powers as head of state in May 1953. ʿAbd al-Ilah thereupon lost his formal powers as regent and was accorded the rank of crown prince. This had little effect, however, either on his determination to play a key role in politics or on his ability to do so through the networks of protégés and associates which he had established over the years. The king himself was young and had been brought up under the aegis of ʿAbd al-Ilah. He therefore had little political vision and had not had the time or opportunity to develop a political personality of his own. His circle of acquaintances was the same as that of the crown prince and

9 Prince ʿAbd al-Ilah (regent of Iraq 1939–53; crown prince 1953–8) and
King Faisal II (King of Iraq 1939–58), 1953

consequently, when Jamil al-Midfaʿi offered his resignation in August
(partly through disillusionment but also for health reasons), the king consulted the crown prince and Nuri before asking Fadhil al-Jamali to form a
government.

Al-Jamali had been associated with a number of the reformist ideas circulating in Iraq during the previous decade. However, he had kept aloof
from the political parties, choosing instead to chart an individual course in
which he was the centre of a grouping of younger officials and academics
thinking about the future of the Iraqi state outside the radical or revolutionary opposition. The bruising experience of having been minister of
foreign affairs under Salih Jabr in the government which negotiated the
Portsmouth Treaty in 1947 turned his attention back to his earlier interests
in domestic reform, with a view to strengthening the efficiency and authority of the state. It was noticeable, therefore, that when he formed his government it was made up of younger men, many of them with known
reformist ideas in relation to land law, the organisation of government and
the provision of social services. It was also noticeable that half of the cabinet
(including the prime minister himself) were Shiʿi, representing the highest
number and proportion of Shiʿa yet included in an Iraqi government.

For those Shiʿa who resented Sunni Arab dominance and favouritism, this was an important symbolic advance. It did not answer their grievances, but it did create a more hopeful atmosphere in which the promise of reform and the promise of better communal representation appeared to go hand in hand. This may explain why Nuri al-Saʿid chose to support al-Jamali's apparently reformist government. Nuri was concerned about the rising tide of grievances among the urban-educated Shiʿa, which Salih Jabr was cultivating in opposition to Nuri's interest. He was also keen to see in office a dynamic government, respectful of his own influence and committed, like him, both to the task of economic development, technocratically conceived, and to the suppression and defeat of revolutionary alternatives, such as the ICP. These qualities appear to have recommended al-Jamali to him, despite the fact that many of al-Jamali's reformist ideas were scarcely sympathetic to much of Nuri's landed, tribal following.

It was also significant that al-Jamali appointed a Kurd, Saʿid Qazzaz, to the sensitive post of minister of the interior, with control over public security. By all accounts, he was a determined and ruthless practitioner in this field. However, as minister, he also had wide powers of patronage and a say in the government's distribution of the growing resources at its disposal. This could be seen as a public signal that Kurdish interests would be accommodated – increasingly necessary as the Kurdish nationalist movement gained definition. With the election of Ibrahim Ahmad as secretary-general of the KDP in 1951, the party had moved in a more radical direction. Its president remained the tribal figure of Mulla Mustafa Barzani, but he had lived in exile in Moscow since the fall of the Mahabad Republic. He was therefore in no position to prevent the KDP from adopting a programme of land reform and workers' and peasants' rights. The KDP also called for the nationalisation of Iraq's oil resources and for the channelling of substantial oil revenues to specifically Kurdish development projects. For al-Jamali it was important to use government patronage not simply to placate the traditional chieftains of Kurdistan, but also to ensure that the KDP with its more radical ideas should not be able to capitalise on the powerful mixture of national and socio-economic grievances in the Kurdish region.

The new government lifted martial law, ended press censorship and allowed party activity to revive in September 1953. At the same time, it maintained pressure on the ICP, encouraged also by factionalism within the ICP itself. Nor was the government any more lenient towards organised labour than its predecessors had been, going so far as to declare martial law in Basra province when oil workers went on strike for better pay and conditions. However, al-Jamali was brought down neither by opposition on the streets nor among the vociferous opposition parties, but by conservative resistance to the relatively modest reform schemes which he tried to introduce. When these touched on questions of land ownership, land settlement or taxation they alarmed the dominant landed interest in parliament. Yet such measures were central to his government's programme, unveiled in December 1953. The opposition of the landed interest then became apparent and it was only through Nuri's influence that the CUP, in which these interests were heavily represented, grudgingly gave its support to al-Jamali. This did not, however, remove the unease which many of its members felt at the government's modest land distribution schemes.

The landowners' fears were compounded by unease in other quarters when the government revealed its plans for civil service reform. These reforms were intended to create a more efficient state, but also one which would be more responsive to the communities which that state claimed to represent. It was a direct threat, therefore, to the groups which had installed themselves in the heart of the state machinery and which used patronage and favouritism to advance their own interests at the expense of other Iraqis. The nature of the power structure in Iraq and its colonisation of the state machinery was such that any reform was potentially dangerous. The administration was chiefly regarded by the politically prominent as a place to build up the networks of clients which gave substance to individuals in political life and caused them to be taken seriously as political actors. It was, therefore, a preserve criss-crossed by special interests, emanating from powerful individuals both within the cabinet and outside it. Any attempt at reform threatened a broad spectrum of these interests. In the case of al-Jamali's cabinet (as in previous instances when Shi'a had been in a position to affect selection and promotion procedures in the civil service) there was the added complication of suspected communal or sectarian favouritism at the expense of the well-established privileges of the Sunnis.

By the spring of 1954 the landed proprietors, both Shi'i and Sunni, had joined forces in parliament and elsewhere to force the government to water down its land reform proposals. At the same time, a campaign of attrition, often less visible, but no less effective, was initiated within the state administration to ensure that al-Jamali's plans for civil service reform were blocked. This was set against a background of allegations of Shi'i favouritism and sectarian prejudice. In the short term, this meant that al-Jamali became ever more dependent on the power and influence of Nuri al-Sa'id. The latter, however, was becoming distracted by the crown prince's eagerness to intervene once again in Syrian affairs, following the fall of al-Shishakli's regime. As a result, Nuri found it difficult to expend much of his political capital shoring up al-Jamali when Nuri's own following within the CUP was so suspicious of the government and when even al-Jamali's colleagues, frustrated at their inability to push through any meaningful reforms, were deserting him. Consequently, when al-Jamali finally offered his resignation in April 1954, Nuri did nothing to dissuade him. Nor did he agree to form an administration himself, but departed instead for Europe, leaving the Palace to sort out the problems to which the crown prince had in some measure contributed.

The king and the crown prince, apprehensive of a backlash against the fall of al-Jamali and the consequences of disappointed hopes for reform, turned to Arshad al-'Umari to form a government and to hold elections. Fearing a repeat of the repression of al-'Umari's 1946 administration, the NDP and the Istiqlal Party unsuccessfully petitioned the Palace and then opened discussions with the ICP, at that time veering towards social democracy. This led to the formation of the National Front in May 1954, composed of the three organisations (the Peace Partisans standing in for the still illegal ICP), in time to contest the general elections the following month. Confounding expectations, these proved to be the freest elections yet held in Iraq, at least in the urban areas. Nuri's CUP still took the largest single block of seats and there was the usual large number of independents, heavily weighted in favour of the rural conservative interest. Nevertheless, the National Front succeeded in winning fourteen seats, giving a significant voice for the first time in parliament to the parties it represented. Believing that the opposition forces would now be harder to contain, al-'Umari resigned the premiership in June.

This move encouraged the National Front and enhanced its members' sense of their own power, as well as their fear of the Palace's reaction. Consequently, they mobilised to put public pressure on the Palace to appoint an acceptable prime minister. Demonstrations and marches were organised in Baghdad, intending to give the impression of the unstoppable force of those asking for change. The effect, however, was quite the reverse. Fearing the consequences of mounting civil disorder, the crown prince flew to Europe to plead with Nuri to return and form a new government. This placed Nuri in a commanding position from which he could dictate his terms, signalling 'Abd al-Ilah's final acknowledgement that Nuri was the 'strong man' the Palace now needed to steer the regime safely through the years ahead, despite the crown prince's misgivings about Nuri.

In August 1954 Nuri formed a government and his terms soon became clear. Parliament was dissolved and Nuri simultaneously disbanded his own party, the CUP, declaring that all other parties should do likewise. Nuri had returned to his familiar argument that parties were unnecessarily fractious and that all should work within the same organisation for the 'good of the country', as defined, of course, by Nuri al-Sa'id himself. Stricter measures were introduced against the ICP and against the communists' front organisations, sympathisers and fellow-travellers, and tighter controls were imposed on all other parties and their newspapers. Parties that protested vigorously, such as the NDP, found themselves and their newspapers closed down.[13]

The campaign of repression, conducted in the name of the fight against communism, was deployed against Nuri's political opponents and indeed against any writers, journalists and academics whom he regarded as critical of the status quo. Some were dismissed from their posts, others arrested and others fled into exile. This set the scene for elections, which produced a parliament in which 116 of the 135 deputies were returned unopposed, allowing the government to revoke the licences of all political parties and to bring all associations under tighter control. At the same time, restrictive legislation was introduced governing such matters as students' and teachers' conduct, the freedom of the press and the right to hold public meetings and organise demonstrations.

Nuri al-Sa'id now felt able to pursue two of his major policy initiatives. The first concerned economic development and was aimed at carrying through the kinds of measures, based on the growing oil revenues of the Iraqi state, that he believed would strengthen both the state and the regime which was shaping the state in its own image and for its own purposes. Since the agreement of 1952, oil had become the leading sector of the Iraqi economy. Production rates had increased and royalties had risen. Thus, in 1951 oil revenues provided about 30 per cent of the Iraqi government's income, but by 1954 this had risen to 65 per cent (by comparison, agriculture accounted for a mere 3 per cent of government income by 1954). However, the oil industry's contribution to the national economy was lopsided. The oil industry purchased almost all its capital equipment outside Iraq itself and employed a relatively small labour force. More than anything else, the rise in oil income placed massive economic power in the hands of those who controlled the state and it was to be the vision of men such as Nuri al-Sa'id which largely determined how that power was to be used and who the beneficiaries were to be.

Since 1952 the Development Board had largely lost its independence and its recommendations needed to be approved by the minister of development. Reinforcing a trend already apparent for some years, it elaborated plans and disbursed funds that substantially favoured the landed interest through massive irrigation and land reclamation schemes. This was undoubtedly important in the long run and to some extent, therefore, it was the result of ideas then current about the development of Iraq as an agricultural country. However, the immediate beneficiaries tended to be confined to those who could lay claim to the newly irrigated lands. Furthermore, these policies tended to encourage the abandonment of lands which had become too saline through previous unrestrained irrigation. Quite apart from the special interests working upon the imaginations and policies of successive Iraqi governments, the board was encountering the increasingly familiar problems involved in trying to use oil revenues to promote development, generally conceived.

In order to address this, the Development Board engaged the economist Lord Salter to investigate the prospects for development in Iraq. His report, which appeared in 1955, criticised the concentration on infrastructure development to the exclusion of all else, as well as the resulting opening up of further acreages of new lands for cultivation. Instead, he recommended that the board make every effort to increase the productivity of lands already under cultivation, through proper investment in drainage. Furthermore, using a rationale that was political as much as economic, he advised the board to spend much greater resources on housing, health, clean water systems and education in order to bring more immediate benefits to wider sections of the population. Many of his recommendations were acted upon, in the sense that substantial funds were allocated to the kinds of projects he had outlined, but the actual expenditure during the following three years proved to be less than planned. It remained the landed interest that gained the greatest benefits. Oil revenues thus provided the basis for a growing provision by the state, but crucially on terms dictated by those who controlled the state itself. This was a recipe for a thoroughgoing patrimonialism in which the underlying social and economic inequality would remain unchallenged.[14]

NURI AL-SAʿID: FOREIGN INITIATIVES AND DOMESTIC CHALLENGES

The other major preoccupation of Nuri during these years lay in Iraqi foreign policy. He continued to believe that Iraq's alignment with the Western powers and its cultivation of close relations with Turkey and Iran were crucial for the security of the state, as well as of the regime. 'Neutralism' was essentially a code for a break with the Western powers which Nuri believed were the main external guarantors of the monarchy.

At the same time, Nuri was ambivalent towards distinctively Arab issues. Dynastic pan-Arabism of the kind advocated by the crown prince was something which Nuri believed to be of only limited utility. It needed a firm controlling Iraqi hand and would unnecessarily complicate Iraq's relationships with Saudi Arabia, as well as Egypt. Nuri was also no enthusiast for the pan-Arabism advocated by the Arab nationalist trend in Iraqi politics. He could dissimulate when required, but much of his political career had been spent thwarting their political ambitions.

Nuri regarded the dogmatic pursuit of pan-Arab goals as potentially divisive. Although unsympathetic to Kurdish demands for autonomy, he knew that pan-Arabism complicated central control of the Kurdish region. Equally, he was aware that many Shiʿa regarded Arab nationalism and Arab unity schemes as attempts by the dominant Arab Sunni minority in Iraq to tie itself to a greater Arab Sunni hinterland which it had lost with the collapse of the Ottoman Empire. Nuri came from these same Sunni Arab circles and was familiar with their prejudices and insecurities in relation to the other communities inhabiting Iraq. He himself shared a number of their preoccupations and he was by no means an ideologically convinced Iraqi nationalist. However, Nuri could see the peculiarly debilitating effect of pan-Arabism on Iraqi political society: it not only tied Iraq's fate to the unstable condition of other Arab polities and threatened to give other Arab leaders a disproportionate say in Iraqi affairs, but it also alienated much of the population, underlining the differences between them and the Sunni Arabs who dominated the state.

By contrast, Nuri was a functional Iraqi nationalist. He believed that Iraq should not ignore Arab issues, but should also look to its non-Arab neighbours and, if necessary, beyond them for the regional order that would secure the boundaries and the very fabric of the state. It was with the idea of reinforcing such ties that Nuri visited Turkey in the autumn of 1954, soon after assuming the premiership. He had become interested in the Turkish–Pakistani agreement of April 1954, seeing it as the possible basis for a larger network of regional alliances which would help to contain the southward expansion of Soviet influence. The example of Soviet involvement in neighbouring Iran in the 1940s, and Nuri's suspicions of the role played in Iraq by the USSR through the ICP, led Iraq to suspend diplomatic relations with the USSR in early 1955.

At the same time, he began conversations with Turkey's prime minister Adnan Menderes and in January 1955 these resulted in the joint declaration that Iraq and Turkey agreed to co-operate in repelling aggression in the region. The formal agreement encapsulating these principles and their detailed implementation was signed in February 1955. The Baghdad Pact, as it came to be known, was also joined by Great Britain which handed over to Iraqi control the two air bases of Habbaniyya and Shuʿaiba in return for air passage and refuelling rights. Great Britain also pledged to come to the aid of Iraq if the latter were attacked and would continue to train and equip the Iraqi armed forces. In this it would be assisted by the United States which had already begun to supply Iraq with military equipment, though it did not become a member of the pact, but fully co-operated with it. (Iran and Pakistan joined the pact later in 1955.) The pact thus served a further purpose for Nuri al-Saʿid: it ended the Anglo-Iraqi Treaty of 1930 without committing Iraq to enter into another bilateral agreement. Nuri thereby hoped to retain the advantages of the alliance with Great Britain (and indeed with the Western powers more generally) whilst at the same time avoiding the uproar which had followed the signing of the Portsmouth Treaty in 1948.

From the beginning of the talks between Iraq and Turkey the Egyptian media had vehemently denounced any pact with the Turkish government. Playing on historical enmity and current suspicions of Turkey and the Western powers in Iraq, Gamal ʿAbd al-Nasser ensured that Egypt maintained an unrelenting campaign of propaganda against Nuri and his government for having entered into the pact. Nuri's riposte was that the terms of the Baghdad Pact were not very different from the terms of the 1954 Anglo-Egyptian agreement and therefore were no more damaging to the idea of Arab collective security than that agreement had been. This touched a raw nerve in the Egyptian regime and, indeed, Nasser had come under attack in his own country for precisely that reason. Nevertheless, the Egyptian tirades found a ready audience in Iraq in the pan-Arab and leftist opposition which denounced Nuri for having undermined 'Arab security' and for continuing Iraq's enslavement to the Western powers.

It was noticeable, however, that the pact failed to provoke the kind of protest demonstrations which had marked the signing of the Portsmouth Treaty. In part, this was due to the effective preventive measures which Nuri's security apparatus had employed precisely to pre-empt any large-scale eruption of public protest. In part, also, it was due to the particular weaknesses of the ICP and the fragmentation of the opposition coalition, as well as to their divergent views about the merits of the pact. The relatively muted public response may also have owed something to the fact that it evoked strong feelings of antipathy amongst only a relatively small section of the Iraqi population and in 1955 (unlike 1948 and 1952) it was harder to mobilise the urban public around the same array of issues which had made the other situations so critical.[15]

However, Nasser's attack on the pact did have an impact on the officer corps. Many resented the lingering ties with Great Britain, regardless of the improved level of military equipment that began to flow into Iraq from both British and American sources. The rapid rearmament and re-equipping of the Iraqi army was a topic of constant concern for Nuri and the government. They believed that much of the unpopularity of the pact would be outweighed in one very important area at least by the influx of substantial quantities of modern weapons into the Iraqi armed forces. According to their calculations, this was a key to cementing the loyalty of the officer corps to the regime. The arms shipments would focus the officers' attention on a professional task, professionally conceived, and would be a visible proof of the relative advantage of alignment with the Western powers.

This did little, of course, to satisfy that small minority of officers who had larger reasons for conspiring against the regime. In the summer of 1956 one such conspiracy was uncovered, although it was inconclusively investigated, leading merely to the reassignment of the suspect officers. For Nuri, the beginning of the Suez Crisis seemed to provide an opportunity to isolate Egypt in the Arab world, but the unfolding sequence of events, culminating in the Anglo-French attack on Egypt in collusion with Israel, profoundly shocked him. He rightly saw it as providing strength and encouragement to those groups in Iraq which had long indicted him for his close association with Great Britain. Consequently, Nuri made an official protest to Great Britain and declared martial law. He also broke relations with France and excluded Great Britain from meetings of the Baghdad Pact, whilst recommending that the king attend the emergency Arab summit in Beirut in a show of pan-Arab solidarity.

This had some effect on the level of protest in Iraq, but whatever measures Nuri took, they could not eradicate his long association with British power. For the opposition forces, restive under Nuri's severe repression since 1954, this was an opportunity to organise by the only means open to them, on the streets of Iraq's major cities. Consequently, demonstrations erupted not only in Baghdad, but also in Mosul and Najaf. In Baghdad itself Nuri used the security forces to ensure that disorder was kept to a minimum, recognising that the political impact of demonstrations in the capital far outweighed events in the provinces. He then went on the offensive, reviving the old charge linking communism with Zionism – given their ties with the USSR and the Soviet position on Palestine, this had always been a weak point of the Arab communist parties. However, in the aftermath of the Suez Crisis, Nuri was particularly concerned about the apparent success of the ICP in shaking off this stigma and in establishing relationships with other sections of the opposition on the basis of an anti-imperialist and pan-Arab alliance.

Some of Nuri's countermeasures may account for the comparatively low level and short duration of the demonstrations. But evidence also suggests that the issues at stake did not engage the range of people who had been involved in previous protests. A section of the political world cared passionately about Arab issues and about Iraq's alignment in global politics, but this was not the foremost concern of most of the country's inhabitants. Thus in Baghdad most of the demonstrations were by teachers, students and schoolchildren – groups which were always readier to protest at issues of general concern and symbolic significance. For this reason, Nuri closed the schools, and when he did so the demonstrations more or less ceased.

In the largely Shi'i towns of Najaf and Hayy, however, the demonstrations took on a more general anti-regime character, providing an opportunity for protest not only against Nuri and his government, but also against the kind of state that produced such a government and the injustices associated with it. These demonstrations met with a more violent response from the security forces. For Nuri's opponents the events of the autumn demonstrated that as long as the triangle of Nuri–Palace–army remained intact, there was little that could be done to shake his hold on power. In response, the opposition parties formed the United National Front of February 1957, grouping together the Istiqlal Party, the NDP, the ICP (now under the conciliatory leadership of Husain al-Radi) and the nascent Ba'th (Renaissance) Party.

The Ba'th Party had originated in Syria in the 1940s, but a branch had been established in Iraq and from 1951 it had been led by Fu'ad al-Rikabi, a young Shi'i engineer from Nasiriyya. Arab nationalist and secular, but not atheistic and vaguely socialist in orientation, the party was critical of the more glaring inequalities of landownership in the Arab world. As such, its message was attractive for students and for others growing restive at the domination of an older, more conservative and more exclusive elite of Arab nationalists. In Iraq, it was significant that it seemed to appeal particularly to a younger generation of Shi'a, critical both of the Shi'i clerical and of the landowning hierarchies, as well as of the Sunni Arab nationalist elite. In common with the Ba'th Party, none of the parties in the Front had large popular followings, but their supporters were concentrated in certain professions, in urban areas, among students and among workers in some key industries. The Front's programme, although critical of Nuri al-Saʿid, was not particularly radical, reiterating the call for democracy and constitutional freedoms, the abolition of martial law, the withdrawal of Iraq from the Baghdad Pact and the pursuit of 'positive neutralism'.[16]

THE COUP D'ÉTAT OF 1958

All of the parties in the United National Front had long cultivated links with the armed forces, having sympathisers or members in the officer corps, as well as in non-commissioned ranks. Some, such as the ICP, had formed distinct organisations for their military members. However, the activities of these officers were uncoordinated and it was clear that other officers were themselves organising, independent of the political parties. The group calling itself the Free Officers had by 1956 come to the attention of the authorities. Some were transferred, but nothing could be proven and their activities continued. It was in these circles that the impact of the Suez Crisis was most significant, leading a large number of officers to adhere to the organisation.

This led, in turn, to a more systematic organisation of the officers themselves: a Supreme Committee was formed, composed of eleven officers from the rank of brigadier to that of major (the majority were colonels). Sub-committees were then formed to study the possibility of carrying out a coup d'état. As might have been expected from any grouping of army officers at the time, the Free Officers were overwhelmingly Arab and Sunni and most of the members of the Supreme Committee were men in their forties who had graduated from the Iraqi Military Academy in the late 1930s. Other than their dislike of the status quo and their resentment of 'imperialism', they had few political principles in common.

The Supreme Committee decided that the most important consideration in planning a coup was to ensure that the commanders of the main military units were either part of their organisation or sympathetic to their aims. This led the committee to approach Brigadier ʿAbd al-Karim Qasim. He had himself formed a loosely organised group of like-minded colleagues and in 1957 he was invited to join the Supreme Committee, becoming its chairman partly because of his seniority. Qasim, 43 years old at the time, in turn introduced the younger, 36-year-old Colonel ʿAbd al-Salam ʿArif, who became the link with the grouping of younger dissident officers, originally recruited by Rifʿat al-Hajj Sirri, the founder of the Free Officers' movement in the 1950s. They attached themselves to the Free Officers' movement at the end of 1957 and remained a key, but distinct, element. Contacts with civilian political parties and organisations were discouraged, but this had little effect. Indeed, when the political parties learned of the existence of the Free Officers, they encouraged their own officer partisans to join. The diversity of these contacts ensured that the Free Officers were neither associated with nor beholden to any one particular faction or party in Iraq. On the other hand, the heterogeneity of the Free Officers made it unlikely that their apparent common purpose would survive in the aftermath of a successful coup d'état.

Nuri al-Saʿid was either unaware of these developments or had heard too faint an echo to take them seriously. Consequently, having successfully managed the crisis over Suez in 1956, he felt confident enough to open up the political system to some degree. Martial law was lifted and there were indications that party activity would be allowed once again, although under a licensing system which would vet the programmes and control the numbers of the parties concerned. With the immediate crisis over, Nuri decided to resign the premiership in June 1957, provoked, as so often, by dissent among his cabinet colleagues, who had focused on the relatively autonomous – and thus resented – status of the Development Board.

The king asked ʿAli Jawdat to form a new government and to oversee elections to inaugurate the new era of more open political activity. In the event, the elections did not take place. ʿAli Jawdat was forced to resign when he fell out with the crown prince by proposing alignment with Egypt. He was replaced as prime minister in December 1957 by ʿAbd al-Wahhab Mirjan, a Shiʿi landowner and protégé of Nuri al-Saʿid, whose influence was to be paramount in the new administration. This was all the more important since developments in the Middle East during the coming months threatened much that Nuri had been trying to achieve.

The formation of the United Arab Republic (UAR) in February 1958, uniting Syria and Egypt, represented a defeat for the pro-Iraqi party in Syrian politics and brought Nasser's influence to the very borders of Iraq. His open hostility to Nuri and to the monarchy made the threat explicit. Nuri's answer was to initiate talks with Jordan, hoping thereby to form a defensive alliance against the UAR and all that it seemed to represent at the time in the Arab world. This resulted in the hasty formation of the Arab Union, composed of Iraq and Jordan, with the possibility of Kuwait's future inclusion left open.

Under these circumstances, it was perhaps inevitable that in March 1958 Mirjan should offer his resignation, opening the way for Nuri's assumption of the premiership. In this, the last of Nuri's cabinets, it was noticeable that he created a more than ordinarily equitable balance between the diverse communities of Iraq. Not only did it contain a good balance of Sunni and Shi'i members, but Nuri was also careful to appoint two Kurdish ministers, aware as he was of Shi'i and Kurdish sensitivity to Arab unity schemes. Parliament was dissolved and elections were held in May, producing a parliament that ratified the act of union between Iraq and Jordan and amended the Iraqi constitution accordingly. Under these amendments, the Iraqi government was responsible for everything except defence and foreign affairs. These would be the responsibility of the government of the Arab Union. Nuri thereupon resigned as prime minister of Iraq and was appointed prime minister of the Arab Union. In his place, Ahmad Mukhtar Baban was asked to form a new Iraqi government, becoming the first Kurd to do so.

Meanwhile, as elections were held, constitutional amendments passed and Nuri and his associates installed as the new government of the Arab Union, a different narrative was unfolding in the armed forces. In early 1958 the Free Officers, despite some underlying political differences, had reached an agreement that Iraq should become a republic and that much of the old elite should be put on trial for treason as collaborators with the imperialists. Furthermore, they agreed that army officers should occupy all the senior posts in the administration and that civilians should in future be strictly subordinate to the officers. The officers' power would be institutionalised in a Revolutionary Command Council (RCC), formed from the membership of the Supreme Committee, and this body would wield supreme executive power in the wake of the overthrow of the monarchy.

The members of the Supreme Committee then proceeded to plan the coup d'état that would carry them to power. The larger and more widespread the organisation became, the greater the chance of discovery. Consequently, the timetable for action was based upon the assumption that the Free Officers would have to act before the end of 1958. The opportunity was in fact provided in the middle of that year by the unfolding of events in the rest of the Middle East. Alarmed by the growing crisis in Lebanon and the enmity of the UAR, Nuri decided to send units of the Iraqi army to the Jordanian border to reinforce Iraq's partner in the Arab Union should the need arise. Originally planned for the first few days of July 1958, the move was postponed until the night of 13–14 July. The Free Officers or, by some accounts, 'Abd al-Karim Qasim and his ally 'Abd al-Salam 'Arif saw their chance.

The units ordered to the western border needed to pass near Baghdad from their stations in the east of the country. Accordingly, when they received the order to move, 'Abd al-Salam 'Arif diverted his forces and those commanded by allied officers into the capital. Executing a classic coup d'état, these troops occupied all the strategic buildings in Baghdad, including the radio station where ʿArif announced the formation of the Iraqi republic. After a brief bombardment, the Royal Guard at the palace surrendered and King Faisal II, Crown Prince ʿAbd al-Ilah and a number of other members of the royal family emerged from the building. Within minutes they had all been shot dead, although it remains a matter of conjecture whether this had been planned by the army conspirators or happened as a result of the tension and passions of the moment. Nuri al-Saʿid's house was also surrounded and, although Nuri managed to escape, he was captured the following day and shot in the street.[17]

The overthrow of the monarchy in the military coup d'état of July 1958 brought to an end one phase in the narrative of the Iraqi state. It had been shaped largely by Great Britain, by the Hashemites and by the coteries of former Ottoman officers and officials who had sought mastery of the new state apparatus, as well as by the landowners and status-conscious elites of the many communities that constituted 'Iraqi society'. They had relied on their economic power, on their networks of patronage and on the deference still shown to them to secure their privileges and to advance their interests. At the same time, they had shown little compunction about relying on coercion when these interests were seriously threatened. Initially concerned to bring all inhabitants of the state into a condition of disciplined acceptance, armed force had been consistently and freely used to overcome provincial resistance. Equally, when resistance moved into the cities and into the newly formed associations connected with the development of a more complex political society, these public spaces also attracted the deployment of force.

Ruthless and effective as this strategy was in the short term, it did little to address the structural causes of grievance. Nor did it deter Iraqis from associating in a number of ways to protect or advance their interests. This faced the regime with a series of challenges in the final decade of the monarchy's existence. Above all, the strategy adopted by Nuri assumed the loyalty and political docility of the major disciplinary instrument – the armed forces – which neither the brief history of the Iraqi officer corps nor the circumstances of its creation and deployment could justify. It was therefore appropriate and possibly even inevitable that a regime created and sustained by authoritarian and conspiratorial ex-officers in their own image should have been overthrown by a new generation of military conspirators.

CHAPTER 5

The republic 1958–68

The seizure of power at the centre in 1958 was possibly quicker and easier than any of the military conspirators had anticipated. By the same token, they found themselves almost immediately in command of all the financial and administrative resources of the state. Some of their civilian allies believed that this would open the way for a radical assault on the systems of privilege and exclusion which characterised Iraq's deeply inegalitarian society, allowing political life to be refounded on a more liberal and democratic basis. However, the very ease of the transfer of power encouraged rather different thoughts among the immediate victors of 1958. 'Abd al-Karim Qasim and his military allies soon discovered the immense powers of patronage conferred upon them. The seductions of office worked on them as powerfully as they had on Nuri al-Sa'id and the sharifian officers who had found themselves, a generation previously, in positions of command in the new state of Iraq.

The gravitational pull of the Iraqi state exerted its force on the men who came to power in 1958. In seeking to master that state and to stay in command, they were destined to follow a logic suggested both by the distinctive politics of Iraq and by the way they had come to power. In the first place, conspiracy within the officer corps and beyond became the practical norm. With this went the use of violence as the ultimate sanction in a polity where there were profound disagreements not only on the substance of policy, but also on the very rules of the political game. Secondly, the tendency to centralise and to dominate negated attempts to create provincial or societal autonomy, frustrating efforts to represent the plurality of Iraq's diverse society in any institutional form. As a consequence, the genuine and widespread hopes for a radical break with the past and for the creation of a more open society that were awakened by the events of 1958 were gradually disappointed in the following decade. Significant changes did take place, but the emerging narratives they seemed to embody were always limited and controlled by those who had seized power by force. The limited imaginations of these men, preoccupied with the immediate struggle for power, shaped the story of Iraq, excluding thereby the many voices which had been raised in the hope of contributing to a refounding of the Iraqi state.

Instead, Iraqis found themselves subject to the command of individuals, more or less skilled at manipulating systems of patronage and coercion, who exercised a power greater than any enjoyed by the politicians under the monarchy. These men ensured that, despite the rhetoric, the various proclaimed 'revolutions' would never be sufficiently radical to challenge an order from which they derived so much strength. Much the same could be said of the growing realisation among the new rulers of Iraq that, despite the initial enthusiasm of some of them for the ideals of Arab nationalism and its associated schemes of Arab unity, only by concentrating on the condition of Iraq itself could they cement the alliances within the state necessary for political survival. Iraq in all its variety was the terrain of a distinctively Iraqi politics and it was this which demanded attention before anything else could be contemplated.

ʿABD AL-KARIM QASIM: DICTATORSHIP AND DISILLUSION

The coup d'état of 14 July 1958 was carried out and consolidated by a diverse collection of groups and individuals. Army officers played the decisive role, with the forces of Colonel ʿAbd al-Salam ʿArif and Brigadier ʿAbd al-Karim Qasim seizing key points in the capital and others preparing for a counter-attack that never came. To the same end, ʿArif used the radio station to urge the crowds into central Baghdad, calling on them to attack imperialism and its agents. In this atmosphere, the initial feeling of celebration gave way to a darker mood, as the Free Officers told the NDP, the ICP, the Baʿth and others to call out their followers in order to give the impression of massive popular support and to discourage any thoughts of outside intervention. During the days that followed, thousands of people poured onto the streets of Baghdad, partly out of curiosity to see the world turned upside down and, in some cases, to exact a violent revenge on figures and symbols of the regime of the Hashemites and their British patrons. There is little doubt that the scale of these demonstrations did make an impression on those within Iraq and beyond who were weighing up the possibilities of intervention to restore the old regime. However, they also alarmed the Free Officers themselves, who brought the crowds under control within the first day through a curfew and by imposing martial law.

It was not long before the spectacle of July 1958 was incorporated into the myth of the Iraqi revolution. Some used it to reinforce the claim that a

10 General ʿAbd al-Karim Qasim (prime minister of Iraq 1958–63), 1961

profound social movement, rather than a coup d'état, had occurred. Others tried to suggest that by participating they had helped to determine the outcome, thereby justifying their claims to share, or indeed to monopolise, the revolutionary inheritance. In fact, the power of the state remained intact. Command now lay in the hands of those who had made the coup, Qasim and ʿArif, with the Free Officers behind them. Popular participation was largely symbolic, despite the thousands of Baghdadis milling around and celebrating the end of the old regime. Once 'the people' had served their purpose during the first few days, many were bundled off the streets and the remainder encouraged to return to the suburbs and *sarifas* of Baghdad. In the capital and in the provinces, the administration continued to function normally and the most urgent task facing officials was to calculate how their own positions were affected by the changes at the top.[1]

Attempts by political parties to build more substantial forms of popular support were dependent on the initiatives of the new ruling elite, vulnerable therefore to their power plays and their prejudices. Thus the ICP's attempt to set up independent centres for Popular Resistance (*al-Muqawama al-Shaʿbiyya*) were soon thwarted by Qasim who took them over himself. Trade unions and peasants' associations were not legalised

until early in 1959 and then enjoyed only a brief period of independent existence before being subsumed into Qasim's system of corporate, patrimonial
control. The same applied to various other forms of associational life which
appeared soon after the fall of the monarchy: professional syndicates and
youth and women's organisations emerged, often with official encouragement and subject to increasingly intrusive state patronage, bringing them
all eventually into line with a system unambiguously dominated by Qasim
himself.

Qasim clearly believed that this degree of direct control was necessary
for his survival, although in retrospect it can be argued that his growing
determination to dominate all facets of public life deprived him of the
major pillars of support which might have helped him when he had to confront conspiracy in the armed forces. 'Abd al-Karim Qasim, 44 years old in
1958, came from a modest background and from a family which was more
representative of the diversity of Iraq's varied population than that of most
of his brother officers (his father was a Sunni Arab from Baghdad, but his
mother was a Faili (Shi'i) Kurd). This may have played a role in the inte-
grative vision he had for an Iraq in which rich and poor, Kurd, Arab, Sunni
and Shi'i, would work together for the common good.

However, more influential in shaping that vision was his growing conviction that he alone should define what constituted the common good. He
tended to present himself as all things to all men, especially at the outset
when he was still uncertain of the kind of support he could command.
Within a year or so, he had come to believe that he really did represent all
Iraqis in his person and increasingly gave the impression that he had a
sacred mission to fulfil. Some have dated his transformation from reticent
and modest army commander to dictator to his survival of an assassination
attempt in October 1959. Others have ascribed it to the inherent instabil-
ity of a rather withdrawn and enigmatic character. Possibly closer to the
truth are those who have stressed the incremental effect upon him as he
drew more power into his hands, discovering the ease of patronage in a
system already geared to central, hierarchical control and thriving on the
sometimes spontaneous, but often pre-arranged, mass adulation he
encountered in his public appearances.

Even at this stage, in late 1958, effective power lay with Qasim and his
growing following. He discovered, as his sharifian predecessors had done in
the 1920s, that vast powers of patronage were conferred upon those who
seized control of the centre and its resources. As his opponents found to
their cost, he used these powers with skill and ruthlessness, ruling over a
state which differed little in many of its particulars from that which he had

inherited from his predecessors. The new constitution proclaimed Iraq a republic and established a three-man Sovereignty Council to fulfil the ceremonial functions of the head of state. However, no representative institutions were established and Qasim himself filled the posts of prime minister and minister of defence, as well as commander in chief. He included 'Arif (as deputy prime minister and minister of the interior) and a few of the Free Officers in his cabinet, but otherwise appointed civilians associated both with the NDP and with the Arab nationalist trend. This disappointed some of the Free Officers who had expected a more prominent political role which the Commanders' Council, composed of Qasim's and 'Arif's military associates, failed to fulfil.

It was not long before tension developed between Qasim and 'Arif. Each believed that he had a claim to precedence over the other – Brigadier Qasim outranked Colonel 'Arif, but the latter had convinced himself that he represented the core of the young Free Officers, that he had been the initiator of the march on Baghdad in July 1958 and that he should therefore be recognised as the leader of the revolution. The rivalry of these two men was not simply personal, but became entangled with the long-unanswered question of the identity of Iraq, as a potential nation-state or as an administrative part of a larger Arab nation. In this respect, the existence of the UAR confronted the new rulers in Baghdad with an immediate test. 'Arif was an admirer of Nasser and seemed to share the Arab nationalist view that immediate adherence of Iraq to the UAR was both desirable in itself and necessary for the defence of the new regime. He was also aware that the slogan of 'Arab unity' gave him a substantial following in the army and beyond. Within days of the coup, he had visited Damascus and Michel Aflaq of the Ba'th Party had visited Baghdad to encourage Iraq to join the UAR.

Qasim, however, was more sympathetic to the views of the NDP and to those who believed that domestic social reform and the building of an Iraqi national community should precede serious engagement with the Arab world. He had support for this view among all those who regarded Arab unity schemes with suspicion – a suspicion openly voiced among the Kurds and the Shi'a and shared by the communists, who were wary of Nasser and the UAR. Consequently, in 1958 'Arif and the enthusiasts for union were held in check by those who wanted to use the Iraqi state as the means of advancing their own ideas of reform. Qasim knew of 'Arif's ambitions – highlighted by 'Arif's attempt to create a popular following in a series of provincial tours which aroused peasants' expectations and led to a number of uprisings against landlords during the late summer months. In September, Qasim dismissed him from his positions of command and ordered him into exile as ambassador to the Federal Republic of Germany. 'Arif had to comply, but returned secretly to Baghdad in late October and was promptly arrested. This temporarily eliminated 'Arif, but failed to neutralise those who shared his views about the need for union with the UAR.

For Qasim, however, this was no longer an option. The arrest of 'Arif had followed a number of moves against Ba'thists and Arab nationalists in the administration, signalling the importance of the 'Iraq first' line under Qasim's leadership. He hoped to build a basis of support among the diverse communities of Iraq but, like many autocrats, Qasim feared any institutional solidity that might eventually call him to account. Thus he helped to reproduce the ambiguity of the Iraqi state itself, divided between the institutional forms of the public state and the less visible, but more important, personal links of patronage and mutual obligation that decided where power lay and who should have access to resources. On the Kurdish question, for instance, the new constitution recognised the bi-national character of the state – but notoriously failed to institutionalise this unprecedented declaration. In the short term, it ensured the return of Mustafa Barzani from exile, leading to a revival of the KDP. This helped Qasim against the Arab nationalists, but he had no intention of granting the Kurds the institutional autonomy that would have satisfied the KDP.

A similar ambiguity characterised Qasim's relations with the Iraqi communists whom he also cultivated as a counterbalance to his Arab nationalist opponents. The ICP, under Husain al-Radi, emerged in 1958 as the best-organised party in the country, with a clear structure and solid foundations in Iraqi urban society and among the peasantry of the south, as well as in the northern Kurdish region. For Qasim, the ICP was a useful ally precisely because of its capacity to organise nationally in areas of Iraqi society largely untouched by other political organisations, even if, ideologically, he was closer to the NDP. Thus, in the aftermath of the coup of 1958, the ICP was allowed to publish freely and to organise, establishing itself in such organisations as the revived Peace Partisans, the League for the Defence of Women's Rights (al-Rabita), the League of Iraqi Youth and eventually in the trade unions and the peasants' associations.

These associations were not simply fronts for political parties, but represented attempts by a wide variety of Iraqis to establish a voice for hitherto neglected sections of society. Nowhere was this more the case than in al-Rabita, established by professional Iraqi women to create widespread access to the kinds of opportunities which their own more privileged backgrounds had granted to them. Since the graduation of the first women doctors and lawyers in Iraq in the late 1940s, a growing number of women had entered the professions, but they still represented a tiny minority of Iraqi women. Literacy rates and educational opportunities for all Iraqis were poor, but for women they were abysmal. Nor, in a patriarchal society such as that of Iraq, was there much encouragement for women to lead lives in public, outside the home, let alone in any overtly political sphere.

In trying to remedy these disadvantages, al-Rabita had some successes, largely in the area of primary education for girls, but it also encountered fierce resistance from those sections of society – both male and female – which saw the advancement of women as deeply subversive of established and accepted values. Consequently, this first concerted attempt to create the possibilities of political expression for a major section of Iraqi society, ignored in the dominant narratives of the Iraqi state, came up against deeply held social prejudices throughout the country. Nor was its task made any easier by the portrayal of the organisation as a front for communist activity. This had the effect of associating the education and indeed the emancipation of women with the package of revolutionary measures which the ICP was accused by its detractors of seeking to impose on Iraqi society.[2]

Yet, in reality, to be a communist or communist sympathiser in Iraq at that time, as in previous decades, did not necessarily mean strict adherence to the doctrines of Marxism-Leninism. When combined with tactical considerations, this allowed and sometimes impelled the ICP to reach accommodation with other political forces. Its focus on the evils of social injustice, economic exploitation and questions of wages and conditions of work won the ICP a wide basis of support and made it the leading party of social reform. In this context, the ICP also emerged as one of the chief advocates of greater democracy in Iraq. However, like other advocates of democracy, the communists had to face the question of how to create the conditions of equitable representation in an inequitable society. Like others before and since, the ICP believed that in the short term only the army had the power to keep in check the forces of established social and economic privilege prior to their dismantling. Consequently, despite its weak representation in the officer corps, it had backed the Free Officers. With the new freedoms after July 1958 it built up its civilian following, believing in the importance of control of the streets to give the impression of mass support and to deter further use of military force. As the balance of Iraqi society had shifted towards the towns, so the streets of the major cities were becoming correspondingly important as sites for public action and thus for forms of symbolic representation.

As far as the reform programme of the new regime was concerned, among its first targets were the vast landed estates whose owners had been among the main pillars of the previous regime. Law 30 of 1958 was aimed at sequestrating the estates of the largest landowners (numbering fewer than 3,000 people, they nevertheless owned over half of Iraq's cultivable land) and distributing them to the landless peasants or to the smaller and middling landowners. In practice, the relatively high limits set on individual landholdings and the choice given to the landlords concerning the land they could retain, as well as the payment of compensation, lessened the measure's radical impact. Equally, the absence of appropriate state machinery, as well as the continuing difficulty of establishing rightful ownership claims in many parts of Iraq, meant that by 1963 only about a quarter of the great estates had been sequestrated and of these less than half had been redistributed. Furthermore, in many areas, redistribution echoed land reform schemes of the Ottoman and monarchical periods in that the prime beneficiaries were those who were best placed to exploit the prevailing regime, as existing small and middling landowners with capital or as friends and clients of the new ruling elite. The landless peasants, as ever, received little.[3]

In 1958, however, the land reform legislation seemed to promise a more radical future, tempting peasants in 'Amara and elsewhere to occupy the lands of their absentee landlords. This happened more rarely than might have been expected. However, for the large landlords, whether tribal shaikhs or urban landowners, these events and the threat of sequestration served notice that their days of power and privilege were numbered. The resulting alarm contributed to Rashid 'Ali al-Kailani's conspiracy. Disappointed at his neglect by the new government following his return to Iraq, he contacted some disgruntled pan-Arab Free Officers and tribal shaikhs worried by the prospect of expropriation with a view to organising a coup d'état modelled on those of the 1930s. In the event, the plot was discovered. Rashid 'Ali was arrested in December 1958, tried and sentenced to death (later commuted to a term of imprisonment).

The arrest and trial of Rashid 'Ali, coinciding with the trial of 'Arif (who was also sentenced to death, but also reprieved), made clear the rift between Qasim and the pan-Arabists. It provided opportunities for the communists and their sympathisers to organise more extensively, not only against the pan-Arabists, but also against the perceived conservative influence of the NDP which threatened to thwart any truly radical reform. Street demonstrations and marches became a marked feature of Baghdad life during this period, as the various factions struggled with each other for command of the streets and for the opportunity to present their case before Qasim in a curious mixture of adulation and overt pressure. Qasim himself was not slow to exploit this, sponsoring marches and factions which could be relied upon to cheer repeatedly for the 'Sole Leader' (*al-Zaʿim al-Awhad*). Counter-demonstrations were organised and the violence that sometimes resulted provided a vivid form of street theatre, heightening the atmosphere of crisis.

The theatre of the streets had its dangers. Demonstrations were no substitute for organised power, institutional or coercive, as the ICP discovered to its cost. Furthermore, they could rouse dangerous passions in a society as divided as that of Iraq. In March 1959, a massive rally organised by the ICP-inspired Peace Partisans in Mosul triggered a coup attempt by the disgruntled pan-Arab Free Officer commanding the Mosul garrison. When sections of the army and the population resisted, violence engulfed the city, representing the conditions of civil war in miniature and going far beyond simple opposition to or support for the government. Instead, ethnic, sectarian, inter-tribal and economic antagonisms showed themselves, with Kurds fighting Arabs, Christians fighting Muslims, Arab clans fighting other Arab clans and the poor fighting the rich. Only after five days were government forces able to restore order.

These events provided Qasim with the pretext for an extensive purge of the armed forces and the administration, targeting officers and officials with known pan-Arab sympathies, as well as those connected to the Mosul conspirators. In their place, he appointed his own protégés, thus extending his own patronage networks. The communists also benefited. More importantly, the ICP gained the impression that, by rallying 'the people', it could effectively check any attempted coup d'état, reinforcing its belief that it could now play an active part in the direction of the Iraqi state. The ICP became more visible on the streets, organising a massive demonstration in Baghdad in May 1959 which called on Qasim to appoint communists to the government and to hold elections for a representative assembly.

Qasim now began to look on the ICP with some concern. Its presence on the streets, its strength in various associations, trade and peasants' unions, its members' mass adherence to the Popular Resistance organisation and the expansion of party membership to an estimated 25,000 made it seem increasingly formidable. More importantly, the very prominence of the party alarmed those whom Qasim did not want to alienate. These included the small industrial entrepreneurs and the middling landowners of the NDP, as well as Qasim's fellow officers, the great majority of whom mistrusted the communists. The events in Mosul had confirmed the belief held by the enduring authoritarian faction within the Iraqi officer corps and civil administration that any uncertainty about the power of the centre and any opportunity for 'the people' to express their opinion without restraint would result in conditions approaching civil war. Ethnic and clannish antagonisms had inevitably been reinforced by the attack on privilege. This was the nightmare of many in Iraq, especially in the officer corps where a consciousness of privilege and a distaste for disorder and indiscipline went hand in hand. To some extent, Qasim himself shared these views, as he was concerned about the need for national cohesion and was sensitive to the many possible fracture lines in Iraqi society.

Consequently, Qasim tightened up on the activities of the Popular Resistance, ensuring that they could never challenge the organised force of the army. He reiterated the ban on all party activities, but also promised the legalisation of political parties within a year. In an attempt to keep the ICP in check and to bind it closer to the government, he appointed a party member, Naziha al-Dulaimi, and two known communist sympathisers to ministerial posts. Although she was fairly junior, al-Dulaimi's appointment was significant in that she was both the first woman and the first member of the ICP to be appointed to an Iraqi government. However, these moves were soon overshadowed by a series of violent events in Kirkuk. Unwisely choosing this city, with its background of Turkmen–Kurdish–Arab antipathies, reinforced by economic inequalities, members of the ICP decided to put on a show of force on the first anniversary of the fall of the monarchy. However, on 14 July the demonstration staged by the communists clashed with one organised by their ideological opponents, supported by those who feared the Kurdish connection with the ICP in Kirkuk. Two days of fighting ensued. As in Mosul, ethnic and economic antagonisms became intertwined, leading to serious intercommunal conflict.

Order was restored by government forces, but the opponents of the ICP and of the Kurds ensured that the events received maximum publicity, particularly their more gruesome details. Qasim himself encouraged this, using the opportunity to curb the ICP and to reinforce the message that his own strong leadership was needed to hold Iraqi society together. During the following months, therefore, large numbers of communists were arrested, some for direct complicity in the events at Kirkuk, but others on a variety of pretexts. At the same time, communists were removed from the peasants' unions and from certain key posts in the trade unions, where a close watch was kept on their activities. A similar purge was initiated in the state administration and in the officer corps, but there was less urgency here because Qasim knew that his own networks and the bias of authoritarian opinion were more formidable than anything which the ICP could organise.[4]

Despite these developments, the communist minister stayed in the government and the party's criticism of Qasim was remarkably mild. The ICP leaders knew that they had little to gain by alienating Qasim since they had few allies and did not have the strength to challenge him, given his hold on the officer corps. The Ba'th Party, by contrast, had decided that the only way of advancing its cause was by assassinating Qasim himself. In October 1959, soon after the execution of the officers responsible for the Mosul revolt, the Ba'thists made an unsuccessful attempt on Qasim's life, in which the future leader of Iraq, the 22-year-old Saddam Husain, participated. The assassination attempt led to arrests and purges of Ba'thist sympathisers and the mobilising of massive demonstrations of support for the 'Sole Leader'. However, these demonstrations could not conceal the fact that Qasim's political survival depended upon his ability to ensure that the bulk of the officer corps remained supportive and that he and the intelligence services which he had inherited from the monarchical regime stayed one step ahead of potential conspirators.

This was the hidden side of politics under Qasim. It was hidden from public view because this was a world of informal contacts and networks of obligation and patronage which were known largely to those who needed to operate within this world. It was not dissimilar to the restricted political world of the Iraqi elite under the monarchy, although paradoxically that had been more generally in the public view because of the relative confidence of the monarchical elite that theirs was the only political world that really mattered. The events of July 1958 had rudely shaken that confidence and those beliefs, but they had not fundamentally altered the terms or principles by which power was handled and mediated among the new rulers of the Iraqi state. Instead, by becoming the focus of effective political decision-making, the circles of the officer corps which now controlled the state ruled in a necessarily more conspiratorial way. Following the various coup attempts, it was dangerous to voice criticism, making any opposition activity equally conspiratorial.

The increasingly dictatorial system ran counter to Qasim's public promises of a more open politics, but effectively determined the outcome when party activity was allowed in January 1960. Only a few parties were granted licences. They included the NDP, but it had no large popular following and many of its leading members were dependent on Qasim's patronage, making criticism difficult and leading to its disintegration within a couple of years. Also granted a licence was the very different organisation of the KDP which brought together in an uneasy alliance two factions headed, respectively, by Mulla Mustafa Barzani (president) and by

Ibrahim Ahmad (secretary-general). Qasim was aware of the incompatibility of many of the Kurdish demands with his own views. Nevertheless, he also knew that Barzani and Ibrahim Ahmad represented very different facets of Kurdish society and had different aspirations. Barzani, despite his association with the short-lived Mahabad Republic, his long exile in the USSR and his use of Marxist rhetoric when it suited him, was primarily a tribal chief and a Naqshabandi shaikh. It was on these features that his very substantial following largely depended. By contrast, Ibrahim Ahmad and most of the politburo of the KDP were urban intellectuals, many of them former members of the ICP, to the ideology of which they remained close, but with which they had a sometimes difficult relationship.

The ICP also applied for a licence to organise as a legal political party, but Qasim prevented it. However, the party was unable to protest effectively since street demonstrations provided merely the semblance of power, not its substance. The ICP's predicament was sharpened by the appearance of an Islamic party. Among the Sunnis and the Shi'a similar processes had been taking place, leading to requests to form two distinct Islamic parties. Initially refused licences because of their sectarian nature, a single religious party was eventually permitted – al-Hizb al-Islami (the Islamic Party). The party's leader was the Sunni layman Nu'man 'Abd al-Razzaq al-Samarrai, but its sponsor was the Shi'i Grand Ayatollah Muhsin al-Hakim. Although it was dedicated to the ultimate goal of forming an Islamic order, its hostility to atheism, materialism and communism was very much to the fore, helping to explain its appeal for Qasim at the time.

The emergence of the Islamic Party was the public symptom of feelings in certain circles among both Sunni and Shi'i Iraqis of a need for the reorientation of political life, not on sectarian or communal grounds, but rather in terms of Islamic obligations, more generally understood. It can also be seen as part of an emerging reaction against the predominantly secularist assumptions of public discourse during the previous two decades. Among the Sunnis, this took shape in al-Ikhwan al-Muslimun (the Muslim Brotherhood), inspired by the example of Egypt and Syria, where similar organisations had long been active. Among the Shi'a, the principal organisation of this kind was al-Da'wa (the (Islamic) Call) which appeared in the late 1950s, organised around the young *'alim*, Muhammad Baqir al-Sadr. It reflected both his own ideas about the nature of the Islamic revival, as well as the feelings of younger clerics and laypeople about the need for a more effective organisation to check the spread of ideologies which they believed threatened both to weaken the Shi'i community and to turn people away from Islam itself.

Al-Daʿwa was opposed by older, more conservative Shiʿi scholars who were wary of some of al-Sadr's innovative ideas and whose own ideas of acceptable political activity were restricted to communal representation and negotiation with the state authorities. At this stage al-Daʿwa, like the Sunni Muslim Brotherhood, was not specifically challenging the regime. However, it seemed radical to some because it used the language and methods of mass politics to mobilise a following among laypeople as well as the *ulama*. These reservations did not deter Ayatollah Muhsin al-Hakim from giving it his endorsement. His sons were also linked to the organisation, having led protests in the autumn of 1958 against the land reform law, arguing that the sequestration of private property was contrary to the *Shariʿa*. This may have contributed to the government's decision to pay compensation to landlords and to exclude *waqf* land (religious endowments) from its rulings, thereby greatly reducing the radical impact of the law.[5]

However, in October 1960, when the Islamic Party criticised aspects of the government's legislative programme for being contrary to the *Shariʿa* a number of its members were arrested, its paper was suspended and some of its branches were closed down. For its part, the ICP came under increasing scrutiny by the security services, its newspaper was suspended for months at a time and its hold on some of the associations it had tried to dominate was constantly challenged. In November 1960 al-Dulaimi was dismissed, to be followed soon afterwards by the other two communist sympathisers in the cabinet. By that stage the main organisations which the ICP had controlled – the Peace Partisans, the League of Iraqi Youth and al-Rabita – had been closed down by the government, further limiting the influence of the ICP.

In this atmosphere, party organisation became less and less sustainable. Qasim refused to create any representative institutions or to hold parliamentary elections. The few political parties could only fall back on their publications and these were highly vulnerable to closure by executive order. This marked the beginning of the end of the remarkable flowering of creative, intellectual activity in Iraq itself which had followed the establishment of the republic in 1958. The overthrow of the old order and the promise of radical new departures not only had stimulated Iraqi writers and artists, but also had provided the space in which new and often contrasting ideas about Iraq's future and the role of the intellectuals in shaping that future could be presented and debated. Books, journals and newspapers, as well as sculpture, painting and theatre, had helped to re-establish lively centres for a literate and concerned public, reminiscent of the moments since 1945 when this had been allowed under the monarchy. However, as under that regime, so under Qasim, this space existed only on the sufferance of those who held political power, exposing the writers and artists themselves not only to arrest and censorship, but also to forms of co-option and patronage that were equally destructive of their creative independence. For many, the only feasible option was self-imposed exile, accelerating the haemorrhage of Iraq's artistic and cultural talent that was so to impoverish the country in the decades to come.

In the political field, clandestine organisation became the rule. Some, such as the ICP, were used to this. Indeed, it was becoming increasingly necessary since the party found itself under attack from government agencies, from al-Daʿwa and from a number of other groups based in the Shiʿi community, which were dedicated to the fight against communism. At the same time a grim covert war was developing. Suspected communists and their families in Baghdad, Mosul and elsewhere were attacked by pan-Arab groups, using murder and intimidation to drive them out. The clandestine revival of the Baʿth Party played a part in this. After the debacle of 1959, ʿAli Salih al-Saʿdi had been sent back to Iraq in secret to rebuild the Baʿth. Following the principles of secret organisation, he created an apparatus that could simultaneously wage a clandestine war against the communists, infiltrate the circles of the regime and bring crowds out onto the streets at key moments. By 1962, when he became effective head of the party in Iraq, he had established a small but well-placed network in a number of strategic locations, creating cells within the state administration, within the armed forces and in the professional syndicates.

For its part, the KDP, despite internal tensions, had used the two years of licensed operation to mobilise and to gain recognition as the foremost organisation in the Kurdish areas of Iraq. The various factions were at least able to unite around the idea of autonomy for all of the Kurdish-speaking regions of the country, despite significant differences about the meaning of autonomy, the territory to be included and the nature of any future regime in the north. The KDP was encouraged by the waning fortunes of the pan-Arab trend in Iraqi politics, but nevertheless had to contend with authoritarian state centralism, justified in the name of Iraqi nationalism and national unity. This attitude was well entrenched in the state administration, limiting the concessions offered to the Kurds and preventing any attempt to realise the promise of Kurdish autonomy contained in the constitution. However, the KDP leaders initially sought to petition, rather than to defy, the regime.

Hoping to exploit the burgeoning relationship between Iraq and the USSR, Barzani visited Moscow in early 1961 with the intention of asking the Soviet leadership to argue the Kurdish case with Qasim. Understandably reluctant to become involved in so sensitive an issue, the USSR declined to help. Qasim had meanwhile begun to harass the KDP in a variety of ways, employing the familiar tactic of lending support to Barzani's rivals among the Kurdish tribes. Consequently, when Barzani's memorandum on autonomy was rejected by the government in July 1961, he returned to his traditional power base in the northern Kurdish region. Soon fighting broke out between his forces and those of the rival tribal leaders whom the government had been assisting. As the fighting escalated, it drew in other sections of the Kurdish population, animated by long-standing rivalries, but also by particular resentments and against a background of growing calls for self-determination. When units of the Iraqi army were attacked in September, the government responded by bombing a number of Kurdish villages, including Barzan itself. The Iraqi army was mobilised, units were sent to the north and by the autumn of 1961 full-scale war had begun.

The fighting was largely confined to the northern 'tribal' areas of the Kurdish mountains and was portrayed by the Iraqi government as a struggle against the 'feudal' and 'reactionary' tribal leaders in that region. This was true insofar as a number of tribal leaders had already been in a state of rebellion because of the land reform laws. Indeed, a section of the KDP itself subscribed to this view of the rebellion and refused to support Barzani. However, Qasim did not help his case by simultaneously outlawing the KDP, causing even those who mistrusted Barzani to join the rebellion. Despite their misgivings, they saw that Barzani was at least keeping the goal of Kurdish autonomy alive and that he alone could command – in the shape of his *peshmerga* (Barzani's guerrilla forces) – the kind of armed force that alone seemed to make an impression on central government. Unlike the other political parties in Iraq, the KDP did not need government patronage to survive, but it did need the protection of Barzani and other tribal leaders. This inevitably influenced its composition and the balance of forces within it, tending to lessen its commitment to radical reform as it became more closely associated with a pan-Kurdish struggle. Its activities would be increasingly governed by the logic of guerrilla warfare and here the key question would be the ability of Barzani's forces to hold their own against the forces of the Iraqi state and of the government's Kurdish tribal allies (dismissively called the *jahsh* (donkeys)).[6]

IRAQI FOREIGN POLICY UNDER QASIM

Barzani's troops succeeded in tying down large sections of the Iraqi army, leading to frustration in the Iraqi officer corps, many of whom saw this as a further indictment of Qasim's leadership. By this stage, other questions were being raised about his rule, particularly his handling of those foreign policy issues which had reverberations within the circles of Iraqi politics. Enmity with the UAR was a constant feature of Qasim's rule, but the assertion of the 'Iraq first' line in politics had not, as under the monarchy, led Qasim to establish closer relations with Iraq's non-Arab neighbours. Indeed, it could hardly do so since the alliance between Iraq, Turkey and Iran in the Baghdad Pact was seen as a symbol of Iraq's subjection to British and to Western interests. Consequently, it was scarcely surprising that Iraq should have withdrawn from the pact in 1959, turning increasingly to the USSR for foreign aid and for military supplies.

The USSR had been much encouraged by the overthrow of the monarchy and the establishment of the republic. The newly tolerated activities of the ICP promised the development of a significant communist force in the politics of an important Middle East state. Equally, the withdrawal of Iraq from the Baghdad Pact was clearly a strategic gain in that it abruptly ended any possibility of the British returning to use the air bases they had handed over to Iraqi control. However, it seems improbable that the Soviet leadership had many illusions about the leanings of the new regime – unlike many in the West and in the region whose Cold War preoccupations led them to overestimate the degree of communist and Soviet influence on Qasim. For his part, it is clear that Qasim saw the USSR as a possible source of diplomatic and economic support, as well as a future supplier of arms. Nevertheless, he had little sympathy with communism as an ideology, he was wary of the ICP and he did not see the Soviet model of economic development as being relevant to Iraq. Furthermore, the close relationship developing between the USSR and Nasser's Egypt meant that Qasim was unable to view the USSR as a regional ally of Iraq.

However, Iraq's break with the Baghdad Pact and the re-establishment of relations with the USSR led to a crisis in relations with Iran, expressed during 1959 by rival claims and counter-claims to the Shatt al-ʿArab. Iran challenged the 1937 agreement and demanded that the waterway be divided along the *Thalweg* for the whole of its length. Iraq rejected this and made claims of its own. In the year that followed, relations deteriorated to such an extent that shots were exchanged across the Shatt al-ʿArab. Neither side had much interest in escalating the conflict, but shipping was prevented from using the ports of Basra and Abadan, eventually bringing the cost of the dispute home to both governments. Consequently, in the spring of 1961, an agreement between Iran and Iraq allowed shipping to use the waterway once again. It did not solve the fundamental difference over the question of sovereignty, but it did commit both sides to seek a negotiated way out of their predicament.

However, deteriorating relations with Iran had two major adverse consequences for Qasim's government and underlined the regional difficulty of pursuing an active policy of 'Iraq first'. On the one hand, partly in reaction to the dominance of the United Arab Republic in the Levant, Qasim tried to carve out a new area of Iraqi interest in the Persian Gulf (now officially renamed by Iraq the 'Arabian Gulf'). This was intended to combine the theme of Arabism with that of distinctively Iraqi national interests. It led to increasing Iraqi attention to the shaikhdoms of the Arab side of the Gulf and the Arabic-speaking populations of the south-western Iranian province of Khuzestan (designated by the Iraqi government by its former name of 'Arabistan').

These moves unsettled the Iranian government, which believed that Iraq was intending to escalate the dispute over the Shatt al-'Arab to take in the politically explosive question of the future of a substantial part of Iran itself. Inevitably, the Iranian government looked to see what levers it could use against the government in Baghdad, and it was not long before relations were established with Mustafa Barzani in the Kurdish mountains. The border was easily crossed and the Iraqi armed forces could not prevent the flow of goods and arms. The quantities were not great at this stage, but they helped Barzani to keep the Iraqi army in check during 1961 and 1962. Equally importantly, they established a precedent which was to be of greater significance in the future.

The second major consequence of this new Iraqi interest in the Persian Gulf lay in the claim made by Qasim in June 1961 to Kuwait. The closure of the Shatt al-'Arab waterway in the earlier part of the year had revived the problem of Iraq's limited access to the waters of the Gulf. Since the 1930s there had been thoughts of developing a port at Umm Qasr near the Kuwaiti border. At that time, these ideas had been associated with Iraqi claims to sovereignty over the whole of Kuwait or at the very least over the Kuwaiti islands of Warba and Bubiyan which overlooked the approaches to Umm Qasr. Similar considerations may have played a part in prompting Qasim to demand that Kuwait be 'returned' to Iraq a few days after Kuwait was declared independent in June 1961. As in the 1930s, Qasim based Iraq's claim on the assertion that Kuwait had been a district of the Ottoman province of Basra, unjustly severed by the British from the main body of the Iraqi state when it had been created in the 1920s.

Qasim underlined his claim by announcing that he was appointing the ruler of Kuwait as *qaimaqam* of the district, subordinate to the governor of

Basra. This corresponded to the rank which had been conferred on the then shaikh of Kuwait by the Ottoman authorities. Qasim was therefore harking back to a recurrent theme in the developing national myth of Iraq – a myth which suggested both that Iraq had 'natural' boundaries, and that these boundaries had been deliberately flouted by the British authorities, to restrict Iraq's access to the sea and thus to reduce its influence in the Gulf. The implication of this was that it was the duty of all true Iraqi patriots to remove this last residue of imperialism and to establish Iraq's rightful place as the dominant power at the headwaters of the Gulf. Qasim's own authority depended in part on his ability to pose as a champion of a distinctive Iraqi patriotism who was also seeking to extend Iraq's influence in the eastern Arab world as a counter-weight to Egypt's dominance of the Levant. He could hardly fail, therefore, to respond to the British withdrawal from Kuwait in 1961.

Qasim did not threaten to pursue his claim by force. Indeed much of the Iraqi army was deployed at the time in the north of the country, preparing to deal with the deteriorating situation in the Kurdish region. Nevertheless, neither the ruler of Kuwait nor the British government could dismiss the Iraqi claims as purely rhetorical. Within days of Qasim's voicing of the Iraqi claim to Kuwait, Great Britain sent forces to Kuwait at the request of the ruler to deter Iraq and called for an emergency meeting of the UN Security Council. The Arab League, dominated at the time by the UAR, admitted Kuwait as a member state, promised to safeguard its independence and asked the ruler to request the withdrawal of British troops. In August, the British forces left Kuwait to be replaced by an Arab League force, composed largely of UAR troops. In response, Iraq withdrew its representative from the Arab League and broke off diplomatic relations with a number of the countries which had recognised Kuwait. However, Iraq was powerless to pursue its claims and, although they surfaced for some years in the Iraqi media, this was the end of the immediate crisis over Kuwait.

In the eyes of the pan-Arab faction in Iraq, represented by the Ba'th and others, particularly in the officer corps, the crisis was a further indictment of Qasim and his regime. They may have sympathised with the idea of annexing Kuwait, but Qasim's tactics had isolated Iraq in the Arab world and had led to a climb-down in the face of British imperialism. The revival of this ever powerful theme in Iraqi politics opened old wounds and shook the confidence even of some of Qasim's supporters. This may have contributed to the government's proclamation in December 1961 of Law 80 under which Iraq took back roughly 99 per cent of the Iraq Petroleum Company's concessionary area without compensation. Having hitherto failed to exploit the vast concessions granted to it, IPC was now effectively frozen out of further development in Iraq, having to content itself with the nevertheless substantial fields it already operated.

These moves followed intermittent and finally unsatisfactory negotiations with IPC during the previous two years over a range of issues, from the price of oil to the desire by the Iraqi government for equity participation in the company. The atmosphere had been soured by the behaviour of the major oil companies during the years of oil glut when the producer countries had been forced to bear the brunt of depressed oil prices. This had led to Iraq's active encouragement of the foundation of the Organization of Petroleum Exporting Countries (OPEC) in September 1960. In this context, Law 80 was a blow aimed specifically at the oil companies (although OPEC refused to endorse the move, regarding it as too extreme). However, it was also presented as a blow against the legacy of British imperial control in Iraq. It fell short of nationalisation, but its implications were regarded at the time as equally radical. IPC responded by slowing down production, penalising the Iraqi government which was, of course, in no position to exploit the concessions it had just taken back and which suffered a corresponding loss of revenue. However, regardless of its economic cost, the move was popular in Iraq and may have helped Qasim to efface the memory of the Kuwait fiasco.[7]

THE POLITICS OF CONSPIRACY AND THE COUP D'ÉTAT OF FEBRUARY 1963

Despite the set-backs he encountered in foreign affairs, Qasim appeared to emerge as a genuinely popular leader of Iraq. Under his direction, oil revenues had been redirected towards the immediate needs of the poorer sections of society. The funds allocated for long-term infrastructural projects were reduced and were committed instead to public housing schemes and housing loans which benefited the *sarifa* dwellers around Baghdad in particular. The numbers of pupils and students at all levels of education trebled during this period and there was a burst of school-building activity. However, the numbers of teachers did not increase proportionately, leading to problems in the provision of education. A similar problem existed in health care where the building of hospitals greatly increased the number of hospital beds, but the numbers of doctors and nurses, given the length and expense of their training, could not be so rapidly increased.

Equally, labour laws had been introduced, designed to reduce the hours of work, raise the minimum wage and give workers some protection against accidents and unemployment. The enactment of these laws had been patchy, to say the least, but they helped to give the impression of a leader concerned about his people's welfare and genuinely determined to improve their standard of living. This was an impression furthered by the state-supervised media which helped to make Qasim the centre of an increasingly elaborate personality cult. Although a creation essentially of Qasim's own office and of his appointees, there is evidence to suggest that he believed firmly in the myths that were being woven around his person. Indeed it is at this time that Qasim felt confident enough to release all those sentenced by the Special Supreme Military Court.

This institution (known as the People's Court and presided over by Colonel al-Mahdawi) had been set up soon after the July coup in 1958 to put on public trial members of the monarchical regime indicted for their 'crimes against the people'. Used chiefly as a public forum for the condemnation of the evils of the old regime, the court had finally handed down four death sentences, despite the large numbers of politicians and officials brought before it. However, it had been kept in session to try a growing list of conspirators against, or merely critics of, Qasim's government. By early 1962, however, Qasim was confident that his own clients dominated the state and that the opposition was in disarray: the NDP was disintegrating; the ICP, denied access to most public associations, was under constant surveillance by Qasim's security agencies; the KDP had come out in support of the guerrilla war in the north, but had little impact in Iraq's major towns where it had few obvious allies. The Kurdish war was a drain on state resources and was demoralising for the officer corps, but for Qasim, as for rulers in Baghdad before and since, the Kurdish question seemed to be a peripheral one.

However, in the winter of 1961–2 elements in the KDP decided that the only way of resolving their dispute with Baghdad was to change the regime. Spurned by the parties which were ideologically closest to them – the NDP and the ICP – the KDP turned to the pan-Arab groups and to the Ba'th Party, largely because of their continuing influence in the armed forces, and offered a cease-fire if Qasim were to be overthrown. These approaches coincided with the growing confidence of the Ba'th Party itself. The core membership of the party remained small, but it was well placed in the state administration and in the armed forces. A much wider circle of 'sympathisers' could also in theory be mobilised at moments of crisis. During 1962 this organisation had been greatly developed through a network of committees intended to bring large numbers of people out onto the streets, once the military had made a decisive move. Emulating the ICP, the Ba'th had realised the importance of being able to control – or to give the impression of being able to control – the 'street' at moments of political crisis. This was meant both to neutralise the ICP and to provide inescapable proof of the popularity and power of the Baʿth.

Al-Saʿdi, a civilian, nevertheless saw the importance of establishing links with Arab nationalist officers, like ʿAbd al-Salam ʿArif, recently released from prison, who shared the Baʿthists' concern about Iraq's isolation in the Arab world and their antipathy to communism. For them, Qasim seemed to epitomise both dangers. During 1962 the Military Bureau of the Baʿth was formed, composed of al-Saʿdi and a number of senior Baʿthist officers, such as Brigadier Ahmad Hasan al-Bakr and Lieutenant-Colonel Salih Mahdi ʿAmmash. The bureau recruited an increasing number of officers, often through their attachment to the personal following of such figures as Hasan al-Bakr. The plans for the overthrow of Qasim's regime were drawn up here and the bureau was also intended to ensure that the Baʿth would remain dominant in the aftermath of the coup, despite having to co-operate with non-Baʿthist officers.

In an echo of the downfall of the monarchy, Qasim had received reports of a conspiracy but, confident of his own networks of control, he merely arrested al-Saʿdi and ʿAmmash. This spurred the remaining conspirators into action since they now feared a more general purge. On 8 February 1963, they assassinated Brigadier Jalal al-Awqati, the communist commander of the air force, and attacked and neutralised the airfield at Rashid military base whilst their own military units headed for Baghdad. The government broadcast news of the coup and the ICP, despite its uneven relationship with Qasim, mobilised its members, bringing thousands into the streets to defend the regime. They converged on Qasim's headquarters at the Ministry of Defence, hoping to forestall the coup by taking over the streets of the capital.

Qasim refused their request for arms, believing to the end that his own forces could deal with the situation. As a military officer he could not bring himself to hand out weapons to the public, despite the fact that he had been willing to use the same public on previous occasions to discourage thoughts of a coup within the military. However, the Baʿth and its allies were not so easily discouraged. Their own popular organisations also took to the streets, well armed and intent on clearing the streets of their political opponents. In the meantime, the military units under the command of Baʿthist and Arab nationalist officers headed straight for the Ministry of Defence, brushing aside civilian resistance. After a day of fierce fighting, the rebel forces broke through, capturing Qasim and his colleagues on 9 February.

They were immediately brought before a tribunal of Baʿthist and pan-Arab officers, sentenced to death and summarily shot.

The circumstances of Qasim's overthrow and death in many ways epitomised the structural problems of Iraqi politics which he had encountered, but which he had also compounded. Power to decide the fate of government lay in the hands of successful conspiracy within the officer corps, just as his own power had depended upon his ability to command the loyalties of key units of the armed forces. Qasim's undoubted personal popularity among many Iraqis and the mesmerising strength of his personality counted for something. In fact, his enemies acknowledged this when they displayed his bullet-riddled corpse on Iraqi television in order to prove that he was dead.

However, Qasim's unwillingness or his inability to devolve power or to create institutions that could mobilise effective popular support meant that he not only focused all animosity on himself, but also that he had no defence against well-organised military conspiracy. Whether through family background or upbringing, Qasim was peculiarly sensitive to the diversity of Iraq's population and thus to the need to encourage some sense of national community if Iraqi politics were not to be continually plagued by intercommunal suspicions and resentments. However, he was unable to see that no common feeling could develop unless people felt that their views were being properly represented in institutions which they could trust. In the absence of any such devolution of power, the already privileged and those with immediate coercive force at their disposal would continue to decide the fate of government according to their own rules and whims. Qasim ruled as an autocrat and died as one, helping thus to reproduce the exclusive structures of Iraqi politics and their authoritarian impulse.

BAʿTHIST CONTROL AND LOSS OF CONTROL IN 1963

On the first day of the coup d'état, a National Council of the Revolutionary Command (NCRC) was formed, composed initially of twelve Baʿthists and four Arab nationalist officers. The Baʿthist contingent was composed equally of officers and civilians and included all six members of the Military Bureau. The NCRC exercised supreme power, but some of its members also held posts in the formal apparatus of government. Thus, ʿAbd al-Salam ʿArif, who commanded a considerable following in the armed forces, but who was not a Baʿthist, became president. His vice-president was the Baʿthist Ahmad Hasan al-Bakr, who also served as prime minister. The deputy prime minister and minister of interior was ʿAli Salih al-Saʿdi, who was also secretary of the Ba'th regional command. As leader of the party in Iraq, al-Sa'di was the most influential and powerful member of the three at the time, although his authority did not go uncontested, as subsequent events were to show.

This was to be a short-lived regime, in large part because of the unresolved conflicts amongst those who had carried out the coup against Qasim. These differences were to some degree personal, made more rancorous by the narrow conspiratorial world of clandestine activity in the preceding years. However, they were also representative of opposing ideas about the identity and the direction of Iraq itself, many of which had been suppressed during the preceding years for the sake of common opposition to Qasim and the forces he was taken to represent. Once the Ba'thists and pan-Arabists had achieved power, disagreements rapidly developed concerning the direction of the state. Unity of purpose gave way to rifts not only between Ba'thists and non-Ba'thists, but also among the Ba'thists themselves as their differing views about Iraq's future and of their place in it became apparent.

Initially, all factions could agree on the need to eliminate the supporters of the previous regime and a savage campaign of arrests, torture and execution was unleashed chiefly against the ICP and its sympathisers. At its most ferocious in the early weeks following the coup when the Ba'thists feared a communist challenge, the campaign continued remorselessly for much of 1963, claiming an estimated 3,000 victims. The relatively public nature of communist and communist-inspired activity during the five preceding years, and the array of their enemies, ranging from Ba'thists and Arab nationalists to the emerging Islamist organisations, made the party and its sympathisers highly vulnerable. Most active in this campaign was the Ba'thist National Guard (Al-Hars al-Qawmi), commanded by Colonel al-Wandawi and formed out of the network of committees established by al-Sa'di to check the power of the communists and other opponents of the Ba'th on the streets. It had been issued with weapons during the coup d'état and grew rapidly into an armed militia numbering over 30,000 members, accountable only to the leadership of the Ba'th.

While the anti-communist campaign was continuing, the government turned to the other pressing legacy of the Qasim regime: the unstable situation in the Kurdish areas of Iraq. Barzani had declared the promised ceasefire and the new government entered into negotiations with the KDP. Al-Sa'di spoke of national reconciliation, two Kurds were appointed to cabinet positions, the economic blockade of the north was lifted and government forces withdrew from some areas. However, negotiations proceeded slowly. The government was prepared to offer only a limited, administrative form of self-rule. By contrast, the KDP's demands included an expanded Kurdish province administered exclusively by Kurds, defended by Kurdish armed forces, with independent finances based on local taxes and on a fixed proportion of oil revenues, with effective Kurdish participation in the main organs of Iraq's government to safeguard Kurdish interests. The government could accept neither the territorial extent of the proposed Kurdish province, which included Kirkuk and the major oil fields, nor the principle of financial and military autonomy. In response, Barzani mobilised his forces once more, manoeuvring into a position which would give him an advantage when, predictably, fighting broke out again in June.

The government, wary of a frustrated officer corps, launched a strong offensive in the north, leading to a string of successes for the Iraqi army, including the capture of Barzan itself in August. However, despite its symbolic resonance, Barzan was relatively accessible, reached by roads which the Iraqi army could control. Beyond these roads and the major settlements, the Iraqi army was powerless. The forces of Barzani and the KDP remained active, benefiting from their mastery of the inaccessible mountain country along the Turkish and Iranian borders, which allowed them to establish de facto autonomy in large areas of the north. The Ba'thist government thus found itself presiding over a demoralising and expensive war, undermining confidence and generating dangerous resentments within the officer corps.

These feelings had, in any case, been exacerbated by the turmoil within the Ba'th itself during the course of the year. The Ba'th Party's advocacy of pan-Arabism and social welfare under the slogan 'Freedom, Unity, Socialism' had always allowed for wide interpretation. In Iraq, as elsewhere, people joined the Ba'th Party for a variety of reasons. Consequently, the Iraqi section of the Ba'th comprised a number of disparate factions, identified as much by the individuals who headed them as by the 'line' that they followed. Al-Sa'di and his associates had built up the clandestine party and now believed that they had a chance to exercise real power. They organised the National Guard not only against the communists, but also potentially against the pan-Arabists with whom the Ba'th was currently allied. They may also have seen the National Guard as a bulwark against the take-over of the party by Ba'thist military officers. In addition, al-Sa'di aligned himself publicly with the more radical socialist tendency in the emerging struggle within the Ba'th Party in the region.

Coming to the Ba'th from a different direction, and seeing it as the vehicle for a rather different programme, were people such as Hazim Jawad and Talib Shabib (the minister of foreign affairs) who were both members of the NCRC and of the Military Bureau. Although labelled by al-Saʿdi as 'rightists', their differences were less ideological than strategic and, to some degree, personal. They had close links with the non-Baʿthist pan-Arab faction and knew the importance of maintaining that alliance, given its influence in the officer corps. They were consequently aware of the alarm caused in these circles by the increasing radicalism of al-Saʿdi and the growth of the National Guard.

In addition to these two developing factions within the civilian wing of the party, different groupings existed among the Baʿthist military officers identified, respectively, with Brigadier Ahmad Hasan al-Bakr, General Salih Mahdi ʿAmmash (minister of defence) and General Tahir Yahya (chief of the general staff). All had been members of the Free Officers' movement and had cultivated their own followings within the armed forces and the party. These were based upon their powers of patronage and, in the case of Hasan al-Bakr at least, upon common provincial backgrounds and clan relationships, rather than on any clear ideological affinities. As a group, they did not represent any very obvious tendency within the party, but as military officers they were also aware of the need for Baʿthists to co-operate with that section of the officer corps which cohered around President ʿAbd al-Salam ʿArif. As events were to show, they also had much in common with the non-Baʿthist officers in the emerging confrontation with al-Saʿdi.

These differences reached a dramatic climax due to a sequence of events which developed initially on the broader stage of the Arab world. As in 1958, so in 1963, the new regime in Baghdad was immediately faced with two questions in Arab politics which were seen by many as tests of pan-Arab commitment. The first concerned relations with the dominant figure of Nasser. Initially, the new regime proclaimed a desire for unity with Egypt. Little of substance followed, but it helped to placate the pan-Arab members of the NCRC, like ʿArif, who were admirers of Nasser. The Baʿthists themselves were more ambivalent about the Egyptian leader, given the party's experiences in Syria during the period of the UAR. Al-Saʿdi was also aware of the delicacy of the question of unification at a time when he was negotiating with the Kurds.

However, all this changed with the Baʿthist coup d'état in Syria in March. Immediately unity talks took on a momentum that the Baʿthists in Baghdad could not resist. The government entered into a tripartite commitment to unification with Egypt and Syria in April 1963, despite the fact that this complicated relations with the Kurds. More seriously for the fate of the Iraqi government, entanglement with the new regime in Damascus embroiled the Iraqis in the barely suppressed power struggle in Syria between the National Command of the Ba'th Party (personified by the party's founder-leaders Michel Aflaq and Salah al-Din al-Bitar) and the Syrian Regional Command of the Ba'th.

In Iraq this struggle polarised pro- and anti-Nasserite sentiment both within the Ba'th Party and within the pan-Arab movement more generally. In the streets of Baghdad clashes erupted between detachments of the National Guard and the Nasserite _al-Harakiyin_ (Harakat al-Qawmiyin al-'Arab, the Arab Nationalist Movement). Al-Sa'di lost his position as minister of the interior, but successfully resisted the demand from Iraq's senior military officers to dissolve the National Guard. In September 1963 he reasserted his own control of the Iraqi branch of the Ba'th Party and chose this moment to announce his support for Marxism. He may have hoped thereby to persuade the USSR to resume the military and development aid which had been suspended during the savage anti-communist campaign of 1963. It also aligned him with the radical socialist faction of the Ba'th in Syria which was in the ascendant in Damascus.

However, these developments spurred the more conservative Hazim Jawad and a number of the military Ba'thists into action. At a meeting of the Regional Congress of the Ba'th in November, they carried out a coup with the assistance of military officers and appointed a new Regional Command, headed by Jawad himself. Al-Sa'di and a number of his associates were immediately put on a plane out of the country. The National Guard came out onto the streets of Baghdad in protest and al-Wandawi led an air attack on the Rashid military base as a warning to the armed forces. This gave him control of Baghdad, but not of the country at large.

In this impasse the military Ba'thists, Hasan al-Bakr and 'Ammash, seized the initiative and invited members of the National Command to Baghdad to help sort out the internal Ba'thist conflict. The arrival of Aflaq and a number of other Syrians was not greeted with much enthusiasm and within a few days they managed to alienate Ba'thists and non-Ba'thists alike by suggesting that they would now be taking charge of Iraqi affairs. However, they lacked any executive powers and the streets continued to be controlled by the ill-disciplined members of the National Guard.

After some days of uncertainty, President 'Abd al-Salam 'Arif decided to act. On 18 November he mobilised those army units on whose loyalty he could rely through his personal and clan networks, co-ordinating his actions with the disillusioned military Ba'thists, General Tahir Yahya (chief of the general staff) and Brigadier Hardan al-Takriti (commander of the air force). 'Arif's forces then launched an attack on the National Guard in

Baghdad and throughout the country. Within hours he had established his control.

The Ba'th had demonstrated that it was less a party than a confederation of cliques. Some of these cohered for ideological reasons, some for professional reasons and some by virtue of the common origins of their members. These same reasons, which created solidarity amongst the cliques and factions within the party, also turned them against each other at critical moments. In particular, the ambiguity of factions of the party towards the primacy of the Iraqi state made them particularly suspect in the eyes of those who were more firmly rooted in the administrative apparatus of that state, particularly in the armed forces. These men found the reality of pan-Arab decision-making considerably less alluring than the ideal. Their power was framed within the military structures of the Iraqi state and founded on the hierarchies of Iraqi society that gave them an advantage. Both of these structures seemed to be under threat from the radical turn of al-Sa'di and from organisations such as the National Guard. When a coalition of factions within the armed forces acted decisively against the Ba'th Party in November 1963, it demonstrated that the key to the armed forces was still the key to power, regardless of the forms of civilian organisation that had emerged under the two preceding regimes.[8]

'ABD AL-SALAM 'ARIF: NASSERIST ASPIRATIONS AND IRAQI REALITIES

This was a lesson reinforced by the regimes of 'Abd al-Salam 'Arif and 'Abd al-Rahman 'Arif, respectively, who were to rule Iraq for the next five years. 'Abd al-Salam made it clear that he intended to monopolise power, sharing it only with those associates whom he trusted or thought worth placating. Consequently, he remained president and commander in chief of the armed forces, ruling by decree and appointing only military colleagues to the NCRC, of which he now became chairman. He formed the Republican Guard as an elite unit in the armed forces, under the command of one of his kinsmen from the tribe of the al-Jumaila, Colonel Sa'id Slaibi, who also ensured that the territory of the al-Jumaila around al-Ramadi was the principal recruiting ground for the Guard. Well armed and stationed strategically near Baghdad, this unit was intended to guard the regime against future coup attempts.

Unlike his predecessors, 'Arif had few illusions either about the strength and reliability of ideological solidarities, or about the capacity of civil organisation to match the striking power of the military, or indeed about

11 President ʿAbd al-Salam ʿArif (president 1963–6), with president Ayub Khan of
Pakistan, c. 1964

his own capacity to resist a determined conspiracy in the armed forces.
With a long history of military conspiracy behind him, ʿArif was well aware
of the importance of personal bonds of trust in establishing power. It was
this which had made him an effective and popular officer. The impetuous
streak which had become so apparent in 1958 and which had made him so

vulnerable to the more taciturn and calculating Qasim seemed to have been played out. Having helped to destroy Qasim, ʿArif seemed also to have settled to his own satisfaction at least that he alone should get the credit for the coup d'état which overthrew the monarchy.

Once installed as president of Iraq, ʿArif could begin to create a regime more in his own image, congenial therefore both to him and to those on whom he relied to maintain the security of the centre. He openly relied on established systems of patronage, kinship and tribal affiliation to cement the core of his power in the armed forces, well aware that this was also a factor in the organisation of some of the rival cliques which might in time challenge him. In the first few months following his coup, he used his knowledge of the rules of this game to dismantle the Baʿth and to compound the divisions amongst its members, removing senior military Baʿthists from positions of command and obliging Hasan al-Bakr to retire from public life.

To some degree, this led ʿArif to rely more heavily upon other pan-Arabists, many of whom strongly identified with Nasser, whom ʿArif admired, but not uncritically. What he seemed to admire most was the power of the state over which Nasser presided, regionally, but also internally. There was, of course, a world of difference between Egyptian and Iraqi societies and histories which had allowed a particular kind of state to emerge in one location, but not in another. Nevertheless, as a model of a powerful Arab state, dominating both its region and its own society, Egypt under Nasser was a seductive example for an Iraqi leader. Considerations such as these played a large part in his initial emulation of the Nasserite model. He could thereby appeal to the pan-Arab *al-Harakiyin* who saw Nasser as a champion of the Arabs, but it also allowed him to bring into the administration men who were more interested in creating a united, orderly and powerful Iraqi state. As ʿArif himself had discovered to his cost under Qasim, this was still an important trend within Iraqi political society and in the officer corps. Indeed, it was a trend that was undergoing a revival and it became increasingly important for ʿArif to encourage it.

These were the factors which led to the decrees of July 1964, nationalising banks, insurance companies and leading industrial firms. However, as the practice soon showed, Iraq was not Egypt. Most obviously, the dominant feature of Iraq's economy, accounting for about one-third of its gross domestic product, was neither agriculture nor industry, but oil. Law 80 had restricted the expansion of IPC, but could not disguise the fact that this sector of the economy was almost wholly foreign-owned. As a way of dealing with Iraq's economic problems, therefore, the nationalisation decrees were in no way comparable to the Egyptian ones, nor did they really address the fundamental structural features of the economy. They seemed to have been principally a way of expressing a desire to emulate Egypt, as well as to signal solidarity with the Egyptian political leadership. In this way, the measures appealed to the 'Iraq first' trend which wanted to build a stronger, more unified state in Iraq, as well as to the pan-Arabists and Nasserists who still looked to the possibility of the unification of the Arab world.

At the time, the latter trend seemed to be in the ascendant. In May 1964 a provisional constitution was promulgated which asserted the Arab character of 'the Iraqi people' and which stressed the aim of Arab unity. It was followed by a preliminary accord on the future unification of Iraq and Egypt. The wording of the accord betrayed the caution of both 'Arif and Nasser, neither of whom were great enthusiasts for the kind of hasty unification which had proved so disastrous in the case of the UAR. Nevertheless, the Nasserists and other pan-Arabists in Iraq took heart and seemed confident that the tide was moving in their direction. Consequently, the nationalisation decrees of July, accompanied by 'Arif's declaration that he was going to establish a political party on the lines of Egypt's Arab Socialist Union, seemed to the Nasserists to be part of a logical progression, bringing Iraq's institutions into line with those of Egypt prior to a genuine merger of the two countries.

The reality of Iraq seen from 'Arif's perspective was very different. He may have briefly entertained the idea that, by creating similar institutions, Iraq would be transformed into a country of Egypt's solidity and homogeneity, but he cannot have believed this for long. The continuing problem of the Kurds, manifested in the renewal of sporadic fighting in the north in the summer of 1964, was one reminder of the vast difference between Iraq and Egypt. 'Arif had announced in the wake of his coup d'état that he wanted to end the war in Kurdistan by peaceful means and had entered into secret negotiations with Barzani. This had resulted in a cease-fire agreement in February 1964, but the politburo of the KDP, led by Jalal Talabani and Ibrahim Ahmad, had not been consulted and denounced the agreement. However, the strength of Barzani's forces on the ground told in his favour. He summoned his own congress of the KDP which endorsed the cease-fire and expelled the dissident members of the politburo and their following. They had little option but to flee across the border into Iran.

The split in Kurdish ranks and Barzani's dominance may have led 'Arif to believe that he had secured peace in the north. However, he reckoned without Barzani's determination to establish his credentials as a genuine national leader of the Kurds, campaigning for national self-determination. Barzani was apprehensive of the Iraqi army's redeployment under the cover of the cease-fire and he rejected Baghdad's demand that his own forces be disbanded. Against this background it was inevitable that 'Arif's accord with Nasser and other indications of 'Arif's commitment to Arab unification should have heightened tensions. Clashes erupted, despite assertions that the cease-fire was still holding and despite intermittent negotiations between Barzani and 'Arif. These events made it clear to 'Arif that unification with Egypt, if seriously pursued, would increase the gulf between Baghdad and the Kurdish leadership. It was also clear that the socialist decrees of July 1964 were as alarming for Barzani and his tribal allies as had been the KDP politburo's radical programme. Emulation of Nasser's Egypt would therefore carry a high price in Kurdistan. In some respects this epitomised much that was different between the two countries.

Protests against these same socialist measures also came from Islamic circles and associations in Iraq, both Sunni and Shi'i, indicating another important difference between Nasser as president of Egypt and 'Arif as president of Iraq. 'Arif had done much to promote himself as a pious Muslim, concerned about the place of Islam in public life. In 1963 he had been instrumental in the repeal of legislation which the Islamic authorities had asserted went contrary to the *Shari'a* and in 1964 he brought in a number of ordinances enforcing stricter public observance of Islam. He did not, however, exercise the kind of control over an Islamic establishment which Nasser enjoyed in Egypt. The revival of Islamic organisations amongst the majority Shi'i community added to the sense of the independence of the *'Atabat* and their *mujtahids* from regimes such as his. They condemned the socialist decrees of July 1964 as they had the land reform measures under Qasim, indicting them as violations of the principle of private property and contrary to the *Shari'a*. 'Arif established a special security unit to monitor the increasingly critical and proliferating Shi'i organisations, but police methods could not curb their influence or that of the senior *mujtahids*. Nor could the *mujtahids* be persuaded to endorse the socialist policies of the government, as the Egyptian *'ulama* had done.

When a Ba'thist plot to overthrow 'Arif was discovered in the armed forces in September 1964, 'Arif was grateful for Nasser's support which included the despatch of Egyptian troops to Iraq. Nasserists were publicly rewarded with additional seats in the cabinet and in December a 'unified political command' was established between Egypt and Iraq, ostensibly to bring the prospect of unification one step closer. However, there was an air of unreality to these moves, since they seemed to accord neither with Nasser's nor with 'Arif's wishes. Both leaders were content to encourage the idea of unification since it seemed to promote the pan-Arab image that was so much part of the legitimation strategies of both men, although in different ways. Concrete rather than symbolic moves in the direction of unity, however, were another matter. Nasser was profoundly cautious about linking the fate of Egypt and his own credibility to a polity so manifestly disturbed and unstable as that of Iraq. For his part, 'Arif was equally cautious about unification since it would have undermined his own position and would have ensured the dominance of the small Nasserist faction in Iraq.

The Iraqi Nasserists were without a significant popular following, depending instead upon the patronage of Nasser himself, as well as of 'Arif, and upon their networks in the officer corps and in the state administration. As with the Ba'thists, the people who chose to identify themselves as Nasserist did not represent a cohesive bloc. Nasserism itself was as ill-defined as Ba'thism and represented instead an amalgam of sentiments focused on Arab nationalism, state socialist development and 'third worldism'. Those who adhered to the Nasserist tendency in Iraq, therefore, were heterogeneous and it was difficult to separate their ideological positions from their personal or factional political ambitions. This, in turn, situated them in the world of Iraqi factional politics, providing them with allies at certain times, but also furnishing them with enemies who distrusted their patrons and their networks of influence as much as they distrusted their policies.

By the winter of 1964–5 the adverse effects of 'Nasserist' policies were becoming apparent in Iraq. Serious fighting had once again broken out in Kurdistan, leading to a temporary reconciliation between Barzani and the KDP politburo. Both factions saw little point in negotiating with a government apparently intent on Arab unity and on submerging the Kurds in the Arab identity of the state. At the same time, the nationalisation measures of the summer of 1964 seemed to be taking their toll on the economy. The flight of capital had accelerated, unemployment had risen sharply and the prospect of land sequestration discouraged investment in agriculture. Meanwhile, negotiations had opened with IPC to try to reach a settlement of outstanding issues and to remedy some of Law 80's negative effects on government revenues. In this context, Nasserist influence was inhibiting any settlement since the Nasserists' instinct was to bring the oil industry and foreign trade in general under more stringent state control.[9]

PATRIMONIALISM AND THE RULE OF THE CLAN

'Arif, confident about the waning of the Ba'thist threat, was determined to free his hands to rule Iraq in accordance with his own political instincts, suggesting a less doctrinaire, more patrimonial form of government. For this he needed to placate the economically conservative, as well as the religiously conservative, sections of society. In many respects, this was a return to the policy adopted under the monarchy. Tribal shaikhs in the countryside, propertied and entrepreneurial elements in the towns and religious dignitaries were all incorporated into a web of patron–client relations, eased by the revenues available to the central government through the export of oil. This provided opportunities and rewards for those whom the government patronised, but it also meant moving against Nasserist influence on a number of fronts.

Blocking the Nasserist plan to increase restrictions on foreign trade, the government reached an agreement with IPC in June 1965. This ensured an immediate increase in government revenues, but restored IPC's right of access, now in conjunction with INOC (the Iraqi National Oil Company, founded in February 1964), to most of the territories from which it had been excluded by Law 80. For the Nasserists, this meant a return to a position in which IPC, having successfully resisted equity participation by the Iraqi government, could once again determine Iraqi production levels and thus the revenues of the Iraqi state on the basis of its own interests, not those of Iraq. In reaction, the six Nasserist ministers resigned in July 1965 and organised a strong campaign of protest against the draft agreement with IPC, effectively making it a dead letter. On this issue 'Arif had to move carefully, since the controversial nature of any agreement with IPC could give Iraqi nationalists and Nasserists common cause.

For the Nasserist factions it seemed that 'Arif was on the verge of abandoning both pan-Arabism and the socialist measures which they believed were imperative for the development of the Iraqi economy and state. These factions were still well represented in the officer corps and – together with the upheavals over the oil agreement – this may account for 'Arif's surprise appointment of one of the most senior military Nasserists, Brigadier 'Arif 'Abd al-Razzaq, as prime minister and minister of defence in September 1965. By appointing him to so senior a position, 'Arif seemed to be placating the Nasserists. However, he was also placing them in the position of having to take responsibility for the war in Kurdistan – perhaps hoping to impress upon 'Abd al-Razzaq and his associates the complexities of a situation that could only be exacerbated by appeals to pan-Arabism.

Full-scale military operations in the Kurdish region had resumed in March 1965 with an Iraqi government offensive which brought together the two factions of the KDP. However, the Iraqi forces had only limited success. In many areas that the Iraqi government nominally controlled, the KDP was able to operate with relative impunity, whilst in other areas there was not even a semblance of Iraqi government control. In order to remedy the government's military weakness, 'Arif had tried once more to drive a wedge between Barzani and the forces of the KDP politburo. However, the military stalemate continued.

In any event, the impatience of 'Abd al-Razzaq and the Nasserists got the better of them and they seized the opportunity of 'Arif's absence from Iraq in September 1965 to launch a coup. It was foiled by Brigadier Slaibi, the commander of the Republican Guard, causing 'Abd al-Razzaq and his colleagues to flee the country and opening the way for 'Arif to make a complete break with the Nasserists. Having himself started as a pan-Arabist, 'Arif had moved increasingly towards an 'Iraq first' position, tutored in its requirements by the experience of governing a country where the pan-Arab idea could seriously alarm significant sections of the population. The logic of the territorial state was thereby overriding the logic of the confessional, ethnic make-up of the society, in which some Sunni Arabs tended to see pan-Arabism as the sole way of restoring their 'wholeness' and their majority status. The irony and the danger was that this same ethnic community – and the corresponding sentiments – were heavily overrepresented in the most powerful agency of that same state, the armed forces.

'Arif signalled the change in direction by appointing as prime minister 'Abd al-Rahman al-Bazzaz, a lawyer and academic of largely conservative inclinations. Although he was an Arab nationalist ideologue with pretensions to being a major theorist of Arab nationalism, he had no links to any political party or to any of the army factions. The power of the latter had in any case been largely eclipsed, due to the succession of attempted coups and purges which had weeded out Ba'thists, Nasserists, communists and others. Officers had instead tended to move into 'Arif's personal orbit, becoming his clients and followers in an extensive network which 'Arif showed great skill in constructing. 'Arif was secure in the knowledge that the Republican Guard formed a strong deterrent to any coup attempt, since he knew that the tribal affiliation of most of the Guard bound them to him personally in a way which eluded many of the ideological factions. The Guard supported him not because of any political programme, but simply for who he was, a member of their own clan, the al-Jumaila, and thus someone who deserved their support more than any of the other military contenders in the officer corps. In return, 'Arif could be expected to fulfil the reciprocal obligations of clan membership by ensuring that they received privileged treatment and special access to resources.

'Arif had thereby succeeded in effectively linking two aspects of patrimonial power long evident in Iraqi politics: he had established a network of clients within the armed forces, many of whose members were also bound to him by other links of affiliation and obligation arising from the structures of Iraqi provincial society. Their support for 'Arif was not unconditional, but depended upon his abiding by certain rules under which most others, by virtue of their identity, were unable to compete. The rules of this game and the reservoir of support it created were as restrictive as anything which had been established under the Hashemite monarchy. However, 'Arif's mastery of the game, as well as the security of the base which it provided, gave him a latitude to act which far exceeded that of previous leaders of Iraq.

This was the background to the appointment of al-Bazzaz, the first civilian to hold the office of prime minister since the overthrow of the monarchy. Reinforcing the impression that a new era of more open government would be introduced, the NCRC was abolished and legislative power was transferred to the cabinet. Al-Bazzaz promised to end the arrest of political opponents and to give people greater opportunity for political expression, hinting that political parties would be licensed once more, parliament revived and elections held. At the same time, al-Bazzaz announced an end to the nationalisations and introduced a number of measures designed to restore business confidence and to give encouragement to private enterprise. Although he did not attempt to reverse the sequestration process, he did seek to ensure that compensation payments to owners and landlords would be increased. Under the slogan 'prudent socialism' he tried to oversee the establishment of an effective mixed economy in Iraq.

This was to be something of an uphill struggle, given the structural problems of the economy and the continued uncertainty of the political background. Those industries which had been nationalised showed a much lower rate of growth after 1964 and, although the surviving private sector operated efficiently enough, there was a marked lack of enthusiasm for substantial capital investment. Consequently, in this sector too, rates of growth slowed down, since potential investors were well aware of the continued Nasserist and socialist inclinations of members of the state administration, as well as of a number of army factions. In the much larger agricultural sector, similar uncertainties and changing government priorities had led to a sharp falling off of investment during the previous few years. When combined with a series of natural disasters, such as droughts, pests and other seasonal hazards, this had led to a constant decline in agricultural productivity since 1958. By the 1960s Iraq was importing substantial amounts of food grains when it should, in theory, have been a net exporter. Indeed, the condition of the peasantry in rural Iraq, especially in the south, and the perceived benefits of living in Baghdad, in particular, where the bulk of government investment seemed to be concentrated, accelerated the migration to the cities visible in most developing countries. This compounded agricultural productivity problems and placed a growing burden on the government's housing and social welfare provision.[10]

Nevertheless, even though faced with problems of this magnitude, al-Bazzaz became the focus and symbol of many hopes in Iraq. For some, he represented a return to the rule of law and to a modicum of political civility, lost in the turbulent events of the preceding years. For others, he was associated with a more liberal economic policy, favouring established property owners and willing to contemplate the re-emergence of a political order based on hierarchies of wealth, albeit different from that under the monarchy. These features also meant that he was associated with the idea that the government of Iraq could return to the hands of the civilians and that the military would be obliged to return to their professional role as the guardians of a civil polity. This notion gained al-Bazzaz supporters and critics in equal measure, if in very different locations, but was in fact the precise opposite of the situation in Iraq. The polity was still dominated by military officers in the shape of 'Arif and the National Defence Council. This had been established upon the demise of the NCRC to ensure that the voice of the military remained pre-eminent in the direction of the Iraqi state. Al-Bazzaz was able to operate as he did only because of the protection afforded him by the patronage of 'Arif. He and some of his supporters, enjoying the apparent licence which 'Arif's protection gave them, began to lose sight of the nature of their dependency and tried to live up to some of the hopes reposing in them. As a result, they became vulnerable to their enemies in the officer corps.

'ABD AL-RAHMAN 'ARIF: A WEAKENING HOLD ON POWER

The dependency and relative weakness of those who had relied solely on the personal patronage of 'Abd al-Salam 'Arif were amply demonstrated in the aftermath of his sudden death in a helicopter crash in April 1966. This appears to have been a genuine accident. There was no opposing faction ready to exploit the situation, but it demonstrated one of the fundamental weaknesses of the patrimonial system. All the lines of patronage, the networks of reciprocal obligation and the informal understandings and loyalties had been drawn into one pair of hands, embodying a key relationship on which the stability of the polity largely depended. It could not be assumed that this would be reproduced by a successor. In the immediate aftermath of 'Arif's death, the feelings of obligation which had tied so many of his colleagues to 'Arif in life nevertheless survived, leading to the election of his brother, General 'Abd al-Rahman 'Arif, the acting chief of staff of the Iraqi army, to the presidency by a joint session of the National Defence Council and the cabinet.

Al-Bazzaz was reappointed prime minister by the new president, who tried to rule much as his brother had done. However, his touch was less sure and the unspoken ties which had been so effective in forming networks of loyalty around 'Abd al-Salam were largely absent in the case of 'Abd al-Rahman. He still relied on the Republican Guard as the guarantor of his rule in the last resort, but his relationship with its officers was not as intimate or as effective as his brother's had been. Nor was he as adept at reinforcing the many ties of mutual obligation that needed to be constantly serviced in order to bind the Guard more firmly to his person. Instead, he took the loyalties of the al-Jumaila largely for granted, leaving it to others to organise the units on his behalf, but failing to integrate them into his circle of intimates as effectively as his brother had. The result of this subtly different relationship with key elements in the officer corps meant that he was less able to keep the factionalism of the officers in check or to use it skilfully for his own purposes. It also meant that he could not protect the civilian government from the mounting hostility to al-Bazzaz in the officer corps.

In the aftermath of 'Abd al-Salam 'Arif's death, the officers' enmity revolved around two issues which touched both on their professional interests and on their accustomed role as political arbiters in Iraqi politics. The first issue concerned the defence budget. Al-Bazzaz and his fellow technocrats wanted to regenerate Iraq's economy by using the very substantial oil revenues of the state, and resented the large proportion of these revenues devoted to the armed forces. It was not long therefore before they proposed a reduction in the defence budget. These moves alarmed the officers, since they feared the implications for the privileges they had so long enjoyed, and they used the pretext of the continuing war with the Kurds as a reason for maintaining existing levels of military expenditure.

It was difficult for al-Bazzaz to argue with this, just as he could have little say in the conduct of the campaign against Barzani's forces. This was regarded as a preserve of the military. For the senior officers the military campaign was part of their professional identity, affecting their personal

12 President 'Abd al-Rahman 'Arif (president 1966–8), 1968

honour, as well as the prestige and ultimately the political role of the Iraqi
armed forces themselves. However, following 'Abd al-Salam 'Arif's death,
al-Bazzaz formed a new cabinet in which he was able to dilute the hard-
line militarist element. This allowed him to contact Barzani and to arrange
a cease-fire when, in May 1966, the Iraqi army and its Kurdish allies
suffered a series of defeats at the hands of Barzani's *peshmerga*. Pressing
home his advantage and playing on the temporary eclipse of the officer
corps, al-Bazzaz announced that he was willing to recognise the force of
Kurdish nationalism and the national rights of the Kurds. As an Arab
nationalist, he even professed a certain respect for Kurdish nationalism,
helping to overcome some of the suspicion with which Kurdish leaders had
always regarded the Arab nationalism of the Iraqi elite. This opened the
way for negotiations between Barzani and the government which was

already holding discussions with Jalal Talabani and the politburo of the KDP.

The result was al-Bazzaz's declaration at the end of June 1966 in which he publicly offered the Kurds a twelve-point programme recognising the bi-national character of the Iraqi state and thus the Kurds' particular cultural and linguistic identity. Furthermore, it promised full representation and self-government to the Kurds within the framework of a parliamentary democracy in Iraq. It did not meet all of the Kurds' demands, but offered more than any previous Iraqi government had done. When taken in conjunction with a number of secret clauses, covering such issues as the territorial extent of the Kurdish province and the legalisation of the KDP, the programme was accepted by Barzani as the basis for a settlement.

However, many officers were becoming seriously alarmed at the course of events. Some opposed any concessions which seemed to derive from military defeat, because of the implications for the prestige of the armed forces. Others were wary of any concession to the principle of Kurdish national self-determination. There was also a fear that peace on these terms would remove the justification for current military expenditure and open the way for al-Bazzaz to cut the military budget. In addition, the prospect of the imminent reintroduction of a parliamentary system alarmed many. By August 1966 such hostility had built up in the officer corps that 'Abd al-Rahman 'Arif felt obliged to dismiss al-Bazzaz, replacing him with a former member of the Free Officers, Naji Talib, who promptly formed a cabinet in which military officers held most of the principal portfolios. Negotiations with Barzani were broken off and the situation in Kurdistan returned to a wary armed truce in which the Iraqi army could achieve little.[11]

'Arif had shown his weakness vis-à-vis the officer corps and his inability to reconstitute effectively the patronage networks that had given his brother an impressive degree of control. Such is the nature of patrimonial politics that factions proliferated, looking not towards 'Arif, but towards other figures of authority keen to make a following for themselves in the armed forces. Naji Talib himself was undermined by the factionalism of the officer corps. Nor did 'Arif solve these problems by taking over the premiership himself in May 1967, filling his cabinet with military officers from virtually all the major factions in the armed forces.

Before any new direction became clear, Iraq and the rest of the Middle East were caught up in the dramatic events of the June 1967 war with Israel. The speed and the scale of the Israeli victory allowed for very little Iraqi participation, despite the bellicose rhetoric of the regime and the official media. Instead, a token Iraqi force was sent to Jordan, but arrived too late to have an impact on the outcome of the fighting. Iraq was not a front-line state and suffered little as a result of the war, but the defeat threw into question the credibility of the successive military regimes which had ruled the country since 1958. This did not prevent 'Arif from appointing yet another military officer, Tahir Yahya, as prime minister in July 1967.

However, this ensured a continued military stand-off in Kurdistan and the absence of any significant effort at negotiation. In the southern regions of the mid-Euphrates and the marshes, the emergence of the revolutionary movement of 'Aziz al-Hajj's Communist Party (Central Command) in the autumn of 1967 led to a series of armed clashes with the security forces. Al-Hajj's split from the mainstream Communist Party (Central Committee), led by 'Aziz Muhammad, had spurred the dormant party into greater activity and it adopted a more hostile attitude to the 'Arif regime. This earned it both the displeasure of the USSR and the close and unwelcome attentions of the government's security forces.[12]

Tahir Yahya's government relied on a variety of factions in the officer corps and the line it took was typical of the period following the June war elsewhere in the Arab world: relations were broken off with the United States and the UK, and closer links were established both with the USSR and with France. These countries were to play important roles in helping Iraq to develop the new oil fields which were designated for exploitation by the increasingly active INOC. No move was made to nationalise IPC, but it was clear that its role was to be restricted relative to that of INOC which entered into an agreement with a French group of companies to exploit areas from which IPC had been excluded. Some saw this as the assertion of Iraq's own control of the foundation of its economy and Yahya's prestige rose accordingly. For others, however, Yahya was too cautious and gave the impression that Iraq was still overanxious to placate foreign interests.

It was at this point that some of Tahir Yahya's enemies began to exploit the clear military weakness of the Iraqi armed forces in Kurdistan and the sense of communist threat caused by 'Aziz al-Hajj's activities in the south. The latter were not particularly serious, but they revived old fears of the power of clandestine communism. This provoked a vocal public response from established Islamic clerics and from Sunni and Shi'i Islamic organisations, some of which had been receiving tacit official backing. Street demonstrations were organised in Baghdad and elsewhere, calling on the government to 'save' the country from the imminent danger of unbelief. The Ba'th Party seized this opportunity to revive its public fortunes by associating itself with these demonstrations, profiting as it had done in the past from the panic created by public fear of a communist threat.

The Baʿth Party had undergone a number of changes since its ejection from power. In 1964 al-Saʿdi and many of his associates were expelled from the party and the remaining members of the Military Bureau, dominated by Ahmad Hasan al-Bakr, took over the leadership. In the summer of 1964 Hasan al-Bakr had appointed his young relative, Saddam Husain, as secretary to the reconstituted Regional Command, and had entrusted him with the task of reconstructing the party, helped by a number of his kinsmen and associates from the time of Baʿthist opposition to Qasim. A Baʿthist coup attempt in the autumn of 1964 swept up large numbers of party activists, including Hasan al-Bakr and Saddam Husain, who was to remain in prison until 1966. However, it did not greatly hamper the process of clandestine recruitment and the establishment of cells within the army, as well as in the country at large. Furthermore, the experience of prison created a certain solidarity between Saddam Husain and some of his fellow prisoners which was to serve him well in the future.

Under ʿAbd al-Rahman ʿArif the campaign against the Baʿthists lessened. He may have thought the Baʿth a spent force. Equally, he may simply have been unable to check the proliferation of factions within the officer corps, of which Hasan al-Bakr's nominally Baʿthist following was one. In any event, a number of Baʿthists were released from prison and were drawn into Saddam Husain's expanding organisation. Hasan al-Bakr had rewarded his kinsman by appointing him deputy secretary-general of the Regional Command of the Baʿth in Iraq in the autumn of 1966, and from this position Saddam Husain was instrumental in laying the groundwork for the party's militia and for the organisation that would help to give the impression once again of Baʿthist control of the streets. In the turbulent days following the June war of 1967, when demonstrations and marches took place in Baghdad and other Iraqi towns, Saddam Husain had plenty of opportunity to extend the party's organisation. This enabled the Baʿthists to come out in strength later in 1967 against the alleged 'communist threat' and then, more directly, against the government of Tahir Yahya itself, attacking its inactivity on the Arab–Israel issue and the corruption of its members.

Such was the atmosphere of crisis to which the Baʿthists helped to contribute that ʿArif considered replacing Tahir Yahya. Having no significant following of his own in the officer corps that could be expected to cohere around a prime minister of his own choosing, ʿArif, in early 1968, consulted a range of senior figures in the armed forces and amongst those who had served in government. This included members of the Baʿth, as well as of various other factions, but the results were inconclusive. ʿArif soon discovered that there was no consensus either on the composition of a new government or on the direction of the country as a whole. On the contrary, scenting weakness and an imminent change in personnel at the top, the animosities of various factions intensified and their demands became more exacting. This led 'Arif to break off his discussions. Some of his interlocutors, including Hasan al-Bakr and the other Ba'thists, followed this up with a petition calling upon 'Arif to form a government of 'national unity', although without apparent irony.

By this stage, however, the Ba'thist Military Bureau and Regional Command had begun laying plans for the installation of a Ba'thist regime once again. As with the coup of 1963, they realised that they needed allies in the officer corps, especially if the Republican Guard were to be neutralised. Contacts were established with a number of senior officers close to the heart of the regime who had become disillusioned with 'Arif or were disappointed in his patronage. The three key officers were all trusted by both 'Arif and Slaibi: 'Abd al-Razzaq al-Nayif (a cousin of Slaibi) was in charge of military intelligence, Ibrahim 'Abd al-Rahman al-Dawud headed the Republican Guard and Sa'dun Ghaidan commanded the Republican Guard's tank regiment. Consequently, they were all well placed to carry out decisive action, but had only a limited following in the armed forces. It was for this reason that they looked to the Ba'thists, believing that they could provide enough support to ensure the docility of the rest of the armed forces when they carried out their coup.

On 17 July 1968, seizing the opportunity of Brigadier Slaibi's absence, the three key officers and their Ba'thist allies acted, seizing Broadcasting House, the Ministry of Defence and the headquarters of the Republican Guard. The prime minister and much of his cabinet were arrested and President 'Arif was put on a plane out of the country. A new regime was formed with Hasan al-Bakr as president and al-Nayif as prime minister, assisted by al-Dawud as minister of defence and the Ba'thist Salih Mahdi 'Ammash as minister of interior. In the armed forces, the Ba'thist Hardan al-Takriti was appointed chief of staff and commander of the air force, but was balanced by Sa'dun Ghaidan as commander of the Republican Guard. In the cabinet a number of portfolios were assigned to Ba'thists, but the majority went to protégés of the three non-Ba'thist leaders of the coup or to representatives of a range of diverse opinion in Iraq, including the leader of the Muslim Brotherhood and four Kurds, one of them acting for Barzani.

The relationship between the Ba'thist and non-Ba'thist elements was a difficult one since neither group wanted to share power. Hardan al-Takriti immediately set about strengthening his hold on the armed forces, in part to pre-empt the minister of defence's attempts to strengthen his own following. However, it was clear that the Ba'thists would eventually lose ground to the overwhelming majority of non-Ba'thists in the officer corps. As a result, they decided to act without delay. Persuading Sa'dun Ghaidan to join them, Hasan al-Bakr and Hardan al-Takriti succeeded in neutralising the Republican Guard. At the same time, they won over the commander of the Baghdad garrison, Hammad Shihab al-Takriti, who was not a Ba'thist but was a tribal kinsman of Hasan al-Bakr. When al-Dawud left the country on a visit to Jordan, the Ba'thists struck. On 30 July an armoured brigade seized the strategic buildings in Baghdad, and al-Nayif, like 'Arif before him, was put on a plane out of the country. The Ba'thists had returned to power.

For all the turbulence of Iraqi politics during the previous decade, some features had remained remarkably constant. The Iraqi people as a whole continued to be denied representation and thus the passing array of military rulers had felt no need to account for their actions beyond the small coterie whom they felt could materially affect their survival. The logic of this process was to place a premium on conspiracy and on personal leadership and trust. Where attempts had been made to break out of this framework and to establish more participatory and consensual forms of political activity, as in the early years of Qasim's rule, or as promised by al-Bazzaz's brief tenure of the premiership, the ruler himself or those on whom he relied for his survival took fright and brought the experiment to an abrupt end.

This reinforced the tendency to look upon the state primarily as an instrument of power, in the service of those who had seized command at the centre. Whatever their larger visions happened to be, whether of economic and social reform, the orientation of Iraq towards a pan-Arab mission or the attempt to build an Iraqi national community, those in command became preoccupied with managing the resources that would allow them to service their patronage networks and the coercive apparatus that guaranteed their tenure of power. In these calculations, it was inevitable that the already powerful and influential sectors of society should have received greatest attention. The voiceless and the powerless were included in the rhetoric, but excluded from calculations of political advantage and thus from playing any significant role in a narrative dominated by those who enjoyed the privilege, often historically established, of close association with the centre of the administrative state.

CHAPTER 6

The Ba'th and the rule of Saddam Husain
1968–2003

The regime established in the summer of 1968 was nominally Ba'thist, but, as subsequent events were to show, this did not mean that the men at the centre could be defined simply with reference to their membership of the party. This was but one identity amongst many and only partially influenced their ideas of Iraq and their methods of operating in Iraqi politics. Equally important was the fact that most of the chief figures of the new regime were army officers. This not only shaped their conduct and their views of the proper ordering of politics, but also ensured their connection to the social networks which had historically provided an important recruiting ground for the officer corps. These groupings, composed of the extended families, clans and tribal networks from the provincial Sunni Arab north-west of Iraq, were disproportionately represented in the new regime. Their codes, status distinctions, insecurities and solidarities formed yet another central influence on the outlook and methods of the men who seized power in 1968.

One consequence of this multitude of influences was the dilution, as under the previous regime of the 'Arifs, of their commitment to pan-Arabism. Arab nationalist rhetoric certainly formed part of their official credo and was adhered to as an ideal by a considerable number of Ba'thists and others in Iraq. However, the men in command showed themselves to be as jealous of Iraqi sovereignty and thus preoccupied with the organisation of power within the territorial state as had any of their predecessors. With the great increase in the government's revenues after the oil price rises of the 1970s, the trend of placing Iraq first was ever more marked. The Arab world came to be seen by the regime as a stage on which Iraq could assert its own primacy and thereby the supremacy of the leader of Iraq, adding to the stature of the dominant figure of Saddam Husain.

The emergence of Saddam Husain and his construction of a dictatorship demanding obedience and using violence on a scale unmatched in Iraq's history were the dominant themes of the politics of this period. The factors which made it possible, as well as its consequences for Iraq's political life, did not suggest a radical break with the past. On the contrary, the methods Saddam Husain used, some of the values he espoused and the political logic of the system that he established in Iraq were all prefigured in previous regimes to varying degrees. Indeed, in many ways they epitomised some of the distinctive characteristics of the Iraqi state itself, as process and as structure. It could be argued that had this not been the case, had the regime not rooted itself in important social networks and had it not taken account of the associated expectations, its power would have been much more limited, whatever the ambitions of its leader.

Equally, it is doubtful that it could have survived for so long the devastating experiences which it was largely responsible for bringing down on the Iraqi people during the last two decades of the twentieth century. This is not to say that Saddam Husain was the necessary outcome of Iraqi history, as he himself would have argued. Nor were the peculiarities of his regime determined in some inescapable way by what had gone before. Rather, Saddam Husain and his dictatorship were the manifestations of a particularly potent narrative in the history of the Iraqi state – one in which exclusivity, communal mistrust, patronage and the exemplary use of violence were the main elements, woven into a system of dependence on and conformity with the will of a small number of men at the centre in the name of social discipline and national destiny. It is important, therefore, to understand not only the constituents of this narrative, but also the circumstances which allowed it, rather than a number of alternatives, to become the force that shaped Iraqi politics in the late twentieth century.

AHMAD HASAN AL-BAKR AND THE CONSOLIDATION OF POWER

Having disposed of the allies who had helped them seize power, Ahmad Hasan al-Bakr, Hardan al-Takriti and Salih Mahdi 'Ammash each tried to enlarge their personal followings at the expense of the other two. Hasan al-Bakr was well placed to emerge triumphant. As president of Iraq, prime minister, chairman of the RCC and secretary-general of the Ba'th Party he had immense powers of patronage at his disposal. He used these to advantage, especially in the armed forces where he had followers not simply amongst Ba'thists, but also in the officer corps more generally. Hasan al-Bakr was in many ways a typical regimental officer, solicitous of the welfare of his subordinates and able to use the language of military collegiality to create a certain bond with fellow officers. Despite the radical Ba'thist rhetoric that he used when occasion demanded, his views were

13 President Ahmad Hasan al-Bakr (president 1968–79), c. 1970

conservative and rather typical of his provincial background: pan-Arab to some degree, but also imbued with a keen awareness of status distinctions between different lineages and clans among the Sunni Arabs which he, along with the greater part of the officer corps, saw as distinct from and superior to the Shi'i Arabs and Kurds of Iraq.

Assisted by his kinsman Saddam Husain, Hasan al-Bakr also dominated the party and the key intelligence services: the party's special security apparatus (al-Jihaz al-Khass) and the presidential security service, as well as the state public security service (al-Amn al-'Am) where Saddam Husain's protégé Nadhim Kazzar was in charge. As a civilian, familiar with the Ba'thist underground and with the urban landscape of Baghdad, Saddam Husain ensured control of the streets through an expanded party militia, intimidating potential opponents and giving the impression of mass support for the new regime. Old scores were settled as a large number of arrests were carried out in the autumn of 1968, rounding up communists, Nasserists, dissident Ba'thists, former politicians, Western-oriented businessmen and others. Simultaneously, purges in the civil service and the officer corps took place against a background of manufactured spy scares and alleged coup plots. Members of Iraq's small Jewish community, amongst others, were accused of spying for Israel or of acting as agents for the shah of Iran, and the sense of crisis was heightened by dramatic televised trials and public hangings in Baghdad.

Most apprehensive of the new regime were the communists, whose memories of the Ba'thist repression of 1963 were still fresh. Surprisingly, Hasan al-Bakr offered them a number of cabinet posts in August 1968. The ICP leadership declined the offer and the party paid the price in a systematic campaign of arrests, torture and imprisonment. This began a curious game whereby the government alternately persecuted and courted the party until finally, in 1972–3, Hasan al-Bakr succeeded in drawing the ICP into the National Patriotic Front. Hasan al-Bakr and Saddam Husain's approaches to the ICP had a number of motives. Initially, there was some idea of ingratiating the new regime with the USSR, Iraq's major arms supplier and aid donor. They also wanted to encourage splits in the ICP itself. Equally important, they wanted to discover the strength of the communist movement in Iraq. The security forces made short work of 'Aziz al-Hajj and his breakaway Communist Party (Central Command) when it launched a 'popular revolutionary war' with raids on police posts and banks in late 1968. By April 1969 al-Hajj and most of his group had been captured and al-Hajj himself had publicly recanted. However, for the Ba'thists communism had taken on mythic aspects, giving an exaggerated impression of the ICP's strength. By luring the party out into the open, Hasan al-Bakr hoped that the ICP would make itself as vulnerable as it had been under Qasim, facilitating the regime's eventual eradication of the movement.

Hasan al-Bakr and Saddam Husain were also concerned about those Ba'thists who, although hostile to the ICP itself, were nevertheless sympathetic to some of its ideas and closer to the radical trend of the Ba'thist regime in Syria under Salah Jadid. These party ideologues posed a danger to Hasan al-Bakr and Saddam Husain since they constituted a reservoir of support for the ideas which had so weakened the party in 1963 and implicitly challenged Saddam Husain's growing domination of both the apparatus and the legitimating language of Ba'thism. This threat haunted the first years of the new regime's existence and did not finally disappear until Saddam Husain had ensured that the party lost any kind of existence independent of the direction which he himself was to give it.

At this stage, powerful as he was in the party, Saddam Husain was not yet in a position to neutralise it as a site of factional dispute and potential threat. Indeed, as the 7th Ba'th Party Regional Congress of early 1969 demonstrated, he and Hasan al-Bakr needed to retain the support of a fairly wide range of tendencies within the party. The more pressing struggle of the moment was with 'Ammash and Hardan al-Takriti whose networks within the armed forces constituted the greater immediate threat. Consequently, the 'left' of the party, as well as the ICP, were encouraged to come out into the open. The language of the 7th Congress was that of radical socialism, with much emphasis on workers' and peasants' rights, and talk of further land reform and the collectivisation of agriculture, as well as of the need to implement a more thoroughgoing socialism in Iraq. Simultaneously, appointments to the Regional Command of the party suggested greater weight for the leftist trend, represented primarily by 'Abd al-Khaliq al-Samarrai, who saw the party as a vehicle for socialist transformation.

There were, however, others rising to prominence, such as Taha Yasin Ramadhan al-Jazrawi and 'Izzat Ibrahim al-Duri, who were close associates of Saddam Husain with no known affiliation in the party other than to him. Their role and importance increased with their appointment to the RCC in November 1969. At the same time Saddam Husain was appointed vice-chairman of the RCC, arguably the second most powerful office in the state. This signalled the decline in the fortunes of Hardan al-Takriti and 'Ammash. Hardan al-Takriti, in particular, was dangerous. As minister of defence and deputy commander in chief he had been trying to insert his men into key positions, relying on clans from Takrit, as well as on others from the Sunni Arab north-west. However, here he came up against other Takritis, as well as the clans from Mosul, Samarra and al-Ramadi which Hasan al-Bakr was cultivating in order to remove any lingering influence of the 'Arif brothers.

This contest was largely hidden from the general public. Occasionally, some event sent out a signal, particularly to the officer corps, about the relative fortunes of the various factions. This led, in turn, to defections, diminishing the influence of perceived losers and providing Hasan al-Bakr and Saddam Husain with further opportunities. During 1970 Hardan and 'Ammash were both dismissed from their ministerial posts, leading to the exile of Hardan al-Takriti and his eventual murder in Kuwait in March 1971. 'Ammash escaped this fate and was merely dropped from the RCC and the Regional Command of the Ba'th, stripped of his title of vice-president and sent off as ambassador to the USSR.

In this way, Hasan al-Bakr and Saddam Husain consolidated their hold on power. There were no obvious ideological differences at stake between them and their rivals. Nor did their enmity stem from such large questions as whether civilians or military officers should be in charge of the party and the country. Saddam Husain, like Hasan al-Bakr, wanted the party to provide disciplined but flexible support, not to act as a forum for debate and thus a site for the potential indictment of the leadership itself. For them, the Ba'th Party was an extension of their personal power through a patronage system which they alone would control. Here the advantage lay with those who could use a small circle of trusted men not to advance some abstract idea, but simply to further the cause of the individual who would be best placed to safeguard the interests of the group. These interests were primarily material, providing the members with the resources they needed to service the networks of contacts, clients and associates that defined and enhanced their social standing. This was the tangible measure of their social identities, corresponding to the values and preconceptions of the only people who mattered to them.

From both a normative and a pragmatic perspective, the people who mattered in this respect tended to come from the same provincial background as Hasan al-Bakr and Saddam Husain, often loosely related to each other through the clans of the larger tribal grouping of the al-Bu Nasir from the region of Takrit. Composed of some 20,000 people, this provided a ready-made network of contacts who would expect to benefit from any privileges flowing from their clansmen's rise to prominence, but who would also provide a trustworthy group to serve their patrons throughout the Iraqi state. The power and reach of Hasan al-Bakr and Saddam Husain, deployed in this way, could also be amplified by bringing into the network members of allied clans from the Sunni Arab north-west who could be relied upon to defend the privileges thus granted against all comers in the new order being established in Iraq.

Their contacts and clients were not confined to these groupings of rural tribesmen, although in some areas of the administration and particularly in the military and security services they soon became conspicuous. Also included were men who had demonstrated their personal loyalties in the conspiratorial days of party opposition and in the turbulent months of the Ba'thist regime of 1963. They were now incorporated into a system of power cemented by the family, clan and shared backgrounds of the chief beneficiaries. They channelled the resources of the state to their clients and used the Ba'th to create the illusion of collective action. In such circumstances, it is difficult to say with any degree of certainty what kind of vision for Iraq Hasan al-Bakr or Saddam Husain entertained. Rooted as they were in a conspiratorial, clannish view of politics and of the state, they could be relatively flexible towards those whom they did not consider an immediate threat. This gave them considerable room for manoeuvre.[1]

KURDISH AND SHI‘I CHALLENGES AND RELATIONS WITH IRAN

These features were visible in the new regime's handling of the challenges it faced, foremost amongst which was the Kurdish question. In July 1968 Hasan al-Bakr appointed three Kurdish ministers, two representing Barzani and the other identified with Talabani's faction of the KDP. This opened the way for negotiations, but also allowed Hasan al-Bakr and his colleagues to play the factions off against each other. Within a month Barzani's supporters had resigned in protest. Negotiations continued, but Barzani was preparing a demonstration of military strength and in December 1968 serious fighting erupted. Within a month the 7th Ba‘thist Congress promised to return to the autonomy declaration of 1966. This encouraged Barzani, who merely stepped up the pressure, simultaneously exploiting the sharp deterioration in relations between Iraq and Iran. In March 1969 his forces launched a spectacular attack on the Kirkuk oil installations, halting much of Iraq's oil production for a number of days.

14 Mustafa Barzani (leader of the Kurdistan Democratic Party until his death in 1979), c. 1973

The government in Baghdad responded with a determined military campaign in the summer of 1969, but soon began secret negotiations with Barzani. For Hasan al-Bakr, despite the ideological affinity of the Talabani faction with aspects of Ba'thism, Barzani represented the real power in the Kurdish region. The secret talks, conducted principally by Saddam Husain, led to the manifesto of March 1970 in which the government seemed to commit itself to a recognition of Kurdish rights that far exceeded anything that had been conceded before: the distinct national identity of the Kurds was recognised, as was their language, and they were promised participation in government and predominance in the local administration. A special, unified administrative region would be created in which distinctive measures would apply and it would incorporate all those areas in which a Kurdish majority lived, according to a census yet to be carried out. A joint committee of government and Kurdish representatives was set up to discuss the detailed application of the manifesto's principles, working towards a 1974 deadline.

Barzani, for his part, broke his links with Iran, implemented a cease-fire and began to co-operate with the newly established committee. He did not, however, trust the government, keeping the *peshmerga* intact and a wary eye on Baghdad. The joint committee meanwhile drew up plans for a Kurdish legislature, for Kurdish language curricula in schools and for some measure of administrative autonomy. However, when Saddam Husain took over the chairmanship of the committee in May 1971, it was clear that the key questions of defence, of finance and of oil were out of bounds. In addition, the government began to encourage Arab families to move to the north, in order to reduce the size of the future Kurdish region. This was specifically the case around Kirkuk where the government was determined to ensure that the oil fields remained outside Kurdish control. A number of assassination attempts against Barzani during 1971 deepened his mistrust of the government since Saddam Husain's involvement was strongly suspected. Against this background Barzani reopened channels of communication with the Iranian authorities in early 1972, foreseeing the possibility of future military action.[2]

Relations between Iraq and Iran had deteriorated since the coming to power of the new regime in Iraq. The shah took the socialist and Arab nationalist rhetoric of the Ba'thist government at face value. Vague, irredentist statements about the Arab character of the Iranian province of Khuzestan took on more concrete form as the small group of Khuzestan's Arab separatists found a congenial refuge in Iraq. They did not represent much of a security threat, but their presence angered the shah. Equally, the socialist rhetoric of the Ba'thist regime, coupled with its burgeoning relationship with the USSR, signified the emergence of a potentially unfriendly power at the headwaters of the Persian Gulf at a time when Iran saw itself as the regionally dominant power after the promised British withdrawal in 1971. At the same time, the new Iraqi regime looked vulnerable: the Ba'thists seemed to have few allies in Iraq or indeed in the Arab world, as their campaigns against a wide spectrum of political opponents indicated; the Iraqi officer corps was clearly riven by factionalism, weakening the armed forces, which were in any case preoccupied by the Kurdish insurrection.

To Iran the Iraqi government looked both weak and rhetorically threatening, encouraging the shah in February 1969 to reopen the question of their common border, demanding that it should lie along the *Thalweg* of the Shatt al-'Arab. Relations deteriorated rapidly. Iran abrogated the 1937 treaty in April, ignoring Iraq's claims to sovereignty in the Shatt al-'Arab, and started providing significant assistance to the Kurds. Iraq, weak militarily vis-à-vis Iran, could do little. The Khuzestan separatists did not constitute a threat comparable to the Kurds. Furthermore, Hasan al-Bakr, in attempting to enlist the public support of the Shi'i hierarchy in Iraq's dispute with Iran, became embroiled in an escalating conflict with those sections of the Shi'i community concerned about the nature of the regime in Iraq. In 1968, the anti-communist record of the Ba'th was remembered, but so too was the power of the socialists within the party. It was also clear from the outset that the new regime was dominated by clans of Sunni army officers not dissimilar to those who had governed Iraq for the previous decade. Nevertheless, Hasan al-Bakr had cultivated a reputation for personal piety and the religious hierarchy took heart from the reference to Islam as the religion of the state in the provisional constitution.

However, any reassurance was soon dispelled by the government's adoption of an increasingly socialist guise. Much of this was rhetorical, but it had some tangible effects, such as the ending of compensation for sequestered land in January 1969, and the appointment to public office of men associated with the secular left of the party. This public face of the secular nature of power was matched by the less manifest secular character of a government that emanated from kinship and clientelist networks born amongst the communities of Iraq's Sunni Arab north-west. From this provincial background, values quite other than those suggested by Islam informed and regulated political behaviour. This may have been understandable and indeed congenial to certain sectors of the lay public, but for the *'ulama* and the Islamic revivalists it was an ominous development.

It was not long, therefore, before conflict erupted. In April 1969, Hasan al-Bakr tried to persuade the senior *mujtahid*, Ayatollah Muhsin al-Hakim, publicly to condemn the Iranian government in its dispute with Iraq over the Shatt al-'Arab. Al-Hakim refused. In response, Hasan al-Bakr took a series of measures aimed as much at the Shi'i hierarchy in Iraq as at Iran: Iranian religious students were arrested and expelled; the independent Kufa University at Najaf was closed down and its endowments confiscated; roughly 20,000 people of allegedly Iranian descent were summarily expelled across the border with Iran. The mounting campaign of harassment of the Shi'a, under the guise of uprooting the 'Iranian threat', brought sharp protests from the Shi'i hierarchy. In June 1969 Ayatollah Muhsin al-Hakim led a protest procession from Najaf to Baghdad, where thousands of Shi'a flocked to pay him their respects. The scale of this demonstration of loyalty so alarmed the authorities that the security services seized his son, Sayyid Mahdi al-Hakim, on trumped-up charges of spying for Israel. The charge was then used to prevent people from visiting the ayatollah. However, this did not stop the protests, which now took the form of sermons and of petitions demanding an end to arbitrary arrest and torture, an end to the expulsions of 'Iranians' and an end to the continued confiscation of the property of those whom the regime judged to be their opponents.

The government responded by arresting *'ulama* who had dared to protest and by executing a Sunni *'alim*, Shaikh 'Abd al-'Aziz al-Badri, who had preached in support of al-Hakim at one of the main Baghdad mosques. These measures were followed by the confiscation of religious endowments in Najaf, the banning of religious processions and the closing of Islamic schools in many of the predominantly Shi'i towns. Alarmed by the apparent formation of a common Islamic front between Sunni and Shi'a, the government abandoned its earlier pretence of respect for Islamic values by prohibiting readings of the Qur'an on the state broadcasting networks and ending Islamic instruction in state schools. Inevitably these measures sparked off protests. Days of rioting and demonstrations followed in the cities of the largely Shi'i south, most notably in Najaf, Karbala and Basra. These were violently suppressed by the government's security forces. For his part, Ayatollah al-Hakim issued a *fatwa* prohibiting membership of the Ba'th, and his son, now released from custody, prudently fled into exile.

Government harassment of the Shi'i hierarchy continued, as did the security services' attacks on lay members of various Islamic organisations. This was intensified in early 1970 when the security apparatus claimed to have discovered a plot aimed at the overthrow of the government, allegedly inspired by Iran. Its discovery served as the pretext for the purge, arrest and execution of more officers and officials suspected of disloyalty, as well as of a number of men thought to be associated with Islamic organisations, both Sunni and Shi'i, such as Generals Muhsin al-Jannabi and Muhammad Faraj. It was also accompanied by further expulsions of 'Iranians' residing in Iraq, which many saw as a straightforward attack on the Shi'i community as a whole and particularly on the urban Shi'a who were the most likely to be associated with active opposition groups such as the Shi'i Islamist organisation al-Da'wa.

The death of Ayatollah al-Hakim in the summer of 1970 opened up the opportunity for one of the founders of al-Da'wa, Sayyid Muhammad Baqir al-Sadr, to become more prominent since many of al-Hakim's followers transferred their allegiance to him. He had been regarded as dangerously radical in his opinions by many of the senior *ulama* and there were still those who had reservations about his active involvement in the political work of al-Da'wa, as well as about the daring nature of some of his interpretations of the *fiqh*. Nevertheless, the large numbers who now acknowledged his authority were a sign of the times. Whilst many remained respectful of the chief *mujtahid*, Ayatollah Abu al-Qasim al-Kho'i, who was known for his disdain for the political world, others were increasingly influenced by the debates among lay people and *ulama* gripping the study circles of Najaf and Karbala.

These debates now revolved around such issues as the form of Islamic society, the proper Islamic regulation of the economy and the nature of truly Islamic authority in the construction of a political community. It was at this time, in early 1970, that the exiled Iranian *alim*, Ayatollah Ruhollah Khomaini, gave a series of lectures on Islamic government at Najaf. He called for the establishment of an Islamic state and asserted the leading political role of the clerics in any such state. Although he had a particular animus against the shah who had exiled him (and his pronouncements were for that reason looked upon indulgently by the Iraqi government), he was nevertheless expressing a perennial concern: the future of Islam in a world dominated by the preoccupations of secular power that owed nothing to a specifically Islamic tradition. In many respects, this concern went far beyond the habitual communal concerns of the Shi'a, and al-Sadr, in particular, sought consciously to broaden his appeal to all Muslims. However, in Iraq the particular status of the Shi'a, subject to a state dominated by Sunni military officers, added a sense of crisis and urgency that gave the message wide currency.

The Shi'i clerics and the concerned members of the community were relatively powerless in the face of the forces which the regime could deploy.

Nevertheless, the capacity of certain Shi'i figures to command respect and to exercise authority within the community clearly unnerved a regime based on narrow circles emanating from the Sunni lands of the north-west. Al-Sadr himself was briefly arrested in 1972 and was deeply suspect in the regime's eyes as a Shi'i leader of stature who was also a political activist with appeal beyond his own community. It was the hidden potential of these forms of social solidarity which worried Hasan al-Bakr and Saddam Husain. Consequently, like previous rulers of Iraq, they tried to undermine that solidarity, channelling resources towards the Shi'i community at large, whilst ensuring that certain groups, families and individuals were more favoured than others. In this way, a patronage network was established, drawing many Shi'a into the widening circle of those who were in some sense complicit in the order being established in Iraq.[3]

ECONOMIC PATRONAGE, POLITICAL CONTROL AND FOREIGN POLICY ALIGNMENTS

Selective patronage was a principle applied to the population as a whole insofar as the economic policies of the new regime were concerned. In its handling of agricultural policy and of business enterprise, and in the general direction of the Iraqi economy, Hasan al-Bakr's government made much use of radical socialist rhetoric, but in fact made sure that all economic directives were geared primarily to enhancing the control of Hasan al-Bakr and his associates. This meant that the chief economic policies of the regime took two main forms. One was largely populist in nature. It took shape in early 1969 in the cancellation of all compensation for sequestered lands. At a stroke, this relieved the beneficiaries of land redistribution of the financial burden which compensation had implied. It also removed a major item of government expenditure. In addition, subsidies of basic commodities were introduced, as were limited social and welfare services and tax relief. These were not to be fully developed until significant resources became available after the massive increase in oil income of the mid-1970s, but they gave the impression of a government concerned about the economic well-being of the people as a whole.

Investment in agriculture was increased and in May 1970 more complex land reform measures were introduced. These attempted to rectify some of the adverse results of previous land reform acts, for instance by paying more attention to the relationship between the type of land (and irrigation system) and the limits of permitted landholding. Co-operatives were established and cultivators were obliged to join them to benefit from the subsidised seed, fertiliser and other benefits through which the government tried to channel investment into agriculture. At the same time a number of collective farms were set up to placate the leftist members of the party whom Hasan al-Bakr and Saddam Husain thought worth courting at the time. However, the numbers involved were never very large and the collectivisation experiment in Iraq was more a result of the symbolic politics being conducted at the senior levels of the regime than a policy adopted out of ideological conviction. The other measures introduced at the time, although they brought immediate benefits for a substantial number of landholding peasants, failed to check the relative decline of Iraqi agriculture. Productivity levels continued to decline and, when faced by the population growth of the previous years, the government resorted to the policy of importing increasing quantities of food. By the early 1970s, Iraq was a net importer of food grains and its food import bill had been subject to a twelvefold increase since the early 1960s.

The provision of subsidised food and removal of financial burdens from the peasantry, although costly, were populist in intent and generally popular in effect. However, they also corresponded to the patrimonial system of Hasan al-Bakr and his circle. The goal was to create a basis of dependent support through selective use of the economic powers now vested in the leading members of the regime. This found various forms of expression. The confiscation of the property of political opponents and, on a much larger scale, the continuing sequestration of landholdings opened up great opportunities for the leading members of the regime to bestow favours on some, as well as to demonstrate to others the cost of disfavour. The slow pace of land distribution was marginally eased by the elimination of compensation, but the state remained the single largest landowner, having at its disposal both sequestered lands and lands brought under cultivation through new irrigation schemes. Consequently, whether through land redistribution or through the leasing of sequestered lands, those who now controlled the state had vast powers of patronage at their disposal. Nor was such a patronage system limited simply to the title to land: the co-operatives provided a useful form of social control through their regulation of crops, supply of fertiliser and marketing mechanisms.

As under all previous regimes, the government of Hasan al-Bakr ensured that land distribution and the role of the state as prime landlord benefited those in power. In some cases, this led to the acquisition of land by individuals close to the political leadership on a scale not seen since the notorious land appropriations by the political elite under the monarchy. Equally useful, as far as the power brokers of Baghdad were concerned, was the distribution of leases to chosen followers and the enlargement of client networks through access to landholdings ultimately controlled by the government. This generally meant favouring those who already held land. In the mid-1970s roughly one-third of the agricultural land in Iraq was still owned by a mere 3 per cent of the landowners – a group which was now deeply enmeshed in networks of government patronage and thus dependent upon those who allowed them to make or to retain their fortunes. This provided Hasan al-Bakr and Saddam Husain with a measure of social control and a bulwark against more radical factions, either from within the party or from outside. By no means convinced Ba'thists, these beneficiaries could nevertheless recognise and appreciate a system of privilege which rewarded them so well.[4]

This was also the policy pursued in relation to business enterprise. Despite the socialist rhetoric, there were no further nationalisations of businesses and individual entrepreneurs were encouraged to help in building up Iraq's weak industrial base. In certain fields, such as contracting and construction, this was the period when a number of people laid the foundations – and created the necessary connections – for the large business concerns that were to emerge with the great increase in oil revenues in the mid-1970s. At this stage, however, although on a more modest scale, the principles had been established whereby economic policy could be used to cement the hold of the leading members of the regime on the expanding world of entrepreneurial activity. This was achieved primarily through patronage, the terms of which were officially made possible by state policy, but the targeting of which was in the hands of those who could command state power.

The setting up of business enterprises, the awarding of contracts by state organs, the issuing of licences for the importation of goods and raw materials, the control of foreign exchange and the domination of negotiations with the reorganised labour unions were amongst the many instruments employed by the government to regulate economic activity. They gave to those who held office the means to create their own power bases, directly and indirectly. A structure was thus being created which was geared not simply or even primarily to the general concern of improving the economic condition of the country, but rather to the particular preoccupation of creating networks of complicity and dependence which would reinforce the position of those in power.

The two themes of populism and patronage were also visible in the other major economic problem facing Hasan al-Bakr and his circle – the question of Iraq's oil resources. Still embroiled in a dispute with IPC over some

of the consequences of Law 80 of 1961, the new regime entered into negotiations with the USSR concerning the exploitation of new Iraqi oil fields,
particularly the North Rumaila field in the south of the country. This
resulted in an agreement between Iraq and the USSR in the summer of
1969 whereby the USSR would help Iraq to exploit its oil fields and would
build a pipeline to a projected oil refinery and oil export facility at al-Faw
on the Persian Gulf. The agreement signalled the beginning of the end of
IPC's dominance of the Iraqi oil industry, souring Iraq's relations with IPC
and reinforcing Hasan al-Bakr's belief in the need to gain eventual control
of the company. Negotiations began in December 1971 and by March 1972
IPC had conceded the long-standing Iraqi demand for a share in the equity
of IPC itself. However, in April, with the start of production from the
North Rumaila field, IPC cut its own production at Kirkuk by half. For the
Iraqi government, this illustrated the arrogance of the company, as well as
the danger of allowing it to play so dominant a role in determining Iraqi
oil production. In June 1972 the Iraqi government nationalised IPC.

This act removed the last – and crucially important – element of foreign
control from Iraq's national life. Despite the austerity measures which the
government introduced to meet the anticipated loss of revenue, the nationalisation was enormously popular. In addition, Hasan al-Bakr and Saddam
Husain had taken steps to ensure that any repercussions would not be too
severe. In January 1972, Saddam Husain had visited Moscow to discuss
Soviet assistance to Iraq. This had resulted both in the Iraqi–Soviet Treaty
of Friendship and Co-operation, signed in April, and in trade agreements
which guaranteed that the USSR would purchase Iraq's oil, softening the
blow of any possible IPC-organised boycott. Equally, the government was
careful not to nationalise two subsidiaries of IPC and further undermined
IPC solidarity by offering special treatment to the French member of the
consortium, ensuring that France purchased nearly a quarter of the former
IPC's production. In the event, Iraq negotiated a settlement with IPC
remarkably quickly, agreeing on compensation terms in February 1973. Iraq
was now well placed to derive full benefit from the massive rises in oil prices
which were to follow the Arab–Israeli war of October 1973. These were also
to place unimaginable wealth in the hands of the small circle of men who
controlled the Iraqi state, providing them with a means of patronage that
far exceeded anything available to their predecessors.[5]

Politically, this coincided with a series of events which placed Hasan
al-Bakr and Saddam Husain in a position of supreme power in the Iraqi
state. It allowed them to put in place the final parts of the framework of
control which was to form the foundation of the distinctive state structure

that carried the power of Saddam Husain forward during the following decades. In November 1971 Hasan al-Bakr had proclaimed the National Action Charter, reiterating the commitment of the Ba'th to state control of the economy and his desire for a coalition among all 'progressive' elements. This was being declared while the security services continued to detain communists on a regular basis. A change came with the increasingly close relationship that developed between the USSR and the Iraqi government, symbolised by Kosygin's visit to Iraq in April 1972. The leadership of the ICP then agreed to join the National Patriotic Front with the Ba'th. In May two members of the ICP were appointed to the cabinet (just prior to the nationalisation of IPC) and harassment of communists ceased abruptly.

It was during this period that the head of the state security services, Nadhim Kazzar, launched an abortive coup attempt. His motives remain obscure, but he was in a good position to see that there was no institutional reality behind the apparently well-entrenched power structures of the state. He may have believed that by killing the entire political leadership he would be able to triumph in the lethal struggle for power that was bound to follow. However, in June 1973 his plan misfired, leading to his own execution. Saddam Husain quickly used the incident to dispose of a number of potential opponents. Over thirty senior officials were executed, including the head of the Military Bureau of the Ba'th. Others were imprisoned, among them 'Abd al-Khaliq al-Samarrai, who had become a focus for those who still believed in the ideological tenets of Ba'thism, rather than simply in the need to follow the leadership uncritically. Hasan al-Bakr took over the Ministry of Defence and Sa'dun Shakir and Barzan al-Takriti (Saddam Husain's half-brother) reorganised the state security services.

It was in these inauspicious circumstances that 'Aziz Muhammad, secretary-general of the ICP, and Hasan al-Bakr signed the National Action Charter of apparently common socialist goals in July 1973. The ICP was legally recognised and was allowed to publish and to organise openly, leading to a revival of its activities in the trade unions, the peasant associations and the youth and women's organisations, as well as in the universities and schools which had been traditional fields of party activity. Communist sympathisers were drawn to its centres throughout the country, thereby providing the security services with a good idea of the extent and location of communist support. It took some months before the ICP began to sense that all was not well. Pressure was repeatedly brought to bear on ICP members when they tried to organise and Ba'thists successfully challenged them in the trade unions and elsewhere. By the autumn of 1974, the relationship was under strain. Realising how vulnerable the party had become, its leadership reduced its public exposure and tried to continue the party's work surreptitiously.

The developing relationship between Iraq and the USSR, in some respects at its zenith during these years, had clearly put pressure on the ICP to associate itself with the regime. On a regional level, it was also in the interests of the USSR that its two allies, Syria and Iraq, should co-operate, but here it was less successful in bridging the gap that existed between these two Ba'thist regimes. Mutual suspicion and hostility between Baghdad and Damascus had characterised the relationship since July 1968 because the leaders of the new Ba'thist regime in Baghdad were held responsible by the Syrian leader, Salah Jadid, for engineering the downfall of the Ba'thist regime in Baghdad in 1963. The ideological divide was compounded and the insecurities, at least on the Syrian side, intensified when a number of exiled Syrian Ba'thists made their way to Baghdad, to be followed in 1970 by Michel Aflaq himself, the Syrian founder of the Ba'th Party. He took up residence in Baghdad and, by his presence, seemed to confer a kind of Ba'thist legitimacy on the Iraqi regime.

When Hafiz al-Asad – whose general outlook was not dissimilar to that of the Iraqi Ba'thists – overthrew Jadid and seized power in Syria in 1970, the war of words continued, although with slightly less rancour. Each regime, uncertain of its own support domestically, seemed intent on disputing the other's legitimacy and was convinced of the subversive intentions of the other. This attitude coloured the handling of all the major issues between the two states during these years, from the vexed question of the dues charged by Syria on Iraqi oil pumped through the pipeline across Syria, to the recriminations that followed the war of October 1973. The Iraqi government was to claim that it had been excluded from the planning for this war by Syria and Egypt. The Syrian government maintained, on the contrary, that Iraq had refused any such participation, fearful as it was at the time of its eastern frontier with Iran.

At any event, Iraq did send an armoured division to help Syria on the Golan, but rather late in the day, after the tide of battle had turned and it seemed as if the Israeli forces were heading for Damascus. The Iraqi forces played an effective role and suffered correspondingly heavy casualties, but this was never publicly acknowledged by the Syrian authorities, whom the Iraqis accused of failing to assist them or, worse, of leading them deliberately into an ambush. Within a week or so of the Iraqi forces' arrival, the Syrian government agreed a cease-fire with Israel without consulting Iraq. This gave the Iraqi government the pretext it needed to withdraw its troops from Syria, expressing disapproval of the cease-fire – a disapproval that turned into vituperative denunciation in 1974 with the Syrian signing of the disengagement agreements with Israel. The Iraqi leadership now saw an opportunity to forge for itself a position of impeccable Arab steadfastness – a position that accorded not only with its desire to undermine the Syrian regime, but also with its growing regional ambitions.[6]

WAR IN KURDISTAN

Nevertheless, these ambitions were to be held in check for a year or so by the outbreak of war in the Kurdish region. Barzani had refused to enter the National Patriotic Front until he could be assured that this would give him substantive control over Kurdish affairs. This was never likely to be the case, as the sluggish pace of negotiations with the government indicated. Consequently, Barzani began to prepare for the possibility of armed conflict once again. He was helped by deteriorating relations between Iran and Iraq. A break in relations had occurred ostensibly because of Iran's occupation of the islands of the Tunbs and Abu Musa in the Persian Gulf when the British forces withdrew in November 1971. However, this had come against a background of arguments over the Shatt al-ʿArab and the continued expulsion of allegedly 'Iranian' Shiʿa from Iraq. One such expulsion, in the autumn of 1971, had particularly angered Barzani and other Kurdish leaders because it had involved nearly 40,000 Faili (Shiʿi) Kurds. For its part, the Iranian government, following the 1972 Soviet–Iraqi Treaty of Friendship and Co-operation, presented its disagreements with the Iraqi regime in the light of its key role in the US-sponsored security system established as part of the Cold War in the Middle East. It appeared that any enemy of the Baghdad regime was a potential ally of the United States. This led to covert American subsidies to Barzani and the KDP from 1972. Encouraged by this and by direct military assistance from Iran, Barzani felt increasingly defiant. By the end of 1972 regular armed clashes between Kurdish and government forces were taking place even as negotiations continued.

Iraq's participation in the war of October 1973 had led to a hasty restoration of diplomatic relations with Iran in a bid to secure Iraq's eastern frontier whilst its forces concentrated in the west. However, surface cordiality soon gave way to disagreement, leading to a series of violent incidents along the two countries' common border. So serious had these become that in February 1974 both Iran and Iraq asked, unsuccessfully, for UN observers to be sent to the region. The significance of this for the Kurdish position was that powerful Iranian and US backing caused Barzani to believe that he could resist Baghdad's attempt to impose its own version of autonomy by the deadline of March 1974. Under these provisions the Kurdish area would have an elected legislative assembly, based in Arbil, which would, in turn, elect an executive committee. However, the president of the committee would be appointed by the president of Iraq who was also empowered to dismiss him and to dissolve the assembly whenever he chose. The Baghdad government would retain control of foreign affairs and defence and security issues, as well as of oil and of the regional budget. Furthermore, the area of the designated Kurdish region would exclude about one-third of the distinctively Kurdish areas of Iraq, including the oil fields in the district of Kirkuk.

Barzani rejected the proposal, but the government pressed ahead with its implementation and persuaded some members of the KDP to co-operate in establishing the assembly in Arbil. This faction, led by ʿAziz al-ʿAqrawi, joined the National Patriotic Front together with two small Kurdish organisations, giving the semblance of a truly national alliance. The reality was quite different. Most of the Kurdish factions, including a number of those historically at odds with Barzani, made common cause with him and, assisted by Iran, confronted the Baghdad government. By the summer of 1974 a full-scale war was in progress. It followed a familiar pattern, with the Iraqi armed forces capturing the more accessible towns, but unable to control the countryside. From this base Barzani and the KDP hit back, relying increasingly on Iranian military support. The escalating war began to take a heavy toll of the Iraqi army, leading to the calling up of reservists and eating into the government's financial reserves. Protests erupted in other parts of the country and when certain Shiʿi *ulama* preached against the war in the ʿAshura sermons of that year, the government responded harshly. Over thirty Shiʿi leaders were arrested and five of them, closely associated with al-Daʿwa, were executed.

However, direct Iranian military involvement in the fighting opened up the possibility of a full-scale war between Iran and Iraq, which neither country wanted. Unknown to Barzani, negotiations began between Tehran and Baghdad. The outcome was the dramatic announcement in Algiers in March 1975 that Iran and Iraq had agreed to resolve their differences. Largely on the initiative of Saddam Husain, Iraq accepted Iran's claim that the *Thalweg* should form the common boundary of the two states in the Shatt al-ʿArab and in exchange Iran agreed to cease all support for Barzani and the KDP. Within days Iran had withdrawn all military assistance and had closed the border. Barzani's forces, heavily reliant on Iranian support, could not resist the renewed Iraqi offensives and the revolt collapsed within

15 Jalal Talabani (leader of the Patriotic Union of Kurdistan,
president of Iraq since 2005), 1996

weeks. Thousands of *peshmerga* accepted the offered amnesty and surrendered, while Barzani himself and the KDP leadership crossed into Iran with
a large number of their followers, joining an estimated 150,000 civilian
refugees who had already fled there. Soon the festering divisions within the
KDP led to a major split between the Barzanis – Mulla Mustafa and his
sons Idris and Masoud – and Jalal Talabani. The latter broke with the KDP
and formed the Patriotic Union of Kurdistan (PUK), attracting many who
had found Barzani's tribal leadership hard to reconcile with their own
nationalist and socialist principles. Barzani himself was to die in exile in the
United States in 1979.

For Hasan al-Bakr and Saddam Husain the disintegration of the KDP
and the end of the Kurdish revolt was the real prize of the Algiers agreement, making it easier to deflect attention from the fact that they had ceded

Iraqi territory to Iran. Baghdad pressed ahead with its plans for the Kurdish region. An appointed assembly began its sessions in Arbil, a Kurd, Taha Muhi al-Din Ma'ruf, was appointed vice-president of Iraq and a massive operation began to relocate entire Kurdish communities away from the Turkish and Iranian border areas into new settlements close to the major towns. Others were transferred to the south of Iraq where they were rehoused among the predominantly Shi'i Arab population. Eventually, it was estimated that nearly half a million Kurds had been moved from their home villages, to which they were forbidden to return on pain of death and many of which had in any case been razed to the ground.

At the same time, the government continued to encourage Arab families to move northward, in order to tip the balance in favour of the Arab inhabitants in certain areas and to justify their exclusion from the Kurdish region. This was accompanied by very substantial investment in the infrastructure of the north, in part to extend the networks of patronage into the Kurdish areas more thoroughly than had hitherto been possible. The government wanted to make it clear to the Kurds that Baghdad's patronage could deliver substantial material rewards, as long as they abided by the dictated rules of the game. Concentration on the development of roads and means of communication also ensured that all of Kurdistan would be accessible to the forces of the central government in the future.[7]

OIL REVENUES, FOREIGN POLICIES AND THE RISE OF SADDAM HUSAIN

The ending of the war in the north and the new warmth in relations with Iran allowed the government to concentrate on realising the potential of Iraq's massively increased oil revenues. These had undergone an eightfold increase since October 1973 such that by the end of 1975 Iraq's annual oil income stood at around $8 billion. The government was quick to capitalise on the opportunities offered by this great increase in resources. On a general level, this led to renewed attention to social security systems, to new housing projects and to impressive investments in health and education. During the next few years the effects of these well-resourced initiatives were felt throughout the country, greatly contributing to the feeling that the government was at last fulfilling its promises even if, at the same time, nearly 40 per cent of the income from oil was being spent on arms purchases. However, it would be increasingly difficult for Iraqis or others to verify Iraq's national income or expenditure since it was at this time that the publication of economic statistics relating to 'strategic areas' was made a criminal offence.

In part this was because these same initiatives provided opportunities for the contractors and other entrepreneurs who were already socially well placed to make the most of this unprecedented injection of funds into the Iraqi economy. Oil revenue offered Hasan al-Bakr, Saddam Husain and their associates the opportunity of creating a wide circle of dependants, deeply implicated in the regime's use of state funds to favour those whom it trusted and to create a client network of countrywide proportions. Much of this went to individuals who were already connected to the principal members of the regime, but Saddam Husain in particular opened up opportunities to others whom he wished to draw into his own circle. Whatever the direction of these funds, it was important for Saddam Husain's growing power that their disposal should not be scrutinised.

In this atmosphere of vast government revenues, of ambitious development plans, of the encouragement and patronage of entrepreneurs in Iraq, it was scarcely surprising that Iraq's relations with Western states should have improved. Iraq had become an important market and, with the resolution of its problems with Iran, it was no longer seen as a strategic ally of the USSR. The Soviet Treaty of Friendship and Co-operation remained in force and the USSR was still Iraq's major supplier of arms, as well as being involved in its oil and other industries. Nevertheless, Iraq's oil income gave its leaders a freedom of choice which inevitably undermined the position of the USSR. None of this boded well for the ICP. Harassment of individual communists began again in autumn 1976 at a low level. Despite official pronouncements to the contrary, tensions were increasingly visible between the ICP and the Iraqi government. If anything, Soviet attempts to heal the rift made it worse, since these efforts tended to be regarded by Saddam Husain as unwarranted interference by the USSR in Iraq's affairs, deepening his already lively suspicions about the ICP.[8]

In the event, the ICP was to be caught up like many others in the series of developments which were to propel Saddam Husain into a position of undisputed leadership during the next few years. By this stage, it was clear that he, rather than Hasan al-Bakr, was the dominant figure in the regime. There was no obvious sign of competition between the two men and it would have been difficult to point to any real policy differences. However, Saddam Husain had established an unchallenged hold on the state security apparatus and on the organisations of the party. This gave him an unparalleled grasp of the administration and from here he made inroads into the officer corps, establishing his own client networks amongst the Takritis and others to whom he opened up the possibilities of enrichment and promotion if they adhered to his cause.

In January 1976 Saddam Husain signalled his ambitions by having Hasan al-Bakr confer upon him the rank of general. At the same time, it was announced that the Popular Army, under the command of Saddam Husain's protégé, Taha Ramadhan al-Jazrawi, was to be doubled in size, effectively deterring any other faction in the party from challenging Saddam Husain's own leadership. Saddam Husain figured increasingly in the publicity of the regime and criticism of him became highly dangerous. He underlined his control of the party by enlarging the Regional Command to twenty-one members in January 1977, rewarding his clients and diluting the influence of those who still had reservations about his ascendancy.

A test of their loyalties was soon to come. In February violent rioting erupted in the Shiʿi cities of Najaf and Karbala. Habitual Shiʿi communal alienation from Iraqi governments and growing resentment at discrimination in the networks of patronage and favouritism under the Baʿth, as well as a renewed and sharp Islamist critique of the secular government, contributed to the unrest. Members of the underground Islamist organisations, such as al-Daʿwa, decided to use the occasion of ʿAshura in 1977 to demonstrate the power of Islamic and anti-government feeling among the Shiʿa of the south. A traditional march of 30,000 from Najaf to Karbala became a prolonged demonstration against the regime, taking the security services by surprise and causing the authorities to send the armed forces to intercept the marchers. Rioting broke out in Najaf and Karbala, leading to a number of deaths, desertions by government soldiers and, eventually, the arrest of over 2,000 people, including a number of *ulama.*

A special court was set up to try the demonstrators and those who were accused of organising the protest. Under the presidency of ʿIzzat Mustafa, a member of the RCC, it included two Shiʿi cabinet ministers who had been appointed to the Regional Command of the Baʿth in January. It sentenced eight of the *ulama* to death and imprisoned a number of others. At the same time, many of the Shiʿi study circles in Najaf, Karbala and elsewhere were closed down and a number of religious scholars fled the country. Nevertheless, Saddam Husain regarded these sentences as too lenient, leading to ʿIzzat Mustafa's dismissal, together with one of the Shiʿi ministers.

Saddam Husain wanted there to be no doubt about his own capacity to dominate the RCC and the government, forcefully showing that independent opposition such as that seen in the Shiʿi cities would not be tolerated. On the other hand, as with the Kurdish question, these events allowed Saddam Husain to put his imprint on relations with the Shiʿi community as a whole. It was noticeable, therefore, that in the summer of 1977 Saddam Husain began to encourage official adoption of more overtly Islamic postures, ostentatiously cultivating certain *ulama* and drawing others into the network of his patronage. Paying lip service to Islamic values was part of a strategy that included patronage as well as intimidation. In the autumn of 1977 the members of the Regional Command of the Ba'th were made members of the RCC, bringing a number of Shi'i Iraqis into the RCC for the first time. These moves had a certain logic at the time, given the scale of unrest among the Shi'a. However, they also indicated that Saddam Husain was carving out for himself a position in which he alone could act as patron of all the diverse sections of Iraqi society. They could expect to enjoy his favour, but also to feel his wrath should they strike out on an independent course.

Accompanying these symbolic moves were measures designed to underpin more concrete forms of power. In September 1977 Saddam Husain took control of all aspects of Iraq's oil policy, giving him unquestioned access to the key resource of the Iraqi state. He determined levels of production and controlled the disbursement of oil revenues. Only Saddam Husain knew the exact levels of income and expenditure and it was from this period that a fixed percentage of Iraq's oil revenues was systematically transferred to deposits abroad, nominally to form the core of a 'Ba'thist fighting fund' should the regime be overthrown – and which was to serve his regime well in the coming decades.

At much the same time, President Hasan al-Bakr relinquished control of the Ministry of Defence to his kinsman, 'Adnan Khairallah Tulfah. Tulfah was the son-in-law of Hasan al-Bakr and the brother-in-law and first cousin of Saddam Husain. The transfer underlined the clannish character of the regime, but it also signified a shift in power within the clan itself. Relative to Saddam Husain's fortunes, those of Hasan al-Bakr were manifestly on the wane. Rumours of Hasan al-Bakr's unspecified health problems circulated, lending credence to the belief that it was only a matter of time before Saddam Husain became president of the republic. Indeed, this was the role which Saddam Husain now played in all but name. The fact that he did not make his move for another couple of years was due to his need to ensure that he had built up sufficient client networks, especially in the armed forces, where 'Adnan Khairallah played a key role. He also used this period to ascertain the nature and scale of opposition to him within the party and the regime. He needed to identify 'his men' (*Ahl al-Thiqa* (people of trust)) when he finally seized control of the state itself. In 1977, there were many who deeply mistrusted Saddam Husain.

Consequently, Saddam Husain used a number of stratagems to flush out the opposition in the senior ranks of the party, where it was potentially most dangerous. In early 1978 he orchestrated a press campaign against the ICP, responding to the party's criticism both of the government's repression in Kurdistan and of its encouragement of capitalism. Party members were arrested and large numbers were executed, accused of organising ICP activity in the armed forces. (In 1976 any non-Ba'thist political activity by members of the armed forces had been made a capital offence – a useful device for suppressing critical political activity in a country in which universal conscription meant that the majority of the adult male population were either serving in or reservists for the armed forces.) As ever, the use of a communist scare was also aimed at members of the Ba'th Party itself. Saddam Husain was testing the degree to which their loyalty was to him personally or to the National Patriotic Front and the socialist ideals which it nominally embodied.

The ICP itself was not a formidable opponent. By the spring of 1979, when the party formally broke with the regime, most of its senior leadership had fled the country. Although pursued relentlessly by the security services, the ICP was less a target than a decoy intended to lure out of concealment those whom Saddam Husain felt he could not wholly trust. Having thereby gauged the strength of the left in the upper echelons of the Ba'th Party, Saddam Husain began to test the attachment of members of the Ba'th to the ideals of Arab nationalism and of Arab unity – the other defining element of a distinctively Ba'thist identity. The opportunity for this stratagem was provided by the Camp David agreements between Egypt and Israel in 1978 which threw much of the Arab world into confusion, but which Saddam Husain tried to exploit by seeking to claim for Iraq the leadership of the Arab world.

His orchestration of an increasingly active and interventionist role in the Arab world had been marked since 1975, once the dispute with Iran was settled, the Kurdish war had ended and the oil revenues were greatly enhancing the state's power regionally as well as domestically. These moves had served to sharpen the rivalry between Iraq and Syria, poisoning a relationship already embittered by the mutual recriminations that followed the 1973 war and by Iraq's conviction that Syria had helped the Kurdish rebels during the war of 1974–5. Syria's invasion of Lebanon in 1976, and its military action against Palestinian forces there, had provided Saddam Husain with further reason to cast doubt on the Syrian leader al-Asad's pan-Arab credentials and to pose as the champion of the Palestinian resistance movements. Direct action against the Syrian regime followed: Iraq started concentrating troops on the Syrian border, stopped all oil exports through the Syrian pipeline (having just opened a pipeline from Kirkuk to al-Faw on the Persian Gulf, it could afford to do so) and initiated an assassination campaign against Syrian officials, accompanied by bomb attacks on government buildings.

In 1977, Iraq hastened to condemn President Sadat's visit to Jerusalem and cut its diplomatic ties with Egypt. At the same time, linked to their efforts to outflank and isolate the Syrian leadership, Hasan al-Bakr and Saddam Husain used the opportunity to urge even more radical action upon the Arab world than even the 1978 Tripoli summit of so-called steadfastness or rejectionist states were willing to contemplate. However, their failure to rally much support for their position led to a decided change in tactics. It was then that Iraq appeared to move towards the 'middle ground', seeing this as ultimately more fruitful in the attempt to position itself as the leading state of the Arab world. The tactic paid off in the sense that the Baghdad summit of November 1978 brought the Arab leaders to Iraq and situated Iraq – and thus Saddam Husain – at the centre of the Arab stage, whilst not wholly alienating Egypt, with which Iraq had already re-established low-level diplomatic ties.

Of equal importance, the summit had been preceded in October by the publication of the Charter of Joint National Action between Syria and Iraq, signalling an unexpected rapprochement between the Syrian and Iraqi leaders. The summer of 1978 had been marked by the usual vituperative exchanges, accusations and counter-accusations. However, by the autumn both regimes seemed to be intent on reconciliation, going so far as to use, once again, the long-neglected language of Iraqi–Syrian unification. For al-Asad the removal of Egypt from any possible military alliance against Israel left Syria dangerously exposed. Iraq and its resources consequently held out the hope of restoring some form of strategic balance, and using unification rhetoric was a small price to pay for the cementing of a strategic alliance. For Saddam Husain a close relationship with Syria would give Iraq a key role in the central Arab–Israeli conflict, providing a platform for Saddam Husain himself and effectively acknowledging Syria's need for Iraqi assistance. Inevitably, a strategic alliance between two Baʿthist regimes raised the question of the union of the two states. Neither al-Asad nor Saddam Husain had any intention of pursuing unification seriously, but it served their purposes to be seen to be preparing the way in the autumn of 1978.[9]

This burgeoning relationship between two bitterly opposed Baʿthist rivals formed the backdrop to Saddam Husain's ruthless purge of the Baʿth in Iraq by allowing him to observe his colleagues during the winter of 1978 and the spring of 1979. He may have had few illusions about their own commitment to unification, but he needed to discover the degree to which they were willing to use this issue as a way of rallying support amongst the lower echelons of the party, playing upon the Arab nationalist sentiment that still enthused many Ba'thists. He could thus discover the degree of their commitment to his person and their attitudes to the 'Iraq first' line that had become increasingly explicit during the years of his ascendancy. The activities of the preparatory committees became more sluggish and those who tried to accelerate the process failed to read the signals of official discouragement. They were marked down as potential dissidents.

Meanwhile, events to the east in Iran were making it more imperative than ever that Saddam Husain should reinforce his absolute control. The Iraqi regime had viewed the growing opposition to the shah unsympathetically, especially since it was linked to the dissident Shi'i hierarchy. For this reason, the Iraqi government had agreed to the shah's request to expel Ayatollah Khomaini from Najaf in October 1978. Ironically, this may have facilitated Khomaini's emergence as leader of the revolutionary movement in Iran which overthrew the shah and established a new regime in February 1979. Despite its concerns, the Iraqi government was quick to recognise the new Iranian government. More important was the effect of the revolutionary example on underground organisations in Iraq, such as al-Da'wa. These took heart from the events in Iran and began to organise attacks on public symbols of the regime in Iraq. The scale of this activity was small, but the Iraqi government, like many governments in the region, had been unnerved by the success of the revolutionaries in Iran and feared the emergence of a similar movement in Iraq. A ferocious campaign of repression therefore began against members of al-Da'wa and other similar organisations.

The repression led to protests from Shi'i leaders. Chief among these was Ayatollah Muhammad Baqir al-Sadr who was placed under house arrest in June 1979. The repercussions awoke the regime's fears of the reservoir of dissent that existed amongst the Shi'a: massive demonstrations of support for al-Sadr, mixed with protest against the government, were organised in Najaf, then in Karbala, Kufa and Madinat al-Thawra, the largely Shi'i public housing quarter of Baghdad. Indeed in Madinat al-Thawra the Ba'th's apparatus of surveillance and repression collapsed under the weight of the protests. These events sharpened Saddam Husain's concerns about the hidden power of the Shi'a and about the doubtful reliability of the Ba'th Party in a crisis. Instead he turned to the more trustworthy security services, bringing the streets under control

16 Ayatollah Sayyid Muhammad Baqir al-Sadr
(Shi'i *mujtahid* executed in 1980), c. 1978

through violence and arresting nearly 5,000 people, including a large
number of Shi'i clerics and even some Sunni *'ulama*. Many were executed
and some of the most prominent Shi'i clergy were expelled from Iraq. Al-
Sadr remained under house arrest, but tapes of his sermons denouncing
the regime were circulated to considerable effect throughout Iraq, listened
to by Shi'i and Sunni alike.[10]

These developments faced the country with a national crisis and the
regime with a crisis of a peculiarly dangerous nature. Saddam Husain
decided to make his move. In the middle of July 1979 Hasan al-Bakr suddenly announced his resignation and within hours Saddam Husain had
been sworn in as president of Iraq, appointing one of his most trusted

subordinates, 'Izzat Ibrahim al-Duri, as vice-president. Saddam Husain's assumption of the presidency was in some ways a formality, but it was symbolically charged and the speed of the operation showed that Saddam Husain would take no chances in allowing opposition to his personal rule to crystallise. This was particularly necessary in view of rumours circulating that Hasan al-Bakr, fearful of what he had created in Saddam Husain, was preparing to nominate Hafiz al-Asad of Syria as his own successor, with the assistance of those Iraqi Ba'thists determined to stop Saddam Husain's relentless rise to the summit of power. Whether or not Hasan al-Bakr really intended to do so – and his physical survival suggests that Saddam Husain did not believe he did – is less important than the fact that alternatives to Saddam Husain's leadership were being discussed within the party.

Saddam Husain acted swiftly and ruthlessly to eliminate all those whom he felt would not give him unquestioning obedience. In late July 1979 Saddam Husain declared that the security forces had uncovered a plot – later alleged to have been masterminded by Syria – aimed at toppling the Iraqi regime through the agency of members of the RCC. This dramatic announcement was accompanied by a special convention of the Ba'th Party at which one of the alleged plotters, RCC member al-Mashhadi, confessed to his own involvement, provided details of the plot and implicated a number of his colleagues. Saddam Husain went on to denounce a long list of other alleged conspirators who were seized and led out of the hall in an atmosphere of increasing frenzy and terror – whilst Saddam Husain himself smoked a large cigar and occasionally pretended to weep at this evidence of betrayal by some of the most trusted members of the party.

Over sixty leading members of the regime were arrested. They were tried by a special court presided over by Saddam Husain's protégé Na'im Haddad and many were sentenced to death, including al-Mashhadi, four other members of the RCC and 'Abd al-Khaliq al-Samarrai who had been in prison since 1973. A number of grudges were paid off at the time, with possibly as many as 500 senior members of the party being executed, whilst others were purged or demoted. They had been associated with the left of the party, or had shown themselves to be overenthusiastic about the prospects of union with Syria, or had belonged to the client followings of the senior members of the regime who had been found guilty of complicity in the 'Syrian plot'. Alternatively, they had simply run foul of the spreading networks of Saddam Husain's influence in some unspecified way.[11]

17 President Saddam Husain (president 1979–2003), 1995

SADDAM HUSAIN'S PRESIDENCY AND THE WAR WITH IRAN IN 1980

The widespread purges of the party and the leadership underlined for those who survived the fact that they held their positions on sufferance. Obedience to Saddam Husain and proximity to him were now to be the criteria for promotion and indeed for political – and sometimes actual – survival. Such obedience could bring its own rewards, but it would also mean accepting the leader's judgement on all matters relating to the state, to the Ba'th and indeed to the fate of any particular individual. Saddam Husain himself, who was 42 at the time of his elevation to the presidency, had triumphed by using the disconcerting combination of charm, generosity and ruthless terror that was to serve him so well in maintaining his position as ruler of Iraq for longer than any predecessor.

In his rise to power, he had initially enjoyed the patronage of his kinsman Hasan al-Bakr, but had soon realised the need to carve out a power base for himself. He could not find this within the established social hierarchies of Iraq because of his low social status as the son of a landless peasant, always dependent on richer and more prestigious relatives. Equally, he was excluded from the crucial networks of the armed forces because of his lack of military background. Consequently, Saddam Husain relied upon his own resources and instincts, trusting few, targeting those who could be useful to him, intimidating others and incorporating all his contacts into a web of obligation and surveillance to which he alone held the key. Scarcely deflected by ideological preoccupations, Saddam Husain was able to deploy his considerable skills to reorganise the Ba'th Party, to develop the intelligence and security services and finally to ensure his indirect control of all the major instruments of state power.

The rise of Saddam Husain, by its nature and its consequences, reinforced the long-apparent ambivalence of the Iraqi state. On the one hand, an elaborate and complex bureaucracy had developed, affecting the lives of Iraqis in all spheres. Formal procedures proliferated, requiring mountains of paperwork and an army of officials to work the system – a system which placed great stress on conformity, on strict spheres of responsibility and on meticulous attention to the details of form and discipline. The very complexity of the state and party bureaucracies made it difficult for any one official to gain an overview of the whole since their immediate task was to fulfil their small role in the larger apparatus – or face the disciplinary procedures which were so prominent a feature of the process. The web of complex procedures thus drew individuals into an operational straitjacket, making them vulnerable to action taken by those who effectively controlled state power.[12]

It was here that the other aspect of the state showed itself. As an engine of power, accumulating resources, deploying patronage and maintaining control over its inhabitants, it was centred on the restrictive circles of Saddam Husain's associates, linked to him either through bonds of kinship and regional background or through a history of personal trust. These men formed the inner circle of the Iraqi regime, having been put to the test on numerous occasions during the preceding fifteen years, when they could have sided with other clansmen, other ideological tendencies in the party or with restless and opportunistic military officers. Instead, they had followed Saddam Husain. This made them the *Ahl al-Thiqa* in whom, for the moment, Saddam Husain could have confidence. His cause had become theirs and they were so closely identified with him that their political fate would be linked to his.

This gave expression to a particular conception of the state, seen primarily as the domain of a small circle of intimates, linked by networks of alliance and advantage, difficult for others to penetrate unless by command of the ruler himself. Such a state, dynastic in its implications, patriarchal and highly personalised, emerged from a social world where a keen aware-ness of status differences between lineages, sects, clans and genders makes all other groupings and factions appear as outsiders. Alliances can be formed with such groups, but at the heart of the system lies a form of trust based on ties that cannot easily be replicated. This trust is a necessary, but not a sufficient, condition for the organisation of such a circle. Nor is it absolute. It can be undermined in a number of ways. By the same token, obedience to the ruler may be thrown into question if he seems incompe-tent, or if he redirects his favours away from the established inner circle. Thus, the ruler, whilst taking account of their expectations, refuses to be dictated to by them, and remains wary of their ambitions.

Saddam Husain had every interest, therefore, in establishing himself as more than simply one amongst a number of Takritis. He needed to under-line his uniqueness and his unparalleled ability to lead his followers to pos-itions of domination and privilege which could not be reproduced by any other potential leader. Consequently, to a degree greater than any prede-cessor, Saddam Husain sought to impose a political unity on Iraq that found its expression chiefly in his person. Obedience to him was to be the common cause of Iraq's heterogeneous inhabitants. Under this leadership distinct myths of Iraqi identity were promulgated, stressing not only the usual qualities of martial prowess, spiritual fulfilment and historical root-edness common to all nationalist myth-making, but also emphasising the succession of absolute rulers who had allegedly presided over the mythical forging of the Iraqi nation. A continuous line of political succession was established between the rulers of the ancient kingdoms of Mesopotamia, the Abbasid caliphs and Saddam Husain himself. He was the historical necessity towards which this long march of absolute rulers was inexorably heading. For these purposes no distinction was made between pre-Islamic and Islamic rulers and any lingering unease about the implications of this for Arab identity was met by transforming all the previous rulers of Mesopotamia into 'proto-Arabs'. The imaginative entity, 'Mesopotamia-as-Iraq', was thus Arabised, although it was acknowledged that minor narra-tives of non-Arab peoples, such as the Kurds, had also figured in the dominant narrative of the Iraqi nation.

Once he assumed the presidency, a personality cult of awesome propor-tions was created around Saddam Husain. It portrayed him as the repre-sentative of all the peoples of Iraq, both in their particular identities as members of different communities, and in their common condition as sub-jects of the Iraqi government. National institutions were created to sustain the national myths. The Ba'th Party was now a countrywide organisation, reaching down to the smallest village and most modest neighbourhood in an unprecedented way. Universal conscription drew in increasing numbers of Iraqis as the expanding defence budget allowed for a spectacular growth in the size of the armed forces. In addition, the Popular Army and the youth organisation brought ever larger numbers into the paramilitary formations established by the regime. Finally, Saddam Husain established a National Assembly in March 1980, setting up the first parliament since the overthrow of the monarchy in 1958. The assembly was a symbolic façade – it was powerless and its members were vetted by the security services. However, it was meant to create the impression of popular supervision of government, to provide another symbol of national unity and to give Saddam Husain another forum for presenting himself as the national leader.[13]

The creation and maintenance of these institutions displayed the ambivalence of the Iraqi state – an ambivalence which Saddam Husain was adept at exploiting. They existed in their present form at the behest of Saddam Husain and his narrow circle of associates. They were 'national' in that they involved people from all sections of Iraqi society and were surrounded by a myth-making apparatus that underlined their national character. For some this did indeed create common experiences. However, they were also instruments of patronage, whereby large numbers of people from different communities could be rewarded with positions of influence, special access to housing and material resources that bound them to the leadership.

For those who refused such patronage, doors were closed and the only alternative for some was to leave Iraq. It is during these years that the exodus of Iraqi professionals and intellectuals began to take on significant proportions, with possibly as many as half a million leaving by the mid-1980s to pursue lives elsewhere free of the intrusive supervision of Saddam Husain's state. The so-called national institutions, therefore, on closer inspection revealed themselves to be webs of patron–client networks, sustained by the violence used against those who challenged the system, dispensing the ruler's patronage along lines which gave the lie to the official myth of a distinctive, unifying Iraqi identity.

This ambiguity pervaded all aspects of associational life, from the trade unions and the peasants' organisations to the General Federation of Iraqi Women. As far as the latter was concerned, it had been established soon after the Ba'thist coup d'état of 1968 ostensibly to voice the concerns and interests of Iraqi women, much on the pattern of the women's organisation al-Rabita in the early 1960s. Insofar as the developmental preoccupations of the government coincided with those of Iraqi women – particularly in the spheres of literacy, education and the opportunity to enter the non-agricultural labour force (of which women had always formed a key part) – the federation was successful. State-sponsored membership grew spectacularly, as did the resources and facilities dedicated to women's education and health. In 1978 the change in the personal status laws which gave courts the power to overrule male members of a woman's family in certain areas appeared to be a substantial advance for women. Some believed that it would allow the long-suppressed public narrative of women in Iraq to emerge from the dominant patriarchal values so closely associated with the development of the state. However, on closer inspection, the concessions were not so dramatic. Nor were women empowered to consolidate the positions granted to them in this law. Like all other Iraqis, they and their interests could be suppressed if it seemed useful to Saddam Husain to do so. In the case of Iraqi women, this was most notoriously expressed in the law of 1988, which not only recognised but also legalised the so-called honour killings in Iraqi society, permitting men to kill their wives or female relatives if they were judged to have dishonoured the family name by committing adultery.[14]

In constructing the core of their power in the state Saddam Husain and his associates looked first to the values and personnel of their own communities, but they also looked beyond this narrow social base. Their patronage was not confined to the clans of the Sunni Arab north-west, although the commanding positions in the regime and the security services without exception went to men from such backgrounds. In areas such as the officer corps, where the Sunni Arab preponderance was an outcome of its history and that of the state itself, it would have been perverse and dangerous to have favoured other groups at their expense. Nevertheless, in many symbolically prominent positions, as well as in local organisations, the whole range of Iraq's diverse population was well represented.

This was very much part of Saddam Husain's strategy. In drawing the people of Iraq under his personal domination, he was seeking to create among the Iraqis a dependent client base that would have a stake in the survival of his regime. In doing so, he hoped both to displace some communal leaders who had hitherto commanded obedience, and to recruit others who could 'deliver' the clan or community which they headed. This gave him a unique position and reassured his intimates that he too could guarantee the social order that allowed them to enjoy their privileges undisturbed. This was all the more important in view of the fears of ethnic and sectarian challenges in 1979.

In the Kurdish areas there was renewed guerrilla activity, organised in the main by the KDP, which had confirmed Idris and Masoud Barzani's dominance at its congress of November 1979 (Mulla Mustafa had died

18 Masoud Barzani (leader of the Kurdistan Democratic Party,
president of the Kurdistan Region since 2005), 1996

earlier that year). Some of the KDP's energies were diverted by clashes with
the rival PUK, but a growing number of attacks on government targets
indicated that the Kurdish region was once again bestirring itself. More
ominously for Baghdad, as its relations with the new regime in Tehran
began to deteriorate, the KDP looked to the Iranian government for
support. Because the Barzani brothers were willing to help the Iranian government in its fight against the Kurdish movement in Iranian Kurdistan –
the KDP-I (Kurdistan Democratic Party – Iran) under 'Abd al-Rahman
Qassemlou – the KDP enjoyed increasingly good relations with Tehran.
Jalal Talabani, on the other hand, because of the PUK's links with
Qassemlou, could not be a party to this and reopened contacts with
Baghdad. Saddam Husain encouraged these overtures, exploiting divisions

among the Kurds, extending his patronage among many of the tribal leaders and among the urban, educated classes who had been drawn into the burgeoning bureaucracy of the Iraqi state, either directly or through the machinery of the 'autonomous region'.

More troubling for the regime was the continued organisation of opposition activity amongst the urban Shi'a of Iraq and the encouragement they seemed to receive from the new Iranian government. Confrontations between the security forces and members of the Shi'i community had continued throughout the summer of 1979, encouraged by the revival of some of the militant Islamist underground organisations, sometimes working in tandem, sometimes acting on their own initiative. Al-Da'wa, Jund al-Imam and the Islamic Task Organisation all agreed on the need for violent action against the regime and in October 1979 this attitude was endorsed by Jama'at al-'Ulama (the Society of Religious Scholars, founded by Ayatollah al-Hakim in 1958), overcoming its earlier scruples. The government responded with mass arrests and executions which were given a semblance of legality by a retroactive decree of March 1980 making membership of al-Da'wa punishable by death. Undeterred, a member of the Islamic Task Organisation tried to kill the deputy prime minister, Tariq 'Aziz, in Baghdad in April. This public attempt on the life of so prominent a member of Saddam Husain's circle unleashed a furious government response.

Within days Ayatollah Baqir al-Sadr and his sister, Bint al-Huda, an influential scholar in her own right, were taken from Najaf to Baghdad where they were hastily executed. This was the first time in the history of Iraq that so senior a cleric had been killed and was an ominous indicator of the regime's determination to force the Shi'i leaders into a posture of obedience. At the same time, the most senior *mujtahid,* Ayatollah al-Kho'i, was placed under virtual house arrest in Najaf and the government stepped up its deportations of so-called Iranian Shi'a, expelling an estimated 40,000 during 1980 alone. Their property was confiscated and in many cases auctioned off, making others effectively complicit in their dispossession. For Saddam Husain this was important, since he was trying to draw as many as possible into the complex network of patronage and obligation that permeated all communities in Iraq. It made the formation of coalitions, grouped around distinctively community-based interests, extraordinarily difficult. The new hierarchies of power and wealth among those Shi'a who depended upon the regime created alternative leaders to the clerics and laymen who had proved so intractable. Many of these had either been executed, imprisoned or had fled into exile in Iran, which was now to become the chief focus of the Iraqi government's attention.[15]

Relations between the two regimes had been deteriorating since 1979. The Iraqi government had initially made friendly overtures to the Bazargan government. However, the antipathy between the new Islamic regime in Shi'i Iran and the Iraqi government which was ruthless in its treatment of Iraq's Shi'i Islamists could not long remain concealed. In Iran the Iraqi regime was portrayed as the embodiment of all that needed to be swept away if the region was to be transformed. For Saddam Husain, this confirmed both the aggressive and sectarian nature of the Iranian regime. It also underlined the questionable loyalties of much of the Iraqi population, reinforcing the insecurity of the narrow circles of the Iraqi regime. Nor could the question of Iran be simply ignored or relegated to a position of relative insignificance. Quite apart from the effect on Iraq's Shi'a, Saddam Husain had to take into account two other factors.

The first was the question of his authority as an Arab leader and the second stemmed from the nature of his authority as head of the territorial state of Iraq. Since at least 1978 Saddam Husain had been manoeuvring to position Iraq under his leadership as the pivotal Arab state. The summits of 1978 and 1979 had been followed in February 1980 by the publication of the Arab Charter in Baghdad, to which most of the states which had attended the Baghdad summits subscribed. It was a restatement of common Arab goals, but the substance of the charter was of less importance than Saddam Husain's sponsorship of it. He was clearly projecting an image of Iraq as a leading power – perhaps the leading power – in the Arab world: wealthy, militarily powerful, politically stable, on relatively good terms with most Arab states and a champion of recognised Arab causes from the Mediterranean to the Gulf.

It was on the Gulf in particular that Saddam Husain focused since it was here that the new, radical regime in Iran seemed to present the greatest threat to the existing order. The assertion of Iraq's leadership of the Arab world was important for Saddam Husain's self-image as a historical Arab leader, but it also helped to secure the allegiance of much of the Sunni Arab population on whose support the extensive networks of his inner circle ultimately depended. Saddam Husain had shown that he was no believer in abstract visions of pan-Arabism. Rather, he saw the Arab world as a stage on which the Iraqi state, constructed as an emanation of his will, should play the leading role, for the benefit of himself and those who sustained his rule in Iraq. Concentrating on the Iranian danger allowed him to assert his dedication to an Arab cause without running the risk of entanglements with Syria. It also allowed him to pose as the protector of the Arab Gulf states which could yield dividends in the future. In particular, increasing trust between Iraq and Kuwait could lead to a territorial settlement favourable to Iraq as it moved to develop the port of Umm Qasr. It was in this context, therefore, that Saddam Husain revived the question of the 'Arab islands' in the Gulf which Iran had annexed in 1971, and reasserted the Arab character of the Iranian province of Khuzestan, suggesting that the time had come for its liberation.

As relations with Iran deteriorated, the question of the fulfilment and status of the treaty of 1975 surfaced. The treaty was a particular problem for Saddam Husain. Few in Iraq knew or cared about its redrawing of the frontier of the two states in the Shatt al-'Arab, but Saddam Husain was well aware both of the concessions forced upon Iraq by Iran's power and of the possibility that these concessions might be used as a potent symbol of his own readiness to sacrifice Iraq's national interests. The latter point became more acute with his assumption of the presidency in 1979. He was now posing as the champion of all Iraq and was repeatedly asserting the distinctive Iraqi character of the population, binding them together in a single political community, dominated and protected by Saddam Husain alone. As he emphasised Iraq's national identity, so it was inevitable that greater attention should be paid to the territory of the state. Consequently, the conflict with Iran began to find territorial expression, focusing on the Shatt al-'Arab in particular, where Iraq revived its claim to exercise full sovereignty over the whole of the waterway.

During the first part of 1980 a few border clashes took place – always a barometer of the poor state of relations. At the same time, the outlines of an unparalleled opportunity began to appear before Saddam Husain and the Iraqi leadership. Revolutionary Iran was volatile and aggressive, but it also seemed weak. Beset by provincial unrest and factionalism at the centre, the regime did not look secure. Furthermore, the notorious mistrust between the revolutionary regime and Iran's armed forces had led to purges of thousands of officers and to administrative chaos in the military. In addition, the break in relations with the United States had severed Iran's main supply of arms and had helped to isolate the new regime internationally. From the perspective of Baghdad, the regime in Tehran looked weak, disorganised and isolated – in some respects a mirror image of the condition of the Iraqi regime in the late 1960s which had so encouraged the shah to press for the concessions which he had eventually won in 1975.

Saddam Husain, by contrast, was confident of his own and his state's strength and relative power. He had destroyed his most intimate opponents to gain undisputed mastery of the Iraqi state, safe for the moment from the factional infighting which had undermined previous Iraqi leaders. The armed forces had been massively reinforced and rearmed as a result of the great increase in the military budget since the mid-1970s, and there was no war in Kurdistan to distract them. Furthermore, Iraq's international relations were in a better condition than they had been for some time: its pre-eminence in the Arab world and in the Gulf was increasingly recognised; its relations with the superpowers were promising, if not particularly cordial, in that the Treaty of Friendship and Co-operation with the USSR remained in force, whilst Iraq had established good trading relations with the Western powers.

It is against this background that Saddam Husain saw a limited war against Iran as a way of forcing the Iranian regime to acknowledge that the balance of power had shifted in favour of Iraq. Tangible proof of such an acknowledgement was to be the scrapping of the 1975 treaty and the restoration of Iraqi sovereignty over the whole of the Shatt al-'Arab. Territorially of little significance in itself, this concession was intended not only to efface Iraq's – and Saddam Husain's – weakness of the mid-1970s, but also to demonstrate that the new and threatening regime in Iran had been brought to heel by the power of Iraq. In terms of symbolic value and thus of the authority of the Iraqi government and the power of Iraq, there was a great deal invested in this desired concession – so much so that Saddam Husain thought it was worth going to war to achieve it.

In a dramatic gesture Saddam Husain publicly abrogated the 1975 treaty and asserted Iraqi sovereignty over the whole of the Shatt al-'Arab before a meeting of the National Assembly on 17 September 1980. This was followed on 22 September by a series of pre-emptive attacks by the Iraqi air force on Iran's military airfields and by the invasion of Iranian territory by Iraqi forces at a number of points. Some Iraqi units had specific targets, such as the towns of Abadan and Khorramshahr on the Shatt al-'Arab, whilst others had orders simply to occupy as much Iranian territory as they could. The campaign was being used as a show of force which would oblige the Iranian government to negotiate a rapid end to the hostilities on terms favourable to Iraq, through territorial concessions and the public acknowledgement of Iraq's superiority.

Saddam Husain believed that the insecure and enfeebled Iranian regime would have to disengage in order to survive. This was a catastrophic miscalculation. Not only were the Iraqi armed forces considerably less competent than Saddam Husain had anticipated, but, more importantly, the Iranian government saw the attack as a test of the revolution itself. Defence of the country and of the revolution became the focus of popular mobilisation in Iran, used by the regime to rally support and to consolidate its control. Within weeks it was clear that the short, demonstrative war planned by Saddam Husain had become something very different and, in a rare moment of public frankness, he admitted as much.[16]

Nevertheless, he tried to turn the situation to his advantage, claiming that the reassertion of Iraqi sovereignty in the Shatt al-'Arab was a matter of national honour and a sacred mission for the nation and its leaders. At the same time, Iraq made claims on the province of Khuzestan. It is unlikely that these claims excited much enthusiasm among most of the Iraqi population – still less among the population of Khuzestan – but, apart from the inhabitants of Basra, few were aware of the effects of the war. The regime ensured that life continued much as usual. Its oil export potential had been damaged by the Iranian destruction of the installations at al-Faw, but the shortfall looked as if it would be temporary and Iraq's massive currency reserves could easily cover it. Despite initial disappointment at the Iranian reaction, the Iraqi leadership still believed that Iran would soon be obliged to negotiate and was thus determined to insulate the people of Iraq from the consequences of war.

This complacency governed the first year or so of the war. After Iraq's initial offensive, little happened on the military front. Domestically, the security forces continued to clamp down on any signs of organised resistance among the Shi'a, responding ferociously to the formation of such groups as the Jama'at al-'Ulama al-Mujahidin in Iran, led by Muhammad Baqir al-Hakim, and dedicated to the establishment of an Islamic order in Iraq. The severity of the government's attack on the Shi'a and their organisations led some militant parties to encourage their followers to make their way to Iran. Here they joined the thousands of alleged 'Iranian' Shi'a who continued to be expelled from Iraq. Taking this further, in 1981 the Iraqi government began to provide financial incentives for Iraqi men to divorce their 'Iranian' wives (generally those connected to families already expelled, or marked down for expulsion), intending to create rifts among the Shi'a and forming part of a government campaign to underline the Arab nature of Iraq's Shi'i population. Playing on themes of Arab identity and superiority, the government hoped to drive a wedge between the Iraqi Shi'a who formed the bulk of the soldiers in Iraq's armed forces and the Shi'i Iranians whom they were being ordered to fight. At the same time, the government brought the Shi'i hierarchy under stricter control, supervising the contents of sermons, taking over control of all Shi'i shrines and mosques, appointing those whom they favoured to positions of responsibility and making all Shi'i *ulama* salaried employees of the state, as their Sunni counterparts had been for some time.

In the Kurdish areas, the KDP looked upon the outbreak of war as an opportunity, but in practice there was little it could do beyond the rather limited hit-and-run attacks of the preceding couple of years. Most of its energies and those of its rivals, the PUK, were devoted to fighting each other and the Kurdish and communist factions which had small armed followings in the Kurdish region. This was reassuring for Baghdad, which granted more than usually lavish quantities of patronage to the tribal leaders of the Kurdish *jahsh* irregular forces. At the same time, it kept channels open to various Kurdish leaders, even hinting that further concessions on autonomy might be made.

As far as Saddam Husain's inner circle was concerned, the confidence of those whom he had already selected as his principal agents, and who in any case had a similar outlook on the world, did not falter. The purges of 1979 had deterred the voicing of doubts. However, at this stage, although they too were exasperated by Iran's failure to respond in the way they desired, they were in no doubt about the depth of Iran's enmity or the links between Iran and some of the forces which these men most despised in Iraqi society, such as the Shi'i hierarchy, the Islamist organisations and the continually disaffected Kurdish rebels. The events of 1982 were to reinforce some of these beliefs, but at the same time, dangerously for Saddam Husain, they momentarily shook the confidence of some in his judgement, throwing into doubt his capacity to command the obedience and respect of the people on whom he most relied for his power.[17]

DEFENDING THE REGIME AND IRAQ AFTER 1982

In 1982 Iran counter-attacked and was more successful than many had anticipated. The Iraqi forces were driven out of most of the territory they had occupied in 1980, suffering heavy casualties, with an estimated 40,000 Iraqi troops taken prisoner. The Iraqi army succeeded in holding the line at the border and prevented the Iranians from pursuing their victory into the heart of Iraq itself, but the defeats of 1982 came as a blow for Saddam Husain. They threw into question his strategic judgement in launching the war in the first place. Furthermore, the mounting toll of casualties and prisoners meant that the human cost of the war could no longer be hidden from the Iraqi people. The economic cost was also evident since Iraq's growing military expenditures and the attempt to maintain a constant level of public investment in the civil infrastructure and the welfare state had reduced Iraq's foreign currency reserves from $30 billion in 1980 to about $3 billion by 1983. Nor could this be made up by oil revenues, since Iraq's oil income had fallen from $26 billion in 1980 to about $9 billion in 1982, following the destruction of the terminal at al-Faw and Syria's closure of the Banias pipeline in April 1982. By 1983, Iraq's foreign debt stood at about $25 billion.[18]

Given the power of the various security agencies, any rumblings of popular dissatisfaction with this state of affairs could be safely ignored by the regime, but it was harder for Saddam Husain to ignore the effect on people within the inner circle. They were all tied to him in some measure, but the gravity of the crisis and the possibility that they might all be swept away unless they in turn sued for peace led to thoughts of how best to extricate themselves. In these circumstances an extraordinary joint meeting was held in June 1982 of the RCC, the Iraqi Military Command and the Regional and National Commands of the Ba'th, in the absence of Saddam Husain. A cease-fire proposal was worked out that offered a return to the status quo ante, abandoning all the claims made by Saddam Husain in 1980. Had this offer been accepted by Iran, Saddam Husain could hardly have survived with his authority intact and might not have survived at all since it was endorsed by the entire leadership, including some of Saddam Husain's most intimate followers. In the event, the offer was rejected out of hand by Khomaini and the Iranian government, now confident that Iran could carry the war into Iraq and achieve its goal of sweeping away the entire Iraqi leadership.

Iran's uncompromising attitude strengthened Saddam Husain. Regardless of his responsibility for the miscalculation of 1980, the Iranian government made it impossible for his colleagues to dissociate themselves from him or from the decision to go to war. Consequently, none of them could pose as a credible alternative leader to negotiate a cease-fire – a point that Saddam Husain repeatedly stressed in responding to the Iranian suggestion that the war could end if he were to give up the presidency. More pertinently for those in a position to act, he let it be known that he had personally shot the minister of health for daring to suggest such a move, although it was publicly given out that the minister had been executed for corruption. Whatever the truth of the minister's death, Saddam Husain was responding to the possibility that some formula might be worked out whereby he would step down temporarily in favour of his predecessor, Hasan al-Bakr, in order to satisfy the Iranian demand that he should leave office. Hasan al-Bakr's sudden death in October 1982 while these dangerous ideas were being floated inevitably strengthened Saddam Husain's hand. It removed a possible focus of inner-circle opposition to his own leadership and added to his already fearsome reputation as someone so ruthless that he would not hesitate to order the death of his kinsman and erstwhile patron.

Saddam Husain used a number of strategies to strengthen his position. He reshuffled the RCC, the Regional Command of the Ba'th and the cabinet in the summer of 1982, identifying each of these bodies even more closely with his person, since they were now all exclusively composed of his closest associates, kinsmen and protégés. He went on to convene the 9th Congress of the Regional Command of the Ba'th, dictating a final report which downplayed all the traditional Ba'thist preoccupations, such as Arab nationalism and socialism, and stressed instead the primacy of Iraq, the significance of religion and the importance of wealth creation and private enterprise. Most important of all was the defining role which was now assigned to Saddam Husain personally (given the awkward epithet of the 'Leader Necessity' (*al-Qa'id al-Durura*)) as presiding genius and ultimate arbiter of the party's ideology. As he himself was to remark a few years later, the ideology of the Ba'th Party was to be whatever he said it was.[19]

In addition to these moves, Saddam Husain made a point of lavishing attention on the armed forces, in part to counteract criticism from within the military of his strategic vision and in part to secure his political base in the military against any threat. Individual officers were promoted and favoured and the officer corps as a whole received generous material rewards and allowances. In some ways, the relationship was made easier by the very plight of Iraq in a war that was now unmistakably defensive. The Iranian threat was very real and the Iraqi officer corps, as professionals occupying a certain position within the Iraqi state, regardless generally of their backgrounds, were determined to deny Iran a military victory. Their principal demand was that they should be given the means to carry out a task which few of them questioned.

There had been general criticism in the early years of the war of the ubiquitous Ba'thist party cadres, keeping watch on the loyalties of the officer corps and ensuring that all initiatives were authorised by the leadership. This clumsy and demeaning referral of all military decisions back to the political leadership in an atmosphere of mistrust had cost the Iraqi armed forces dear in the first years of the war. Their task was made harder by the toll on professionalism taken by years of political shuffling and personal factionalism which had led incompetents to be promoted on grounds of political reliability. However, in 1982 the military task was greatly simplified. The political leadership redefined the war aims in terms of the survival of the Iraqi state and could be confident that this was a goal shared by the officer corps. At the same time, the rapid expansion of the armed forces and the massive purchases of military equipment enhanced the officers' position. Surveillance was not relaxed and there were repeated reports of assassination plots and purges, but material and professional incentives were used to good effect. The officer corps was now focused on a professional task entirely in keeping with the regime's view of the armed forces' responsibilities, although the development of a marked professionalism in the armed forces was eventually to create problems for Saddam Husain.

In the meantime, however, the Iraqi leaders, both political and military, were preoccupied with the task of developing an effective counter-strategy that would oblige the Iranian government to accept a cease-fire. To this end it invested massively – through funds lent to Iraq chiefly by Saudi Arabia, Kuwait and the other Gulf states, as well as through arms deals with the USSR and France – in the purchase of conventional weapons, with military expenditures averaging about $15 billion per year for the eight years of the war. Furthermore, the government accelerated its programme for the acquisition and development of non-conventional weapons of mass destruction. In June 1981, an Israeli air raid on the Osirak nuclear reactor drew general attention to the military potential of the Iraqi nuclear programme which had been initiated under Saddam Husain's auspices in the early 1970s. Chemical and biological weapons programmes had also been started, receiving large amounts of government funding by the late 1970s and benefiting from elaborate networks set up in Europe and elsewhere for the acquisition of expertise and the necessary materials. Starting in 1984, chemical weapons were used intermittently on the front when conditions seemed favourable, but their direct military impact was less great than their effect on the morale of the Iranian soldiers. In certain engagements, the knowledge that Iraq was prepared to use such weapons could be decisive.

At this stage these weapons were essentially defensive in nature. Iraq's strategy in the war had become focused on holding the land front and preventing any Iranian breakthrough to Iraq's major cities. Its growing superiority in conventional weaponry, the construction of massive fortifications and defensive works and the selective use of chemical weapons gave Iraq an edge over the repeated offensives launched by Iran. Nevertheless, despite the high human cost this inflicted on the Iranian forces, the Iranian leadership maintained its strategy of relentless pressure on the land front. This forced the Iraqi leadership to devise other strategies. Resources were poured into Iraq's surface-to-surface missile development, in which Soviet Scud missiles were adapted for use on targets deep inside Iran. This initiated the 'war of the cities' in 1985 which came to an end when Iran showed that it too could inflict damage on Iraq's cities. At the same time, with the assistance of France, Iraq was developing its air force to attack economic targets – principally the oil industry – in Iran, hoping thereby to cripple Iran's economy.

By 1984–5 Iraq's air force was inflicting serious damage on Iran's oil installations at Kharg island, scaring off much of the international shipping on which Iran depended for its oil exports. The success of these tactics led to longer-range attacks on Iran's oil terminals further down the Gulf at Sirri and Lavan islands. Inevitably, Iraq's attacks on Iran's oil industry and on shipping trading with Iran led to Iranian reprisals against ships doing business with Iraq or with Iraq's Arab Gulf allies which were by now financing Iraq's war effort. This potential danger to the flow of oil led, in turn, to the increased presence of Western naval forces in the Gulf. Headed by the United States, other Western countries, principally Great Britain and France, maintained naval flotillas in the area, with the express purpose of deterring Iranian attacks on international shipping.

So great had the dangers of the escalating 'tanker war' become by 1987 that Kuwait started leasing Soviet and US tankers, deliberately intensifying international and particularly American naval involvement. In these circumstances, US forces clashed repeatedly with Iranian naval units, culminating in 1988 with the destruction of much of Iran's naval capability and creating the conditions in which US naval forces shot down a civilian Iranian airliner. The economic cost of Iraq's sustained attacks on Iran's oil installations had been high. However, it was the apparently open-ended commitment of US naval forces to the war in the waters of the Gulf, effectively on Iraq's side, which seems to have been a decisive factor in inducing the Iranian government in the summer of 1988 to accept the terms of the UN cease-fire, laid out in UN SC Resolution 598 of 1987. It appeared to Tehran that Iran was now involved in a war not simply with Iraq, but also with the Western powers with which Iraq had been developing an increasingly close relationship during the war years.

Saddam Husain's view of the role of the superpowers had formed a central part of his war strategy from the outset. As he had demonstrated in the 1970s, he was very conscious of the ability of the superpowers to determine the success or otherwise of his regional initiatives. However, like other leaders of third world states during the Cold War he had few scruples about playing one off against the other or about courting both simultaneously. In 1980 Iran's rupture with the United States and its relative isolation at the

UN had been important in Saddam Husain's calculation of the risks involved in invading Iranian territory. The general failure to condemn the Iraqi invasion tended to prove him right. Only the reaction of the Soviet Union in immediately stopping arms shipments to Iraq because of its own developing relationship with Iran appeared to take Saddam Husain by surprise. However, this provided an opportunity for Iraq to draw closer to the Western states which could help to sustain the Iraqi war effort in a variety of ways. Furthermore, when the tide of battle turned in 1982, the Soviet Union began to resupply Iraq on a massive scale, generally subscribing to the common assumption, within the region and beyond, that an Iranian military victory would radically destabilise the Middle East as a whole in a way that would be to the advantage of 'neither East nor West' (to use the Iranian slogan of the time). As Iran discovered, use of this slogan exacted a heavy price since by 1988 it found that both 'East' and 'West' were actively supporting Iraq's war effort.[20]

By the mid-1980s, not only had Iraq re-established full diplomatic relations with the United States, but it was also benefiting from the material support of a range of Western states, most notably the United States itself, France and Great Britain. Some of this assistance came in the form of financial credits, some in consumer goods and some in military supplies directly useful to Iraq's war effort. Iraq found itself in the happy position of being courted and supplied by both superpowers and their allies, successfully enlisting their assistance for its war effort in the waters of the Gulf and on the land front. As the relationship with the United States blossomed, Iraq was provided with detailed satellite information, giving the Iraqi forces immediate and accurate intelligence of Iranian military initiatives and positions. This was to play an important role in defeating Iranian attacks and in ensuring Iraq's success when its own forces went on the offensive in 1988.

Iran's decision to accept the cease-fire terms that year was strongly influenced by these reversals on the land front, where repeated attempts to break through the Iraqi lines had only limited success and had cost the lives of hundreds of thousands of Iranians. By 1988, the superior condition of the Iraqi armed forces was beginning to tell. The success of the Iraqi armed forces and the decision to go on the offensive was due not simply to better intelligence and to the massive superiority of their weaponry, but also to basic changes in the way in which the armed forces were used. These had come about as a result of the crisis between Saddam Husain and his military commanders in the summer of 1986. He had emerged dominant politically, but there had been a significant shift in the patterns of authority that underpinned his regime. It was a shift which he found difficult to tolerate, but it was forced upon him by the perilous situation in the war at the time.

In the years following 1982 Iran had repeatedly launched costly, but futile, offensives against the Iraqi lines. The front held and the large numbers of casualties inflicted on Iran gave hope that it might reconsider its war aims. However, this relatively static position changed dramatically in February 1986 when Iranian troops captured and held the al-Faw peninsula at the mouth of the Shatt al-'Arab. The importance Saddam Husain attached to recovering al-Faw was demonstrated by the fact that he ordered the elite units of the Republican Guard into battle. These units, recruited from and officered by members of Saddam Husain's tribal group and allied clans from the region of Takrit, had hitherto been kept in reserve. Their function – like the Republican Guard under the 'Arif brothers – was primarily to defend the regime itself from internal attack by other army units in the event of a coup d'état. For that very reason they had been manned almost exclusively by individuals who shared Saddam Husain's background and were thus identified with him in important ways. However, they suffered heavy casualties at al-Faw, leading their officers to join others in recommending disengagement.

This led to a confrontation between Saddam Husain and some of the senior military command in which, ominously for him, officers of the Republican Guard and other kinsmen and clansmen in the Iraqi army made common cause with their fellow officers. Arguing from a professional military standpoint, they made it clear that they could not commit the forces under their command to futile military exercises simply to accord with the political priorities of the leadership. This was a challenge to Saddam Husain's claim to be all knowing and all powerful and, as such, it was a political challenge. However, when faced by professional solidarity of this kind which seemed to cut through all his carefully established networks of clan and familial patronage and control, Saddam Husain was obliged to bow to the advice of his senior commanders. He consoled himself by planning a way of regaining the military initiative.

This resulted in the ill-fated offensive at Mehran in May 1986. Hailed in the Iraqi media as an example of Saddam Husain's military genius, the occupation of this town was portrayed as a form of revenge for the Iranian capture of the territory of al-Faw. In fact, it dangerously exposed the Iraqi forces and fell to an Iranian counter-attack in July. This incident appears to have led to a second confrontation between Saddam Husain and his senior military commanders. For many of the Iraqi high command the occupation of Mehran epitomised the danger of allowing the political leadership to dictate war strategy at this level. The years of war, the great improvements in the Iraqi armed forces and the immediacy of the Iranian military threat had created a degree of corporate professional solidarity which had eroded the network of clientelistic and kinship solidarities on which Saddam Husain relied to ensure the subordination of the military to his dictatorship. These had not been displaced and had indeed proliferated, as any glance at the identities of the senior unit commanders and of the high command would have confirmed. However, first al-Faw and then Mehran indicated that there were occasions when professional or corporate solidarity and the specialist demands to which this gave rise could confront Saddam Husain in a way that his own systems of control appeared powerless to prevent.

Whatever form the confrontation took, the results were significant. Greater independence of military planning from the political leadership of Saddam Husain and the RCC allowed Iraqi military commanders greater freedom to respond to Iranian attacks without referring to Baghdad. Equally, the Iraqi air force returned to the field as an operational arm of the armed forces, having disappeared from the land front since its failure at the outset of the war to establish air superiority over Iran. Saddam Husain feared the cost of attrition of this particular branch of the Iraqi services, seeing the air force largely as a 'weapon of last resort'. His reluctance to use the air force in this way may also have been due in part to his mistrust of its political allegiances, since its officers were not so easily controlled by networks of clan affiliation.

Given the situation on the war front, Saddam Husain recognised that he was in no position to do anything about this crystallising of corporate feeling at the time. However, he could also see that giving the armed forces professional, institutional definition would undermine his political leadership, eroding his methods of control and questioning his chosen strategies. Consequently, whilst ceding to the demands of the military, he also tightened up his control of the state apparatus, dismissing some officials, transferring others and relying ever more heavily on the narrow circle of kinsmen and associates who formed the core of his regime. He was determined that the same processes of 'institutional answerability' should not take hold within the political leadership and its extended networks of control. His insertion of kinsmen and members of other trusted clans to positions of command in the armed forces naturally continued but, as Iraq's military fortunes demonstrated over the next couple of years, they could not seriously interfere with the professional competence of the Iraqi military.[21]

RESISTANCE AMONGST THE KURDS AND THE SHIʿA

This combination of factors helped Saddam Husain to turn his attention once again to the situation in Kurdistan – a situation which had been largely neglected during the previous few years because of its seeming marginality to the struggle on the southern front. However, in 1987, with the apparent stalling of the Iranian offensives in the south, Iran's military planners turned their attention to the Kurdish areas where an alliance between the KDP and the PUK in 1985 had led to more sustained and effective military operations against Iraqi government positions. For his part, Saddam Husain, already concerned about the erosion of his authority caused by the continued failure of the Iraqi forces to recapture al-Faw and by his new relationship with the Iraqi military command, saw Kurdistan as a field of opportunity for demonstrating his power and ruthlessness. This combination of factors prompted him in March 1987 to appoint his cousin ʿAli Hasan al-Majid (hitherto the head of the state security service and member of the Regional Command of the Baʿth) as his viceroy in the north. As such, he was in absolute command of all state and party agencies, including all military forces and intelligence organisations, and was answerable only to Saddam Husain.

The situation which al-Majid faced and over which he was to assert control in a fearsome manner was one which had developed since July 1983 when the Iranian high command launched a major offensive across the border into the Kurdish region. This led to the capture of the town of Hajj ʿUmran and to Iranian occupation of areas near Penjwin in the south-east of the Kurdish region. The KDP had assisted the Iranian forces, providing invaluable local support and intelligence. In revenge and as an example to others who might have been thinking of collaborating with Iran, the Iraqi security forces rounded up an estimated 8,000 men and boys of the Barzani clan and almost certainly killed them. One other consequence of the Iranian advance in 1983 was to drive the PUK closer to the government in Baghdad, since its leadership felt threatened by the Iranian forces and by the advantage this would give to its KDP rivals. Saddam Husain opened negotiations with the leader of the PUK, Jalal Talabani, and held out the possibility of a favourable renegotiation of the terms of the autonomy agreement. This proved to be illusory, but the split between the PUK and the KDP deepened and the eighteen months during which these negotiations dragged on had helped Baghdad to limit further gains by Iran or its allies in the Kurdish region.

By January 1985, it was clear that Saddam Husain was unwilling to accede to the PUK's demands concerning financial autonomy, Kurdish control of the Kirkuk oil fields or the question of local control of the security forces in the Kurdish region. In essence, these had been the sticking points in all previous negotiations between Baghdad and the Kurds and, as on previous occasions, they led to the collapse of the talks. The PUK reverted to opposition, mobilised its own guerrilla forces and established links with Tehran. Consequently, by mid-1985, Baghdad was facing a deteriorating security situation. Iran's efforts to mediate between the two rival Kurdish parties had some success and an informal military division of labour developed, with the KDP and the PUK carving out areas of de facto autonomy in the parts of Kurdistan where their social support was greatest. Consequently, by late 1986 Iraqi government forces controlled only the principal cities and towns, the oil pipelines and the major roads linking the population centres. Elsewhere, the KDP, the PUK and a number of other smaller Kurdish parties and local defence organisations had established themselves, in many cases neutralising the *jahsh*, whose leaders were increasingly reluctant to provide even the minimal support that they had once supplied to the government forces.

It was against this background and with the knowledge that Saddam Husain was now determined to reassert government control over Kurdistan at all costs that 'Ali Hasan al-Majid took up his new post and initiated the violent campaign known as *al-Anfal* (the spoils of war). Chemical weapons were used (their first recorded use by Iraqi forces in Kurdistan was in April 1987), as much to inspire terror as to achieve any strictly military purpose. Men suspected of belonging to the guerrilla organisations or who had deserted from the Iraqi army were captured and executed. Villages in the designated areas were demolished, agriculture destroyed and all surviving inhabitants were transferred to government-controlled resettlement camps. During 1987 these campaigns were intermittent and, although they gave an indication of the capabilities and intentions of the Iraqi regime, they did not succeed in reversing the military situation in the Kurdish region.

In part this was due to uncertainty about Iranian intentions on the southern front and the concern of the Iraqi authorities to conserve their resources. However, by early 1988 it was clear that no major Iranian offensive would materialise and indeed that the Iranian military capacity was much reduced. Consequently, the Iraqi government turned its full attention on the Kurdish region, providing 'Ali Hasan al-Majid with the resources he needed to destroy all Kurdish resistance. In February 1988 *al-Anfal* proper began. Iraqi forces carried out a scorched-earth policy in all those areas associated with one or other of the Kurdish guerrilla organisations, killing all the inhabitants and demolishing their villages. Chemical weapons were now used routinely and the victims included women and children, as well as the men of military age who had always been targeted. Few were given the option of moving to resettlement camps. Faced by such an onslaught, the Kurdish guerrilla organisations were powerless and tried instead to get their people to safety. Iranian assistance was minimal and when Iranian forces did intervene, as in the capture of the Kurdish town of Halabja in March 1988, the Iraqi forces responded with such ferocity that the cost to the local civilian population could not be sustained. In the case of Halabja, chemical weapons killed an estimated 5,000 people, causing the rest of the population to flee to the Iranian border.

By the end of March 1988, the PUK headquarters had been captured and it became difficult for the PUK to organise any sustained resistance in the devastated countryside. KDP resistance continued, but, after the cease-fire between Iran and Iraq in July 1988, the Iraqi government threw the full power of their armed forces against the last strongholds of the KDP. Faced by this assault, the KDP advised its men to offer minimal resistance and to ensure that their families escaped to safety across the Turkish border. By the end of August, all organised resistance was at an end and the Iraqi armed forces were in control of the whole of the Kurdish region. In the three governorates of the Kurdish autonomous region, roughly 80 per cent of all the villages had been destroyed, much of the agricultural land was declared 'prohibited territory' and possibly 100,000 people had lost their lives. Executions of those captured during the *al-Anfal* campaigns continued, but in early September 1988, the government declared an amnesty, allowing even former *peshmerga* to return to Iraq, although their home villages had usually been destroyed.

Al-Anfal was the logical if brutal conclusion of the policies pursued by the regime towards the Kurds. Those who were willing to accept Baghdad's patronage were tolerated, if not wholly trusted. Nevertheless, they were used and rewarded in the fight against those who rejected the authority of Saddam Husain and the government in Baghdad. The KDP and the PUK, having successfully challenged the central government, had set a dangerous precedent and Saddam Husain was determined to make an example of them and of the people on whom they depended. Iraqis were told that the punishment of the Kurds was due to their treacherous behaviour in siding with Iran, but their real crime was to have successfully defied Saddam Husain's will. The devastation of *al-Anfal* had demonstrated not only to the Kurds, but to all Iraqis, in the circles of power as elsewhere, the fate of those who stepped out of the 'national ranks', as defined by Saddam Husain himself.[22]

In some respects, a not dissimilar attitude shaped the policies of the regime towards the Shi'a of Iraq during these years. Since they formed the majority of Iraq's population and thus the bulk of the armed forces, their subordination required rather different tactics. This was also necessary because the regime was seeking to mobilise them en masse against Iran, whose government was adamant in stressing its Shi'i identity and thus, potentially, the common cause of Iraqi and Iranian Shi'a. To counter this, the Iraqi government pursued a number of strategies that not only tried to make a clear divide between Iraqis and Iranians, but that also brought out the many identities amongst the Shi'a of Iraq. These identities were not created by the regime and, although encouraged by Saddam Husain, bore testimony as much to the various ways in which differently situated groups of Shi'i Iraqis had engaged historically with the Iraqi state. The rural Shi'a, whose social world was still largely influenced by considerations of particular kinship, family and clan codes of honour and behaviour, differed markedly from the various established groups of urban Shi'a, whether these comprised the clerics, the lay professionals or the urban poor in places like the vast housing project of Madinat Saddam (formerly Madinat al-Thawra, renamed in 1982) in Baghdad. Amongst these groups too there were differences in terms of wealth, status, piety and ideological predilection.

Prior to the war, the Iraqi government had expended considerable effort on encouraging division amongst the Shi'a, using government patronage amongst the clerics, separating off and expelling those Shi'a it labelled as 'Persian' because of their family origins and, rhetorically at least, stressing both Iraqi and Arab identities to distinguish Iraq's Shi'a from those of Iran. This had been accompanied by the suppression of distinctively Shi'i political organisations such as al-Da'wa which were campaigning for the establishment of an Islamic state in Iraq, leading to the flight of many of their members to Iran. There, under the auspices of the Iranian government, the Supreme Council for the Islamic Revolution in Iraq (SCIRI) was formed in 1982. Led by Muhammad Baqir al-Hakim, this began as an umbrella organisation, but increasingly resembled a political party under the command of al-Hakim. Heavily patronised by the Iranian government, al-Hakim seemed increasingly willing to subscribe to the official Iranian Islamic republican doctrine of *velayat-e faqih* (rule of the jurisconsult or chief cleric) as a formula for the future government of Iraq. This alienated other Iraqi Shi'i organisations, such as al-Da'wa, which were wary both of this doctrine and of the close association of SCIRI with the Iranian government. Consequently, they tended to keep their distance from SCIRI.

However, Iranian government sponsorship did allow al-Hakim to create a small military force, the Badr Brigade, recruited in part from Iraqi prisoners of war, which played a limited role in a few engagements, most notably in Kurdistan.

The bulk of Iraq's Shi'i population was unconnected to these political organisations and endured the hardships of the war in much the same spirit as other Iraqis. Whilst the officer corps of the armed forces remained disproportionately filled with Sunni Arabs, as had always been the case, a growing number of Shi'i officers were promoted to positions of prestige and responsibility in which they demonstrated their competence and loyalty in the war against Iran. Rates of desertion from the army were high at certain moments of crisis, but considerably less than those from largely Kurdish units and possibly little different from those of their Sunni compatriots. Fearing the allegiances of the Shi'i footsoldiers who formed the bulk of Iraq's conscript army, the Iraqi government maintained a powerful propaganda campaign throughout the war years which stressed the unity of all Iraqis, the Arab identity of the Iraqi Shi'a, the Islamic credentials of the regime (going so far as to claim Saddam Husain's direct descent from Caliph 'Ali) and the perverted Islam of the non-Arab Persians. Whether this convinced many in Iraq that Iran was indeed a necessary and inveterate enemy of all Iraqis is unknown. It is impossible to judge how far the active participation of Shi'i Iraqis in the war effort was due to their overwhelming sense of their Arab and Iraqi identities. Probably more decisive were pragmatic considerations such as the need to defend themselves against the attacking forces of Iran or the dire consequences for them and their families should they refuse to fight.[23]

In April 1988 the new co-ordinated strategy of the Iraqi high command allowed the Iraqi forces to recapture the al-Faw peninsula in a matter of days. During the following months Iraqi forces went on the offensive in other sectors of the front, breaking the morale of the Iranian troops and demonstrating clearly to the Iranian leadership that Iran now had no hope of achieving its war aims. When the cease-fire was accepted by Iran in July 1988 Saddam Husain trumpeted the victory of Iraq. In terms of his redefinition of the country's war aims, Iraq had indeed been victorious since it had thwarted Iran's attempt to overthrow his regime. It had survived the strains of eight years of war with its principal figures still in place. There had been a number of assassination attempts against Saddam Husain and reports of conspiracies in the armed forces. However, by comparison with previous episodes in Iraqi history, these were relatively isolated events, organised generally by groups which came not from the favoured circles of the regime's social base, but from disgruntled outsiders, particularly amongst the Shiʿa.

Nevertheless, there was a hollowness in Iraq's so-called victory. The goals of September 1980 had been only partially achieved: Iran had finally acknowledged that there were limits to its capacity to carry the Islamic revolution forward and had seemingly been fought to a standstill on the battlefield. Nevertheless, the Shatt al-ʿArab remained blocked and there was no sign that the Iranian government was willing to make the territorial concessions once demanded by Saddam Husain. Furthermore, eight years of war had taken a terrible toll of the Iraqi population: the war had cost Iraq an estimated quarter of a million dead, although possibly a quarter of those had been victims of the Iraqi government's own campaigns against the Iraqi Kurds; over 60,000 Iraqis remained prisoners of the Iranians; nearly 1 million Iraqis now served in the armed forces.

In order to fight the war once its foreign currency reserves had been exhausted, Iraq had run up a debt of over $80 billion. At the same time, although the volume of its oil exports had recovered somewhat, due to the construction of pipelines through Turkey and Saudi Arabia during the war, the collapse of world prices meant that Iraq's oil revenues in 1988 amounted to $11 billion, less than half its 1980 revenue. With the threat of war removed, Iraq's international creditors were likely to be less forgiving. The same was true of some of the men on whom Saddam Husain had relied during the war: with the danger of the external enemy removed, his stature was diminished, since he could no longer present himself as the bulwark, protecting the privileges of the elite from the prospect of an Iranian-sponsored Islamic political order in Iraq.[24]

THE AFTERMATH OF WAR AND THE INVASION OF KUWAIT 1988–90

Saddam Husain was well aware of the fact that the ending of the war with Iran, the crushing of the Kurdish rebellion and the continued effective suppression of Shiʿi Islamist organisations did not remove political challenges to his own position. On the contrary, these were more likely to come from the circles of those whom he had favoured and who had been regarded as the insiders of the regime. Two particular legacies of the war needed to be dealt with immediately if they were not to undermine his own position as supreme leader. The first was the apparent corporate solidarity of the Iraqi officer corps. The second was the economic predicament of the country. Both of these developments presented a challenge of a particularly acute kind to the form of neo-patrimonialism that sustained Saddam Husain's power in Iraq. At this stage, no direct bid to oust him had emerged, but, knowing as he did the true costs of the war, this could be only a matter of time and he moved to pre-empt any such threat.

His first target was the officer corps itself. In some respects, he was helped by the fact that the Iraqi armed forces were now so large that the officer corps was quite heterogeneous and could not easily act as a corporate body, even when some of its members were threatened. Using the tested means of patronage and discrimination, Saddam Husain favoured and promoted some, whilst demoting and retiring others. In other cases, senior officers who had made their names during the war met with fatal 'accidents', or were placed under house arrest. In this way, Saddam Husain was seeking to break many of the bonds which had formed during the war years and to destroy the institutional memory which could make the Iraqi officer corps as a whole so formidable a challenge to his leadership.

This was the case even when the officers concerned came from his own provincial background and, as in the example of General Maher 'Abd al-Rashid, were related to Saddam Husain by marriage. The killing of 'Abd al-Rashid's brother (also a general), and his own forced retirement and virtual disappearance from public life, not only broke his connections with the substantial body of officers loyal to him, but also served as an example to others. Saddam Husain's attempts to forestall a coup d'état seem to have brought the plans for his overthrow forward, but the plots to assassinate him in late 1988 and early 1989 were discovered by the authorities. The purges which followed were used to accelerate the re-establishment of Saddam Husain's personal control over the armed forces. More seriously for the regime, however, the very existence of such plots, coupled with a hint that they might have been aimed at replacing Saddam Husain with one of his kinsmen rather than overthrowing the regime as a whole, led to a deepening suspicion of 'Adnan Khairallah Tulfah, the minister of defence and Saddam Husain's brother-in-law. Tulfah's position was not helped by the fact that, as a close relative of Saddam Husain, he was also embroiled in a family quarrel at the time which was causing rifts among the small circle of Saddam Husain's kinsmen. His sudden death in May 1989, allegedly in a helicopter crash, may not therefore have been wholly coincidental.

As Saddam Husain was well aware, reliance on the circles of family and kin may have been a key to his political survival, but it could also have its disadvantages. In the 1980s, fearing an overbearing solidarity amongst one grouping of clans from the al-Bu Nasir (which included Hasan al-Bakr, 'Adnan Khairallah Tulfah and Saddam Husain's three half-brothers), he relieved his half-brothers of their posts in the intelligence and security networks. In their place, members of Saddam Husain's own al-Majid clan were promoted. Thus ruling through and with the family required a balancing act of some skill. Family members might be trusted more than other Iraqis, but they also tended to be jealous of each other and ambitious, and might begin to think of themselves as immune from retribution. Saddam Husain's eldest son, ʿUday, clearly thought as much, but when he publicly murdered one of his father's circle of intimate servants in 1989, he overstepped the mark and was imprisoned – only to be released a few days later and sent into exile in Switzerland. Tulfah's death may thus have been a warning as much to Saddam Husain's own kinsmen as to Iraq at large.

It was against this restless background of military conspiracies, family feuds and general expectations of change that Saddam Husain promised the opening up of the public realm to greater political diversity, initially embodied in greater competition for National Assembly seats and the encouragement of criticism of government ministers and the state bureaucracy. Most of the promises were not kept and the 'opening' remained a highly controlled process. Non-Baʿthists were able to stand as 'independents' in the assembly elections of April 1989 and a number won seats, but they were, as ever, vetted by the security services. Criticism was permitted only of certain government ministers – essentially the technocrats employed to try to manage Iraq's deteriorating economy in order to shift the blame for strategic miscalculation away from the political leadership. The president, his relatives and other members of his inner circle were of course immune from criticism, as were most key areas of the state and state policy.

It was in the area of economic policy that Saddam Husain was facing his greatest obvious challenge. The shortage of funds to keep the wheels of patronage turning and to maintain the subsidised, import-based, consumption-oriented economy of Iraq was something that could potentially create a tide of resentment against a leader who now seemed incompetent rather than heroic. Furthermore, the very indebtedness of Iraq to a wide range of creditors placed the country in the position of a petitioner, again undermining the credibility of Saddam Husain's image as an all-powerful leader. The economic liberalisation process which had begun during the war was extended and reinforced, at least on the statute book. Price controls were removed, entrepreneurial activity was encouraged and a number of state factories were sold off to private individuals, as were some other minor state assets, presaging, it seemed, the final dismantling of the large public sector. Licences were granted for private industrial projects, the private sector accounted for nearly a quarter of all imports and there was clearly some hope that inward investment from the other Arab Gulf states would materialise. These activities provided excellent opportunities for profit-making by a few individuals and family concerns, especially those well connected to the ruling circles of the regime who benefited from special licences and the selling off of state farms in particular. However, they led to massive inflation which became so serious that regulations had to be reimposed in a number of areas.[25]

All of this activity, although beneficial for those in a position to profit, could not make any serious dent in the overall economic predicament of the country. Given the debt repayment burden (amounting to over 50 per cent of Iraq's oil income in 1990), the massive costs of reconstruction, the continuing weakness in the price of oil and a military and a civil – especially food – import bill which far exceeded Iraq's projected oil revenues, a more drastic solution was needed. Attempts by Saddam Husain to reshuffle his economic team in 1989 amounted to little. Austerity measures, such as reductions in the number of government employees or the demobilisation of thousands of troops from the armed forces, only added to the problem of unemployment and led, in the case of the armed forces, to the rescinding of the measures concerned.

It was in these circumstances that Iraq tried to increase its oil revenues by seeking to persuade OPEC to raise the price of oil through new restrictive quotas. In particular, Saddam Husain looked to Iraq's Gulf neighbours, Saudi Arabia and Kuwait, to help extricate it from its financial plight in a number of ways. They were supposed to co-operate in maintaining a high price for oil, through restraint of their own production and pressure on others. Furthermore, they were asked repeatedly, but unsuccessfully, by Iraq to declare that the $40 billion financial aid they had given to Iraq during the war with Iran should be considered a grant and not a loan. In addition, it was suggested that they should contribute very substantially to Iraq's economic reconstruction. The disappointing answers received by Iraq led Saddam Husain and his associates to use ever more threatening – and indeed desperate – language in the first six months of 1990, hinting that, if these resources were not granted freely, Iraq might use other means to extract them.

During this period the idea of using military force began to take shape among Saddam Husain's circle. Kuwait was to be the immediate target, but the longer-term aim was to extract resources and concessions from the Gulf states generally and particularly from Saudi Arabia. In this calculation, Kuwait itself was to be a commodity which could either be retained through a puppet government or through annexation. Alternatively, it could be exchanged for substantial concessions. These would alleviate Iraq's financial position, greatly enhance Saddam Husain's authority and establish Iraq as both the dominant power in the Gulf and a leader in the oil market.

The calculation shared many features with the decision ten years before to use force against Iran. It was based on the belief that the Arab Gulf states would see the Iraqi move as an opening gambit and make terms accordingly. It was also based on a supposition that the international community and the great powers, the United States in particular, would take their lead from the Gulf states and would therefore acquiesce in the negotiated outcome of a crisis created by Iraqi force of arms. Furthermore, as in 1980, it was driven to some degree by the intangible but potent consideration that Saddam Husain's claim to be the 'necessary leader' of the Iraqi territorial nation-state demanded forceful action to 'restore the rights of the Iraqi people'. In 1980 this had been aimed at re-establishing Iraqi control of the Shatt al-'Arab and the humbling of the Iranian government. In 1990, it was aimed at establishing a controlling influence for Iraq in the affairs of Kuwait and at humbling the oil-rich Arab rulers of the Gulf states.

Having failed to wring substantial concessions out of the Gulf states, despite an increasingly menacing tone, and having established to his satisfaction at least the probable acquiescence of the Arab states and of the United States, Saddam Husain ordered his forces to invade Kuwait on 2 August 1990. The occupation was completed within twenty-four hours. The ruler of Kuwait, Shaikh Jabir al-Sabah, and most of the ruling family succeeded in escaping to Saudi Arabia, soon to be joined by an estimated 300,000 other Kuwaitis. Meanwhile, Iraq established a Kuwaiti 'provisional government' to provide the fiction that the Iraqi forces had been invited into the country to defend a revolution against the ruling al-Sabah family. However, within a matter of days, the Iraqi government announced that it would be annexing Kuwait, 'returning' it to the Iraqi homeland. This was formally achieved by the end of August when Kuwait became the nineteenth province of Iraq.

The annexation was presented as Saddam Husain's culminating achievement of Iraq's national goals, rectifying the injustice committed by British imperialism in 'separating' Kuwait from Iraq when the boundaries of the Iraqi state were drawn. The heavy use of Iraqi nationalist symbolism and propaganda to justify this move after the event, combined with a certain amount of Arab nationalist unification rhetoric, could hardly divert attention from the spectacular miscalculation which Saddam Husain had made in invading Kuwait. Far from facing a supine Arab world or an acquiescent international community, Iraq found itself roundly condemned in the Arab League and at the United Nations. Iraqi and Kuwaiti assets were frozen, the UN Security Council imposed a total economic and trade embargo on Iraq and Iraq's only oil export pipelines through Turkey and Saudi Arabia were promptly cut. Furthermore, Saudi Arabia, alarmed by the Iraqi forces on its border and believing that it was either the direct or indirect target of the Iraqi invasion, asked for US military assistance. The United States, committing itself to the unconditional withdrawal of Iraq from Kuwait and the restoration of the status quo, began a military airlift that was to lead to the stationing of over half a million American troops in Saudi Arabia within six months.[26]

THE WAR FOR KUWAIT AND THE UPRISINGS OF 1991

During this time, Saddam Husain tried to devise a strategy that would allow him to recoup something from the disastrous decision to invade Kuwait. Annexation was a way of demonstrating his resolve to the international coalition of Arab as well as non-Arab states ranged against Iraq, obliging them to think of the ways in which Iraq could be persuaded to withdraw. Similar ploys involved Saddam Husain's linkage of the Israeli occupation of Arab lands to his occupation of Kuwait. Neither these strategies nor Iraq's attempts to split the international coalition were to much avail. In November the UN Security Council passed Resolution 678, which demanded Iraq's unconditional withdrawal from Kuwait by 15 January 1991 and authorised the use of military force if Iraq failed to comply. With the imposition of this deadline and the consequent reinforcement of US and allied military forces in the Gulf, it became harder for Saddam Husain to believe that his initial post-invasion strategy of 'advantageous withdrawal' would be possible. It seemed inevitable that war would result, and Saddam Husain's priority now became 'survivable withdrawal'.

As the events of early 1991 demonstrated, this was a strategy for which, as in the war with Iran, he and his regime were well prepared. At the heart of power lay the self-reinforcing oligarchy of his kinsmen, headed by Saddam Husain himself. It included his cousin and son-in-law Husain Kamil al-Majid (formerly minister of military industrialisation and oil), another cousin from the same family 'Ali Hasan al-Majid (briefly governor of Kuwait), his half-brothers Barzan, Wathban and Sib'awi Ibrahim (all occupying key posts in the intelligence networks), his kinsman General Husain Rashid al-Takriti (commander of the Presidential Guard) and three long-term associates Taha Yasin Ramadhan al-Jazrawi (commander of the Popular Army), Tariq 'Aziz (minister of foreign affairs) and 'Izzat Ibrahim al-Duri.

This group, inextricably associated with Saddam Husain, closed ranks as the likelihood of war increased. 'Ali Hasan al-Majid, who had initially been installed as governor of Kuwait, was brought back to Baghdad in November. At the same time, Husain Rashid al-Takriti was promoted from commander of the Presidential Guard to chief of the general staff. The divisions of the Republican Guard were deployed in such a way as to ensure both that the heart of the regime in central and northern Iraq was secure and to block any attempted invasion of the country from the south. With these forces in place it now appeared that Saddam Husain was confident that he could survive any attack, sacrificing his forces in Kuwait if necessary to guarantee the safety of the heartland.

When the allied attack began on 16 January it subjected Iraq to the devastating experience of modern aerial bombardment for six weeks before ground troops became seriously engaged. Iraq had no effective defence against such an attack and responded instead politically, firing a number of missiles against Israel, in symbolic defiance and possibly in the hope that an Israeli retaliation would disrupt the coalition by causing its Arab members, Syria and Egypt in particular, to withdraw. However, this failed to have the desired effect and the allied bombardment continued unabated, targeting not only Iraq's military apparatus but also much of its civil infrastructure. Because of the speed and scale of the eventual allied ground offensive into Kuwait and Iraq, it is difficult to tell how seriously Saddam Husain intended to defend Kuwait itself. It seems likely that the decision to abandon Kuwait had been taken some time before, even if the unfortunate Iraqi troops stationed there were unaware of the fact. Meanwhile, a scorched-earth policy was implemented: having systematically looted Kuwait during the occupation, the Iraqi forces fired Kuwait's oil wells and destroyed its major public buildings and installations. Saddam Husain seemed determined to inflict one last act of humiliation on the al-Sabah, very much in keeping with his and his circle's view of what had been at stake in the crisis.

Driving through southern Iraq and cutting off the divisions of the Republican Guard supposedly held in reserve, the scale and direction of the allied ground offensive on 24 February caught the Iraqis by surprise. The Iraqi forces in and around Kuwait City were routed, surrendering en masse or fleeing in confusion towards Basra. Iraqi units caught without air cover in southern Iraq broke and fled across the Euphrates. Within a matter of days Kuwait had been liberated by the allied forces and Iraq asked for a cease-fire to prevent further destruction of its forces. The allied coalition had by then achieved its objective and had neither a mandate nor much desire to press on into Iraq itself. Accordingly, a cease-fire agreement was signed at Safwan on 28 February 1991.

Startling as the speed and scale of the defeat had been, for the Iraqi leadership the crucial question was how to survive the repercussions of the defeat. It was less the loss of Kuwait that mattered than what else might be lost in the losing of it. It is here that Saddam Husain's underlying strategy came into play. The very smoothness of the transition from external military defeat to internal military repression suggests that by the end of February Kuwait – and the Iraqi forces trying to defend it – had virtually become an irrelevance in the strategic calculations of the regime. That strategy was now geared to the more familiar task of securing the political order against internal enemies: crushing open rebellion by force and re-establishing the networks of terror and surveillance which briefly – and dangerously for Saddam Husain – evaporated in the aftermath of the defeat in Kuwait.

In early March 1991 uprisings broke out across southern Iraq, centring principally on the predominantly Shi'i cities of Basra, 'Amara, Nasiriyya, Najaf and Karbala. These were largely spontaneous revolts against a hated regime when it seemed that the power of that regime was broken. In each town local leaderships emerged, some, but by no means all, associated with underground Islamic organisations, such as al-Da'wa. Baqir al-Hakim, head of SCIRI in exile in Iran, sent a few thousand of his organisation's Badr Brigade across the border to help the rebels, whose numbers were swollen by army deserters fleeing the military disaster in the south. In the towns seized by the rebels, a terrible revenge was wrought on those whom they regarded as agents of or collaborators with the regime. However, despite the fact that the rebels succeeded in persuading the senior *mujtahid*, Ayatollah Abu al-Qasim al-Kho'i, to give his public approval of the formation of a committee to preserve order and security in Iraq, it was clear that there was no overall leadership or direction of the rebellion. Furthermore, it also became clear that support for the rebellion was largely confined to the cities and towns of the south. In many rural districts, the inhabitants bided their time, waiting to see the outcome. In some areas prominent shaikhs of major tribes even helped government forces to reassert control.

Faced with this situation, the rebel forces proved to be no match for those now deployed by the regime. Within a couple of weeks the Republican

Guard divisions, kept in reserve for just such a purpose, had recaptured all the towns held by the rebels, inflicting massive loss of life and destruction in the Shiʿi cities of the south. On 21 March the authorities forced Ayatollah al-Khoʾi to declare his support for Saddam Husain and to call for an end to the rebellion. More than 50,000 refugees poured over the border into Saudi Arabia and thousands of others sought sanctuary in Iran, whilst many fled to the marshes of the south in an attempt to escape the vengeful pursuit of the Iraqi armed forces. These exacted a terrible price on those whom they suspected of having joined the rebellion, leaving tens of thousands dead in their wake and seizing thousands more, many of whom were to perish in Iraqi prisons during the coming years.

19 Ayatollah Sayyid Abu al-Qasim al-Khoʾi (senior Shiʿi cleric until his death in 1992), c. 1985

Having dealt a death-blow to the Shi'i rebellion in the south, Saddam Husain now turned his forces on the rebellions that had broken out simultaneously amongst the Kurds of the north. Encouraged by the defeat of the Iraqi armed forces in Kuwait and by news of the southern rebellions, Kurds had also risen in revolt. Again, as in the south, the initial revolt was spontaneous, emerging from countless local grievances against a regime that had shown such brutality in its rule of Kurdistan. The main parties of the Kurdistan Front, the KDP and the PUK, soon seized the opportunity to reassert their leadership, but it was noticeable that in this rebellion many of the local chieftains of the *jahsh*, hitherto the paid clients of the central government, also rose in revolt. The strength of the rebels and the weakness and distraction of the government troops led to a string of successes as one town after another fell to the Kurdish forces, culminating in the capture of Kirkuk itself on 19 March. However, this was the high point of the rebellion. Within ten days, Iraqi government forces, led by the units of the Republican Guard, hit back, recapturing Kirkuk, driving into the rebel-held areas and inflicting heavy casualties on the Kurds. Memories of *al-Anfal* and its chemical attacks, as well as rumours of the killings of civilians, led to the mass exodus of hundreds of thousands of Kurds, fleeing for the relative safety of the borders of Iran and Turkey. Nearly 2 million people were on the move within the space of a few days, leading to the disintegration of the rebel forces.

However, this mass exodus also led in April 1991 to the passing of UN SC Resolution 688 which called on Iraq to end its repression of its own population and paved the way for the creation by the coalition powers of a 'safe haven' north of the 36th parallel in Iraq (a line just south of Arbil). Iraqi aircraft were forbidden to fly in this zone and the Iraqi leadership called a halt to the advance of the Iraqi forces, evidently fearing further military action by the coalition powers. Hitherto it had been noticeable that the Iraqi authorities had enjoyed an almost completely free hand to suppress the rebellions as they chose. Despite the American president's call on the Iraqi people to rise up and overthrow Saddam Husain in February, no help had been forthcoming from the United States or their coalition partners when revolts erupted in the south and the north. It was clear that the United States and others in the region and beyond were as fearful about the possible fragmentation of Iraq as many in Iraq itself. They may have viewed Saddam Husain with distaste, but they still favoured the idea of a strong leader, backed by the bulk of Iraq's armed forces, over a possible breakdown of order, a general civil war or the intervention of regional powers, especially Iran.

This attitude on the part of foreign powers was echoed by many in Iraq and greatly helped Saddam Husain in his efforts to salvage something from the military defeat and to restore his own hold over the country. Faced by the rebellions in north and south, he could rely on the cohesion not only of the inner circle of his clansmen, but also on all those whose obedience allowed the regime to function. Whatever their opinions of the political leadership, the spectre of communal conflict and civil war evidently terrified them more. In the case of many communities in the rural south, for instance, prudent self-interest deterred them from joining the rebellion until the outcome seemed clear. For that reason, the Iraqi armed forces were able to move with impunity through much of the southern countryside, picking off the rebellious towns one by one.

Nor was Saddam Husain slow to make public gestures of reconciliation. A few days after the crushing of the rebellion in the Shiʿi south he appointed a Shiʿi member of the RCC, Saʿdun Hammadi, as prime minister, hinting that he was the harbinger of fundamental change. Similarly, whilst his forces were driving back the Kurdish rebels, he opened a dialogue with the leaders of the Kurdish Front, suggesting that new, more wide-ranging autonomy proposals were on offer. This led Talabani to visit Baghdad, where he publicly embraced Saddam Husain and seemed to endorse the Iraqi government's unlikely promise of a federal, democratic Iraq.

Needless to say, these promises were not kept. Saddam Husain had used them to buy time, to split the rebels and to convince the international community that there was no reason for further intervention in Iraq. Although successful in part, he was unable to persuade the UN that Iraq under his leadership could easily or soon be rehabilitated. Instead, the sanctions regime, imposed in 1990 to force Iraq out of Kuwait, was maintained in the hope of achieving a number of further objectives. Most prominent here was the attempted elimination of Iraq's weapons of mass destruction and its missile capability, which made it a potential military threat in the region. However, the UN Security Council resolutions, when taken in their entirety, also implied that the sanctions would not be lifted until the Iraqi government had fulfilled a long list of other conditions.

These conditions included recognising the sovereignty and territorial boundaries of Kuwait, agreeing to the payment of war reparations, accounting for the many Kuwaitis who had disappeared during the occupation, ceasing to pose a threat to regional security and ending the repression of its own citizens. The requirement that Iraq meet these conditions was used both to justify a formidable sanctions regime crippling Iraq's economy and to establish intrusive forms of inspection and intervention which took little notice of Iraqi sovereignty. It was scarcely surprising in these circumstances that Saddam Husain became convinced that these were the instruments which the United States in particular wanted to use to destroy him and his regime. Accordingly, he and his circle became determined to survive this siege as they had the assaults of Iran during their eight-year war.[27]

IRAQ UNDER SANCTIONS AND THE LONG AFTERMATH
OF THE GULF WAR

The ability of Saddam Husain to maintain his regime and much of his ruling circle intact during the years that followed the defeat of 1991 was a testimony to the resilience of the system he had constructed. To some degree also, it was a testimony to his skill in reading Iraq's diverse communities, knowing whom to favour and whom to exclude, and when. This strange and devastating period in Iraq's history arguably brought out more sharply, therefore, the character of the Iraqi state under the rule of Saddam Husain. This was partly of his own devising, but it can also be traced back to the dominant narratives of that state as they drew in increasing numbers of its inhabitants during the twentieth century. Beset by hostile international and regional powers, faced by the drying up of oil revenues and the virtual secession of the Kurdish territories, as well as by rifts and factionalism within his own family and clan, Saddam Husain nevertheless proceeded much as always. In large part this was possible precisely because these were threats which he had long anticipated and with which the system he had devised was able to cope.

In the immediate aftermath of Iraq's defeat, there was a clear consensus in the UN Security Council that Iraq should be prevented from launching similar aggression in the future. To this end Iraq was required to give formal recognition to the independent state of Kuwait, to commit itself to the payment of war reparations and to open up all sites in Iraq for inspection by UN teams searching for evidence of Iraq's suspected programmes of nuclear, chemical and biological weapons development. Once discovered, these would be destroyed, as would the remaining long-range surface-to-surface missiles. Only when the Security Council was satisfied that Iraq no longer possessed these capabilities, had allowed monitoring systems to be installed and had complied with the other stipulations contained in the UN resolutions would the punitive sanctions be lifted. In May 1991 the first UNSCOM (United Nations Special Commission on Disarmament) teams began their work in Iraq.

For Iraq's closed and secretive regime random, intrusive investigations by foreign nationals into the most sensitive aspects of Iraq's military industrial complex were hard to accept. However, Saddam Husain was left in no doubt by the United States and the leading members of the Security Council that any failure to comply would result in punitive military action. Grudgingly and slowly, therefore, the UNSCOM teams were permitted to visit a number of sites, and a disturbing picture of Iraq's nuclear, chemical and biological weapons programmes emerged. This process took many years of effort and persistence on the part of UNSCOM, matched by the denial, deception and obstruction of the Iraqi authorities. Occasionally a crisis would result and Iraq would be threatened once more with military action by the United States and some of its coalition partners in the name of the UN Security Council.

The investigations revealed the scale and sophistication of Iraq's various weapons programmes, proving that Iraq not only had an arsenal of chemical weapons and had succeeded in adapting biological organisms, such as anthrax, for use as weapons, but also that it was on the verge of developing its own nuclear device. Even eight years after the initial inspections, the UNSCOM teams still feared that Iraq had retained a substantial capacity for manufacturing and delivering chemical and biological weapons. This was not surprising. Saddam Husain had a predatory view of international relations and particularly of the region in which Iraq is situated. It was clearly not his intention that Iraq should emerge from the humiliating process of weapons inspections naked and vulnerable. For that reason, he needed something that would effectively deter regional states from exploiting Iraq's obvious weakness. A suspicion of Iraq's continuing possession of chemical and biological weapons, combined with knowledge of the regime's ruthlessness and past use of such weapons, would be deterrent enough and not something that Saddam Husain would easily yield. Ironically, this was to contribute to his downfall in 2003.[28]

The ferocity of his determination to maintain this posture can be measured in part by the price Iraq was made to pay for doing so. Iraq had suffered extensive damage in the war with the allied coalition. Within the space of six weeks, the air bombardment had destroyed more of Iraq's economic infrastructure countrywide than had the eight years of war with Iran. At the same time, Iraq still suffered under the burden of debt created by that war and by additional financial burdens such as the reparations demanded for its aggression against Kuwait. Yet the continuing UN sanctions regime meant that Iraq was unable to sell its oil to earn foreign currency and was severely limited as to what it could import. Food and medicines were theoretically exempt from the embargo. However, the import of fertilisers, agricultural machinery, pesticides and chemicals that might have a dual use, as well as parts for restoring Iraq's ruined electricity and water purification systems, was forbidden. Within a relatively short time, the effects of these enforced shortages were being felt by the Iraqi population, as malnutrition and disease took their toll, causing infant mortality rates to rise to levels not seen in Iraq for over forty years. This had little impact on the regime's priorities.

The UN attempted to alleviate some of the hardship suffered by the Iraqi population by offering the Iraqi government the opportunity to sell $1.6 billion worth of oil in 1992 to pay for the import of food and medicine. This was rejected by Saddam Husain since the UN also insisted on controlling the funds realised and this included retaining some 30 per cent to pay towards war reparations. Regarding this as too great an infringement on his freedom of action and too great an insult to his authority, Saddam Husain continued to block similar offers, possibly hoping that the early lifting of sanctions would make such a deal unnecessary. Only in 1996 did the Iraqi government finally agree to the terms of UN SC Resolution 986, allowing Iraq to sell $2 billion worth of oil every six months for the purchase of supplies for its population (this was raised to $5.52 billion worth of oil every six months in UN SC Resolution 1153 of 1998 and in October 1999 to $8.3 billion for the period May–November 1999). In agreeing to the scheme the Iraqi government was also agreeing to the UN's management of the funds, releasing to Iraq only the sum left after the removal of a fixed percentage to pay for war reparations and the work of UNSCOM, as well as a given sum to go directly to the Kurdish region in northern Iraq. In addition, the UN demanded that the distribution of the supplies thus purchased should be supervised by teams of UN inspectors, hoping to ensure as wide and equitable a distribution as possible amongst the Iraqi population.

For Saddam Husain, the main advantage of this agreement was not merely that it placed additional revenues in his hands, but also that it might be a prelude to the end of sanctions since it brought Iraq back into the world market as an oil producer and, potentially, as a major consumer of industrial goods. It was clearly his hope that this would help to build momentum within the UN for the lifting of sanctions. It was a momentum which the Iraqi government had been seeking to encourage since at least 1992. In particular, Iraq had targeted Russia and France as members of the UN Security Council which were owed roughly $10 billion and $7 billion, respectively, by Iraq, largely for weapons purchased during the

1980s. They had every interest, therefore, in seeing Iraq's reinstatement as a major oil-producing power and the Iraqi government reinforced these interests by signing a number of agreements with Russia and with French companies for the development of Iraq's oil industry once sanctions were lifted.[29]

These moves were accompanied by other diplomatic initiatives on the part of Iraq. The more remote Gulf states were cultivated, leading Oman, Qatar and the United Arab Emirates to join the ranks of those who called for the immediate end to the UN sanctions and the rehabilitation of Iraq. In November 1994 Iraq recognised Kuwait as an independent sovereign state, thereby formally abandoning its earlier claims to sovereignty and recognising the Iraq–Kuwait border which had been finally demarcated by the UN in Kuwait's favour in May 1993. Furthermore, Iraq made an effort to ensure that China too, as a permanent member of the Security Council, added its voice to the demand that sanctions be lifted, playing upon the Chinese government's dislike that human rights issues should be used to penalise any state.

This was particularly necessary for Iraq. The UN had appointed a Special Rapporteur on Human Rights in 1991 and his regular damning reports on the Iraqi government's continued violations of the human rights of large numbers of its citizens were used by the United States, Great Britain and others to argue for the maintenance of the sanctions as a means of weakening and containing the Iraq of Saddam Husain. However, these reports also illustrated the cruel paradox of which the Iraqi people as a whole were the victim. Not only did they show that the years of sanctions had had no appreciable effect on the power of Saddam Husain's dictatorship over Iraq, but the reports also increasingly made clear that the sanctions themselves were contributing to the widespread and terrible suffering of the Iraqis.[30]

The 'oil for food' deals were intended by the dominant powers at the UN to resolve this paradox. They were meant to keep sanctions in place, whilst alleviating the living conditions and health problems inside Iraq that were causing real concern at the UN and elsewhere about the morality of economic sanctions, given their effects on the weakest sections of the Iraqi population. The realisation that this was the case led Saddam Husain to try to force the pace and to repeat his demand for an end to the sanctions. A series of crises manufactured by Iraq during 1997 and 1998, threatening to prevent UNSCOM from carrying out its duties, obliged the UN to focus on the weapons inspection programme as the sole reason for maintaining the sanctions regime. This was a risky strategy for Iraq since it brought forward the possibility of renewed US military action to force compliance, and made it seem as if the Iraqi government was indeed concealing a weapons development programme.

After going to the brink of military action several times during 1997 and 1998, the United States, assisted by British forces, finally launched a four-day aerial bombardment of Iraq, codenamed 'Desert Fox', in December 1998. The targets were primarily military ones, including those sites which the United States suspected played a role in the concealment of Iraq's weapons programme. Publicly justified by the United States and British governments in terms of the continuing military threat which Iraq posed to the region, the attack was intended both to force Iraqi compliance with UNSCOM and to weaken the regime of Saddam Husain in the hope of accelerating its overthrow. This mixture of motives and the methods used seriously compromised its objectives. The future of UNSCOM itself was thrown into doubt as Iraq exploited disarray at the UN over the United States' overwhelming use of force, refusing the UNSCOM teams access to its territories. Furthermore, Saddam Husain's power was not much affected by such military action. Equally frustrating and often puzzling for those who wished to see a change of regime in Baghdad, even the punitive sanctions regime seemed to have had less impact on the power of Saddam Husain than had been imagined, despite the destruction of the Iraqi economy and the destitution of the vast majority of Iraq's inhabitants.

KURDISH AUTONOMY AND KURDISH POLITICS

Nor was the power of the regime in Baghdad much affected by the emergence of a virtually independent Kurdish region in the north-east of Iraq during the 1990s. After the failed uprisings of 1991, the problem created by Kurdish refugees pouring over the Turkish border led to direct intervention by the allied forces: a 'safe haven' zone was created in the north of Iraq from which all Iraqi forces were excluded while all Iraqi flights were forbidden north of the 36th parallel (a line running south of Mosul and Arbil). These measures led to the withdrawal of the Iraqi armed forces from large areas of the north, finally establishing a cease-fire line in October 1991 which roughly matched the boundary of the Kurdish region as defined in 1974.

Allied intervention and protection had led to the de facto creation of an autonomous Kurdish entity in northern Iraq. Within this zone, the KDP established itself once again as the major local power in the north, whilst the PUK reasserted its control around its traditional base of Sulaimaniyya in the south. Under international auspices, relatively free elections were held throughout the Kurdish zone in May 1992, producing more or less equal representation for the KDP and the PUK (each gained roughly 45 per cent of the vote) with a variety of smaller parties – Assyrian, Kurdish Christian and socialist – gaining some seats as well. In June 1992 the Kurdish Assembly began its sessions in Arbil.

However, from the beginning, the Kurdish region found itself in an invidious position. Negotiations with Baghdad had been broken off in early 1992 and in their place the Iraqi government imposed a complete economic blockade on the Kurdish region, stopping the payment of salaries and preventing the import of goods. Shortages became widespread, exacerbating existing social conflicts and eventually testing the ability of the two main parties to co-operate with each other. Instead of joining the new Kurdish Regional Government, formed in July 1992, the leaders of the KDP and the PUK, Masoud Barzani and Jalal Talabani, stood aside, appointing subordinates to represent them. This allowed them to maintain and to extend their party networks and encouraged the development of two parallel administrations in the Kurdish region, one dealing largely with the north and the other with the south. It also wholly undermined the authority of the Kurdish government itself. Inevitably disputes erupted between the two parties, exacerbated by historical mistrust, but also more immediately by arguments over where the jurisdiction of one party began and the other ended. These issues revolved around questions of territory, but also around questions of the distribution of international economic aid and the revenues derived from lucrative oil and commodity smuggling across the Iranian and particularly the Turkish borders. In December 1993 the first open armed clashes between the forces of the two rival parties broke out.

Various attempts were made to arrange cease-fires, but these were short-lived. In December 1994, PUK forces seized Arbil and the administration of the region ground to a halt. Attempts by interested outside parties, particularly the United States, to bring the two sides together seemed to have little effect and by the end of 1995 the death toll of the sporadic fighting between the two sides had reached into the thousands. Despite the economic and human cost of the conflict, neither the KDP nor the PUK seemed able to reconcile their differences, seizing instead upon every point at dispute to drive home their case, backed up by force of arms. In these circumstances, it was inevitable that the parties should look beyond the Kurdish region for help. Initially, the KDP looked to Turkey, providing assistance for several massive and prolonged incursions by Turkish troops during these years as the Turkish armed forces tried to destroy units of the PKK (the radical Kurdish separatist movement in Turkey). Meanwhile, the

PUK cultivated Iran, despite earlier misgivings, as the power best placed to lend them immediate support.

Nor had either party neglected to keep a channel open to Baghdad. This served the KDP well when, in the summer of 1996, Iranian forces entered the territories of the PUK allegedly in pursuit of units of the KDP-I (the Kurdish autonomy movement in Iran). Accusing the PUK of enlisting Iranian military support, the KDP turned to Baghdad and asked for military assistance from the Iraqi government. Within a short space of time, 30,000 Iraqi government troops had entered the Kurdish region, helping the KDP to capture Arbil from the PUK and using the opportunity to hunt down opponents of the Iraqi regime who had taken refuge there. Although the major part of the Iraqi forces withdrew within a couple of months, Saddam Husain had reasserted his power in the north. The KDP's action had shown how difficult it was to break free from the gravitational pull at the centre of the Iraqi state – however diminished its power might be. It had also greatly boosted Saddam Husain's prestige. The threatening gestures made by the United States during the military operation had not deterred him. Instead he had the satisfaction of seeing the dispersal of the Iraqi opposition organisations which had congregated in the Kurdish region, as well as the evacuation by the United States of some 5,000 Iraqis, both Kurdish and non-Kurdish, whom they now regarded as being at risk from the Iraqi security forces.

American concern about the re-establishment of Saddam Husain's control in the north and the continued fighting in areas of Kurdistan spurred the United States to try to reconcile the two warring Kurdish factions. The resulting Ankara Accords of October 1996 contained a number of expressions of good intent, but the situation in the Kurdish region remained unchanged. Disputes over revenues, over territory and over alliances forged with Baghdad, Tehran and Ankara underlined the differences between the PUK and the KDP and produced a destructive cycle of sporadic fighting interspersed with shaky cease-fires. Casualties mounted, the administration was paralysed and all hope of a unified, let alone exemplary, Kurdish region appeared to have been lost.

Given the commitment of the United States over the years to establishing a viable autonomous region in Iraqi Kurdistan and given its continuing attempts to contain the Iraqi government, it could not let the Kurdish question go. The events of 1996 had shown that internecine Kurdish fighting threatened to bring Baghdad's forces back to Kurdistan, and also encouraged Iranian intervention. Intense American mediation and pressure finally resulted in the Washington Agreement of September 1998 whereby Barzani and Talabani committed themselves to power-sharing in the region. This ended the fighting between the KDP and the PUK, but there was slow progress in other spheres. Promised elections for a new Regional Assembly failed to take place and two Kurdish Regional Governments persisted, one based in Arbil, controlled by the KDP, and one in Sulaimaniyya, controlled by the PUK. Only in January 2001 did Masoud Barzani and Jalal Talabani, the leaders of the two rival Kurdish parties, meet face to face – for the first time in three years – to discuss their differences.

However, during the decade or so after 1991, a new and distinctively Kurdish order was taking shape in the Kurdish region, despite the insecurity and upheavals of intra-party fighting. New institutions had been established, school curricula had been revised, the Kurdish language was given understandable prominence and the inhabitants of the region were getting used to dealing entirely with the regional governments in their daily affairs. Contact with the rest of Iraq was largely confined to senior government officials or to the trading and smuggling networks which provided the backbone of an economy largely dominated by the KDP and its clients. It was not surprising, therefore, that the two parties should have begun to reflect these trends, with a more self-confident assertion of the need for a future federal Iraqi state and an enjoyment in the meantime of effective independence from Baghdad. This enhanced Barzani's control over the KDP, which he reinforced by promoting family members to positions of prominence, with his nephew Nechervan appointed as prime minister in Arbil and his son Masrour gaining a seat on the politburo. In the PUK, where less centralised control allowed for a more disputed politics, the *peshmerga*, especially those from Kirkuk (still under Iraqi government control), became more prominent in the leadership, suggesting the reassertion of claims to territory and oil resources by a future Kurdish government.[31]

With the changes taking place in the region and the growing prospects of confrontation between the new US administration and the government of Saddam Husain, the process of reconciliation in Kurdistan gained pace. So too did the fears and ambitions suggested by the possible imminent change of regime in Baghdad. Between them, the two Kurdish parties commanded armed forces some 80,000 strong. For US strategic planners, the nature of these forces, lightly armed and irregular from a conventional military point of view, could only have a minor role to play in any future military operation. However, the example of Kurdish development during the previous decade or so, both economic and political, was held up as a demonstration of the possibility of establishing an open and plural politics in Iraq. Given the actual record of internecine fighting, clientelism and corruption behind the façade of representative, plural politics this called for a certain suspension of disbelief.

Nevertheless, the Kurdish question as it was then represented epitomised certain American views of the larger question of Iraqi identities and the political order that could be built upon them. The Washington Agreement explicitly recognised the multi-ethnic composition of the Kurdish region and thus of Iraq as a whole, placing the aspirations of such groupings as the Turkmen, the Assyrians and the Chaldeans on an equal footing with those of the Kurds. At the same time, it pledged the commitment of all parties to the territorial integrity and unity of Iraq, but on the basis of a pluralistic, democratic and federal political structure. The de facto autonomy created by the events of 1991 in much of the Kurdish region allowed distinctive forms of political expression to emerge, encouraging the formation of parties based on ideas of ethnic and sectarian identity, such as the three separate Turkmen parties, the Islamic Movement of Kurdistan and its more radical Islamist offshoots, as well as Assyrian and other Christian parties. The increasing involvement of the United States in this process helped to call such parties into being, placing them in a political framework designated as liberal, plural and democratic, regardless in many respects of the aims and methods of some of the parties themselves. For some in the US administration and in the Iraqi opposition, this version of the Kurdish model seemed to hold out a kind of hope for the future politics of Iraq itself.

The Kurdish leadership was willing to play along with this since it was a way of binding the United States to the future autonomy of Kurdistan. In 2002, it was increasingly clear that the United States was going to act to bring down Saddam Husain and, with regime change imminent in Baghdad, it became all the more important for the Kurdish parties to demonstrate their value to the United States. A change of regime in Iraq to one supported by the United States could mean that Kurdish demands for autonomy would no longer be looked upon so indulgently. At the same time, the ending of the UN sanctions regime that would follow would have profound effects on a Kurdish economy that had grown up on the back of the illicit and semi-licit trade with the rest of Iraq. As the countdown to war began in 2003, the KDP and PUK prepared to give what assistance they could, as well as to seize the opportunities offered by major military action against Baghdad by the United States and its allies.

THE 'SHADOW STATE' IN IRAQ

The fact that war and invasion were being considered by 2002 as the only way of dislodging Saddam Husain from power was a testimony, amongst other things, to the curious resilience of his regime. Thirteen years of punitive sanctions, the slashing of Iraq's oil income, the break-away of the northern, Kurdish provinces, the impoverishment of the vast majority of the population and the persistent violation of Iraqi sovereignty through American and British patrolling of no-fly zones in north and south, interspersed with periodic bombardment of Iraq's air defences, appeared to have made little impact on Saddam Husain's hold on the country. On the contrary, it could be argued that during these years, his hold had tightened in a way unimaginable hitherto.

In part this could be explained by the nature of Saddam Husain's power in Iraq and the state forms that reproduced that power. There existed in Iraq a dual state. The elaborate bureaucracy of government agencies, state-run enterprises and organisations formed the public state in Iraq. They comprised the ministries, the official associations, the armed forces and the Ba'th party. But behind this lay a 'shadow state', formed by networks of associates, chains of patrons and clients, circles of exclusion and privilege emanating from the office and person of the president. This was the real nexus of power. It stood behind all public state organisations, turning their hierarchies upside down and answering to a very different set of commands. At its heart were the men attached to the president through common regional background, family or tribal affiliation or tried-and-tested dedication to his personal service. Beyond them spread the networks of patronage and association that gave them weight in Iraqi society and established their worth to Saddam Husain himself, whilst reinforcing their dependence on his favour. Although implicating large numbers of people across Iraq in the direct or indirect service of the president, they represented a small proportion of the 26 million inhabitants of the state whose fates they controlled. Estimated at 500,000 or so, including dependants, these were the people whom Saddam Husain needed to convince both that his leadership was better for their interests than that of any imaginable alternative and that they would lose everything were he to be overthrown.

They came predominantly, but not exclusively, from the Sunni Arab population of Iraq, especially those whose origins lay in the regions northwest of Baghdad from which Saddam Husain originated, and were known as *umana' Saddam* (Saddam's faithful). They vied with each other to be close to the president, to catch his eye and gain his favour whilst implicitly accepting the principles of the system itself. To have failed to do so might not only have been fatal to the individual concerned, but might also have seriously damaged the grouping with which he was identified – be it a faction within Saddam Husain's immediate family, an allied clan, a particular village, tribal grouping or family in Iraq, or simply a network of associates. These were the people whose privileged access to the hoarded resources of the Iraqi state and to the various oil and commodity-smuggling enterprises set up by Saddam Husain to evade sanctions largely insulated them from the effects of those sanctions – and thereby marked them off from the vast majority of the Iraqi population. In the final analysis it was the president who decided which individuals should benefit, which should be reminded of his power in some exemplary way and how far competition amongst them should be encouraged as a means of fragmenting them and harnessing their ambitions to his cause.

Throughout his rule, Saddam Husain showed unnerving skill at manipulating the rivalries and ambitions of these people. Sometimes it produced violent resentment and conspiracy. For instance, it was noteworthy that the alleged plots in the armed forces which were used to execute and imprison large numbers of officers in the 1990s came principally from hitherto trusted groupings of officers from al-Ramadi, al-Dur, Samarra and even Takrit itself – the clan territories from which the regime had always drawn most of the senior officers of the key security forces. In thwarting conspiracies, Saddam Husain not only made use of his intelligence networks – generally commanded by members of his immediate family – but also relied on other clans and groupings within the officer corps, conspicuously favouring them in the aftermath at the expense of their rivals.

On a more general level across Iraq, these tactics reflected the favour shown by Saddam Husain to the hierarchies of tribal shaikhs, inducing them to co-operate with the regime and to 'deliver' the loyalty or at least the acquiescence of their fellow tribesmen to the head of state. Officially, this led to edicts in the 1990s which recognised the authority of tribal shaikhs to settle disputes and to regulate affairs amongst their tribesmen and with other tribes, bringing back a form of separate jurisdiction for the 'tribal areas' (situated in many cases within the towns of Iraq) that recalled the days of the monarchy. Unofficially, Saddam Husain favoured the most co-operative of the tribal shaikhs, granting them land rights, promoting their tribesmen and allowing them to arm their followers. As a means of social control, this has been a tried-and-tested instrument of successive Iraqi governments, although the particular predicament – and ethos – of the regime of Saddam Husain made it an integral part of the state's organisation of support.

It was accompanied by official encouragement of the virtues of 'Arab' and 'tribal' culture. This was a construction, no less than any other narrative taken up and developed by Iraqi state media. It was thus selective and largely instrumental, although, of course, it was presented as a 'natural' characteristic of the bulk of the Iraqi population. Yet it was entwined with the particular regime of power that was the state of Iraq under Saddam Husain. By rewarding them, it gave meaning to notions of tribal identity whereby townsmen, several generations removed from the countryside, rediscovered their 'tribal' affiliations and identities, or consciously sought out a tribal shaikh to ask permission to affiliate to his tribal following, where their own lineage had become obscure. Such identifications made a good deal of sense in the 'shadow state' of Iraq, where networks for protection and advancement could so dramatically affect the life chances of individuals.

The systems of favouritism, of inclusion and exclusion, associated with this process and reproduced across Iraq as a whole, served Saddam Husain well. Most intimately, and occasionally dramatically, he used the same system to keep his immediate family in line. His conception of the state was largely a dynastic one, formed by notions of lineage which continue to be important markers of identity and status in the communities of rural Iraq from which Saddam Husain and his closest lieutenants came. Transferred to the level of the state, this favoured the kin of the ruler who were drawn into the heart of power and were granted unrivalled access and privileges, the better to serve him. But they themselves were riven by factions, as cousins, sons and half-brothers of the president competed for advantage within this circle.

Saddam Husain used these men to cement his power, but also ensured that no single one of them or indeed grouping amongst them could challenge him. Nor were any allowed to assume that they had a right to the favours he alone dispensed. On the contrary, they were constantly reminded, through reassignment and through the granting of land and of economic concessions, as well as through the withdrawal of the same, that they were all creatures of the president. Inevitably, as in Iraq at large, much energy and skill was devoted to playing one group off against another, favouring now one, now another, but opening to all the possibility of privileged access if they could curry favour with the president.

In 1995 a series of events exposed the ruthless logic of this process. It was then that the declining fortunes of some of the al-Majid clan ('Ali Hasan al-Majid was dismissed as minister of defence and his nephew, Husain Kamil al-Majid, a son-in-law of Saddam Husain, lost control over most of

20 President Saddam Husain, his wife, sons, daughters and sons-in-law, c. 1989

the lucrative oil-smuggling business to the president's elder son 'Uday) led
to the flight to Jordan of Husain Kamil and his brother Saddam Kamil with
their wives, two of Saddam Husain's daughters. Husain Kamil revealed
details of Iraq's weapons of mass destruction (as minister of industry and
military production in the 1980s he had been instrumental in building up
these programmes), but his intimate association with the regime meant
that he was shunned by other Iraqi exiles.

Disillusioned with the treatment they received and reassured by the
promise of a presidential pardon, as well as by more traditional guarantees
given to their father by Saddam Husain, the brothers returned in February
1996. Once back in Iraq, they were promptly killed, together with their
father and other close family members, allegedly by outraged clansmen,
determined to wipe this stain off the family's honour. Saddam Husain
thereby demonstrated once again not only the price of defiance, but also
the fact that he would not hesitate to eliminate close relatives if he thought
they were overreaching themselves. Indeed, he may have been responsible
for spreading the rumour that the children of the two brothers – his own
grandchildren – had also been killed, making the point that if he could act
this way towards his own family, no one else could expect any pity. In a
world such as this, where not only kinship but also revenge are important,

21   President Husain and family portrayed in the Iraqi magazine *Alif-Ba*, 1996,
omitting the two disgraced and murdered sons-in-law

it was possible that the nearly fatal shooting of Saddam Husain's elder son,
ʿUday, in December 1996 and the attempt on the life of his younger son,
Qusay, in early 1997 were repercussions of the elimination of an entire sub-
branch of Saddam Husain's own family.[32]

Others attributed these attempts on the lives of Saddam Husain's sons
to organised forces of the Islamist opposition based in the Shiʿi community. They had been sporadically active since the crushing of the rebellions
in the south in 1991. Despite their losses at the hands of the regime's security forces, al-Daʿwa, in particular, could still maintain networks of resistance in urban areas such as the largely Shiʿi Madinat Saddam in Baghdad,
as well as in cities of the south. However, neither al-Daʿwa nor the Iran-
based SCIRI was able to achieve much against the formidably armed circles
of the regime.

The clannish and personalised system constructed by Saddam Husain
was based on the patronage and inclusion of selected individuals and
groups from known communities. This meant the exclusion and marginalisation of the members of other communities, less trusted and less
amenable to the kind of co-option favoured by Saddam Husain – or simply
less important in his eyes for his own well-being and survival. As a consequence, after 1990 communities across Iraq suffered under the burden of

two sets of sanctions. One was imposed by the UN and the other had long formed the basis of Saddam Husain's distribution-and-reward system at the heart of the 'shadow state'. What in times of relative prosperity had been a social disadvantage became in times of absolute shortage a matter of desperation as families tried to cope with the destitution of their condition.

This was not a situation which the UN was able to remedy even after the 'oil for food' deals of 1996–9 allowed Iraq to spend massively once again on importing food and other necessities. The inspectorate system devised by the UN to ensure that these goods reached the weakest sections of the Iraqi population was inadequate not simply to cover the whole of the country, but also to penetrate and expose the networks of patronage and favouritism whereby the imports were distributed. Indeed, the 'oil for food' administration at the UN itself became entangled in the seductions and corruption of the system operated by the Iraqi government. The Iraqi government continued to use the example of the suffering of its own people in its campaign to have sanctions lifted and at the same time explained the shortages to the Iraqis themselves in terms of the malice of the external powers, led by the United States, which had master-minded the 'thirty-country aggression', as the war for Kuwait came to be officially known. Meanwhile, it continued to operate the system of penalty and reward which had served it so well in the past and which ensured that the majority of the population lived in misery.[33]

For some, targeted by the regime for special or exemplary treatment, this misery was intensified. Thus the Shi'i tribal peoples of the vast marshlands of southern Iraq were subjected to prolonged persecution during the 1990s. This involved an economic blockade and repeated bombardment by the Iraqi army, as well as the completion of the 'third river project' which diverted the main rivers and effectively destroyed large areas of the marshlands. The inhabitants either fled across the border into Iran or found themselves resettled in new villages, denied their traditional means of livelihood and under the watchful eye of the security forces. They were suffering because the marshes had long provided sanctuary for those fleeing from the agents of the regime. During the Iran–Iraq war they had become a refuge for thousands of army deserters. Similarly, after the failed uprisings of 1991, thousands fled to the marshes, hoping to escape the Republican Guard. The harsh treatment now meted out to the population of the marshes and the destruction of one of Iraq's oldest communities was publicly justified by the regime in the name of security and modernisation, claiming that this underdeveloped and uncontrolled area represented a threat to the identity and progress of Iraq. At the same time, the regime denigrated the peoples of the marshes, playing upon racial and sectarian prejudices to persuade other Iraqis that these were people of no account who should indeed be dispersed and whose communities should be destroyed.

Also targeted were those among the Shi'a who looked for guidance to clerics independent of the regime. Saddam Husain had always been careful to patronise both the tribal leaders of the rural Shi'i south and those clerics, such as 'Ali Kashif al-Ghita, who were willing to serve as the regime's intermediaries. Any sign of independence generally led to exemplary violence. Thus, in the wake of the revolts of 1991, Grand Ayatollah Abu al-Qasim al-Kho'i was placed under house arrest, members of his family and of his circle of advisers were imprisoned and a number of them killed. When he died in August 1992, a close watch was kept on his sons and on the other Shi'i clerics who disdained government patronage. Any who became too active or too prominent as leaders in their own right were harassed and in some cases murdered. Thus one of al-Kho'i's sons, Muhammad Taqi, was killed in 1994 on the road between Najaf and Karbala. Ayatollah Murtada Borujerdi and Ayatollah 'Ali al-Gharawi were both shot by 'unknown assailants' in the first half of 1998. In February 1999, a similar fate befell Ayatollah Muhammad Sadiq al-Sadr and two of his sons. By no means a public critic of the regime, al-Sadr was nevertheless becoming a focus of mass loyalty among the Shi'a – a loyalty amply demonstrated by the violent anti-government protests that erupted in Shi'i towns and in Madinat Saddam when news of his death became known. Meanwhile, the senior Shi'i *mujtahid*, Grand Ayatollah 'Ali al-Sistani, was placed under effective house arrest in 1994 precisely to limit his contacts with the community. In this way the regime hoped to intimidate and to destroy any semblance of independent leadership amongst the Shi'a.[34]

This system of control posed a formidable challenge to those working to undermine Saddam Husain. They had to contend not simply with the ruthlessness and brutality of the regime, but also with the apparent resilience of a regime able to exercise control through the co-option of large numbers of Iraqis. They also had to suffer the consequences of their own disunity. Notoriously fragmented and mutually hostile, Iraqi opposition groupings encapsulated much of the country's troubled and fractious political history. Apparently irreconcilable ideological formations and powerful personalities nursing histories of antagonism and betrayal, as well as a multitude of ethnic and sectarian groupings, represented competing narratives in Iraqi politics – all displaced at the time by the dominant figure of Saddam Husain. The inability of these groups to formulate a coherent strategy during the crisis of 1990–1 and to present a united front as interlocutor for the United States and others contributed to the failure of the revolts, reinforcing the reluctance of the allies to intervene on behalf of the rebels.

Sobered by this experience and heartened by the existence of the de facto autonomous Kurdish region, the Iraqi opposition parties agreed to suspend their differences and came together in Vienna in June 1992 to form the Iraqi National Congress (INC) as an umbrella organisation to encourage co-operation. In October 1992 the INC met at Salahuddin, near Arbil in the Kurdish region. It established an assembly that included representatives of all the Iraqi opposition groups, save for some dissident Baʿthist and Arab nationalist groupings, and elected an executive committee that confirmed the leadership of Ahmad Chalabi, an academic and banker from a promin-ent Iraqi Shiʿi family. He was well regarded in Washington, but had little authority over Iraqis either inside or outside the country.

Although it made much of the fact that this was the first time a unified Iraqi opposition had established itself on Iraqi soil since the Baʿthist coup of 1968, the INC soon found itself entangled in the increasingly complex and fractious politics of the Kurdish region. The KDP and the PUK were its largest constituent members with a real claim to be representative of sub-stantial numbers of Iraqis and in command of financial and military resources. As their relations deteriorated and as various parties on the left and in the Shiʿi Islamist movement took sides, it became harder to sustain the fiction that the INC spoke with one voice. Chalabi and the executive tried to mediate and ironically found themselves using the small military units at their disposal to separate the armed militias of the warring Kurdish parties. By 1995, they were fighting alongside the PUK against units of the Iraqi armed forces. Their success in this engagement was short-lived. The KDP and others now no longer looked upon the INC as neutral mediators and, when the KDP invited Iraqi government forces back into the Kurdish region in 1996, the offices of the INC in Arbil, Salahuddin and elsewhere in KDP-controlled territory were ransacked whilst all INC personnel who did not succeed in escaping were killed by the Iraqi security forces.

With its diminished capacity to speak for the Iraqi opposition as a whole, the INC emerged as simply one grouping amongst many, facing all the frustrations of trying to organise effective opposition to the regime in Iraq from the isolation of exile. Its problems were shared by a rival grouping of Iraqi opposition forces: the Iraqi National Accord (al-Wifaq al-Watani), or INA. Emerging in 1990 and composed of many who had shunned the INC, it represented a view of Iraq closer in some respects to that of Saddam Husain. As a result, it was thought by outsiders to have a better chance of undermining the regime in Baghdad. Led by the secular, ex-Baʿthist Ayad ʿAllawi (also from a prominent Shiʿi family), it attracted dissident Baʿthists and a number of defectors from those social groups favoured by Baghdad – chiefly the Sunni Arabs of the north-west who predominated in the security services and the officer corps. The INA's principal strategy was to try to organise conspiracies within the very organs of the Iraqi state on which Saddam Husain relied, exploiting kinship and other informal links within the armed forces as he himself had done. However, it too faced failure, frustration and the arrest and execution of its associates within the country, most dramatically in the summer of 1996.

This was the dilemma faced by those who wanted to organise against the regime of Saddam Husain. The main instruments of state power remained the preserve of Saddam Husain himself and his trusted few. Little opportunity was therefore provided for those who wanted to act against the regime. This fact applied with equal force to the United States and to other outside powers which made no secret of their desire to see the overthrow of Saddam Husain whose downfall was not brought about, as might once have been expected, by economic sanctions, nor by conspiracies within the security forces or the ruling elite. Frustrated by these failures, and cultivated in particular by Ahmad Chalabi of the INC, those in the United States pressing for a change of regime in Iraq succeeded in getting the Iraq Liberation Act passed by the US Congress in the autumn of 1998. It committed around $100 million to the assistance of a number of approved Iraqi opposition groups, but these still faced the problem that they could themselves make few inroads into the 'shadow state' that sustained the rule of Saddam Husain.

WAR AND THE FALL OF SADDAM HUSAIN

Nevertheless, the passing of the 1998 Act signalled a change in the political balance in Washington. It was here that the plan to bring down the government of Saddam Husain and to end the Baʿthist regime in Iraq was drawn up. However, the condition of its success was to be a full-scale invasion of the country by American and other foreign forces. During the years that followed, accelerating after 2001, it was the drive to war in Washington which sealed the fate of Saddam Husain and his regime. Although encouraged by some sections of the Iraqi exiled opposition, it was clear that they would have no role to play in this, as their startled representatives were reminded in Ankara in February 2003, a month before the invasion. The United States intended to be in complete control not simply of the military operation, but also of the entire country for at least a year following the overthrow of its government. Iraqis would merely be called upon to act as advisers.

One reason for the change in the United States was the realisation that the obduracy and resilience of Saddam Husain's regime, and Iraq's re-emergence as a major oil producer and regional economic power, meant that Iraq was poised on the verge of international rehabilitation. This not only made a mockery of the UN sanctions, but also explicitly challenged American power at a time when the United States, as the sole superpower, seemed set to enjoy the fruits of what had been prematurely called 'The New American Century'.[35]

By 2001–2 Iraq was producing an estimated 2.8 million barrels of oil per day, exporting 1.7 million barrels per day under the UN's 'oil for food' arrangement, bringing in roughly $12 billion annually. After the removal of a fixed percentage to pay for compensation claims, meet UN expenses and provide the Kurdish Regional Government with 13 per cent of the proceeds, the Iraqi government retained some 50 per cent to spend on imports. It supplemented these revenues by charging purchasers a levy on the oil it exported, as well as by exporting oil semi-covertly outside UN control through Turkey, Iran, Jordan and, after the reopening of the Syrian pipeline in late 2000, through Syria. These operations brought in an estimated additional $2 billion each year.

The economic activity these revenues generated and the widening scope of its imports made Iraq once again a hub of regional trade. Although substantial numbers of contracts for imported commodities and equipment had been held up by the UN Sanctions Committee during the years since the implementation of UN SC Resolution 986 (amounting to roughly $4 billion worth by January 2002), over the same period contracts worth about $30 billion had been approved. Companies and countries which had hitherto been wary of re-entering the Iraqi market could not pass up the opportunities and inducements offered by an Iraqi government eager to encourage its commercial re-integration into the world economic system. For ordinary Iraqis, at least those living in the major towns, a wide range of goods was now available on the market at increasingly affordable prices. For the Iraqi government, this was a political asset in more senses than one. As its revenues increased it made a point of encouraging trade deals with neighbouring states and with three of the permanent members of the UN Security Council – Russia, France and China – as a means of giving these countries a stake in their continued access to the Iraqi market.[36]

The decay of the sanctions regime and its political consequences under-lined a further contradiction. Unintentionally, the sanctions had appeared to strengthen the networks of the repressive patrimonial state, both mater-ially and by fostering a kind of beleaguered solidarity. Nor had the sanc-tions prevented the Iraqi government from maintaining a large military establishment which, although much reduced in terms of size and equip-ment from its peak in 1990, was still formidable domestically. Of greater concern for the international community was the possibility that, despite the sanctions, Saddam Husain had restarted Iraq's programme for the development of weapons of mass destruction after the departure of the UN weapons inspectors in 1998.

The difficulties posed by these contradictions became apparent at the UN where an attempt was made to re-establish an effective weapons inspec-tion regime in Iraq. In December 1999, the UN Security Council passed Resolution 1284 replacing UNSCOM with the United Nations Monitoring, Verification and Inspection Commission (UNMOVIC). However, four countries abstained, including three permanent members of the Security Council – Russia, France and China. This encouraged Iraq to reject the resolution, claiming it would turn Iraq into a 'protectorate' of the UN. Resentful of the UN's continued control of its oil revenues and the embargo on military and 'dual-use' items, Iraq refused to allow UN weapons inspectors back into the country prior to the unconditional lifting of economic sanctions. For some, this suggested that the resolution had been ill thought out and needed greater refinement. For others, however, it was a sign that Iraq was indeed concealing biological and chemical weapons, as well as possibly restarting its nuclear weapons programmes.[37]

Iraq found further ways of testing the resolve of the UN Security Council. During the year that followed, it reopened Iraqi air space to civil-ian flights and reopened the civil airport. This was not in violation of UN resolutions, but it drew attention to and in some respects complicated the task of the US and British planes patrolling the 'no-fly zones' in northern and southern Iraq. These patrols continued on a regular basis and Iraq's defiance of what its government regarded as an unacceptable infringement of its sovereignty led to repeated military engagements during 2000 and 2001 in which Iraqi anti-aircraft batteries paid a high price.

For the administration of President Clinton this situation was irksome, if bearable. It recognised that the more extensive Iraq's economic rehabil-itation, the harder it would be to enforce UN resolutions through inter-vention, but there was in fact little incentive to intervene. The experience of 1996, when American efforts to foment internal conspiracy against

Saddam Husain had unravelled in a spectacular and violent way, discouraged thoughts of actively promoting regime change. Since that time the United States had relied on the instruments of the status quo – sanctions, overflights and explicit support for Kuwaiti and Saudi security – to keep in place its policies of containment and deterrence. Unsatisfactory as this was recognised to be, it was nevertheless thought more effective and less costly than the alternatives as a means of preventing Iraq from posing a threat to regional order.

There were others in the United States, particularly in the Republican Party and the US Congress, who thought such inaction both shameful and short-sighted. For them the 'problem of Iraq' demanded the overthrow of Saddam Husain since they believed that the only acceptable way of re-integrating Iraq into the world community and neutralising it as a military threat was by establishing a regime in Baghdad friendly to the United States and more in tune with its wider interests in the Middle East. These supporters of the Iraq Liberation Act of 1998 had watched in frustration as the subsequent cautious disbursement of funds failed to translate into a strategy that would seriously threaten the regime in Baghdad. Lobbied with considerable success by the INC, which had switched its major field of operations to Washington, these same figures, collectively labelled the 'neocons', associated themselves with the campaign of George W. Bush for the presidency in 2000.[38]

With Bush's victory and the formation of a new US administration in 2001, there seemed to be an opportunity for the United States to reshape its policy towards Iraq. The repeated failure at the UN to tighten up the sanctions regime or to get UN weapons inspectors back into Iraq encouraged those within the US administration who felt that more forceful and, if necessary, unilateral methods were needed. Centred chiefly at the Pentagon, this group had long advocated the overthrow of Saddam Husain as the only certain way of dealing with the threat Iraq was believed to represent. Whilst there were differences of opinion about the best way of achieving this aim, there was unanimity about the goal. They held to the idea that the Gulf War of 1991 had left unfinished business which could be resumed a decade later by similar means. However, this presented a set of practical problems which the president and his closest advisers were unwilling to take on immediately.

These perceptions were altered by the dramatic attacks on New York and Washington by members of the Islamist organisation al-Qa'ida on 11 September 2001. Some were prepared to see an Iraqi hand in these events, based on Iraq's known enmity to the United States and on the suspicion that it might have used Islamist organisations in the past to attack American targets rather than on any evidence linking the Iraqi authorities to these particular acts.[39] In the tense weeks that followed, when Bush declared his 'war on terror', Saddam Husain did little to ingratiate himself. He was the sole Arab leader who failed to condemn the attacks of September, pointing out instead that the United States had brought them on itself through the policies it had pursued over the years in the Middle East.

However, with the continuing absence of evidence to link Iraq to the attacks, and the concentration of the United States on its military campaign in Afghanistan, Iraq seemed to fade into the background. Nevertheless, there were many within the administration, including President Bush, who saw the 'war on terror' as having longer-term implications than simply the uprooting of al-Qaʾida or the overthrow of the Taleban regime in Kabul. It was intended to embody a more ambitious vision of American power by capitalising on the United States' dominant position in the international order to secure American interests globally. In this view, the threat to these interests came from those who had the will and the means to launch terrorist attacks like those of 11 September.

In such an atmosphere it was inevitable that attention should have turned to states seen as hostile to the United States, especially those suspected of possessing the capacity to make chemical, biological or nuclear weapons. Accordingly, the grounds for the indictment of Iraq shifted to its alleged development of weapons of mass destruction. This referred both to stocks which it might have concealed since 1991 and to the possibility that it had resumed its weapons development programmes after 1998. A succession of defectors, many of them planted by the INC and others who wanted to goad the United States into action against Iraq, had encouraged the belief that Iraq retained chemical and biological weapons and that it had both the human resources and the political will to resume its nuclear weapons programme.[40] The truth of these allegations could not, in any case, be verified unless and until the UN weapons inspectors returned to Iraq, but in November 2001 Iraq repeated its refusal to allow UNMOVIC into the country.

The United States publicly confined its moves vis-à-vis Iraq to the UN Security Council. Less visible was the planning that had already started at the Pentagon for an invasion of Iraq. The success of the US-led military campaign in overthrowing the Taleban regime in Afghanistan, hunting down al-Qaʾida forces and installing a more amenable regime in Kabul gave heart to those who advocated this as a pattern for successful intervention elsewhere, especially in Iraq. President Bush's reference to the 'axis of evil' comprising Iraq, Iran and North Korea in a speech in January 2002 seemed to map out the contours of a newly confident interventionism, enunciated in the 'Bush Doctrine', fleshed out later in the year by the National Security Council.[41] This outlined a strategy for the United States that combined preventive war against terrorists or rogue states producing weapons of mass destruction, pre-emptive attack, unilateralism and intervention to promote democracy in all parts of the world. It seemed tailor-made to justify the invasion of Iraq, plans for which had been submitted to President Bush as early as December 2001.[42]

The US administration was faced not simply with the military challenge of planning a successful invasion and occupation of Iraq, but also with trying to assess which of the Iraqi opposition groupings could form the basis of a viable successor regime. To the consternation of some, this became a site of fierce personal and ideological rivalry within various branches of the US government, as different agencies laid claim to the future of Iraq. Given the power and influence of the Pentagon in the wake of the September attacks, the security fears they had provoked and the success of the war in Afghanistan, it was the Defense Department, headed by Donald Rumsfeld, that prevailed – with fateful results for the shaping of Iraq's history.[43]

For his part, Saddam Husain, adept at thwarting internal conspiracy, was less skilled at countering the challenge of direct military intervention of the kind threatened by the United States in 2002. Rather belatedly, Iraq tried to cultivate its neighbours. Having heaped abuse on Kuwait and Saudi Arabia for more than a decade for providing bases for the US military in the region, the Iraqi government changed tack and effected a symbolic reconciliation with Saudi Arabia in Beirut in March 2002, consoling itself with a resolution that an attack on any one Arab state would be regarded as an attack on all. A similar strategy was pursued towards Iran, leading to an exchange of official visits and friendly communiqués in 2002 between these mistrustful neighbours.

Iraq also tried to enlist support for its position at the UN, where the possibility of unilateral American military action against Iraq caused general alarm. Following the adoption of UN SC Resolution 1441 in November 2002, UNMOVIC, headed by Hans Blix, was finally allowed into Iraq to begin its work, and in December Iraq submitted what it claimed was the full documentation of its now terminated weapons programmes and of the measures taken to destroy stocks and capabilities. Given the suspicions that existed at the time, this was treated with some scepticism and various aspects of the Iraqi presentation did little to allay these suspicions.

In fact, Iraq neither possessed weapons of mass destruction, nor had developed programmes designed to restart their production. The Iraqi case was not helped, however, by two aspects of the regime which were to contribute to its downfall. In the first place, it appears to have been part of Saddam Husain's strategy to maintain a degree of ambiguity about Iraq's capabilities, in order to retain some of the deterrent value conferred upon those thought to possess weapons of mass destruction. Iran, always suspected of nursing thoughts of revenge for the war of the 1980s, was the principal audience. This policy also influenced others, lower down in the security and scientific establishments, who could not be sure what other branches of government were up to, but who were terrified of giving the game away and so colluded in this dangerous game of ambiguity.

The US administration, however, had already finalised its plans for the invasion of Iraq as early as the summer of 2002. In October, a compliant US Congress passed a resolution authorising the use of force against Iraq, opening the way for the president to order military action as and when he saw fit. It was not surprising, therefore, that the United States and its close ally the United Kingdom, when faced with Iraq's ambivalence, chose to believe the worst. They pressed for a further UN resolution which would condemn Iraq for failing to comply with UN SC Resolution 1441 and which would explicitly sanction the use of force against Iraq. To the exasperation of those who believed now that only war and the downfall of the regime in Baghdad would solve the problem, the IAEA (International Atomic Energy Authority) and UNMOVIC made generally positive reports to the UN Security Council in the first months of 2003, citing Iraqi co-operation and stating that they had found no evidence of prohibited weapons or activities.

By this stage, however, there was no doubt that the United States and some of its allies, most notably the United Kingdom, Australia, Spain and Italy, were planning a full-scale invasion of Iraq. Forces were already in place in the Persian Gulf and elsewhere. Under these circumstances, and in view of the continued positive reports by UNMOVIC, it was clear that a further resolution authorising the use of force against Iraq was not going to get past the opposition of two of the permanent members of the UN Security Council, France and Russia. Their governments saw it merely as a ploy to allow unilateral action by the United States and the United Kingdom against Iraq. By mid-March efforts to get explicit UN authorisation for war had collapsed, and the United States and its allies prepared for the invasion, relying on previous UN resolutions to justify a war regarded by some as illegal.[44]

On 17 March President Bush gave Saddam Husain an ultimatum to leave Iraq within forty-eight hours and the UNMOVIC teams were evacuated. Two days later 'Operation Iraqi Freedom' was launched with an air attack designed to kill Saddam Husain and his close associates. It failed, and a full-scale aerial bombardment of political and military targets began – part of the 'shock and awe' tactics advocated by the US military to demoralise and possibly to paralyse the command structures of the Iraqi armed forces. Having failed to gain Turkish acquiescence in the opening of a 'northern front', on 21 March the US-led invading forces came up from Kuwait, with the British contingent turning towards Basra and the main US force driving northwards towards Baghdad both through the desert and, via Nasiriyya, Diwaniyya and Kut, through the farmlands between the Euphrates and the Tigris.

In view of the overwhelming firepower of the allied forces and their complete command of the air, the Iraqi forces crumbled, many surrendering en masse or fading away into the civilian population. More tenacious were irregular formations, like the Fidayi Saddam, whose guerrilla-style activities caused some initial problems for the conventional forces ranged against them. However, this could only be a delaying tactic and by 7 April British forces had taken Basra, followed on 9 April by the US army's capture of Baghdad, where the threatened street-by-street fighting failed to materialise.

On the contrary, by the time US forces reached the capital, there was remarkably little organised resistance. Saddam Husain himself fled the city, pausing only to give a brief speech exhorting resistance until victory to a somewhat bemused crowd in al-'Adhamiyya. He then sped off in a convoy of cars and went into hiding. Meanwhile, US forces pressed on northwards, meeting sporadic resistance, but little that hampered their onward march which speeded up when it seemed that the Kurdish *peshmerga* were about to capture Mosul. PUK forces had already taken Kirkuk, where Jalal Talabani had given an emotional press conference on 10 April, but had been persuaded by the United States to leave the city. Alarmed by Turkish and more general Iraqi reactions to this expression of Kurdish irredentism, US forces raced on to Mosul, bringing it under American control by 11 April. In the space of three weeks, therefore, the United States and its allies found themselves in occupation of Iraq.[45]

For the Iraqi population, the pace and violence of these events had made them bystanders or victims. The bewildering speed of the collapse of Saddam Husain's apparently formidable security forces had delighted many, especially those who remembered the terrible events of 1991.

However, an estimated 4–7,000 Iraqi civilians were killed during the invasion, in addition to 7–12,000 members of Iraq's security forces. The very lack of precision of these figures is a testimony to the confusion of war, but also to the breakdown of all Iraqi record-keeping, as well as to the declared indifference of the allied command, whose forces suffered few casualties by comparison, with some 140 Americans and 33 British service personnel killed during the campaign.[46]

Indifference bordering on neglect on the part of the allied forces was reproduced across the country when, in the days following the capture of Baghdad and other major cities, widespread looting took place. Not only were government ministries and other official buildings ransacked by crowds of Iraqis, so too were schools, universities, hospitals, museums, libraries, factories, power stations – effectively any installation that looked as if it might contain something worth stealing, and which was not protected by armed guards. The relatively small number of allied troops used to invade Iraq (totalling 173,218 – of which 150,816 were US forces and 22,402 belonged to the coalition) chose to guard very few of the country's public buildings and, indeed, across large swathes of the country there were no allied troops to be found. Instead, the allied forces concentrated on their own security and stood by whilst a population long repressed and impoverished took their revenge not only on the symbols of authority, such as the many statues of Saddam Husain that crashed to the ground, but also on the whole infrastructure of the public state.

The ending of Saddam Husain's rule in Iraq was as violent as many had predicted. The methods he had used to dominate Iraq and the hold this had given him over his countrymen had granted him vast scope for his ambitions, plunging Iraq into two major wars and two bloody insurrections, the scars of which remained in a fragmented and destitute population. His continuing defiance of the international community and the price his population paid for this under more than twelve years of sanctions compounded the problems and degraded the faltering public institutions of the Iraqi state. In the 1970s they had looked set to become an outstanding example of successful centrally directed development fuelled by oil revenues, but gradually, starved of resources and subject to the whims of the coterie that surrounded the president, they decayed.

Paradoxically, whilst the public state faltered, the 'shadow state' thrived, mobilising local networks to serve the personal rule of Saddam Husain. The massive force represented by the US-led invasion attacked the heart of this powerful and repressive system, physically dislodging Saddam Husain and his immediate circle and wrenching from their hands the main levers of power. In doing so, however, the invaders oversaw the final collapse of the public institutions of the Iraqi state. They also found that the 'shadow state' itself disintegrated into its myriad components and that these, far from evaporating, fell back on their local ties and communities, positioning themselves to re-form according to the new dispensations of power. This was a legacy of over thirty years of Ba'thist rule, in particular under the leadership of Saddam Husain, with which those who now found themselves ruling Iraq would have to grapple for years to come.

CHAPTER 7

The American occupation and the parliamentary republic

The military occupation of Iraq by the United States and its allies was intended to last for at least a year. In fact, large numbers of American and allied forces remained in Iraq for much longer, but sovereignty was formally handed over to an Iraqi government in June 2004. Nevertheless, the brief period of direct American rule brought out certain trends in Iraqi politics, reflecting different possibilities in Iraq's history, but leaving an ambivalent legacy. On the one hand, the US administration seemed intent on setting up a fully functioning liberal democracy within a very short space of time, encouraging the development of a market economy and providing a secure environment by reconstructing the Iraqi security establishment, gearing it to police a thriving civil society. Yet the way the US administration set about this ambitious task was at odds with its declared goals. The result was a troubled and increasingly insecure country in which insurgency, lawlessness and sectarian conflict claimed growing numbers of Iraqi lives, in addition to taking a mounting toll of the occupation forces.

During this period the gradual establishment of formally representative institutions could have given the impression of the emergence of a new, democratic Iraq from the ruins of Saddam Husain's dictatorship – were it not for the backdrop of mounting violence, the flight of hundreds of thousands of Iraqis into exile, the sectarian murders and the widespread corruption that depleted still further the uncertain income of the Iraqi state. A closer look at the governments that came to power as a result of the elections of 2005 would reveal that, once again, all was not what it seemed. Public ministries became partisan fiefdoms, farmed out to powerful factions, made more powerful by their ability to command militias that were used to terrorise political enemies and whole neighbourhoods or communities seen as hostile to their sponsors. The elected National Assembly, although the formal seat of authority, was not where power resided. This lay in the hands of men made powerful by the support they could muster in local ethnic and sectarian communities, by the weapons at their disposal, by the share of the national resources which they had managed to appropriate or by the patronage of the United States. In short, a range of mutually suspicious leaders were being encouraged to emerge as the new oligarchy of Iraq.

Yet there were thousands of Iraqis who hoped it could be otherwise. As in 1958, that other year when many possible futures stood before Iraq after decades of repressive rule, so in 2003 there were those who saw the collapse of the old regime as a golden opportunity to recapture some of what Iraq might have been. They sought to build organisations to give a voice to the voiceless – all those who had been written out of the narrative of Iraqi history by the strident commands of the Ba'thist vanguard and its instruments of repression. The array of new media, the possibilities offered for NGO (nongovernmental organisation) and trade union activities, as well as the novel freedom to communicate and debate, were avidly seized upon, bringing a host of new and original Iraqi voices to the fore. However, they faced a hard struggle trying to carve out a secure space in which to enjoy these freedoms. They had to ensure that what they built could withstand the assaults of government agencies, repressive local authorities, partisan militias, foreign occupying forces and the ruthless violence of those who were organising an insurgency against the emerging order in Iraq. This has been their story during the years since the invasion of 2003.

THE RULE OF THE COALITION PROVISIONAL AUTHORITY (CPA)

The Pentagon, which had won the internal political struggle in Washington to shape the US occupation of Iraq, had done little to plan for its future. Detailed and meticulous planning had gone into the military campaign, and a division of labour for the occupation had been worked out between the allied states that had signed up to 'Operation Iraqi Freedom'. Thus, British forces would occupy and control the four southern provinces of Iraq, centred on Basra, whilst the four provinces north of these would be controlled by contingents from ten other members of the coalition, under overall Polish command. The remaining provinces would come under direct US military occupation, although in the three provinces of the autonomous Kurdish region US forces were kept to a minimum.

However, there had been no corresponding effort to think about how the politics of Iraq might develop in the aftermath of the fall of Saddam Husain. Other branches of the US administration had been working on this, but the results of their deliberations had fallen victim to the notorious inter-agency rivalries of Washington. Only in mid-January 2003 did the

Pentagon focus on the question of post-war Iraq, leading the White House to establish, under Pentagon auspices, the Office of Reconstruction and Humanitarian Assistance (ORHA), headed by a retired general, Jay Garner, who had helped to set up the Kurdish 'safe haven' in northern Iraq in 1991.

Aware that he would be working under a limited mandate, Garner's plans for post-war Iraq focused on questions such as humanitarian relief, refugees, maintaining basic services and ensuring law and order. However, when Garner and his staff finally reached Baghdad in the third week of April, they found a chaotic situation. Assumptions they had made about using the existing Iraqi administration had been undermined by the break-down of law and order, the widespread looting and the physical destruction of much of the state infrastructure. ORHA thereupon adopted two strategies. The first was to try to reconstitute as much of the old Iraqi administration as they could by recalling people to their posts, setting up temporary offices and guaranteeing salaries. Given his small staff, limited resources and the scale of the problem, Garner faced a formidable challenge and made little headway.

Garner also tried to start a process to involve Iraqis themselves in discussing the future. He was hampered by the fact that the US government had stated that it would not cede any powers of decision to Iraqis for at least a year, thereby discouraging participation in a process that seemed at best advisory and at worst a form of collaboration with foreign military occupation. He and the US administration more generally were also at a disadvantage since the only Iraqi political figures they knew at all well were either the Kurdish leaders or long-exiled opposition figures. A number of these were well connected in Washington and were correspondingly influential there, but their authority in Iraq was unknown.

Equally obscure were the true power brokers of Iraqi political society. Under the previous regime, public prominence was only allowed on terms set by Saddam Husain and this generally meant public subservience to his wishes – a disqualifying condition for holding power in post-invasion Iraq. It was far harder to determine who enjoyed authority in their own right of a kind that would be immediately useful to the US-led occupation. To this end, Garner organised a series of public meetings at which he hoped that a leadership pool of suitable Iraqis would appear.

It was a naïve hope. Interested individuals turned up, but many stayed away, particularly those who were already making other plans for the future. The fall of the old regime had allowed the return of the exiles and their followers, all seeking to carve out a place for themselves in post-Ba'thist politics. Some, such as Ahmed Chalabi or his rival Ayad 'Allawi,

hoped that their future prominence would be assured through their connections with US government agencies. Others, such as Ibrahim al-Jaʿfari
of al-Daʿwa and ʿAbd al-ʿAziz al-Hakim of SCIRI, returned to revive their
organisations, assisted by the armed units which had grown up in exile or
in the underground resistance. At the same time, the Iraqi Islamic Party
(outgrowth of the Sunni-based Muslim Brotherhood), under Muhsin ʿAbd
al-Hamid, emerged into public view, and the secretary-general of the Iraqi
Communist Party, Hamid Majid Mousa, hoped to revive the fortunes of a
party that had once played so prominent a role in Iraqi history. Even Sharif
ʿAli, the Hashemite pretender to the Iraqi throne, returned to ascertain if
there was a role for his dynasty in Iraq.[1]

However, the exiles were not the only ones hoping to shape the future.
It would be mistaken to suppose that 'politics' returned to Iraq with the
ingathering of the exiles. On the contrary, many who had stayed in Iraq
throughout the years of repression and sanctions believed that they had
more right than the exiles to determine the future and they often had the
advantage of commanding powerful local networks. The poor Shiʿi mass
housing district of east Baghdad, once called Madinat al-Thawra, then
Madinat Saddam, was re-labelled Madinat al-Sadr (Sadr City) when
Muqtada al-Sadr, a son of the late Ayatollah Sadiq al-Sadr, asserted his leadership with a speed and success made possible by the organisation originally set up by his father for welfare distribution. Muqtada used his
connection to his distinguished clerical family, but his authority did not
rest on his own scholarly pre-eminence. On the contrary, he emerged as a
populist leader, claiming to protect and provide for his community, whilst
using systematic violence against those who opposed him. This was seen
early on as his militia, Jaish al-Mahdi (the Mahdi Army), extended his
power beyond Sadr City, throughout the largely Shiʿi south of Iraq.

In doing so, he came up against other authorities amongst the Shiʿa.
Almost certainly responsible for the murder of Sayyid ʿAbd al-Majid
al-Khoʾi who had returned to Najaf in April, al-Sadr's forces were met
by opposition from those supporting the *marjaʿ* of the Shiʿa, Ayatollah
ʿAli al-Sistani. Al-Sistani was looked upon by most of Iraq's Shiʿa as the
chief authority in their community and his opinions carried a weight
unmatched by others. He was thus effectively the head of the *hawza*, the
Shiʿi clerical establishment, but he also held to the view that clerics should
not themselves become politicians. Rather, they should offer advice to
ensure that the welfare of the community, both spiritual and material, came
first. This set him at odds with the Iranian-influenced Shiʿi activists of
SCIRI, some of al-Daʿwa and with the radical populism of al-Sadr.

However, there was no denying his authority and many who sought power tried to associate themselves with him. They and their supporters came to his defence when he himself was physically threatened by al-Sadr's forces in Najaf.[2]

Elsewhere in the south, local associations, some tribal, some based on religious community and Islamist feeling, others preoccupied with order in their neighbourhood or locality, sprang up to guard their communities and to make sure that their voices would be heard. Thus, the British authorities in Basra and the southern provinces co-operated with various local figures and organisations – the armed irregulars who had taken over 'Amara before the allied forces arrived, the romantically named 'Prince of the Marshes', 'Abd al-Karim al-Muhammadawi, organiser of local resistance during the 1990s, and tribal shaikhs whom the British believed could help in keeping order.

However, the British had only a weak grasp of the personal histories, relationships, rivalries and status differences behind these provincial networks. This was knowledge that came gradually, and by that stage people had already inserted themselves into positions of influence in local government. They used these posts to build up local fiefdoms, pursue feuds with rivals and initiate complex relationships with the emerging parties and leaders in Basra and Baghdad. In short, a distinctively Iraqi politics was developing which escaped the supervision, let alone the control, of the allied forces in occupation of the country.[3]

Similar developments were taking place in Baghdad and in the northern provinces under the auspices of the United States. In the rural areas and in some of the provincial towns, tribal shaikhs were enlisted to keep order and their men allowed to bear arms, especially those, such as certain shaikhs of the Dulaim, who had been in close contact with the Americans prior to the invasion. However, for the most part, the US authorities had no way of reading local society in northern and western Iraq and a series of violent incidents, such as the shooting of demonstrators by US forces in Falluja at the end of April, heightened tensions.

At the time of the invasion, the lack of organised resistance even in places like Takrit, Saddam Husain's home town, had surprised the US authorities. However, across this part of Iraq, peopled mainly by Sunni Arabs, there was an undercurrent of apprehension about what a new regime in Iraq might mean for them. Quite apart from their resentment at foreign military occupation, the fact that the principal allies of the United States seemed to be Kurdish nationalists in the north and parties led by Shi'i clerics in the south caused alarm and fear for the future.

22 L. Paul Bremer III (administrator of the Coalition Provisional Authority
2003–4), 2003

These fears were redoubled in mid-May 2003 when the US administration abruptly ended Garner's tenure, abolished ORHA and sent Paul Bremer to run the newly constituted Coalition Provisional Authority (CPA) in Baghdad. He was an official with no Middle Eastern experience, but his good connections, ideological and professional, to senior figures in the US administration won him the post. As head of the CPA, Bremer was to exercise supreme executive, legislative and judicial authority in Iraq until June 2004, when sovereignty was transferred to an Iraqi government. Signalling an abrupt break with the past, but also with the gradualist approach of his predecessor, Bremer issued two edicts in quick succession that were to have fateful consequences.

The first was the order dissolving the Baʿth party and banning all members of the party above a certain rank from holding any position in the public services. The second was the order dissolving the Iraqi armed forces and the entire security apparatus of the old regime. The adverse effects of these two decisions were to be felt for years to come. They put some 300,000 armed young men out of work at a stroke, stopped the pensions of tens of thousands of ex-officers and purged the slowly recovering government ministries of roughly 30,000 people, including their most experienced administrators. Whoever was finally responsible for this decision, it showed little knowledge of Iraqi society, of the reasons why people had joined the Ba'th party, or even of the role of the armed forces under Saddam Husain. It appeared that the US administration had been persuaded, either by the few Iraqis who had access to it, or by its own ideological preconceptions, that this was the only way to clear the path for the liberal, democratic Iraq which it had proclaimed was its goal.

Before the full impact of these and other decisions had become clear, the United States and the United Kingdom had obtained UN approval for their occupation of Iraq. UN SC Resolution 1483 of May 2003 recognised the military occupation, ended thirteen years of economic sanctions and authorised Sergio de Mello, the UN Secretary General's special representative, to work on reconstruction, humanitarian aid and the establishment of an Iraqi government. These moves seemed to promise international involvement in Iraq's political future, but the question facing the United States, and the Iraqis, was how to get from the reality of foreign military occupation to the professed ideal of an independent, stable, responsive and democratic political system.

In this respect, the United States found itself in a situation reminiscent of that of Great Britain in Iraq in the 1920s. Whilst claiming to bring the benefits of democratic governance to the Iraqis, the United States was nevertheless reluctant to give up control of the process to the Iraqis themselves. On the contrary, they wanted to ensure that when the Iraqis did regain their sovereignty, it would be within a framework fixed by the United States. Since the establishment of democracy was being used retrospectively by the American and British governments to justify the invasion of Iraq (given the awkward failure to discover any of Iraq's alleged chemical, biological or nuclear weapons)[4] it was believed in Washington and London to be crucial to lock the Iraqis into a political system founded on these values.

Understandably, this was not a view shared in Baghdad, or in Najaf. It was here, in early July, that Ayatollah al-Sistani issued a *fatwa* in which he stated that it was unacceptable for an Iraqi constitution to be drafted and passed into law by people who were appointed, rather than elected. He was responding to the fears of many Iraqis that the United States was trying to impose a secular, federal constitution upon the country, backed by its chosen protégés among the exiled politicians and the Kurdish leadership. Al-Sistani called for direct elections to a constitutional convention, followed by a referendum of the entire Iraqi electorate to decide on the draft's acceptability. It was a testimony to his authority in those years that, after prevarication and attempts to retain control of the process, Bremer finally agreed to a timetable based more or less on this pattern.

23 Ayatollah Sayyid ʿAli al-Sistani (senior Shiʿi cleric in Iraq
since 1992) on a poster carried by supporters, 2005

   This was announced in November by the Iraqi Governing Council
(IGC). The IGC itself was an American concession to the increasingly
vocal demands by Iraqis for some say in the process by which they were to
be governed. In mid-July Bremer appointed a twenty-five-member council
of Iraqis to act as advisers, with limited authority to appoint ministers,
draft laws and draw up a budget, governed by the US power of veto.
Significantly, the composition of the IGC was an indicator of how the
United States read the politics of Iraq at the time and laid down a precedent for its future. Thus, of the twenty-five members thirteen were Shiʿi
Arab, five were Kurdish, five were Sunni Arab, one was Turkmen and one
was Assyrian Christian. Three of the members were women and nine were
returnees from political exile. Some of them were chosen because they led
substantial political organisations – especially the Kurds and leaders of Shiʿi

Islamist parties – but most were selected because they were believed to reflect different facets of a communally divided Iraqi society, or because they had long-established links with the US administration.[5]

Bremer's decision to include Iraqis in the governance of the country sooner than intended was partly due to the fact that, by the summer of 2003, it was clear that ruling Iraq was not going to be as straightforward as had once been thought. On the contrary, violent resistance was on the rise. By July attacks against US and allied forces were becoming so systematic, and taking such a toll, that the US military authorities were forced to admit that they were now facing a 'classical guerrilla-type campaign'. Nor, to the disappointment of many, was the impetus of this campaign lessened when Saddam Husain's two sons, 'Uday and Qusay, were trapped and killed by US forces in Mosul. On the contrary, a rapid escalation of violence followed, with suicide bombers, car bombs and gunmen targeting not simply US forces, but all those who were seen to be assisting or benefiting from the US occupation.

In August, the UN headquarters in Baghdad was blown up, killing many, including de Mello, a few days after the UN Security Council had passed UN SC Resolution 1500 welcoming the creation of the IGC. In the same month a massive bomb in Najaf killed the recently returned leader of SCIRI, Ayatollah Baqir al-Hakim, and many others. With a growing number of attacks, particularly on those seeking work with the new Iraqi security forces or administration, and on public spaces, such as markets or public gatherings, especially in the Shi'i areas, the security situation deteriorated rapidly. Fearing for their safety, the UN withdrew its staff from Iraq after a further attack on its premises and was followed by many other relief organisations whose workers' lives were in danger.

For their part, the CPA, the IGC and the representatives of the allied forces of occupation retreated inside the 'Green Zone' that had been created as a kind of citadel in the centre of Baghdad. Occupying several acres along the Tigris, and including many public buildings, with the presidential palace at its heart, this became the centre of the CPA's – and later the Iraqi government's – operations in Iraq. But it was actually and symbolically cut off from the rest of the city by high anti-blast walls, gates guarded by US forces and increasingly by a mentality – understandable in the circumstances – which saw the world outside its walls as a potential killing zone, especially of those associated with the occupation authorities.

It was in this environment and against this backdrop that the CPA developed a timetable for the transfer of power to a sovereign Iraqi government, possibly hoping that the prospect of greater public involvement and the imminent restoration of sovereignty to Iraqis would cut the ground from under the insurgency. Thus, in November it was announced that an appointed transitional Iraqi government would take over from the CPA in June 2004, charged with organising elections for a constituent assembly by January 2005. To the relief of the CPA, Ayatollah al-Sistani, who had been pressing for immediate national elections to a constituent assembly, finally gave his approval to the plan.

This allowed the drawing up of a 'fundamental law' (effectively a provisional constitution) to begin in January 2004 and caused all the interested parties to start outlining their negotiating positions. The Kurdish leader Masoud Barzani made it clear that the Kurds demanded nothing less than a fully federal state, drawing attention to the way the balance of forces now stood in the Kurds' favour. Representatives of SCIRI and al-Daʿwa, the Shiʿi Islamist parties, were equally insistent that the law of Iraq should be based on the *shariʿa*. These moves by well-defined and self-confident ethnic and sectarian organisations even pushed the Sunni Arabs of Iraq into an attempt to create a united front. Unused to thinking in communal terms, since there has never existed a Sunni community as such in Iraq, the parties and individuals involved – Islamist, secular nationalist and tribal – found it difficult to formulate a clear-cut agenda that would carry much weight. They were also conscious of the fact that they were regarded with deep suspicion, since the heart of the developing insurgency lay among the Sunni Arabs, whether Baʿthist, nationalist or Islamist. For that very reason, of course, they had to tread carefully when appearing to collaborate in the establishment of a political order under foreign occupation.

Eventually, in March 2004, the IGC approved the final draft of the Law of Administration for the State of Iraq for the Transitional Period (TAL). It confirmed the sequence of events whereby the CPA would be dissolved in June, and an Interim Iraqi Government would oversee elections for an assembly which would then draft a constitution to be put to a national referendum in autumn 2005. The TAL itself affirmed the republican, federal, democratic and pluralistic nature of the Iraqi state. It also asserted that Iraq's federalism would be based on geography and history, not on ethnicity or sect, and that Islam would be the official religion of the state, as well as a source of its legislation.

Almost immediately, manoeuvring began to choose the Iraqi who would head the Interim Government – manoeuvres into which the UN was briefly drawn. The outcome, however, bore the imprimatur of the United States, since the successful candidate, finally agreed upon by the IGC at the end of May, was Ayad ʿAllawi, a returning exile who had long enjoyed the patronage of the United States. He encouraged the view that he was a potential 'strong man' who knew how to deal with disorder and had the right connections to defuse the opposition of the 'regime remnants', as the insurgents were sometimes dismissively called.

By this stage there was certainly need for a combination of these skills, since the security situation was deteriorating week by week. The dramatic capture of Saddam Husain in mid-December 2003 had made no difference to the strength or vehemence of the insurgency. There were Ba'thist loyalists organising attacks on allied forces, but generally the insurgency had taken on a much more local shape, fragmenting into dozens of groupings, some of which co-operated, but none of which submitted to an overall national command. Thus, units of the old Iraqi army, often based on the villages and localities from which they had been recruited, had reformed as guerrilla bands, using their military training, their knowledge of the country and their access to the vast quantities of weapons and explosives circulating in Iraq following the systematic looting of the Iraqi army's unguarded arsenals and camps in the aftermath of the 2003 invasion. These were now turned with devastating effect on US, British and other allied forces, as well as on fledgling units of the new Iraqi security services, or were used to disrupt communications and to sabotage efforts at reconstruction in the energy, oil and water sectors.

The Iraqi and Arab nationalist armed resistance was joined by Sunni Islamists hostile to the occupation – and to the Shi'a who seemed to be on the verge of taking over. These groups had their origins both in Iraqi underground Islamist groups which had flourished in the 1990s and in the growing numbers of Islamists from other Arab countries who crossed Iraq's now unguarded borders to join what they saw as a *jihad* against the United States and its allies. Some of these, such as the grouping led by the Jordanian Abu Mus'ab al-Zarqawi, affiliated themselves with al-Qa'ida, at least by name. He gained thereby considerable kudos amongst the young militants who had come to Iraq to strike a blow against the United States in the hope of humbling a superpower as the USSR had been humbled in Afghanistan in the 1980s. Others linked up with Iraqi groupings and became central to the strategy of suicide bombings, used with increasingly devastating effect across Iraq.

With this broadening of the insurgency, the targets and thus the fighting took on a sectarian aspect. Bombs set off in Shi'i quarters triggered reprisals against Sunni mosques and neighbourhoods by the militias of the Shi'i organisations, the Badr brigade and the Mahdi Army. This in turn provoked further attacks against specifically Shi'i targets, and so a vicious cycle of revenge and atrocity was initiated. Under the cover of this violence, patterns of power and recruitment were being established, neighbourhoods were arming themselves and out of these vigilante groups further conflicts developed. The situation was particularly ominous in Baghdad, a city of some 6 million and very mixed in terms of its religious communities and neighbourhoods. But it was also developing in other cities: in Basra, Kirkuk, Baquba and Mosul ethnic and sectarian tensions and violence surfaced. Calls for restraint came from community leaders, but it was the voice of communal fear and anger that rapidly gained a wider hearing.[6]

For ordinary Iraqis, the unpredictable violence of the suicide bombers and the dangers of being caught in an attack on US forces, or of being attacked by the same forces, suspicious now of all civilians, was only part of the insecurity of everyday life. This was compounded by the sharp increase in criminality that had taken place since the invasion of 2003. It was not simply that all the prisons had been opened in the last weeks of the old regime. It was also that the disappearance of the police across the country, the general lawlessness of the months that followed and the wholly unguarded borders of the state opened up new possibilities for criminal activity. Theft of private and public assets, oil and drug smuggling and kidnapping had become widespread, and it appeared that neither the allied forces of occupation nor the slowly re-emerging Iraqi security forces were able to do much about it. Indeed, there was growing evidence to suggest that in many places the newly formed police forces were themselves implicated in many of these activities.

For some Iraqis, their profession or position in society placed them in danger. In the aftermath of the fall of the old regime, many scores had been settled against those with a link to the old order. Potentially very large numbers of Iraqis were involved and the murders formed a grisly counterpoint to much of the official optimism voiced by the allied authorities, which nevertheless appeared to turn a blind eye to these activities. More puzzling and far more ominous were the murders of professional Iraqis, including doctors, school teachers, university professors and scientists. Some of these killings may have been the result of personal grudges, or of sectarian targeting, but many appeared to be part of systematic attempts to intimidate or silence independent voices by organisations which now wanted to impose their own imprint on Iraq's future. This campaign was being waged by extreme Islamists, both Sunni and Shi'i, as well as by embittered Ba'thists determined to maintain their fearful hold on people's imaginations and to forestall efforts at reconstruction. The result was a steady flight of Iraqi professionals from the country which they had hoped to help rebuild.[7]

In this they were joined by increasing numbers of Iraqis fearful not only of the physical dangers, but also of rapidly deteriorating conditions of life, as far as electricity, water, sanitation, health and employment were concerned. Iraq's public infrastructure had been degraded during the sanctions years. The war and the lawlessness that followed had also taken its toll. However, the rebuilding of the public utilities and the restoration of normal conditions of life were painfully slow and, to many Iraqis, it seemed that things were rapidly getting worse. Electricity was restricted to a couple of hours a day, or was cut off altogether, along with water supplies and sewage services, and the unemployment rate was estimated at between 30 and 60 per cent. Yet, paradoxically, the United States had pledged some $22 billion for reconstruction, which had been augmented by pledges of $5 billion from the international community. Meanwhile, Iraq's oil income, although diminished, was still substantial. At the same time, foreign investment in Iraq was being vigorously encouraged and private enterprise, at least in some sectors of the economy, seemed to be making the most of the opportunities promised by the US assertion that Iraq would be regenerated by transforming it into a liberal, market-based economy.

The answer to this paradox could be found in three factors which undermined economic reconstruction and recovery. These were the inadequacy of the CPA in the face of the scale of the economic challenge, the bias, corruption and inefficiencies which beset the allocation of funds and the rapidly deteriorating security situation which discouraged further investment, or sabotaged the few projects that were up and running. The vast majority of the expanding staff of the CPA, often serving on very short-term contracts, were wholly unfamiliar with Iraqi conditions or Middle Eastern society. They had little contact with Iraqis and were caught up in a system where the financial mismanagement was breathtaking. It was characterised by inadequate accounting procedures and supervision by untrained and ill-prepared individuals in the opaque, often fractious, bureaucracy that burgeoned in the Green Zone under the gaze of Bremer, who was evidently overwhelmed by the magnitude of the task before him.[8]

Bremer shared all the prejudices of those who had appointed him in Washington against the role of the public sector in the economy. He also shared their belief that the reconstruction of Iraq could best, and most profitably, be handled by massive American private enterprises with which senior members of the US administration had been linked. To many Iraqis, it appeared that the stream of decree laws coming out of the CPA was chiefly geared to facilitating this objective. The abolition of customs dues and tariffs, the tax-free repatriation of all funds, including profits, the opening up of the banking system to foreign involvement, the plans for widespread privatisation of state-owned industries and the flat tax rate of 15 per cent imposed on individuals and corporations alike – all of this seemed to be opening up Iraq to a free-for-all of economic opportunity, in which Iraqis themselves could only play a minor role. At the same time, it was noticeable that the CPA, despite the energy with which it was sweeping away so many of the decrees of the old regime, nevertheless kept on the statute books legislation that restricted the powers of the trade unions. Inevitably, this irritated nationalist sensibilities even amongst those Iraqis who had welcomed the initial US intervention. For others, it merely confirmed their worst suspicions about what the United States was really after in Iraq.[9]

It was in the oil sector that these suspicions were at their sharpest. Partly in acknowledgement of this, the CPA left the state-run Northern and Southern Oil Companies untouched – despite vigorous lobbying in Washington by those who believed that the oil sector should be broken up and privatised. Powerful voices against this had come from the major international oil companies which preferred to deal with a single national authority, fearing that wholesale privatisation might eventually exclude them. In the view of some, their perseverance paid off, since the influence of these companies was thought to have played a role in the drafting of a law put before the Iraqi parliament in 2007 incorporating production-sharing agreements with major oil companies. These would give the oil companies long-term rights in the production and profits of Iraqi oil in exchange for investment, exploration and the rehabilitation of the oil industry. UN SC Resolution 1483 had stipulated that all Iraq's oil revenues should be paid into a newly established Development Fund for Iraq (DFI), under the control of the CPA, but independently audited. Since no independent auditor was appointed for about a year, the amount of oil revenue Iraq earned in 2003–4 (estimates ranged between $10 and 13 billion) and the fate of the revenues were largely unknown.[10]

It was known, however, that the CPA used Iraqi oil revenues in preference to funds allocated by the US Congress because of the lack of accountability and that of the $1.5 billion of contracts awarded from Iraqi funds, 74 per cent went to US firms and only 2 per cent to Iraqi contractors, with little competitive bidding. The increasingly vocal and critical Iraqi media pointed out that it was strange for the United States to declare that it intended to encourage the growth of Iraqi private enterprise and the entrepreneurial class, when it so consistently excluded Iraqi contractors in favour of American ones. Favouritism at the top and mismanagement at all descending levels in Iraq itself provided enormous scope for the inflation of budgets, the misappropriation of funds and the squandering of resources. For many, it seemed as if the old system had been re-established, whereby those with political connections to the powerful were rewarded through economic patronage, immune from any responsibility to the Iraqi public. This was a lesson and a model that was not lost on those who were aspiring to replace the CPA as the future power brokers of Iraq.[11]

The last few months of the CPA's rule of Iraq were taken up in trying to manage the different worlds that now formed the fractured politics of Iraq. Despite the financial and military resources at its disposal, the CPA's command of events in the country at large was minimal. In the Green Zone detailed plans were laid for the formal political framework which the US administration was insistent would root democracy firmly in the soil of Iraq. However, beyond its walls other worlds were coming into being. Quite apart from the deteriorating economy, the general destitution and the poor prospects which fuelled public resentment of the authorities, both American and Iraqi, there was the world of military occupation and resistance. US military authorities still nominally controlled Iraq and, in the climate of a developing insurgency, based often in very specific parts of the country, this led to major military operations that could devastate particular locations and cost large numbers of civilian lives.

One such operation was in April 2004 against insurgent groups in Falluja, one of the main towns in al-Anbar province where the resistance against the US forces was at its strongest and most lethal. However, it was called off within weeks because of the opposition of the IGC and the international outcry at this full-scale assault. The city was then placed under the command of a former general in the old Iraqi army and soon reverted to the control of a variety of nationalist and Islamist insurgent groups. At more or less the same time, US forces fought units of the Mahdi Army, which was making one of its periodical bids for control of the city of Najaf. In this case, the IGC had better connections with the militia and a cease-fire was negotiated. As an indication that security conditions were deteriorating across the country, British forces in Basra gave up the pretence that they were merely a civil protection force and imitated the Americans by wearing helmets and body armour when on patrol.

In the midst of these unsettling developments, the systematic abuse and torture of Iraqi prisoners by US military units in the notorious Abu Ghraib prison became widely known, with the leaking of an internal US report and the publication of graphic and shocking photos. This publicity drew attention not only to the methods used, but also to the fact that some 10,000

Iraqis languished without trial in various US-run prisons, often arrested on the basis of anonymous tip-offs. Not only did these features of military occupation contradict the kind of Iraq the United States was claiming to build, they also bore an uncanny resemblance to the practices of the defunct regime. Inevitably, these aspects of the occupation formed a powerful indictment of American military control of Iraq.

Nevertheless, this control was to persist for some years to come, since the United States had insisted that even after the return of sovereignty to an Iraqi government, the United States would only hand over security responsibility to Iraqi forces as and when they were considered ready. Continued control of this kind, however, with the inevitable violent fall-out from military action and the deaths of civilians at road blocks or in bombardments of residential neighbourhoods, together with the occasional criminal acts of violence by US service personnel, would take its toll on the authority of the US presence in Iraq, as well as on that of the Iraqi politicians who seemed to acquiesce in these arrangements.

As if in acknowledgement of the growing dangers facing all participants, even in the Green Zone, Bremer's formal handover of sovereignty to the newly designated prime minister, Ayad 'Allawi, on 28 June 2004 was a strikingly low-key affair. The media were allowed to witness it, but not to broadcast it live and, immediately after handing over a letter ceding authority, Bremer was flown by helicopter to Baghdad airport (the airport road was too dangerous) where fear of anti-aircraft fire made him take part in an elaborate subterfuge to conceal the identity of the plane on which he finally left Iraq.[12]

This strange end to the formal rule of Iraq by the United States was testimony to the unsatisfactory and ambiguous nature of the handover. Fear of the insurgents dictated its almost covert finale and its ambiguity was underlined by the fact that, despite the appointment of an Iraqi prime minister and a government recognised as sovereign by the UN Security Council in resolution 1546, power still lay in the hands of the US military and political authorities in Iraq. Thereafter, despite elections, referenda and all the attributes of representative life, the uneasy question of direct command and indirect influence on the part of the United States persisted, rankling with future Iraqi governments, and at the same time undermining their authority amongst many of their compatriots.

NEW INSTITUTIONS AND OLD POLITICS

As head of the Interim Government, 'Allawi's powers were limited, not simply because of the continued US presence, but also because he was seen as a caretaker prime minister, preparing the way for elections to the constituent assembly. The IGC had agreed to his nomination and so his cabinet included representatives of its member organisations, some independents and a few of his trusted allies. Reproducing the dominant theme of sectarian and ethnic representation that increasingly marked the composition of all public bodies in Iraq, the role of head of state was given to the Sunni Arab, Ghazi al-Yawar, shaikh of the Shammar tribe, flanked by a Kurdish and a Shi'i vice-president.

Cultivating the image of a 'strong man', 'Allawi proceeded to govern accordingly. Announcing that he would show no mercy to those responsible for the rising levels of violence, he concentrated on the deteriorating security situation, but he did this in a way which arguably made the situation worse. On the one hand, he created a new internal intelligence agency, reinstating many of the Ba'thists dismissed earlier, and continuing the confusingly named 'de-de-Ba'thification' process started in the last months of the CPA and enraging his political rival Ahmad Chalabi who had won control of the National De-Ba'thification Commission. On the other hand, he encouraged the growth of military and paramilitary units, such as the Special Police Commandos, with obscure lines of responsibility, led by people trusted by him alone. At the ministry of defence, his appointee was responsible for a $1 billion budget for the new Iraqi army, but within a year a warrant was out for his arrest on charges of buying substandard equipment and of stealing ministry funds.

As far as the security situation more generally was concerned, 'Allawi had little impact on the violent criminality, kidnapping and smuggling rings that had become a part of everyday life in Iraq. Instead, he concentrated on the forces of resistance that had shown such an alarming capacity to set the agenda. In this task he had to rely wholly on US forces, which were eager to give 'Allawi's security project their full support, since the levels of terrorism, assassination and violence were frustrating most of the plans for the reconstruction of Iraq. They also provided an unwelcome reminder to the US public of the lack of success of American plans for the country – something of which President Bush and his campaign team were acutely aware in the run-up to the US presidential elections of November 2004.

This strategy led to violent confrontations with the Mahdi Army of Muqtada al-Sadr in the summer of 2004 in and around Najaf. But as US forces neared the centre of the city, getting perilously close to the shrine of Imam 'Ali in which al-Sadr's men had prudently taken refuge, energetic mediation efforts brought the fighting to an end. Nevertheless, the strength of the Mahdi Army remained. A similar impulse led to the more

24 Sayyid Muqtada al-Sadr (populist cleric and head of Mahdi Army), 2005

destructive US assault on Falluja in November 2004. 'Allawi declared martial law across Iraq and warned the population of Falluja to evacuate the city so that the insurgents, 'foreign fighters' and Islamist terrorists alleged to be holed up there could be crushed. Some 70 to 80 per cent of the population fled, adding to the growing numbers of Iraq's displaced internal refugees. Unfortunately for the success of the mission, however, many of the very insurgents who formed its target also left the city unobserved. At the same time, many civilian inhabitants remained, to be caught in ten days of bombardments and fighting which left an estimated 5,000 dead and caused extensive damage to the city. It is not known exactly how many died, nor how many of them were armed insurgents, although very few were identified as the 'foreign Islamist fighters' who had been blamed for much of the violence of the insurgency.

US forces thus secured the city, but it was a ghost town to which only half of its population had returned even two years later. The political and security consequences were equally serious. The Sunni Iraqi Islamic Party (IIP) withdrew in protest from 'Allawi's government, reinforcing the impression that the Sunni Arab minority was now to be the target of vindictive 'security operations' – a suspicion reinforced by the use of Kurdish and Shiʿi troops in Falluja. This only strengthened the determination of the Sunni Arab-based parties, especially the Islamists, to boycott the forthcoming elections. Equally, the operation appeared to heighten the violence in Iraq. Those insurgents who had escaped from the city sought to avenge those they had left behind, and the mass exodus of the inhabitants, who found little or no state provision to help them, brought tales of anger and humiliation to large swathes of the Sunni Arab population. Thus, far from 'rooting out' the insurgency, 'Allawi and his American backers found that they had intensified the feelings on which it thrived and had caused it to spread.[13]

It was not surprising, therefore, that US military deaths, which had reached the symbolic 1,000 mark shortly before the Falluja operation, began to climb steadily – as did the deaths of Iraqi civilians and members of the security forces. In October 2004 a report was published, based on statistical sampling, suggesting that since the invasion of March 2003 some 100,000 Iraqis had died violent deaths at the hands of the allied forces, or as a result of the bombs and assassinations of the various insurgent groups and militias, or through violent crime. This was strenuously disputed by allied and Iraqi authorities, as well as by those who relied on press and published accounts for their own tallies and who claimed that the figure was closer to 30,000. The truth was that no one knew or could know exactly how many had died during this period precisely because of the chaos and insecurity which was the very cause of the deaths. Whatever the absolute figure, the toll went on rising.[14]

It was against this background that preparations were set in train for the first general elections of the new era. The boycott by much of the Sunni Arab population and threats by various insurgent groups did not prevent the poll going ahead in mid-January 2005. The whole country was treated as one constituency for the 275-seat Transitional National Assembly, with party lists competing against each other, the outcome decided on the basis of proportional representation. Some 58 per cent of the national electorate turned out (although there were great variations between the high turnout in some of the Kurdish provinces and the scarcely visible turnout in the pre-dominantly Sunni Arab province of al-Anbar). They voted for dozens of different party lists, including over two dozen coalitions, but many of them were very local, comprising just one or two candidates.

The result confirmed the demographic shift in the balance of power, as well as the prominence of sectarian and ethnic communal politics. The overall winner was the United Iraqi Alliance (UIA) – a coalition dominated by the Shi'i-based Islamist parties, SCIRI and al-Da'wa – headed by 'Abd al-'Aziz al-Hakim and endorsed by Ayatollah al-Sistani. It won nearly 50 per cent of the vote and 140 of the assembly's seats. The next largest bloc was the Democratic Patriotic Alliance of Kurdistan (a joint list dominated by the KDP and the PUK), with 75 seats, followed by 'Allawi's secular Iraqi List which won 40 seats.

These elections formed the assembly that was to draft and submit the constitution to the Iraqi electorate later in the year. It was significant that some 20 per cent of the Iraqi population – the Sunni Arabs – were virtually unrepresented, that the secular left and liberal traditions had secured too few votes to be effectively represented and that Shi'i Islamists and Kurdish nationalists now commanded over three-quarters of the seats. The lines were set therefore for a lively debate about the future of Iraq, divided between those who wanted to see a strong, even exclusive, emphasis on Islamic law and those who believed a secular, federal state would be the only guarantee of their own national autonomy and identity. Few other voices were heard. In fact, although these issues were vigorously debated in the Iraqi media, the assembly itself played a minor role. In May a Constitutional Committee was established, but of its fifty-five members over half were nominees of the UIA and only two were Sunni Arabs. Meanwhile, the sparsely attended assembly became something of an irrelevance, openly derided in Iraq's satirical press.

This was partly due to the fact that the elections had brought to the fore a range of interests which now felt that they were justified in staking a claim to power. At the same time as the national elections, elections had taken place for the eighteen provincial councils and for the Kurdish Regional Assembly. In the latter case this had confirmed the division of Kurdistan into spheres of influence dominated by the KDP and PUK, but in many of the provincial elections the bewildering variety of local parties and indi-viduals showed that there was a lively, contested politics behind the façade of unity which the electoral coalitions had presented to the national electorate. Thus, although there was no doubt that the UIA would form the new government, its leader, 'Abd al-'Aziz al-Hakim, aware of the ambi-tions within his own party and within the coalition, realised the need to distribute posts more widely to give the impression of national consensus. This led to a delay of some three months whilst the struggle to determine who would receive which portfolio proceeded, preoccupying the politicians to the exclusion of virtually all else.

Finally, in early April 2005, the shape of the new government became clearer. The National Assembly approved Jalal Talabani as the largely ceremonial president of Iraq, flanked by two Arab vice-presidents, one Shi'i and one Sunni, and elected a Sunni Arab as Speaker of Parliament. This paved the way for the nomination and approval of Ibrahim al-Ja'fari, from the Islamist Shi'a-based al-Da'wa party, as prime minister. He headed a government that reflected the shift in the balance of power, with a preponderance of Shi'i ministers, chiefly from the UIA, outnumbering the Kurdish, Sunni Arab and Christian members. Its composition testified to the fractured and mutually suspicious nature of the factions which now dominated Iraqi politics, all of which were reluctant to cede overall power to al-Ja'fari himself. On the contrary, he was expected to give each the opportunity to entrench itself within the ministry it had been allocated – an opportunity which they seized with alacrity.

Purges began, ousting not simply civil servants from the era of the old regime's administration, but also those who had been favoured by the previous government. The ministry of the interior, with its key internal security role, was given to a representative of SCIRI, who lost no time in installing his own partisans within it and its proliferating intelligence and security forces. The ministry of defence was placed under a former Ba'thist army officer who advocated extreme force to crush the insurgency, but who, as a Sunni Arab returnee, had no power base of his own. He thus oversaw the colonisation of the ministry and the armed forces by Kurdish and Shi'i officers. The same pattern of patronage and favouritism, whether on personal, political or communal grounds, was repeated at various levels across many of the ministries.[15]

The demoralisation, corruption and waste to which this gave rise did little to enhance the authority of a government which was already seen by some 20 per cent of the population as a hostile administration in the service of foreign powers. The increasing use of the derogatory label '*safawi*' (the Iranian Shi'i Safavid Empire had occupied Baghdad and much of Mesopotamia in the sixteenth to seventeenth centuries) to describe the inner core of ministers indicated the focus of suspicions about their loyalties. Added to this, Sunni Arab leaders such as the cleric Hareth al-Dhari, who had emerged as leader of one of the main Sunni organisations, the Association of Muslim Scholars, voiced in more extreme form the fear of many when he accused the minister of the interior of using units of the Badr Brigade (the militia of SCIRI) to murder Sunni clerics and to terrorise Sunni communities in Baghdad and elsewhere. The growing number of attacks on Sunni mosques, preachers and neighbourhoods, and the frequent discovery of murder victims, apparently killed simply because of their religious identity, were becoming marked features of the violence and disorder that persisted in Iraq, raising the spectre of sustained sectarian conflict. This was especially the case when it was set against the continued attacks by various insurgent groups, through car bombs, suicide bombs and shootings, which aimed to kill as many Shiʿa as possible, whether or not they were connected to the government.

In addition to this underlying and sinister trend which the government of al-Jaʿfari seemed unwilling or unable to confront, there was rising public discontent and protest associated with deteriorating economic conditions. The pace of reconstruction of public utilities was painfully slow, with little to show for the money and effort that had allegedly gone into this sector since 2003, and unemployment remained high in most parts of the country, adding to the destitution and insecurity of much of the population. In addition, as Iraq sought assistance from institutions such as the International Monetary Fund (IMF), it came under increasing pressure to apply the prescriptions set down by these organisations for financial health.

However, in a country where the bulk of the population still relied on the old ration system and on an array of public subsidies for their basic necessities, the social cost of these measures would be high. The fear and desperation which any move to withdraw such subsidies evoked led to demonstrations and protests across Iraq, regardless of ethnic or sectarian affiliations, and caused rifts within the government. In many towns during 2005 demonstrators voiced their anger and in some places they were met by a violent response from security forces unused to dealing with social protest.

Nor was the government much more sympathetic to the re-emerging trade union movement in Iraq. In May 2003, trade unionists hostile to the old Baʿthist state union had formed the Iraqi Federation of Trade Unions (IFTU), electing a leadership that included Subhi Abdallah al-Mashhadani as general secretary and, as international secretary, Hadi Saleh, who from exile had helped to keep alive an independent union movement. Within a year thirteen unions had been established under its aegis, incorporating some 200,000 members, amongst them the first woman leader of an Iraqi trade union, Hashimiya Husain, president of the Basra Electricity and Energy Workers' Union.

Vigorously campaigning against the working conditions, insecurity and threats of redundancy facing its members, the IFTU (which became the General Federation of Iraqi Workers (GFIW) in 2005 after amalgamating with two smaller union federations) became a powerful independent voice, critical of American plans for privatisation and of the repressive anti-union legislation from the Ba'thist era that had been kept on the statute book. Despite gaining recognition from the IGC in early 2004, the IFTU's stance angered many both in authority and in the resistance. In 2003, US forces seized and closed down the headquarters of the IFTU until July 2004 on the pretext of its threat to security. In January 2005, Saleh himself was murdered by a death squad linked to the insurgency, where his opposition to the old regime was remembered.

For its part, al-Ja'fari's government not only retained the Ba'thist-era anti-union laws, but in August 2005 introduced its own law aimed at giving the Iraqi government power over the union movement by authorising it to seize the assets of any union. This would be overseen by a Committee for Labour and Social Rights, comprising the ministers of national security and the interior, as well as those of finance and justice. Government attempts to interfere in union elections, as well as to retain overall control of their finances and to enforce a restrictive legal framework for their operation, indicated that the impulse to curb the potential of an independent union movement was strong in the Islamist parties of the UIA. They seemed to be aiming for the system operating in the Kurdish region where, for some time, independent union activity had been squeezed out by the two major federations of Kurdish unions, each linked to one of the two major Kurdish nationalist parties. In these circumstances, it became increasingly difficult to organise effectively – a difficulty compounded by the constant threat of violence from those who saw the very existence of an independent union movement as the precursor of an Iraq which they were determined should never emerge.[16]

The widespread resentment by Iraqis who already felt sharply the degradation of public services and the insecurity of living in a country where political and criminal violence were inexorably rising was further fuelled by stories of corruption within various branches of government at both national and local levels. Al-Ja'fari had been eager to pursue corruption charges against members of the 'Allawi government and against a range of officials from different ministries. But this could not dispel the impression that similar practices were still condoned, shielded by the immunity which the perpetrators' political patrons enjoyed from systematic public scrutiny. It was clear that such immunity could not be lifted without some fundamental realignment in the political constitution of the government – a power which was specifically denied to al-Ja'fari by those on whom he had to rely.[17]

Nor was al-Ja'fari expected to bring about any major policy initiatives in Iraq by his own colleagues or by the US administration. He too was regarded in some respects as a caretaker prime minister, charged with overseeing the drafting of the Iraqi constitution, the holding of a referendum to allow the Iraqis to vote on the draft and, were it to pass, organising general elections to determine the nature of the Iraqi government for the next four to five years. It was to this task that the Constitutional Committee finally turned in July and August 2005, after both Ayatollah al-Sistani and the US Embassy put pressure on the government to ensure that an additional sixteen members (fifteen Sunni Arabs and one Sabaean) should join it.

In the event, this had little effect on its most contentious aspect – the question of the future federal structure of the Iraqi state. The federal option was wholly rejected by the Sunni Arabs, but it also caused a rift amongst the Shi'i parties. Within the ruling coalition, al-Hakim and SCIRI favoured a form of federalism which would allow the nine, overwhelmingly Shi'i, southern provinces to form a confederation in the future, with a claim to a percentage of the southern oil fields' production. This was opposed by the prime minister and al-Da'wa, as well as by Ayatollah al-Sistani. It was also vociferously opposed outside parliament by Muqtada al-Sadr, who organised massive demonstrations across the south, vehemently denouncing federalism as part of an Iranian and American plot to divide Iraq. Possibly these considerations, as much as any concern about the Sunni Arabs, led to the decision that it should eventually be resolved by a simple majority vote in the new National Assembly.

Thus the draft constitution that was presented to the assembly at the end of August was suitably vague. Article 1 stated that Iraq has a federal, as well as democratic, parliamentary and republican, system of government (supplemented in the version put to the plebiscite in October by the statement that Iraq is a 'single, independent federal state', with the constitution 'the guarantor of its unity'). Article 2 stated that 'Islam is the official religion of the state and it is a fundamental source of legislation'. Furthermore, it stipulated that 'no law that contradicts the undisputed rules of Islam may be established', appearing to give the clerical authorities the right to make final judgement on all legislation, even if it also went on to stipulate that 'no law that contradicts the principles of democracy may be established'. It was a draft which left a number of issues, such as the relationship between local and central government or the distribution of oil revenues, as well as federalism, to be filled in by parliament in the future. To many it seemed to have been thrashed out between the Kurdish and Shi'i leaders, bypassing the Constitutional Committee as a whole – an impression reinforced when its Sunni Arab members boycotted the presentation of the constitution to a very sparsely attended session of the assembly. Those members present neither debated nor voted on the draft, but merely agreed to put it to the Iraqi people in a referendum on 15 October.

Most of the Sunni Arab parties called for the constitution's rejection and insurgent groups threatened violence against those who took part, but they did not prevent 63 per cent of the electorate from voting. The results were predictable. The Kurdish and mainly Shi'i provinces voted overwhelmingly for the constitution, whereas it was rejected in three mainly Sunni Arab provinces. However, only two provinces rejected it by more than a two-thirds majority, allowing the constitution to become law, since it would only have failed if two-thirds had voted against it in at least three provinces. Understandably, in Ninawah province, where over half had rejected it, there were allegations of vote-rigging.

In this way, the constitution of Iraq became the foundation for the new Iraqi state. It was not a promising start. Rejected by a large section of the Sunni Arab population, as well as by many of the secular Arabs of Iraq, it was also a crucially incomplete document which left some of the most contentious issues to be resolved through future political struggle. Since the UIA was convinced that it would dominate the field for the foreseeable future, it seemed to some that the process would allow the UIA to draw up a final constitution to suit its own interests. In some respects, this was borne out in October 2006 when a session of the National Assembly attended by just over half its members voted for a law which would allow all of Iraq's eighteen provinces to hold referendums to decide whether or not to amalgamate into federal units similar to that of the Kurdistan region. Although there was an agreement that there would be no attempt to implement this until 2008, the session was boycotted by all the parties, Sunni and Shi'i Islamist, as well as secular nationalist, which were vehemently opposed to the idea of a federal Iraq.[18]

Nevertheless, the approval of the constitution cleared the way for general elections in December 2005. The UIA entered the election campaign, still incorporating SCIRI and al-Da'wa, although others had left to fight the elections independently. The major addition were the followers of Muqtada al-Sadr whose exclusion from the parliamentary process had caused such disruption in 2005. Their inclusion now may have been seen by some as a way of diluting the influence of al-Hakim, with whom al-Sadr had often been at loggerheads. The other main development was the participation in the elections of Sunni Islamist parties which had concluded that their previous boycott had done them little good. It also ensured a polling day relatively free of violence.

The results, when they were finally published at the end of January 2006, showed a turnout of nearly 80 per cent, with voting mainly along sectarian, ethnic and communal lines. Thus, the UIA was still the largest bloc, with more than twice as many seats as the next largest bloc, the Kurdish alliance, but both had fewer seats than before. 'Allawi's Iraqi National List was pushed into fourth place by the Sunni Arab Iraqi Accord Front (an alliance of the IIP and two other groupings of Sunni Arab parties, mostly Islamist, but including some Arab nationalists). The Iraqi National Dialogue Front, a coalition of largely secular parties, chiefly based in the Sunni Arab population, but also including a number of Christian Arab nationalists, was in fifth place. The remaining seats were divided amongst secular nationalists and representatives of Turkmen, Assyrian and Yazidi communities.

Although clearly the victor, the UIA was in a weaker position than before, unable to command an overall majority in the assembly. This position was

25 Ibrahim al-Ja'fari (prime minister 2005–6), Nuri al-Maliki (prime minister since 2006), and Sayyid 'Abd al-'Aziz al-Hakim (head of the Supreme Council for the Islamic Revolution in Iraq), 2006

weakened further by the withdrawal of al-Fadhila (the Islamic Virtue Party) from the UIA bloc in May 2006, disappointed by the allocation of ministries. These developments, as well as the stresses and strains within the UIA itself, and the attempt by the United States to influence events, meant that the process of forming a new government was as protracted as in 2005. As before, there was fairly rapid agreement on the election of Jalal Talabani as president, assisted by two vice-presidents – one Sunni Arab and one Shiʿi Arab. Finally, in May 2006, al-Jaʿfari, in whom large sections of the Iraqi public, as well as the United States and its allies, had lost confidence, gave way and the premiership was conferred on a fellow member of al-Daʿwa, Nuri al-Maliki.

INSURGENCY, SECTARIANISM AND THE SPECTRE OF CIVIL WAR

As the first prime minister of a democratically elected, constitutional government, al-Maliki was the focus of many hopes. The difficult phase of establishing an independent and sovereign Iraq, with a new constitutional basis for political life, appeared to be at an end, allowing al-Maliki's government to tackle the pressing issues of insecurity, reconstruction, insurgency, unemployment and collapsing public services. However, the record of its first year in office showed it to be little different from its predecessor, despite being more broadly based. It included not only the Sadrists, but also representatives of the Sunni Arab, mainly Islamist, Iraqi Accord Front and of ʿAllawi's secular Iraqi National List, but it was formed through the same protracted bargaining processes and with a similar outcome. Ministers entrenched themselves in their ministries and used them as power bases, appropriating resources not simply for their ministerial duties, but also to exercise patronage, even to raise their own paramilitary units in the name of security. The ministry of the interior again went to SCIRI, and again, the ministry of defence was assigned to an independent Sunni Arab former army officer who had no power base of his own. Meanwhile the prime minister ensured that the increasingly influential ministry of national security went to an ally in al-Daʿwa.

Surrounded by ministers who were reluctant to let him exercise much authority, al-Maliki found himself presiding over a country sliding towards civil war. Iraq thus presented a strange spectacle. All the formal trappings of constitutional and democratic government seemed to be in place, but were little connected to the life-and-death struggles that formed the texture of a much more local, violent and communal politics across the country. Indeed, the distribution of portfolios in al-Maliki's government reflected the power relationships established not simply by the electoral weight of their main figures, but also by the force they could command on the ground in particular localities, the hold they could exercise there and their capacity to inflict serious damage on any who tried to interfere with the absolute control they enjoyed within their fiefdoms. It appeared to give tacit, even explicit, endorsement of powerful local leaders who would form the new oligarchy of the emerging order.

Echoing the politics of the 'shadow state', the fragmented networks of which had become so integral to patterns of politics and resistance across Iraq, some referred to this as the 'ghost politics' of the new Iraq: an arena in which the rules of the game were not explicit and where loyalties were uncertain, but which had to be navigated by those who knew that to err was to risk death and collective punishment. Local courts and summary justice, militia violence, intimidation and the infiltration and use of local security forces marked the emergence of new networks of power, some based on existing status, some on success within the often violent environment these trends encouraged – these were the symptoms of a lively and often intolerant communal politics across Iraq.

It rapidly became apparent that this demanded a conformity of ideas and behaviour which was often ruthlessly enforced. Nowhere was this felt more sharply than amongst the women of Iraq, many of whom had hoped that the overthrow of the dictatorship and the opening up of new political space would allow their voices to be heard in public life. Taking seriously the emancipatory promise of the early months of the occupation, women's organisations emerged in 2003 to protect women against discrimination, to combat insidious and often hidden forms of violence against women, to organise and to make women aware of their rights. NGOs such as the Iraqi Women's Network (IWN), the Organisation of Women's Freedom in Iraq (OWFI), led by Yanar Muhammad, and the Women's Alliance for Democratic Iraq (WAFDI) took the place of the defunct Ba'thist General Federation of Iraqi Women.

Their work was supplemented and co-ordinated by the national councils set up by Rajaa Khuza and Nesreen Berwari, members of the IGC in 2004. In addition, American, British and other aid agencies had set aside substantial funds to encourage the emergence of women's associations and workshops. At a formal, official level, the CPA had tried to ensure women's representation in government, appointing three women to the IGC, including anti-discrimination clauses within the TAL and stipulating that in the elections of January 2005 every third candidate on each electoral list should be a woman. This had the effect of boosting the parliamentary representation of women. The new constitution stated that at least one-quarter of the seats in the National Assembly should be held by women and this was almost exactly the number allocated after the December 2005 elections, where women won 70 of the assembly's 275 seats, although they were only allocated four posts in al-Maliki's government.

However, behind these developments a darker picture was emerging. On the one hand, there were concerns that governments dominated by socially conservative Islamist men would seek to alter the status of women, hitherto protected by liberal secular laws, such as the 1959 law on personal status. Indeed, an attempt had been made to repeal key aspects of this as early as 2004 when the Islamists on the IGC pushed through Resolution 137 which would have abolished the 1959 law, placing all family matters under the jurisdiction of the *shari'a* courts. This was only prevented by concerted action by women and secularists on the IGC, working in conjunction with the CPA, which led to the resolution's repeal. Equally, ambiguities in the constitution suggested to some that the socially conservative Islamists had managed to re-introduce a degree of *shari'a* and thus clerical jurisdiction over women.

Of more immediate concern to most Iraqi women were the effects of the insecurity and violence across Iraq, as well as the increasingly repressive forms of local power which targeted women in particular. Some of the violence was symbolic, whereby women in positions of authority were attacked because of their prominence or their association with the new order. This was the fate of Aqila al-Hashimi, a member of the IGC, assassinated in September 2003, Salama al-Khafaji, also a member of the IGC, who narrowly escaped death in an assassination attempt in May 2004 in which her eldest son died, and Amal al-Ma'malchi, a women's activist and adviser to the ministry of municipalities and public works, who was gunned down in November 2004.

With the escalation of the insurgency, the number of attacks on women in public life, or merely working as independent professionals, as well as on those involved in the new women's organisations, increased sharply. Ominously, these attacks often occurred in situations and areas which suggested that they came not simply from the Sunni Islamists and Ba'thists, but also from Shi'a-based Islamists who seemed equally determined to discourage the emancipation of women. The enforcement of dress codes in certain areas, the public humiliation of women who would not conform and the lack of recourse to a legal system that might protect their rights added to the predicament of women in Iraq who were also, by 2006, the principal victims of the epidemic of kidnappings that severely restricted women's movements outside their homes.[19]

This and other symptoms of the local and communal nature of politics in Iraq were only connected to the formal political processes unfolding in the Green Zone in Baghdad, insofar as powerful patrons congregated there, channelling resources and protection to their clients, in exchange for support against rivals within the governing structure, as well as against those networks across the country working for their downfall. The consequences were visible everywhere, in the communal boundaries that sprang up across the country and in the proliferation of armed units, official and unofficial, patrolling them. By the end of 2006 there were many more Iraqis under arms than there had been in the final years of the old regime – but they were now serving a variety of masters, often mutually hostile, whether in the state security forces, or in the militias controlled by the ruling parties. They were confronted by armed cohorts of the nationalist and Islamist resistance whose fighters were variously estimated at 30–40,000, but whose numbers were periodically swollen by vigilante groups and community protection forces, as the communal and sectarian violence escalated, particularly in Baghdad, Baquba, Kirkuk and other towns of mixed population.[20]

In February 2006, insurgents had heightened already existing sectarian tensions by blowing up one of the most sacred monuments of the Shiʿa in Iraq – the al-ʿAskariyya shrine in the predominantly Sunni Arab town of Samarra. In response, Sunni mosques across the country were attacked, causing death and destruction of an explicitly sectarian kind and setting up a vicious cycle of revenge and retribution. Calls by senior clerics, both Sunni and Shiʿi, for calm and unity in the name of Islam went unheeded and the violence spread. At the very time when the post-election manoeuvrings were taking place, prior to al-Maliki's eventual assumption of the premiership, the situation seemed to provoke a response in which violence was to be the main currency.

Militarisation and its associated violence were to be the themes of the first year or so of al-Maliki's administration. In part, this was due to the various forms of armed revolt that constituted 'the insurgency'. The organisations which made up these networks were generally concentrated in the Sunni Arab populations of al-Anbar, Ninawah, Salah al-Din and Diyala provinces, as well as in Baghdad, but they brought death to every part of the country. Well armed and well financed, they used relentless violence against a range of targets, taking on nationalist and Islamic labels to justify their actions and to attract support in a Sunni Arab population disillusioned with the chaos and corruption of post-war Iraq and fearful of discrimination by an alien government. In this world of shadowy resistance, a number of identifiable organisations emerged, with confusingly similar names, such as the Islamic Army in Iraq, the Islamic Resistance Movement, with its 1920 Revolution Brigade, the Islamic Front for the Iraqi Resistance, Muhammad's Army, the Islamic State of Iraq and the Army of the Rightly Guided Caliphs.

Some of these organisations were clearly shaped by Iraqi nationalist, as well as Ba'thist, ideas and cadres, even if they generally appeared in Islamist guise, the ideals of which, in a radicalised *salafi* form, seemed to drive the majority of the resistance organisations. They were fighting against Western occupation and against what they saw as a puppet regime installed by the United States. They were also fiercely opposed to the Iranian influence which they believed lay behind most of the Shi'a-based parties, and they had little time for such notions as majority rule or representative government. Some confined their attacks to US and other allied forces in the country, as well as to government figures and the new Iraqi security forces. For others, the targets were clearly sectarian, as the murders of Shi'a and the bombs in Shi'i quarters showed. In many other cases, the aim seemed to be to disrupt by terrible violence normal life and thus the reconstruction of Iraq. Some of them may have believed that their struggle would soon bring them to power, but more were seeking to impress upon the government the fact that Iraq could not be governed without their co-operation. However, the very fragmentation of these groups meant that there was no unified national leadership with which to deal and their political demands only emerged fitfully.[21]

They were facing not only 150,000 or so US troops, and nearly 9,000 British and allied forces, but also the Iraqi state security forces. These were being developed in a variety of ways, all of which suggested a troubled future. A relatively small army was being formed by the United States, specifically designed for internal security duties, its units generally recruited on communal and regional lines which established networks within the allegedly 'national' army. These were supplemented by a proliferation of security forces and commando units in the ministry of the interior under the control of SCIRI.

Playing a key part in all of this were the many militias affiliated to specific political organisations – the Badr Brigade in the service of SCIRI, the veterans of resistance attached to al-Da'wa, the Mahdi Army of al-Sadr, the armed units working for al-Fadhila in Basra or the militia of Hizbullah in 'Amara. These forces, together with the formidable *peshmerga* of the two main Kurdish parties, the KDP and PUK, and the embryonic forces of the IIP, were simply the militias of the parties in government. Beyond them the country was filled with village and neighbourhood armed vigilante organisations and an array of tribal forces, as well as with militias set up by ethnic minority and communal parties, such as those of the Turkmen, the Assyrians and the Yazidis. They testified to the continuing insecurity of all in Iraq, but also helped to reproduce the very conditions of insecurity.

This was the landscape in which the notorious and shadowy death squads operated, killing political opponents, as well as those selected simply because of their sectarian or ethnic identities. Al-Maliki seemed powerless to prevent this. The intermeshing of militias and death squads with the official security forces meant that their mentors were often his political allies or those on whom he depended for support, limiting his freedom of manoeuvre. Increasing pressure on him by the United States to act forcefully placed him in a difficult position, whereby he would have to risk becoming more dependent on US reinforcements if he were to assert his own control of the situation. These were the circumstances which witnessed the resurgence of a 'shadow state', but reflecting the fragmentation of power since the collapse of the central dictatorship.[22]

The effect was to mark out the strategic ground for a civil war, especially in Baghdad where neighbourhoods were purged of one community or another, creating defensible boundaries, 'safe zones' and all the apparatus of a city at war. A similar process had already been underway for some time in the disputed city of Kirkuk where the promise of an imminent referendum to decide on its inclusion in the Kurdish region accelerated Kurdish displacement of Sunni Arabs and Turkmen, as well as the many Shi'i Arabs who had been settled there in one of the Ba'thist drives to 'Arabise' the city. In Basra, meanwhile, a large proportion of the Sunni Arab minority had fled. Evidence of similar processes were at work in the mixed cities of Mosul and Baquba and minorities in all locations in Iraq felt increasingly threatened and insecure.

Quite apart from the rising death toll – during 2006 and early 2007 an estimated 100 Iraqi civilians were being killed each day – there were other indicators of a society being torn apart by internecine violence.[23] By the end of 2006 it was estimated that nearly 2 million Iraqis had become internal refugees. Fearful of sectarian killing, of the intimidation of whole quarters by forces of the insurgency or by government-protected militias and death squads, of the insecurity of being Sunni in a largely Shi'i area, or vice versa, hundreds of thousands of Iraqis were on the move. They sought refuge with family and friends in other parts of the country, or simply moved to areas where they would feel more secure amongst members of their own sect or ethnic group.

Others who had the means to do so or had skills that they thought would make them employable elsewhere fled the country. In November 2006, as hundreds died every week in Iraq, it was estimated that 2–3,000 Iraqis were crossing the Syrian border each day and similar numbers were fleeing to Jordan. They added to the outflow of over 2 million Iraqis who were thought to have left the country since 2003, unable to deal with the danger and uncertainty of everyday life and representing the largest movement of refugees in the Middle East since 1948. A large proportion of this new wave of exiles came from the professional middle class which had been expected to be the backbone of reconstruction but which, possibly for that very reason, had been a particular target of assassination, intimidation and kidnapping.[24]

It was only in those provinces where the insurgency was weak, or where the political balance of power was more or less agreed, that any serious reconstruction and development could proceed. Thus, the three Kurdish provinces of the recognised 'Kurdistan region' enjoyed the kind of political stability and security, despite the occasional bomb attacks, that allowed economic development, encouraged foreign investment and ensured that per capita income was about 25 per cent higher than in the rest of Iraq. The region was dominated by the KDP and the PUK, with their overwhelming majority in the Kurdish parliament and with Masoud Barzani, leader of the KDP, now president of the Kurdistan region, assisted by his nephew Nechervan Barzani as prime minister. Associational life flourished, as did the press, although in both cases almost all the main NGOs and media outlets were co-opted by either the KDP or the PUK.

Yet there were signs of dissent in Kurdistan, where the patrimonial, familial rule of these parties, the dynastic inclinations of their leaders and the inequalities of Kurdish society were becoming a matter of public protest. Demonstrations by residents of Halabja in March 2006 against the complacency and neglect of the Kurdish authorities, who nevertheless continued to exploit the symbolic impact of the gassing of thousands of its inhabitants by Iraqi forces in 1988, were suppressed by local security forces with considerable violence. Equally, demonstrations in the summer of 2006 protesting about poor public services, government corruption and inequality indicated a restive younger generation. They felt excluded from the networks of patronage and privilege, often founded on the war experience of an ageing *peshmerga* elite, that constituted the core of politics in Kurdistan. For the Kurdish leadership, these were warning signs of a new kind of politics, fuelled not simply by social protest, but also by the demand for complete independence from Iraq which every poll suggested was the wish of the vast majority of the Kurds. To some extent they played up to this, continuing to refuse to fly the Iraqi national flag next to the Kurdish flag on public buildings in the Kurdistan region. But they were also wary of the international and regional repercussions of any premature move towards formal Kurdish independence beyond the recognised autonomy which they now enjoyed within Iraq.[25]

Part of this concern revolved around the possible responses of the Turkish government should it believe an independent Kurdish state was about to be established on its southern borders. Perennially suspicious of Kurdish autonomy in its own territories, the Turkish security establishment was also angered by the re-emergence of the Partiya Karkeren Kurdistan (PKK or Kurdistan Workers' Party) in south-eastern Anatolia and believed it to be operating from bases inside the Kurdistan region in Iraq. This was denied by the Kurdish authorities and the PKK itself, which claimed that it had merely a 'political presence' in Arbil and elsewhere. However, this did not satisfy the Turkish authorities, who put on a show of military force on the Iraqi border in the summer of 2006. This operation seems to have been co-ordinated with the Iranian authorities, who had their own Kurdish separatists to pursue, the KDP-I, whom they also accused of seeking sanctuary in Iraq. Scores of villagers fled from the border region when the Iranian military – and possibly also the Turkish armed forces – drove home their point by shelling the territory of the Kurdistan region, despite protests from the Kurdish Regional Government.

Iran's direct violation of Iraqi sovereignty touched on the much larger question of the relationship between the Islamic Republic of Iran and the newly established government of Iraq. The US invasion of Iraq and overthrow of Saddam Husain had given a great boost to Iran's influence in the region. Yet this had been far from the intention of the Bush administration, which continued to see Iran as its major strategic adversary in the area. One of the constant themes of the following years, therefore, was the tension between attempts by the United States to prevent Iran from capitalising on developments in Iraq, whilst simultaneously creating the conditions in which Iranian influence would be sure to increase. The return of Shi'i political organisations, such as SCIRI and al-Da'wa, which had established themselves in Iran for more than twenty years, with all the personal, financial and ideological ties that implied, and the support they enjoyed amongst the majority Shi'i population, meant that the electoral process could only work in Iran's favour. It was not surprising therefore that Iranians were said to have been active in encouraging Iraqis to register to vote.

The election of Iraqi governments dominated by the very parties which had such close ties with Iran led to a spate of official visits between ministers of the two countries. These occasions were used to stress the close bilateral relations and, on the part of al-Maliki and his foreign minister in the summer of 2006, to reassure Iran that Iraqi territory would never be used as a launchpad for an attack on Iran. This was a reference to the deteriorating relationship between the United States and Iran, especially after the election of Mahmud Ahmedinejad as president of Iran in 2005. The growing dispute over the possible Iranian development of a nuclear capability and the US administration's belief that agencies of the Iranian government were both supplying Iraqi insurgent groups and assisting the numerous Shi'i militias in Iraq heightened the tension to such an extent that armed confrontation seemed possible.

For its part, the Iraqi government found itself caught between impatient US authorities, eager to curb Iranian influence, if necessary by force of arms, and the various forms of Iranian leverage, some of which was accepted with gratitude, some with pragmatism and some wholly resented as evidence of an overbearing neighbour. Thus, within the Iraqi government itself and its component parts, very different attitudes existed towards the desirability of Iranian assistance and towards the diverse elements that comprise the Iranian state. Meanwhile, the situation was no less complex for the US administration. It could invite 'Abd al-'Aziz al-Hakim of SCIRI to the White House, whilst at the same time US forces were raiding the SCIRI compound in Baghdad and arresting alleged Iranian 'agents' whom they accused of helping to destabilise Iraq. Equally, President Talabani could visit Iran in November 2006 to reaffirm 'fraternal relations' between Iraq and Iran and to lay the ground for the reopening of Iranian consulates in Arbil and Basra, yet not long afterwards US forces were raiding an Iranian government building in Arbil and arresting further Iranian 'agents', despite Iraqi government protests.[26]

Similarly, the role of Syria in the years following the US-led invasion came in for increasing criticism by the US administration. It was suspected that a number of senior Ba'thists had found refuge in Syria and that the Syrian government made it easy for them to help the insurgency, the heart of which lay in Iraq's north-western provinces. There were undoubtedly Syrians helping the Iraqi insurgents, whether for Ba'thist, nationalist or Islamist motives, but the length of the common border meant that it was as poorly guarded by Syrian forces on the one side as it was by US forces on the other. This invited cross-border traffic of various kinds. The Syrian authorities made some effort to tighten border security, but they had little incentive to assist the United States in Iraq whilst the US administration continued to pursue policies seen as harmful to Syrian interests elsewhere in the Middle East.

Syria did, however, see the value of cultivating the Iraqi government, leading to a restoration of diplomatic relations in late 2006 after a lapse of some twenty-four years. In January 2007, Jalal Talabani visited Syria to sign co-operation agreements and to give substance to the new relationship. However, the cordiality between the two governments came under increasing strain. Some in the Iraqi government believed that financial aid, weapons and fighters were coming into Iraq from Syria to reinforce the insurgency. For their part, the Syrian authorities, concerned about the thousands of Iraqi refugees pouring into the country, imposed unprecedented restrictions which were much resented in Iraq. As if to epitomise the scale of the problem, but also underlining the difficulty of dealing with it, in February 2007 Iraq closed its borders with both Syria and Iran, as part of the security plan for Baghdad. Apart from the question of whether this was even relevant to the security situation in the capital, there was a belief that this could be no more than a token gesture, given the hundreds of kilometres of unguarded and porous borders between Iraq and its neighbours.

In the south of Iraq, the British were also suspicious of what they regarded as growing Iranian influence on militias responsible for an increasing number of attacks on their forces. Nevertheless, they were able to hand over full control of the sparsely inhabited and relatively stable Muthanna province to the Iraqi authorities in July 2006, followed by Dhi Qar in September. The situation in Maysan province, bordering Iran, was more complicated. With the forces of Muqtada al-Sadr effectively in control of 'Amara, the provincial capital, the British handed over their military base, which was promptly looted, retaining a small, mobile force in the province and watching an increasingly vehement and often violent political struggle develop between Sadrists and SCIRI that threatened to draw British forces back in.

In Basra itself a complex situation had developed, but one over which the British also had little control. In some quarters of the city, Shi'i Islamist militias imposed a tight and intolerant rule, but in so doing ensured a kind of stability. The governor, representative of the Shi'i al-Fadhila party, had a defiant relationship with central government and used his patronage – and militia – effectively, but was faced by split loyalties in his administration. The British meanwhile became involved in trying to purge the local police and paramilitary forces of the criminal and partisan elements which had made them key players in drug- and oil-smuggling networks, as well as in the notorious death squads. Some success was achieved, but at the cost of increased attacks on British forces and officials. Nor could it dispel the fear that the same conditions might re-establish themselves once British intervention had ended.[27]

Against this background, the ability of the central government to shape events in the provinces, let alone to tackle those which still defied its authority, seemed very limited. On a symbolic level, the trial of Saddam Husain and his associates proceeded, but had little bearing on events in the country at large. Held in US custody since his capture in December 2003, Saddam Husain was finally indicted on the first of many charges in the summer of 2005. A statute was passed setting up the Iraqi High Tribunal, a special courtroom was constructed within the Green Zone and, in October 2005, the trial began. Saddam Husain and the others were charged with the unlawful killing in 1982 of 148 villagers in the predominantly Shi'i village of Dujail following a failed assassination attempt. In the summer of 2006, while this first trial was proceeding, a second trial began in which Saddam Husain and another group of associates faced charges for the crime against humanity that was *al-Anfal*– the killing of over 100,000 Iraqi Kurds in 1988.

26 Saddam Husain on trial (before the Iraqi High Tribunal), 2005

Saddam Husain, aware that the proceedings were being televised, sought to use the trial as a platform to indict the Iraqi government, denouncing it as a mere puppet of the United States. For their part, the Iraqi government and, behind them, the United States and its allies also sought to use the trial to remind Iraqis and the world of the crimes of the old regime, to allow the relatives of its many victims to get the satisfaction of seeing the fallen dictator brought to account and, through the proceedings, to demonstrate the new rule of law that now applied in Iraq. In none of these areas was either the accused or the prosecution particularly successful. Saddam Husain overestimated his capacity to mobilise Iraqis against the occupation. There was little sympathy for him and, after the first few days of fascinated viewing, the sight of him in the dock began to pall. However, politically motivated dismissals of judges, assassinations of defence lawyers, mishandling of evidence and the occasional blanking out of the trial did not suggest that the proceedings were a model of new judicial standards of integrity. On the contrary, it looked like a very familiar form of victors' justice. It was little surprise, therefore, when, in November 2006, a verdict of guilty was returned by the court and Saddam Husain and two of his associates, including his half-brother Barzan, were sentenced to death. The appeal was rejected some weeks later and on 30 December Saddam Husain was hanged in a form of televised public execution.[28]

To many in Iraq and beyond, the passing of Saddam Husain was less significant than the manner of his passing. Not only had the government chosen to execute him on the day that Sunni Iraqis (but not the Shiʿa) celebrated the ʿId al-Adha (feast of sacrifice), but the unofficial video, widely broadcast, showed that men loyal to Muqtada al-Sadr were in the execution party, using the opportunity to revile Saddam Husain, who in turn denounced them from the scaffold. There could be little clearer indication of the forces now dominating Iraq and of the kind of conflict playing itself out beyond the execution chamber.

It was this which was having the greatest impact, with all the attendant violence, frustration and disappointment that it generated. A form of sectarian civil war had engulfed whole areas of the country, particularly the capital Baghdad. In the face of this and of the rising death toll of US troops, who appeared unable to suppress the insurgency or to do anything to lessen the horrors of the incipient civil war, it was not surprising that disillusionment about the US mission in Iraq made itself felt in the United States itself. Support ebbed away from President Bush and his administration, since for many in the United States the violent chaos of Iraqi politics and the little that had been achieved in political or economic terms no longer seemed to be worth the cost in American lives or expenditure. In the mid-term elections of November 2006 these feelings helped the Democratic Party to capture both houses of Congress, changing the political balance in Washington.

However, the US and the Iraqi governments were caught in a characteristic dilemma. President Bush hoped that with one last push – the 'surge' of 28,000 extra troops in 2007 – the urban civil war in Baghdad could be ended. But this required pushing Iraqi troops into action against forces that were linked to the government itself. Al-Maliki feared that this would undermine his already fragile authority and could raise the spectre of serious resistance. Yet at the same time, he knew that the Iraqi government forces on their own were not capable of coping with the insurgency, in Baghdad or elsewhere. Thus, despite the bold, occasionally defiant talk, his anxiety about a sudden US withdrawal was greater. He therefore authorised a series of measures to be taken against the supporters of Muqtada al-Sadr in particular, exploiting the rivalry between factions in the UIA as well as in the coalition government to win some backing for a policy that could be presented as an even-handed clampdown on Shiʿi militias and Sunni insurgents alike.

Whether or not this would succeed in bringing security to Baghdad and its inhabitants, the forms of power emerging in Iraq had become clearer four years after the US-led invasion. The manner of the collapse of the old order and the fear amongst many sections of the Iraqi population about their fate under a highly centralised state, given their historical experiences of the way it could devastate their lives, had ensured that power would be fragmented and localised. It fell largely into the hands of men who could command loyalty, and if necessary force obedience, on the basis of communal identification, ethnic, sectarian, tribal or regional.

Their leadership claims did not go uncontested, making for a lively, sometimes violent, local politics across Iraq that seemed to undermine attempts to reconstitute a truly national politics. Ironically, the electoral processes begun in 2005 had encouraged this form of communal populism, making it harder for those who held secular nationalist ideals to influence the outcome. Instead, the field of Iraqi politics seemed to be dominated by men who had fought their way to recognition by each other – and by a US administration desperate for stability. Only once this was achieved could they think of dividing the spoils, but on the basis of devolved power fuelled by oil revenues and policed by often unaccountable paramilitary forces. It would be a fragile framework, depending on a host of untested factors – the internal cohesion of the different parties, the degree of their immunity to cultivation by regional and outside powers, and their changing views about the unity of the Iraqi state. Nevertheless, for many Iraqis, despite misgivings about the inequalities it implied and the patterns of local authoritarian control it established, such an arrangement was preferable to the open violence and bloodshed of the first years of the parliamentary republic.

Conclusion

The political history of Iraq is a continuing one. The uncertainty about its future hovering over the turbulent years since the overthrow of Saddam Husain's dictatorship testified to many of the suppressed narratives that have been a feature of Iraq's complex history. The new spaces that opened up, encouraging forms of political behaviour unimaginable only a few years before, created opportunities for a variety of groups and interests to shape Iraqi history. In doing so, they came up against others with very different versions of Iraq to tell and who believed they had the right and the power to make their versions the new reality. All had to deal with the legacies of the fallen regime, the relationships of compromise, betrayal and advantage which had allowed it to maintain its ferocious hold on power for so long. Sadly, they and the Western allies whose military intervention gave many Iraqis hope for a radical break in their history often failed to recognise how much they were part of this same history and thus ran the risk once more of succumbing to its baneful logic.

The Iraqi state, no less than any other state, embodies a certain hierarchy, expressing differentials of power and status, and using sanctions, sometimes violent, to maintain an order suggested by the values and material interests of those who rule. As such, one of their main preoccupations has been to maintain boundaries, both territorially and socially, within Iraq. Given the origins of the Iraqi state and the processes of its formation, certain social groups had always been favoured over others. They used the power thus acquired to protect privilege and to give it dimensions of property, status and position. Although initially characterised as Sunni Arabs associated with the hierarchies of the defunct Ottoman state, this is too crude a label to capture the rivalries, conflicts and struggles of the early Iraqi state. Here politics was defined as much by antagonisms within these circles as by attempts to exclude others on the basis of their status, sect, ethnic grouping, gender or economic position.

Naturally, there were exclusions. Indeed the whole system could be said to have been built upon them from the very beginning. The pattern of Iraqi politics never allowed systematic popular representation or a genuine answerability of the rulers to the ruled, despite rhetorical flourishes and the aspirations of many Iraqis who saw this as the only way of breaking the cycle of authoritarian rule. It was collusion and conspiracy that prevailed, based on narrow and self-selected circles of landowners, military officers, and state and party elites. They brought with them their prejudices, rivalries and networks of trust, becoming ever more restrictive as the ruling elite narrowed itself down to the followers of one man. Under Saddam Husain, they were the men whom he trusted personally, privileging his kin, his clan and those who could be counted as 'insiders' because they came from his own region. Although not a communal regime in any sense, the vast majority of the inner circle came from distinct groups within the Sunni Arab population, perpetuating thereby the grip which men from these communities had had on the levers of state since its foundation.

With the overthrow of this regime in 2003 and the dismantling of the very levers that had reproduced these forms of control, the possibility of a new, democratic politics founded on principles of consent and the rights of the citizen was opened up. If fully realised, this would indeed represent a significant break in Iraqi history, changing the balance of power in society, not between one 'community' and another, but rather between the mass of the excluded and those who had always appointed themselves to speak in their name. This was a different kind of narrative, opening itself up to new forms of power and to the telling of the stories of Iraq by countless millions whose voices had never been heard.

The concern has been that the early years of this possible new course have been dominated instead by the assertion of a communal and sectarian politics which leaves little room for a politics of consent. Rather than opening out the space for a truly national political community to emerge, it has made way instead for a shift in power towards those who assert the claims of their own communities, with the Shi'i leaders, as representatives of the major part of the population, claiming the lion's share of posts and resources for their people. This threatens to re-establish the networks of privilege, exclusion and power witnessed so often before in Iraqi history, operating along the same lines but clearly with a different cast of beneficiaries.

It was also the case that certain parts of the state apparatus were privileged over others not simply because of the origins of their personnel, but because of the immediate power they could bring to bear in any conflict.

Thus, the armed forces always enjoyed pre-eminence, creating the very conditions which perpetuated that pre-eminence and making those who would challenge their hold operate along very similar lines. This has not necessarily meant that military commanders have wielded political power themselves, but it has meant that those who held power or who aspired to do so have paid close attention to the loyalties and political allegiances of the security forces. This has been no less the case in the aftermath of the US occupation of 2003. It was then that the disbanding of the formal military establishment and its slow rebuilding only served to underline the primacy of military force, as an array of militias, special security forces and insurgent groups fought each other to stake their claims to shape Iraqi politics.

These twin, interlinked features – the restricted circles of the rulers and the primacy of military force – have combined with the massive financial power granted to successive Iraqi governments by oil revenues to create dominant narratives marked by powerful, authoritarian leadership. The ideas of politics as discipline and of participation as conformity have figured prominently, facing many Iraqis with a choice between submission and flight. Beginning in the 1920s, as the space for autonomous activity became gradually more restricted or the price of obedience was too much to bear, the urge to escape has seized various groups of Iraqis, propelling them into exile of one form or another. For the peasants of the south, even the slums of Baghdad seemed preferable to the conditions they endured on the vast estates in ʿAmara province. For Assyrians, Jews, Chaldeans, Kurds and Yazidis, migration and exile seemed at times to be the only way to escape the sometimes murderous power of those who had seized the state. For the creative and independently minded intellectuals associated with the remarkable flowering of artistic talent in Iraq, exit was often the only way to ensure that their voices did not become drowned in the barked commands of the centre. For many of the Shiʿa the example of those *mujtahids* who had performed an inner, spiritual migration was a powerful one, causing them to turn their backs on a political world which had so little to offer them. For those trying desperately to avoid the systematic communal and criminal violence unleashed in the aftermath of the 2003 invasion, flight within the country or across its borders seemed to be the only safe path before them. Never have these processes been so pronounced as during the past thirty years – a time when the wars, civil strife and destitution that have been so much a feature of recent Iraqi history have impelled hundreds of thousands to flee their country in a desperate search for survival. Yet for the majority of Iraq's 26 million or so inhabitants, this cannot be an option. Instead, they must endure the kind of state that Iraq has become. The toll has been great, exacted by the forces that at present define the predicament of the state of Iraq. In his thirty-year domination of the country, Saddam Husain reinforced certain tendencies in Iraq's history, building up a powerful apparatus that brooked no opposition and provided scarcely any space for political activity other than on his own terms. With his removal, there is an opportunity to imagine other futures for Iraq, to ensure that other narratives come to the fore, reshaped or reworked to take account of a society and a history that has undergone decades of tyranny, as well as years of war and of economic siege. However, the key question of which alternatives will prevail or engage significant numbers of Iraqis remains open. The developments of the past few years provide some clues about the major contenders. Fragmented, devolved and broken up amongst different communities and groups, military force still has a powerful role to play, but no longer as a single military establishment with its own identity and ethos. Instead, it is in the service of a variety of competing visions, making armed units throughout Iraq serious and often ruthless political players.

Another important element that was reinforced during the years of Saddam Husain's rule were the social networks of kinship and patronage. Used to reinforce the 'shadow state' that sustained the regime, this system was so effective that it drew in millions of Iraqis, even if many abhorred its implications for the kind of political society that it reproduced. So widespread has it become as a practice, even amongst those most vehemently opposed to the previous regime, that it raises the question of whether such networks can be truly integrated into a national state of accountable institutions. By their very ability to get things done, organising power and channelling resources, these forms of political activity may once again delay or even prevent the emergence of such a state.

Under the conditions created by the overthrow of the Ba'thist regime, another important element in Iraqi politics has come to the fore which various governments had tried to control, even to appropriate. This is the Islamic vision of an alternative Iraqi state and the structures that have long sustained it amongst Iraq's Shi'a, but equally amongst the Sunni Muslims of Iraq. The strong Shi'i communal basis allowed this vision to thrive on the historic sense of injustice felt by many of Iraq's Shi'a as the excluded majority of Iraqi politics. However, this sense of exclusion has not led all Shi'a to see their identity and interests in terms of the reconstruction of the Iraqi state by clerics working to a self-consciously Islamic programme. Rather, a variety of Shi'i Islamist ideologues have emerged, championing different versions of the ideal Islamic order and competing for the power that would allow them to make theirs the dominant version. This is complicated by the emergence of Sunni Islamist voices, portraying themselves as the oppressed minority of the new Iraq and calling for yet other kinds of Islamic order. Thus there is no more a single Islamist narrative in Iraqi politics, whether Shiʿi or Sunni, than there is an Iraqi one itself.

Similar questions arise in relation to the Kurds and their role in the history of Iraq. Although historically they have seemed less central to the narrative of the Iraqi state, their treatment and the rights granted or denied to them as Iraqi citizens and as inhabitants of a distinctive Kurdish region have been powerful indicators of the nature of that state. The events of the 1980s convinced many of them that their future did not lie within Iraq at all, and the autonomy enjoyed since 1991 has provided the space to make an independent Kurdistan more than simply a nationalist dream. In some respects this sharpened differences amongst the Kurds themselves, but it also hardened the Kurds' determination to preserve their autonomy. Difficult as the achievement of true independence will be, the present engagement of the Kurdish leadership in the construction of a new political order in Iraq is based on a refusal to return to the old formula of ad hoc co-option and intimidation by the centre – and a belief that, if necessary, the history of Iraq may yet proceed separated from that of the Kurdistan region.

Meanwhile, it must be acknowledged that, as in the past, none of these competing visions for the redefinition of the Iraqi state will be operating in a regional vacuum. As in the past, outside powers will seek to play a role and may be actively invited to do so by Iraqi groups trying to enlist outside support. The question then arises about whether outsiders' visions of order will be pursued through the vehicle of the reconstituted state of Iraq. This will be a temptation hard to resist for those who believe that only some extraneous power is sufficient to hold in check the forces hostile to their own vision of order in Iraq itself. The despair and frustration born of the past few decades have prompted many of the would-be players in Iraqi politics to look beyond Iraq itself for their salvation. In doing so, of course, they have ensured that the narrative of Iraqi history cannot be an Iraqi one alone.

The dictatorship of Saddam Husain and the violence that followed its demise have been in part the result of just such competitive and ruthless struggles, conducted with a view to excluding and suppressing alternative narratives in the shaping of the history of Iraq. New possibilities have been imagined and the space for their expression has been created, but not yet safeguarded. The fear is that this is taking place in conditions of regional and domestic crisis of such magnitude that – as on previous occasions – those best placed to act will take fright, reinforcing closed and repressive communal orders, however unequal and stifling of other possibilities these may be. The contest for control of the narrative of the Iraqi state will continue, but in these circumstances there is a strong possibility that newly won privileges will be entrenched and Iraqis will have good reason to fear subjection once more to a regime that equates power with force and dissent with treason.

Notes

1 THE OTTOMAN PROVINCES OF BAGHDAD, BASRA AND MOSUL

1 D. R. Khoury, *State and Provincial Society in the Ottoman Empire: Mosul 1540–1834* (Cambridge, 1997).

2 Y. Nakash, *The Shi'is of Iraq* (Princeton, 1994), pp. 13–48; M. Litvak, *Shi'i Scholars of Nineteenth-Century Iraq* (Cambridge, 1998); J. Cole and M. Momen, 'Mafia, Mob and Shiism in Iraq: the rebellion of Ottoman Karbala, 1824–1843', *Past and Present*, 112 (1986), pp. 112–43.

3 E. B. Howell, 'The Qanun Al Aradhi', *Journal of the Royal Central Asian Society* (1922), pp. 21–39; A. Jwaideh, 'Midhat Pasha and the Land System of Lower Iraq', *St Antony's Papers*, No. 16, ed. A. Hourani (London, 1963), pp. 106–36; Jwaideh, 'Aspects of Land Tenure and Social Change in Lower Iraq During the Late Ottoman Times', in T. Khalidi (ed.), *Land and Social Transformation in the Middle East* (Beirut, 1984), pp. 333–56; M. Farouk-Sluglett and P. Sluglett, 'The Transformation of Land Tenure and Rural Social Structure in Central and Southern Iraq, 1870–1958', *International Journal of Middle East Studies*, 15 (1983), pp. 491–505.

4 P.-J. Luizard, 'La confédération des Muntafik: une représentation en miniature de la "question irakienne"', *Monde Arabe Maghreb-Machrek*, 147 (Jan.–Mar. 1995), pp. 72–80; S. H. Longrigg, *Four Centuries of Modern Iraq* (Oxford, 1925), pp. 305–24.

5 G. Atiyyah, *Iraq: 1908–1921, a socio-political study* (Beirut, 1973); H. Batatu, *The Old Social Classes and the Revolutionary Movements of Iraq* (Princeton, 1978), pp. 5–318; G. Cetinsaya, 'The Ottoman Administration of Iraq 1890–1908' (University of Manchester Ph.D., 1994); E. Tauber, *The Arab Movements in World War I* (London, 1993); H. Kayali, *Arabs and Young Turks* (Berkeley, 1993).

2 THE BRITISH MANDATE

1 H. Fattah, *The Politics of Regional Trade in Iraq, Arabia and the Gulf 1745–1900* (Albany, 1997).

2 'Ali al-Wardi, *Lamahat Ijtima'iyya min Ta'rikh al-'Iraq al-Hadith*, vol. IV (Baghdad, 1974); 'Abd al-Halim al-Rahimi, *Ta'rikh al-Haraka al-Islamiyya fi al-'Iraq 1900–1924* (Beirut, 1985).

3 C. J. Edmonds, *Kurds, Turks and Arabs: travel and research in north-eastern Iraq 1919–1925* (London, 1957); S. B. Eskander, 'Britain's Policy Towards the Kurdish Question 1915–1923' (University of London Ph.D., 1999); W. R. Hay, *Two Years in Kurdistan: experiences of a political officer 1918–1920* (London, 1921).

4 Lady Bell (sel. and ed.), *The Letters of Gertrude Bell*, vol. II (London, 1927); E. Burgoyne, *Gertrude Bell, from Her Personal Papers 1914–1926*, vol. II (London, 1961); S. H. Longrigg, *Iraq, 1900–1950* (London, 1953), pp. 92–121; A. T. Wilson, *Loyalties, Mesopotamia 1914–1917* (London, 1930), and *Mesopotamia 1917–1920: a clash of loyalties* (London, 1931); P. Sluglett, *Britain in Iraq 1914–1932* (London, 1976), pp. 9–65.

5 G. Atiyyah, *Iraq: 1908–1921, a socio-political study* (Beirut, 1973); Sir Aylmer Haldane, *The Insurrection in Mesopotamia, 1920* (Edinburgh, 1920); W. J. O. Nadhmi, 'The Political, Social and Intellectual Roots of the Iraqi Independence Movement of 1920' (University of Durham Ph.D., 1974); E. Tauber, *The Formation of Modern Syria and Iraq* (London, 1995); Wilson, *Mesopotamia 1917–1920*, pp. 270–302; 'Abd al-Razzaq al-Hasani, *Al-Thawra al-'Iraqiyya al-Kubra Sana 1920* (Beirut, 1978); al-Wardi, *Lamahat Ijtima'iyya min Ta'rikh al-'Iraq al-Hadith*, vol. V (pts 1 and 2) (Baghdad, 1977–8); A. Vinogradov, 'The 1920 Revolt in Iraq Reconsidered: the role of the tribes in national politics', *International Journal of Middle East Studies* (1972), pp. 123–39.

6 M. Tarbush, *The Role of the Military in Politics: a case study of Iraq to 1941* (London, 1982), pp. 73–94; P. P. J. Hemphill, 'The Formation of the Iraqi Army 1921–1935', in A. Kelidar (ed.), *The Integration of Modern Iraq* (London, 1979), pp. 88–110.

7 See King Faisal's 'Memorandum on Iraq' of 1933 in 'Abd al-Razzaq al-Hasani, *Ta'rikh al-Wizarat al-'Iraqiyya*, vol. III (Beirut, 1982), pp. 313–19.

8 Sluglett, *Britain in Iraq*, pp. 231–58; H. Batatu, *The Old Social Classes and the Revolutionary Movements of Iraq* (Princeton, 1978), pp. 319–61; N. T. al-Hasso, 'Administrative Politics in the Middle East: the case of monarchical Iraq 1920–1958' (University of Texas at Austin Ph.D., 1976), pp. 148–70.

9 E. Kedourie, *England and the Middle East* (London, 1987); Longrigg, *Iraq, 1900–1950*, pp. 126–52; P. Marr, *The Modern History of Iraq* (Boulder, Colo., 1985), pp. 34–43; al-Hasani, *Ta'rikh al-Wizarat*, vols. I–III.

10 M. Kent, *Oil and Empire: British policy and Mesopotamian oil 1900–1920* (London, 1976); H. Mejcher, *Imperial Quest for Oil: Iraq 1910–1928* (London, 1976); R. W. Ferrier, *The History of the British Petroleum Company*, vol. I, *1901–1932* (Cambridge, 1982); B. Shwadran, *The Middle East, Oil and the Great Powers* (London, 1955).

11 Mir Basri, *A'lam al-Adab al-'Iraq al-Hadith*, vol. I (London, 1994), pp. 97–186; Yusuf Izz al-Din, *Poetry and Iraqi Society 1900–1945* (Baghdad, 1962), pp. 15–57; Muhammad Mahdi al-Jawahiri, *Dhikriyati*, vol. I (Damascus, 1988), pp. 137–395.

12 D. McDowall, *A Modern History of the Kurds* (London, 1996), pp. 151–83; W. Jwaideh, 'The Kurdish Nationalist Movement: its origins and development' (Syracuse University Ph.D., 1960), pp. 460–592.

13 S. Haj, *The Making of Iraq 1900–1963: capital, power and ideology* (Albany, 1997), pp. 27–32, 44–9; Sluglett, *Britain in Iraq*, pp. 231–58; D. Pool, 'From Elite to Class: the transformation of Iraqi leadership 1920–1939', *International Journal of Middle East Studies*, 12 (1980), pp. 331–50; R. Abu al-Haj, 'Capital Formation in Iraq, 1922–1957', *Economic Development and Cultural Change*, 9 (1961), pp. 604–17.

14 E. Dowson, *An Inquiry into Land Tenure and Related Questions* (Letchworth, 1931).

15 Sluglett, *Britain in Iraq*, p. 198.

16 Batatu, *The Old Social Classes*, pp. 53–361; D. Pool, 'The Politics of Patronage: elites and social structure in Iraq' (Princeton University Ph.D., 1972); Sluglett, *Britain in Iraq*, pp. 206–10; M. Farouk-Sluglett and P. Sluglett, 'Labour and National Liberation: the trades union movement in Iraq, 1920–1958', *Arab Studies Quarterly* (1983), pp. 139–54.

17 A. Wigram, *Our Smallest Ally: a brief account of the Assyrian nation in the Great War* (London, 1920); D. Omissi, 'Britain, the Assyrians and the Iraq Levies 1919–1932', *Journal of Imperial and Commonwealth History*, 17/3 (1989), pp. 310–22; N. Fuccaro, *The Other Kurds: Yazidis in colonial Iraq* (London, 1999), pp. 149–65.

3 THE HASHEMITE MONARCHY 1932–41

1 For British accounts sympathetic to the plight of the Assyrians, see S. H. Longrigg, *Iraq, 1900–1950* (London, 1953), pp. 229–37; and R. S. Stafford, *The Tragedy of the Assyrians* (London, 1935). For an account which leans more towards the Arab and Iraqi nationalist versions, see K. S. Husry, 'The Assyrian Affair of 1933', *International Journal of Middle East Studies*, 5 (1974), pp. 161–76, 344–60.

2 M. Khadduri, *Independent Iraq* (London, 1962), pp. 49–68; A. D. MacDonald, 'The Political Developments in Iraq Leading to the Rising in the Spring of 1935', *Journal of the Royal Central Asian Society* (1936), pp. 27–44; 'Abdallah al-Nafisi, *Dawr al-Shi'a fi Tatawwur al-'Iraq al-Siyasi* (Beirut, 1973); Y. Nakash, *The Shi'is of Iraq* (Princeton, 1994), pp. 75–125.

3 H. Batatu, *The Old Social Classes and the Revolutionary Movements of Iraq* (Princeton, 1978), pp. 300–6, 411–38; 'Abd al-Fattah Ibrahim, *Mutala'a fi al-Sha'biyya* (Baghdad, 1935).

4 N. Fuccaro, 'Ethnicity, State Formation and Conscription in Postcolonial Iraq: the case of the Yazidi Kurds of Jabal Sinjar', *International Journal of Middle East Studies*, 29 (1997), pp. 559–80.

5 T. Y. Ismael, *Iraq and Iran: roots of conflict* (Syracuse, 1982), pp. 14–18, 57–60; Khadduri, *Independent Iraq*, pp. 324–32; A. Shikara, *Iraqi Politics 1921–1941: the interaction between domestic politics and foreign policy* (London, 1987), pp. 125–40.

6 Kamil al-Chadirchi, *Mudhakkirat Kamil al-Chadirchi wa-Ta'rikh Hizb al-Watani al-Dimuqrati*, vol. II (Beirut, 1970), pp. 42–52; P. Marr, *The Modern History of Iraq* (Boulder, Colo., 1985), pp. 55–75.

7 A. Baram, 'A Case of Imported Identity: the modernising secular ruling elites of Iraq and the concept of Mesopotamian-inspired territorial nationalism, 1922–1992', *Poetics Today* (1994), pp. 279–319; W. L. Cleveland, *The Making of an Arab Nationalist* (Princeton, 1971); R. Simon, *Iraq Between Two World Wars: the creation and implementation of a national ideology* (New York, 1986); Sati' al-Husri, *Mudhakkirati fi al-'Iraq 1921–1941*, 2 vols. (Beirut, 1967–8); Muhammad Mahdi Kubba, *Mudhakkirati fi Samim al-Ahdath 1918–1958* (Beirut, 1965); Sami Shawkat, *Hadhihi Ahdafuna* (Baghdad, 1939); P. Marr, 'The Development of a Nationalist Ideology in Iraq 1920–1941', *The Muslim World* (1985), pp. 85–101; B. Tibi (ed.), *Arab Nationalism: a critical enquiry* (London, 1990), pp. 123–58.

8 M. Eppel, *The Palestine Conflict in the History of Modern Iraq: the dynamics of involvement 1928–1948* (London, 1994), pp. 30–79.

9 M. Tarbush, *The Role of the Military in Politics: a case study of Iraq to 1941* (London, 1982), pp. 150–82; Khadduri, *Independent Iraq*, pp. 126–243; Marr, *Modern History of Iraq*, pp. 76–85.

10 R. El-Solh, *Britain's Two Wars with Iraq* (Reading, 1996), pp. 101–36; W. Hamdi, *Rashid Ali al-Gailani: the nationalist movement in Iraq 1939–1941* (London, 1987); 'Abd al-Razzaq al-Hasani, *Ta'rikh al-Wizarat al-'Iraqiyya* (Beirut, 1982), vol. V; L. Hirszowicz, *The Third Reich and the Arab East* (London, 1966), pp. 134–72; Ayad al-Qazzaz, 'The Iraqi–British War of 1941: a review article', *International Journal of Middle East Studies*, 7 (1976), pp. 591–6; Salah al-Din al-Sabbagh, *Mudhakkirati* (Damascus, 1956); D. Silverfarb, *Britain's Informal Empire in the Middle East: a case study of Iraq 1929–1941* (New York, 1986), pp. 118–41.

11 E. Kedourie, 'The Sack of Basra and the *Farhud* in Baghdad', in Kedourie, *Arabic Political Memoirs* (London, 1974), pp. 283–314; H. J. Cohen, 'The Anti-Jewish *Farhud* in Baghdad 1941', *Middle Eastern Studies*, 3/1 (1966), pp. 2–17.

4 THE HASHEMITE MONARCHY 1941–58

1 For a sympathetic view of Regent 'Abd al-Ilah, see G. de Gaury, *Three Kings in Baghdad 1921–1958* (London, 1961), pp. 136–73. The picture that emerges from other accounts, including the British Foreign Office archives, series FO 371, is rather less flattering.

2 D. McDowall, *A Modern History of the Kurds* (London, 1996), pp. 287–95; C. Kutschéra, *Le Mouvement National Kurde* (Paris, 1979), pp. 133–85.

3 H. Batatu, *The Old Social Classes and the Revolutionary Movements of Iraq* (Princeton, 1978), pp. 485–536.

4 *Ibid.*, pp. 465–82; Edith Penrose and E. F. Penrose, *Iraq: international relations and national development* (London, 1978), pp. 150–62; S. Haj, *The Making of Iraq 1900–1963: capital, power and ideology* (Albany, 1997), pp. 99–102; J. Sassoon, *Economic Policy in Iraq 1932–1950* (London, 1987), pp. 114–36.

5 M. Khadduri, *Independent Iraq* (London, 1962), pp. 252–8; P. Marr, *The Modern History of Iraq* (Boulder, Colo., 1985), pp. 96–101; D. Silverfarb, *The Twilight of British Ascendancy in the Middle East: a case study of Iraq 1941–1950* (London, 1994), pp. 81–92.

6 Nuri al-Saʿid, *Arab Independence and Unity: a note* (Baghdad, 1943), pp. 1–12; Y. Porath, *In Search of Arab Unity 1930–1945* (London, 1986), pp. 39–57, 175–85, 216–23.

7 Batatu, *The Old Social Classes*, pp. 545–66; M. Elliott, *'Independent Iraq': the monarchy and British influence 1941–1958* (London, 1996), pp. 62–5.

8 C. Tripp, 'Iraq in the 1948 War: mirror of Iraq's disorder', in A. Shlaim and E. Rogan (eds.), *Rewriting the Palestine War: 1948 and the history of the Arab–Israeli conflict* (Cambridge, 2000); M. Eppel, *The Palestine Conflict in the History of Modern Iraq: the dynamics of involvement 1928–1948* (London, 1994), pp. 177–94.

9 *Taqrir Lajnat al-Tahqiq al-Niyabiyya fi Qadhiyyat Falastin* (Baghdad, 1949), pp. 14–46.

10 M. Gat, *The Jewish Exodus from Iraq 1948–1951* (London, 1997); E. Kedourie, 'The Break Between Muslims and Jews in Iraq', in M. R. Cohen and A. R. Udovitch (eds.), *Jews Among Arabs: contacts and boundaries* (Princeton, 1989), pp. 21–63; Abbas Shiblak, *The Lure of Zion: the case of the Iraqi Jews* (London, 1986).

11 Penrose and Penrose, *Iraq*, pp. 163–71; F. Jalal, *The Role of Government in the Industrialization of Iraq 1950–1965* (London, 1972), pp. 7–18.

12 Batatu, *The Old Social Classes*, pp. 666–70.

13 Kamil al-Chadirchi, *Mudhakkirat Kamil al-Chadirchi wa-Ta'rikh Hizb al-Watani al-Dimuqrati* (Beirut, 1970), vol. II, pp. 641–76; Ibrahim al-Jaburi, *Sanawat min Ta'rikh al-ʿIraq 1952–1959* (Baghdad, n.d.), pp. 219–42.

14 R. Abu al-Haj, 'Capital Formation in Iraq, 1922–1957', *Economic Development and Cultural Change*, 9 (1961), pp. 604–17; W. E. Adams, 'The Pre-Revolutionary Decade of Land Reform in Iraq', *Economic Development and Cultural Change* (1963), pp. 267–88; G. Baer, 'Agrarian Problems in Iraq', *Middle Eastern Affairs* (1952), pp. 381–91; Haj, *The Making of Iraq*, pp. 32–9, 49–53, 70–5; Penrose and Penrose, *Iraq*, pp. 163–96; Lord James Salter, *The Development of Iraq* (London, 1955); D. Warriner, *Land Reform and Development in the Middle East* (London, 1957), pp. 113–83; M. Farouk-Sluglett and P. Sluglett, *Iraq Since 1958* (London, 1990), pp. 30–45.

15 R. A. Fernea and W. R. Louis (eds.), *The Iraqi Revolution of 1958: the old social classes revisited* (London, 1991), chapters by W. Roger Louis, N. G. Thacher and F. W. Axelgard; C. Tripp, 'Iraq', in A. Shlaim and Y. Sayigh (eds.), *The Middle East and the Cold War* (Oxford, 1997), pp. 186–215; Marr, *Modern History of Iraq*, pp. 116–25.

16 Batatu, *The Old Social Classes*, pp. 709–63.

17 *Ibid.*, pp. 764–807; Sabih ʿAli Ghalib, *Qissa Thawra al-Rabiʿ ʿAshar min Tammuz wa-l-Dubbat al-Ahrar* (Beirut, 1968).

5 THE REPUBLIC 1958–68

1 H. Batatu, *The Old Social Classes and the Revolutionary Movements of Iraq* (Princeton, 1978), pp. 800–7; G. de Gaury, *Three Kings in Baghdad 1921–1958* (London, 1961), pp. 190–201; Lord C. B. Birdwood, *Nuri as-Said* (London, 1959), pp. 264–70; S. Falle, *My Lucky Life* (Lewes, 1996), pp. 139–48; F. Handhal, *Asrar Maqtal al-'A'ila al-Malika fi al-'Iraq* (Beirut, 1971); Edith Penrose and E. F. Penrose, *Iraq: international relations and national development* (London, 1978), pp. 202–10; Caractacus (pseud.), *Revolution in Iraq* (London, 1959), pp. 117–36.

2 M. Farouk-Sluglett, 'Liberation or Repression?: pan-Arab nationalism and the women's movement in Iraq', in D. Hopwood, H. Ishow and T. Koszinowski (eds.), *Iraq: power and society* (Reading, 1993), p. 64.

3 S. Haj, *The Making of Modern Iraq 1900–1963: capital, power and ideology* (Albany, 1997), pp. 121–5; Penrose and Penrose, *Iraq*, pp. 240–7; M. Farouk-Sluglett and P. Sluglett, *Iraq Since 1958* (London, 1990), pp. 76–8, 215–17; Batatu, *The Old Social Classes*, pp. 835–43; R. Gabbay, *Communism and Agrarian Reform in Iraq* (London, 1978), pp. 108–51.

4 The best description of the turbulence, optimism and frustration of the period is to be found in Batatu, *The Old Social Classes*, pp. 764–925.

5 T. M. Aziz, 'The Role of Muhammad Baqir al-Sadr in Shi'i Political Activism in Iraq from 1958 to 1980', *International Journal of Middle East Studies*, 25 (1993), pp. 207–22; A. Baram, 'The Radical Shi'ite Opposition Movements in Iraq', in E. Sivan and M. Friedman (eds.), *Religious Radicalism and Politics in the Middle East* (Albany, 1990), pp. 95–126; H. Batatu, 'Shi'i Organisations in Iraq: al-Da'wah al-Islamiyah and al-Mujahidin', in J. Cole and N. Keddie (eds.), *Shi'ism and Social Protest* (New Haven, 1986), pp. 179–200; C. Mallat, *The Renewal of Islamic Law: Muhammad Baqer as-Sadr, Najaf and the Shi'i International* (Cambridge, 1993), pp. 1–19; J. N. Wiley, *The Islamic Movement of Iraqi Shi'as* (Boulder, Colo., 1992), pp. 31–9.

6 U. Dann, *Iraq Under Qassem* (London, 1969), pp. 332–47; D. McDowall, *A Modern History of the Kurds* (London, 1996), pp. 302–13; Sa'd Jawad, *Al-'Iraq wa-l-Mas'alat al-Kurdiyya 1958–1970* (London, 1990), pp. 51–74; C. Kutschéra, *Le Mouvement National Kurde* (Paris, 1979), pp. 200–28; L. M. Wenner, 'Arab–Kurdish Rivalries in Iraq', *Middle East Journal*, 17 (1963), pp. 68–82; I. C. Vanly, *Le Kurdistan Irakien* (Neuchatel, 1970), pp. 81–177.

7 Dann, *Iraq under Qassem*, pp. 348–55; M. Khadduri, *Republican Iraq* (London, 1969), pp. 166–87; R. Schofield, *Kuwait and Iraq: historical claims and territorial disputes* (London, 1991), pp. 101–11; Penrose and Penrose, *Iraq*, pp. 254–81; M. Mufti, *Sovereign Creations: pan-Arabism and political order in Syria and Iraq* (Ithaca, 1996), pp. 121–40.

8 J. F. Devlin, *The Ba'th Party: a history from its origins to 1966* (Stanford, 1976), pp. 255–79; Munif al-Razzaz, *Al-Tajriba al-Murra* (Beirut, 1967); Batatu, *The Old Social Classes*, pp. 1003–26; Hani al-Fakaiki, *Awkar al-Hazima: tajribati fi Hizb al-Ba'th al-'Iraqi* (London, 1993), pp. 267–372.

9 Penrose and Penrose, *Iraq*, pp. 381–8.

10 A. Alnasrawi, *The Economy of Iraq: oil, wars, destruction of development and prospects 1950–2010* (Westport, Conn., 1994), pp. 35–53; Penrose and Penrose, *Iraq*, pp. 452–76; Farouk-Sluglett and Sluglett, *Iraq Since 1958*, pp. 219–26.

11 McDowall, *Modern History of the Kurds*, pp. 315–22; E. O'Ballance, *The Kurdish Revolt 1961–1970* (London, 1973), pp. 116–80; Jawad, *Al-'Iraq wa-l-Mas'alat al-Kurdiyya*, pp. 125–41; Vanly, *Le Kurdistan Irakien*, pp. 256–82; Kutschéra, *Mouvement National Kurde*, pp. 244–66.

12 Batatu, *The Old Social Classes*, pp. 1069–72; 'Aziz al-Hajj, *Dhakirat al-Nakhil* (Beirut, 1993), pp. 171–6; A. Kelidar, 'Aziz al-Haj: a communist radical', in Kelidar (ed.), *The Integration of Modern Iraq* (London, 1979), pp. 183–92.

6 THE BA'TH AND THE RULE OF SADDAM HUSAIN 1968–2003

1 H. Batatu, *The Old Social Classes and the Revolutionary Movements of Iraq* (Princeton, 1978), pp. 1073–93; A. Baram, *Building Towards a Crisis: Saddam Husayn's strategy for survival* (WINEP Policy Paper 47; Washington, D.C., 1998), pp. 7–36; A. Baram, 'The Ruling Political Elite in Ba'thi Iraq, 1968–1986', *International Journal of Middle East Studies*, 21 (1989), pp. 447–93.

2 C. Kutschéra, *Le Mouvement National Kurde* (Paris, 1979), pp. 264–79.

3 J. N. Wiley, *The Islamic Movement of Iraqi Shi'as* (Boulder, Colo., 1992), pp. 45–9; T. M. Aziz, 'The Role of Muhammad Baqir al-Sadr in Shi'i Political Activism in Iraq from 1958 to 1980', *International Journal of Middle East Studies*, 25 (1993), pp. 211–14.

4 H. Ishow, 'The Development of Agrarian Policies since 1958', in D. Hopwood, H. Ishow and T. Koszinowski (eds.), *Iraq: power and society* (Reading, 1993), pp. 180–3; A. Alnasrawi, *The Economy of Iraq: oil, wars, destruction of development and prospects 1950–2010* (Westport, Conn., 1994), pp. 55–71; Edith Penrose and E. F. Penrose, *Iraq: international relations and national development* (London, 1978), pp. 452–60, 492–6.

5 M. Farouk-Sluglett and P. Sluglett, *Iraq Since 1958* (London, 1990), pp. 145–8, 227–31; Penrose and Penrose, *Iraq*, pp. 394–417.

6 E. Kienle, *Ba'th v. Ba'th* (London, 1990), pp. 31–86.

7 For an account broadly sympathetic to the position of the Iraqi government, see E. Ghareeb, *The Kurdish Question in Iraq* (Syracuse, 1981), pp. 113–93. For other accounts, more critical of Baghdad's position, see I. C. Vanly, 'Le Kurdistan d'Irak', in G. Chaliand (ed.), *Les Kurdes et le Kurdistan* (Paris, 1978), pp. 244–71; Kutschéra, *Mouvement National Kurde*, pp. 277–300; D. McDowall, *A Modern History of the Kurds* (London, 1996), pp. 323–42.

8 O. M. Smolansky and B. M. Smolansky, *The USSR and Iraq: the Soviet quest for influence* (Durham, N.C., 1991), pp. 117–27.

9 Kienle, *Ba'th v. Ba'th*, pp. 87–134; M. Mufti, *Sovereign Creations: pan-Arabism and political order in Syria and Iraq* (Ithaca, 1996), pp. 207–13.

10 H. Batatu, 'Shi'i Organisations in Iraq: al-Da'wah al-Islamiyah and al-Mujahidin', in J. Cole and N. Keddie (eds.), *Shi'ism and Social Protest* (New Haven, 1986), pp. 192–7; O. Bengio, 'Shi'is and Politics in Ba'thi Iraq', *Middle*

Eastern Studies (1985), pp. 1–7; Wiley, *The Islamic Movement of Iraqi Shiʿas*, pp. 51–5.

11 S. al-Khalil, *The Republic of Fear* (London, 1989), pp. 70–2.

12 *Ibid.*, pp. 3–45; Human Rights Watch/Middle East, *The Bureaucracy of Repression* (New York, 1994).

13 A. Baram, *Culture, History and Ideology in the Formation of Baʿthist Iraq 1968–1989* (London, 1991), pp. 97–116; O. Bengio, *Saddam's Word: political discourse in Iraq* (New York, 1998), pp. 69–85; al-Khalil, *The Republic of Fear*, pp. 110–46; al-Khalil, *The Monument: art, vulgarity and responsibility in Iraq* (London, 1991).

14 M. Farouk-Sluglett, 'Liberation or Repression?: pan-Arab nationalism and the women's movement in Iraq', in Hopwood, Ishow and Koszinowski, *Iraq*, pp. 65–73; T. Niblock (ed.), *Iraq: the contemporary state* (London, 1982), chapters by A. Rassam and A. Sharqi; Sana al-Khayyat, *Honour and Shame: women in modern Iraq* (London, 1990), pp. 185–94; A. Baram, 'Re-inventing Nationalism in Baʿthi Iraq 1968–1994', in C. Issawi and B. Lewis (eds.), *Princeton Papers: Interdisciplinary Journal of Middle Eastern Studies*, 5 (1996), p. 39. The 1988 law itself was repealed a couple of years later, but the authorities continued to turn a blind eye to honour killings.

15 Aziz, 'The Role of Muhammad Baqir al-Sadr', pp. 214–22; Batatu, 'Shiʿi Organisations in Iraq', pp. 197–200; Bengio, 'Shiʿis and Politics', pp. 8–12; Wiley, *The Islamic Movement of Iraqi Shiʿas*, pp. 54–9.

16 Saddam Husain's speech to the Iraqi National Assembly, November 1980, in *BBC Summary of World Broadcasts* (Middle East), 6 November 1980, pp. 5–10.

17 S. Chubin and C. Tripp, *Iran and Iraq at War* (London, 1988), pp. 13–30, 53–7.

18 E. Kanovsky, 'Economic Implications for the Region and World Oil Market', in E. Karsh (ed.), *The Iran–Iraq War: impact and implications* (London, 1987), pp. 234–5.

19 Saddam Husain's speech to the mayors of Najaf, Misan and Karbala, 7 June 1987, in Saddam Husain, *Al-Muʾallafat al-Kamila*, vol. XV (Baghdad, 1990), pp. 424–5; Arab Baʿth Socialist Party Iraq, *The Central Report of the Ninth Regional Congress June 1982* (Baghdad, 1983).

20 M. S. Navias and E. R. Hooton, *Tanker Wars: the assault on merchant shipping during the Iran–Iraq conflict 1980–1988* (London, 1996), pp. 70–188.

21 Chubin and Tripp, *Iran and Iraq at War*, pp. 61–7, 114–22, 188–202; D. Hiro, *The Longest War: the Iran–Iraq military conflict* (London, 1989), pp. 167–212; E. O'Ballance, *The Gulf War* (London, 1988), pp. 173–205.

22 Human Rights Watch/Middle East, *Iraq's Crime of Genocide: the Anfal campaign against the Kurds* (New Haven, 1995); Kanan Makiya, *Cruelty and Silence* (London, 1993), pp. 151–99.

23 A. Baram, 'Two Roads to Revolutionary Shiʿite Fundamentalism in Iraq', in M. E. Marty and R. S. Appleby (eds.), *Accounting for Fundamentalisms* (Chicago, 1994), pp. 541–51; Chubin and Tripp, *Iran and Iraq at War*, pp. 98–104.

24 K. Mofid, *Economic Consequences of the Gulf War* (London, 1990), pp. 35–52, 120–42.

25 I. al-Khafaji, 'State Incubation of Iraqi Capitalism', *Middle East Report and Information Project*, 142 (1986), pp. 4–9; R. Springborg, 'Infitah, Agrarian Transformation and Elite Consolidation in Contemporary Iraq', *Middle East Journal*, 40 (Winter, 1986), pp. 33–53; M. Farouk-Sluglett, 'The Meaning of Infitah in Iraq', *Review of Middle Eastern Studies*, 6 (1993), pp. 35–49.

26 C. Tripp, 'Symbol and Strategy: Iraq and the war for Kuwait', in W. Danspeckgruber and Tripp (eds.), *The Iraqi Aggression Against Kuwait* (Boulder, Colo., 1996), pp. 21–38; L. Freedman and E. Karsh, *The Gulf Conflict 1990–1991* (London, 1993), pp. 42–94.

27 Freedman and Karsh, *The Gulf Conflict*, pp. 297–427.

28 United Nations Security Council, *Reports of the Executive Chairman of the Special Commission Established by the Secretary-General Pursuant to Paragraph 9 (b) (i) of Security Council Resolution 687 (1991)* (1991–8); T. Trevan, *Saddam's Secrets* (London, 1999).

29 S. Graham-Brown, *Sanctioning Saddam: the politics of intervention in Iraq* (London, 1999), pp. 56–104.

30 United Nations Economic and Social Council Commission on Human Rights, *Reports on the Situation of Human Rights in Iraq, Prepared by Mr Max van der Stoel, Special Rapporteur on Human Rights* (1992–9).

31 M. M. Gunter, *The Kurdish Predicament in Iraq* (London, 1999), pp. 67–126; I. al-Khafaji, 'The Destruction of Iraqi Kurdistan', *Middle East Report*, 201 (Oct.–Dec. 1996), pp. 35–8, 42; D. McDowall, 'Addressing the Kurdish Issue', in G. Kemp and J. Gross Stein (eds.), *Powder Keg in the Middle East: the struggle for Gulf security* (London, 1995), pp. 211–36; Gareth R. V. Stansfield, *Iraqi Kurdistan: political development and emergent democracy* (London, 2003), pp. 153–85.

32 Baram, *Building Towards a Crisis*, pp. 8–20; A. Baram, 'Neo-Tribalism in Iraq: Saddam Hussein's tribal policies 1991–1996', *International Journal of Middle East Studies*, 29 (1997), pp. 1–31.

33 Graham-Brown, *Sanctioning Saddam*, pp. 267–91; Independent Inquiry Committee into the United Nations Oil-for-Food Programme, *Manipulation of the Oil-for-Food Programme by the Iraqi Regime* (Chair: Paul Volcker), 27 October 2005.

34 B. Stapleton, *The Shias of Iraq* (London, 1993); Middle East Watch, *Endless Torment: the 1991 uprising in Iraq and its aftermath* (New York, 1992); Minority Rights Group, *The Marsh Arabs of Iraq* (London, 1993); E. Nicholson and P. Clark (eds.), *The Iraqi Marshlands: a human and environmental study* (London, 2002).

35 *Rebuilding America's Defenses: Strategy, Forces and Resources for a New Century* (Report of the Project for the New American Century, September 2000), www.newamericancentury.org

36 R. Alkadiri, 'The Iraqi Klondike: oil and regional trade', *Middle East Report*, 220 (Fall 2001), pp. 30–5; *Middle East Economic Survey*, 45/4 (28 Jan. 2002), pp. B1–B7.

37 David M. Malone, *The International Struggle over Iraq: politics in the UN Security Council 1980–2005* (Oxford, 2006), pp. 158–84.

38 The label 'neocons' or 'neoconservatives' was often used in a derogatory way by those critical of the stance of individuals associated with the Washington think-tank the American Enterprise Institute. They seemed to share a common set of beliefs that encompassed not simply a commitment to free trade, but also the maintenance of the military superiority of the United States, intervention abroad to export democracy and American values and a general contempt for international institutions that could prevent the United States from acting unilaterally.

39 L. Mylroie, *The War Against America* (New York, 2001); Michael Isikoff and David Corn, *Hubris: the inside story of spin, scandal, and the selling of the Iraq war* (New York, 2006), pp. 67–84. On 9 February 2007, the acting Inspector General of the Department of Defense presented a report to the US Senate Armed Services Committee highly critical of the Office of Special Plans within the Pentagon, accusing it of manipulating intelligence to establish non-existent links between the Iraqi government and al-Qa'ida. Suzanne Goldenberg, 'Pentagon unit defied CIA advice to justify Iraq war', *Guardian* 10 February 2007, p. 26; Department of Defense Office of Inspector General, Report No. 07-INTEL-04, *Review of Pre-Iraqi War Activities of the Office of the Under Secretary of Defense for Policy*, 9 February 2007.

40 'Weapons of Mass Destruction Programs in Iraq', testimony of Charles A. Duelfer and 'Iraq and the Risk Posed by Weapons of Mass Destruction', testimony of Anthony H. Cordesman to the Subcommittee on Emerging Threats and Capabilities of the Armed Services Committee of the United States Senate, 27 February 2002 (*CSIS on the Hill* – www.csis.org/hill); K. Hamza with J. Stein, *Saddam's Bombmaker* (New York, 2000); T. Trevan, *Saddam's Secrets* (London, 1999); S. Ritter, *Endgame* (New York, 1999).

41 The White House, *The National Security Strategy of the United States of America*, September 2002 www.whitehouse.gov/nsc/nss.html

42 Michael Gordon and Bernard Trainor, *Cobra II: the inside story of the invasion and occupation of Iraq* (London, 2006), pp. 21–37.

43 Andrew Rathmell, 'Planning post-conflict reconstruction in Iraq: what can we learn?', *International Affairs*, 81/5 (2005), pp. 1020–3; Thomas F. Ricks, *Fiasco: the American military adventure in Iraq* (London, 2006), pp. 78–84, 104–11.

44 Philippe Sands, *Lawless World* (London, 2006), pp. 174–204; Malone, *International Struggle over Iraq*, pp. 190–221.

45 For a detailed account of the military campaign in 2003, see Gordon and Trainor, *Cobra II*, pp. 182–456.

46 www.iraqbodycount.net/database/; www.icasualties.org/oif/

7 THE AMERICAN OCCUPATION AND THE PARLIAMENTARY REPUBLIC

1 Michael Gordon and Bernard Taylor, *Cobra II: the inside story of the invasion and occupation of Iraq* (London, 2006), pp. 463–74; George Packer, *The Assassins' Gate: America in Iraq* (London, 2006), pp. 130–44.

2 Vali Nasr, *The Shia Revival* (New York, 2006), pp. 169–74.

3 For a good sense of this process see Rory Stewart, *Occupational Hazards: my time governing in Iraq* (London, 2006) and Mark Etherington, *Revolt on the Tigris: the al-Sadr uprising and the governing of Iraq* (London, 2005).

4 The Iraq Survey Group (ISG) had been set up in May 2003 by the United States to search for evidence of weapons of mass destruction (WMD) production. Within a year its first head resigned, saying there was no evidence of the existence of any such weapons or programmes. In September 2004 the final report of the ISG confirmed this, making it clear that Iraq had been effectively disarmed by the UNSCOM inspections of the 1990s and had not restarted any programmes. *Comprehensive Report of the Special Advisor to the DCI on Iraq's WMD*, 30 September 2004 www.cia.gov/cia/reports/iraq_wmd_2004/index.html

5 Packer, *Assassins' Gate*, pp. 180–212; Eric Herring and Glen Rangwala *Iraq in Fragments* (London, 2006), pp. 83–8, 107–12; Nasr, *Shia Revival*, pp. 174–8.

6 Nir Rosen, *In the Belly of the Green Bird: the triumph of the martyrs in Iraq* (New York, 2006), pp. 101–38; Ahmed Hashim, *Insurgency and Counter-Insurgency in Iraq* (London, 2006), pp. 17–40.

7 In January 2007 the BBC provided a forum for Iraqi voices to give their account of this violent process – http://news.bbc.co.uk/1/hi/talking_point/6224427.stm; see also the site run by the Council for Assisting Refugee Academics (CARA) – www.academic-refugees.org/content/view/100/173/ – which gives extensive press coverage of the violence affecting universities in Iraq, with regard to both students and staff, during the period 2003 to 2007.

8 A critical but not unsympathetic view of the life of those within the Green Zone during this period can be found in Rajiv Chandrasekaran, *Imperial Life in the Emerald City: inside Iraq's Green Zone* (New York, 2006).

9 Stephen Zunes, 'The United States in Iraq: the consequences of occupation', *International Journal of Contemporary Iraqi Studies*, 1/1, pp. 61–71; CPA Orders Number 12 (8 June 2003), 37 (15 September 2003), 39 (19 September 2003) and 40 (19 September 2003) www.cpa-iraq.org/; Herring and Rangwala, *Iraq in Fragments*, pp. 210–59.

10 Robert Springborg (ed.), *Oil and Democracy in Iraq* [SOAS Middle East Issues] (London, 2007) pp. 7–32; 'Blood and Oil', *Independent on Sunday* (London), 7 January 2007, pp. 2, 6–9; James Glanz, 'Iraq produces draft law governing oil industry', *International Herald Tribune*, 19 January 2007.

11 Open Society Institute – Iraq Revenue Watch, *Iraqi Fire Sale* (Briefing No. 7, June 2004) and *Audit finds more irregularities and mismanagement of Iraq's revenues* (Briefing No. 9, December 2004) www.iraqrevenuewatch.org/; Christian Aid, *Iraq: the missing billions – transition and transparency in post-war Iraq* (London, October 2003) and *Fuelling Suspicion: the coalition and Iraq's oil billions* (London, June 2004); Ed Harriman 'Where has all the money gone?' *London Review of Books* 27/13 7 July 2005, 'Cronyism and kickbacks' *LRB* 28/2 26 January 2006, 'The least accountable regime in the Middle East' *LRB* 28/21 2 November 2006.

12 L. Paul Bremer III, *My Year in Iraq* (New York, 2006), pp. 388–95.

13 Hashim, *Insurgency and Counter-Insurgency*, pp. 38–47; Patrick Cockburn, *The Occupation: war and resistance in Iraq* (London, 2006), pp. 162–6.

14 L. Roberts, R. Lafta, R. Garfield, J. Khudairi and G. Burnham, 'Mortality before and after the 2003 invasion of Iraq: cluster sample survey' *The Lancet* 364/9448, 20 November 2004, pp. 1857–64; this was disputed by the organisation Iraq Body Count, which monitors Iraqi deaths from published sources: www.iraqbodycount.net/

15 Herring and Rangwala, *Iraq in Fragments*, pp. 36–8; Cockburn, *Occupation*, pp. 182–96.

16 Abdullah Muhsin and Alan Johnson, *Hadi Never Died: Hadi Saleh and the Iraqi trade unions* (London, 2006); see also the IFTU website www.iraqitrade-unions.org/en/

17 Cockburn, *Occupation*, pp. 172–81.

18 Steve Negus 'Iraq approves controversial federalism law', *Financial Times* 11 October 2006; Reidar Visser 'Iraq federalism bill adopted amid joint Shiite–Sunni boycott' 12 October 2006 http://historiae.org

19 Amnesty International *Iraq: decades of suffering, now women deserve better* (Report MDE14/001/2005, 22 February 2005); Peter Beaumont 'Hidden victims of a brutal conflict: Iraq's women' *Observer* (London) 8 October 2006; Efrati Noga 'Negotiating Rights in Iraq: Women and the Personal Status Law', *Middle East Journal* 59/4 (2005), pp. 577–95; Lucy Brown and David Romano 'Women in Post-Saddam Iraq: one step forward, two steps back?' Inter-university Consortium for Arab and Middle East Studies (ICAMES) report, June 2004 (final revision December, 2006) www.mcgill.ca/icames/events/iraq/

20 Herring and Rangwala, *Iraq in Fragments*, pp. 164–72.

21 International Crisis Group (ICG) *In Their own Words: the Iraqi insurgency*, Middle East Report, 50, 15 February 2006; Robert Fisk 'Iraqi insurgents offer peace in return for US concessions' *Independent* (London) 9 February 2007.

22 James A. Baker III and Lee H. Hamilton (co-chairs) *Iraq Study Group Report* (New York, December 2006); ICG *The Next Iraqi War? Sectarianism and civil conflict*, Middle East Report, 52, 27 February 2006, pp. 14–27; ICG *Iraq's Muqtada al-Sadr: spoiler or stabiliser?*, Middle East Report, 55, 11 July 2006, pp. 17–24; Paul Richter 'U.S. frustrated by pace of change in Iraq' *Los Angeles Times*, 16 September 2006, p. A1.

23 G. Burnham, R. Lafta, S. Doocy and L. Roberts 'Mortality after the 2003 invasion of Iraq: a cross-sectional cluster sample survey' *The Lancet* 368/9545, 21 October 2006, pp. 1421–8 suggested that there have been 654,965 war-related deaths, of which 601,027 have been due to violence. This has been disputed by the Iraq Body Count, which estimates civilian deaths 2003–2007 as 55,441–61,133, the latter figure corresponding to the estimate of the Brookings Institution's Iraq Index (www.brookings.edu/iraqindex). The UN estimated that some 34,000 civilians had been killed in 2006 alone, but was criticised for underreporting since it only counted registered deaths.

24 UNHCR *Supplementary Appeal: Iraq Situation Response*, January 2007 www.unhcr.org/news/NEWS/45a270954.html

25 Herring and Rangwala, *Iraq in Fragments*, pp. 22–6; Patrick Cockburn 'The End of Iraq', *London Review of Books*, 28/7, 6 April 2006.

26 ICG *Iran in Iraq: how much influence?* Middle East Report, 38, 21 March 2005; Herring and Rangwala, *Iraq in Fragments*, pp. 136–40.

27 Jonathan Finer 'An end to the soft sell by the British in Basra', *Washington Post*, 26 February 2006, p. A16; 'Discussions to follow Basra raid', 26 December 2006, http://news.bbc.co.uk/1/hi/world/middle_east/6209249.stm

28 Human Rights Watch, *Judging Dujail: the first trial before the Iraqi High Tribunal*, 18/9, November 2006; M. P. Scharf and G. S. McNeal, *Saddam on Trial: understanding and debating the Iraqi High Tribunal* (Durham, N.C., 2006).

Bibliography

Adams, W. E., 'The Pre-Revolutionary Decade of Land Reform in Iraq', *Economic Development and Cultural Change* (1963), pp. 267–88

Alkadiri, R., 'The Iraqi Klondike: oil and regional trade', *Middle East Report*, (Fall 2001), pp. 30–5

Allawi, Ali A., *The Occupation of Iraq* (London, 2007)

Alnasrawi, A., *The Economy of Iraq: oil, wars, destruction of development and prospects 1950–2010* (Westport, Conn., 1994)

al-Askari, J., *A Soldier's Story: from Ottoman rule to independent Iraq: the memoirs of Jafar Pasha Al-Askari (1885–1936)* (ed. W. Facey and N. F. Safwat) (London, 2003)

Atiyyah, G., *Iraq: 1908–1921, a socio-political study* (Beirut, 1973)

Aziz, T. M., 'The Role of Muhammad Baqir al-Sadr in Shi'i Political Activism in Iraq from 1958 to 1980', *International Journal of Middle East Studies*, 25 (1993), pp. 207–22

Baer, G., 'Agrarian Problems in Iraq', *Middle Eastern Affairs* (1952), pp. 381–91

Baram, A., *Building Towards a Crisis: Saddam Husayn's strategy for survival* (WINEP Policy Paper 47; Washington, D.C., 1998)

'A Case of Imported Identity: the modernising secular ruling elites of Iraq and the concept of Mesopotamian-inspired territorial nationalism, 1922–1992', *Poetics Today* (1994), pp. 279–319

Culture, History and Ideology in the Formation of Ba'thist Iraq 1968–1989 (London, 1991)

'Neo-Tribalism in Iraq: Saddam Hussein's tribal policies 1991–1996', *International Journal of Middle Eastern Studies*, 29 (1997), pp. 1–31

'The Radical Shi'ite Opposition Movements in Iraq', in E. Sivan and M. Friedman (eds.), *Religious Radicalism and Politics in the Middle East* (Albany, 1990), pp. 95–126

'Re-inventing Nationalism in Ba'thi Iraq 1968–1994', in C. Issawi and B. Lewis (eds.), *Princeton Papers: Interdisciplinary Journal of Middle Eastern Studies*, 5 (1996), pp. 29–56

'The Ruling Political Elite in Ba'thi Iraq, 1968–1986', *International Journal of Middle East Studies*, 21 (1989), pp. 447–93

'Two Roads to Revolutionary Shi'ite Fundamentalism in Iraq', in M. E. Marty and R. S. Appleby (eds.), *Accounting for Fundamentalisms* (Chicago, 1994), pp. 531–88

Batatu, H., *The Old Social Classes and the Revolutionary Movements of Iraq* (Princeton, 1978)
'Shiʿi Organisations in Iraq: al-Daʿwah al-Islamiyah and al-Mujahidin', in J. Cole and N. Keddie (eds.), *Shiʿism and Social Protest* (New Haven, 1986), pp. 179–200
Bell, Lady (sel. and ed.), *The Letters of Gertrude Bell*, 2 vols. (London, 1927)
Bengio, O., *Saddam's Word: political discourse in Iraq* (New York, 1998)
'Shiʿis and Politics in Baʿthi Iraq', *Middle Eastern Studies* (1985), pp. 1–14
Birdwood, Lord C. B., *Nuri as-Said* (London, 1959)
Blix, H., *Disarming Iraq: the search for weapons of mass destruction* (London, 2004)
Bremer, L. P. III, *My Year in Iraq: the struggle to build a future of hope* (New York, 2006)
Burgoyne, E., *Gertrude Bell, from Her Personal Papers 1914–1926*, 2 vols. (London, 1961)
CARDRI, *Iraq: revolution or reaction?* (London, 1989)
Chandrasekaran, R., *Imperial Life in the Emerald City: inside Iraq's Green Zone* (New York, 2006)
Christian Aid, *Fuelling Suspicion: the coalition and Iraq's oil billions* (London, June 2004)
Iraq: the missing billions – transition and transparency in post-war Iraq (London, October 2003)
Chubin, S. and C. Tripp, *Iran and Iraq at War* (London, 1988)
Cleveland, W. L., *The Making of an Arab Nationalist* (Princeton, 1971)
Cockburn, P., *The Occupation: war and resistance in Iraq* (London, 2006)
Cohen, H. J., 'The Anti-Jewish *Farhud* in Baghdad 1941', *Middle Eastern Studies*, 3/1 (1966), pp. 2–17
Cohen, S. A., *British Policy in Mesopotamia 1903–1914* (London, 1976)
Cole, J. and M. Momen, 'Mafia, Mob and Shiism in Iraq: the rebellion of Ottoman Karbala, 1824–1843', *Past and Present*, 112 (1986), pp. 112–43
Dann, U., *Iraq Under Qassem* (London, 1969)
Davis, E., *Memories of State: politics, history, and collective identity in modern Iraq* (Berkeley, Calif., 2005)
Davison, R., *Reform in the Ottoman Empire 1856–1876* (New York, 1973)
de Gaury, G., *Three Kings in Baghdad 1921–1958* (London, 1961)
Department of Defense Office of Inspector General, Report No. 07-INTEL-04, *Review of Pre-Iraqi War Activities of the Office of the Under Secretary of Defense for Policy*, 9 February 2007.
Devlin, J. F., *The Baʿth Party: a history from its origins to 1966* (Stanford, 1976)
Dodge, T., *Inventing Iraq: the failure of nation building and a history denied* (New York, 2003)
Edmonds, C. J., *Kurds, Turks and Arabs: travel and research in north-eastern Iraq 1919–1925* (London, 1957)
Elliott, M., *'Independent Iraq': the monarchy and British influence 1941–1958* (London, 1996)
El-Solh, R., *Britain's Two Wars with Iraq* (Reading, 1996)

Eppel, M., *The Palestine Conflict in the History of Modern Iraq: the dynamics of involvement 1928–1948* (London, 1994)

Etherington, M., *Revolt on the Tigris: the al-Sadr uprising and the governing of Iraq* (London, 2005)

Falle, S., *My Lucky Life* (Lewes, 1996)

Farouk-Sluglett, M., 'Liberation or Repression?: pan-Arab nationalism and the women's movement in Iraq', in Hopwood, Ishow and Koszinowski, *Iraq*, pp. 65–73

'The Meaning of Infitah in Iraq', *Review of Middle Eastern Studies*, 6 (1993), pp. 35–49

Farouk-Sluglett, M. and P. Sluglett, *Iraq Since 1958* (London, 1990)

'Labour and National Liberation: the trades union movement in Iraq, 1920–1958', *Arab Studies Quarterly* (1983), pp. 139–54

'The Transformation of Land Tenure and Rural Social Structure in Central and Southern Iraq, 1870–1958', *International Journal of Middle East Studies*, 15 (1983), pp. 491–505

Fattah, H., *The Politics of Regional Trade in Iraq, Arabia and the Gulf 1745–1900* (Albany, 1997)

Fernea, E. W., *Guests of the Sheik* (New York, 1965)

Fernea, R. A., *Shaykh and Effendi: changing patterns of authority among the El Shabana of southern Iraq* (Cambridge, Mass., 1970)

Fernea, R. A. and W. R. Louis (eds.), *The Iraqi Revolution of 1958: the old social classes revisited* (London, 1991)

Ferrier, R. W., *The History of the British Petroleum Company*, vol. I, 1901–1932 (Cambridge, 1982)

Freedman, L. and E. Karsh, *The Gulf Conflict 1990–1991* (London, 1993)

Fuccaro, N., 'Ethnicity, State Formation and Conscription in Postcolonial Iraq: the case of the Yazidi Kurds of Jabal Sinjar', *International Journal of Middle East Studies*, 29 (1997), pp. 559–80

The Other Kurds: Yazidis in colonial Iraq (London, 1999)

Gabbay, R., *Communism and Agrarian Reform in Iraq* (London, 1978)

Galbraith, P., *The End of Iraq: how American incompetence created a war without end* (New York, 2006)

Gat, M., *The Jewish Exodus from Iraq 1948–1951* (London, 1997)

Ghareeb, E., *The Kurdish Question in Iraq* (Syracuse, 1981)

Gordon, M. and B. Trainor, *Cobra II: the inside story of the invasion and occupation of Iraq* (London, 2006)

Graham-Brown, S., *Sanctioning Saddam: the politics of intervention in Iraq* (London, 1999)

Gunter, M. M., *The Kurdish Predicament in Iraq* (London, 1999)

al-Haj, R. Abu, 'Capital Formation in Iraq, 1922–1957', *Economic Development and Cultural Change*, 9 (1961), pp. 604–17

Haj, S., *The Making of Iraq 1900–1963: capital, power and ideology* (Albany, 1997)

Haldane, Sir Aylmer, *The Insurrection in Mesopotamia, 1920* (Edinburgh, 1920)

Hamza, K. with J. Stein, *Saddam's Bombmaker* (New York, 2000)

Hashim, A. S., *Insurgency and Counter-Insurgency in Iraq* (London, 2006)

Hay, W. R., *Two Years in Kurdistan: experiences of a political officer 1918–1920* (London, 1921)

Hemphill, P. P. J., 'The Formation of the Iraqi Army 1921–1935', in Kelidar, *The Integration of Modern Iraq*, pp. 88–110

Herring, E. and G. Rangwala, *Iraq in Fragments* (London, 2006)

Hiro, D., *The Longest War: the Iran–Iraq military conflict* (London, 1989)

Hirszowicz, L., *The Third Reich and the Arab East* (London, 1966)

Hopwood, D., H. Ishow and T. Koszinowski (eds.), *Iraq: power and society* (Reading, 1993)

Howell, E. B., 'The Qanun Al Aradhi', *Journal of the Royal Central Asian Society* (1922), pp. 21–39

Human Rights Watch/Middle East, *The Bureaucracy of Repression* (New York, 1994) *Iraq's Crime of Genocide: the Anfal campaign against the Kurds* (New Haven, 1995)

Husry, K. S., 'The Assyrian Affair of 1933', *International Journal of Middle East Studies*, 5 (1974), pp. 161–76, 344–60

Independent Inquiry Committee into the United Nations Oil-for-Food Programme, *Manipulation of Oil-for-Food Programme by the Iraqi Regime* (Chair: Paul Volcker) 27 October 2005.

International Crisis Group (ICG) *In their own words: the Iraqi insurgency*, Middle East Report, 50, 15 February 2006 *Iraq's Muqtada al-Sadr: spoiler or stabiliser*, Middle East Report, 55, 11 July 2006 *Iran in Iraq: how much influence?* Middle East Report, 38, 21 March 2005 *The Next Iraqi War? Sectarianism and civil conflict*, Middle East Report, 52, 27 February 2006

Ishow, H., 'The Development of Agrarian Policies since 1958', in Hopwood, Ishow and Koszinowski, *Iraq*, pp. 171–92

Isikoff, M. and D. Corn, *Hubris: the inside story of spin, scandal, and the selling of the Iraq war* (New York, 2006)

Ismael, T. Y., *Iraq and Iran: roots of conflict* (Syracuse, 1982)

Issawi, C. (ed.), *The Fertile Crescent 1800–1914: a documentary economic history* (New York, 1988)

Jabar, F. A., *The Shiʿite Movement in Iraq* (London, 2003)

Jalal, F., *The Role of Government in the Industrialization of Iraq 1950–1965* (London, 1972)

Jwaideh, A., 'Aspects of Land Tenure and Social Change in Lower Iraq During the Late Ottoman Times', in T. Khalidi (ed.), *Land and Social Transformation in the Middle East* (Beirut, 1984), pp. 333–56 'Midhat Pasha and the Land System of Lower Iraq', *St Antony's Papers*, No. 16, ed. A. Hourani (London, 1963), pp. 106–36

Kanovsky, E., 'Economic Implications for the Region and World Oil Market', in E. Karsh (ed.), *The Iran–Iraq War: impact and implications* (London, 1987), pp. 231–52

Karsh, E. and I. Rautsi, *Saddam Hussein: a political biography* (New York, 1991)

Kayali, H., *Arabs and Young Turks* (Berkeley, 1993)

Kedourie, E., 'The Break Between Muslims and Jews in Iraq', in M. R. Cohen and
A. R. Udovitch (eds.), *Jews Among Arabs: contacts and boundaries* (Princeton,
1989), pp. 21–63
England and the Middle East (London, 1987)
'The Sack of Basra and the *Farhud* in Baghdad', in Kedourie, *Arabic Political
Memoirs* (London, 1974), pp. 283–314
Kelidar, A., 'Aziz al-Haj: a communist radical', in Kelidar, *The Integration of
Modern Iraq*, pp. 183–92
(ed.), *The Integration of Modern Iraq* (London, 1979)
Kent, M., *Oil and Empire: British policy and Mesopotamian oil 1900–1920* (London,
1976)
Khadduri, M., *Independent Iraq* (London, 1962)
Republican Iraq (London, 1969)
al-Khafaji, I., 'The Destruction of Iraqi Kurdistan', *Middle East Report*, 201
(Oct.–Dec. 1996), pp. 35–8, 42
'State Incubation of Iraqi Capitalism', *Middle East Report and Information
Project*, 142 (1986), pp. 4–9
Tormented Births: passages to modernity in Europe and the Middle East (London, 2004)
al-Khalil, S., *The Monument: art, vulgarity and responsibility in Iraq* (London, 1991)
The Republic of Fear (London, 1989)
al-Khayyat, Sana, *Honour and Shame: women in modern Iraq* (London, 1990)
Khoury, D. R., *State and Provincial Society in the Ottoman Empire: Mosul 1540–1834*
(Cambridge, 1997)
Kienle, E., *Ba'th v. Ba'th* (London, 1990)
Kutschéra, C., *Le Mouvement National Kurde* (Paris, 1979)
Litvak, M., *Shi'i Scholars of Nineteenth-Century Iraq* (Cambridge, 1998)
Longrigg, S. H., *Four Centuries of Modern Iraq* (Oxford, 1925)
Iraq, 1900–1950 (London, 1953)
Louis, W. R., *The British Empire in the Middle East 1945–1951* (Oxford, 1984)
Luizard, P.-J., 'La confédération des Muntafik: une représentation en miniature de
la "question irakienne"', *Monde Arabe Maghreb-Machrek*, 147 (Jan.–Mar.
1995), pp. 72–92
MacDonald, A. D., 'The Political Developments in Iraq Leading to the Rising in
the Spring of 1935', *Journal of the Royal Central Asian Society* (1936), pp. 27–44
McDowall, D., 'Addressing the Kurdish Issue', in G. Kemp and J. Gross Stein (eds.),
Powder Keg in the Middle East: the struggle for Gulf security (London, 1995),
pp. 211–36
A Modern History of the Kurds (London, 1996)
Makiya, Kanan, *Cruelty and Silence* (London, 1993)
Mallat, C., *The Renewal of Islamic Law: Muhammad Baqer as-Sadr, Najaf and the
Shi'i International* (Cambridge, 1993)
Malone, D. M., *The International Struggle over Iraq: politics in the UN Security
Council 1980–2005* (Oxford, 2006)
Marr, P., 'The Development of a Nationalist Ideology in Iraq 1920–1941', *The
Muslim World* (1985), pp. 85–101

The Modern History of Iraq, 2nd edition (Boulder, Colo., 2004)

Mejcher, H., *Imperial Quest for Oil: Iraq 1910–1928* (London, 1976)

Middle East Watch, *Endless Torment: the 1991 uprising in Iraq and its aftermath* (New York, 1992)

Minority Rights Group, *The Marsh Arabs of Iraq* (London, 1993)

Mofid, K., *Economic Consequences of the Gulf War* (London, 1990)

Mufti, M., *Sovereign Creations: pan-Arabism and political order in Syria and Iraq* (Ithaca, 1996)

Muhsin, A. and A. Johnson, *Hadi Never Died: Hadi Saleh and the Iraqi trade unions* (London, 2006)

Mylroie, L., *The War Against America* (New York, 2001)

Nakash, Y., *The Shi'is of Iraq* (Princeton, 1994)

Nasr, V., *The Shia Revival* (New York, 2006)

Navias, M. S. and E. R. Hooton, *Tanker Wars: the assault on merchant shipping during the Iran–Iraq conflict 1980–1988* (London, 1996)

Niblock, T. (ed.), *Iraq: the contemporary state* (London, 1982)

Nicholson, E. and P. Clark (eds.), *The Iraqi Marshlands: a human and environmental study* (London, 2002)

Nieuwenhuis, T., *Politics and Society in Early Modern Iraq: mamluk pashas, tribal shaykhs and local rule between 1802 and 1831* (The Hague, 1982)

Noga, E., 'Negotiating Rights in Iraq: women and the Personal Status Law', *Middle East Journal*, 59/4 (2005), pp. 577–95

O'Ballance, E., *The Gulf War* (London, 1988)

The Kurdish Revolt 1961–1970 (London, 1973)

Omissi, D., 'Britain, the Assyrians and the Iraq Levies 1919–1932', *Journal of Imperial and Commonwealth History*, 17/3 (1989), pp. 310–22

Owen, R., 'Reconstructing the Performance of the Iraqi Economy 1950–2006', *International Journal of Contemporary Iraqi Studies*, 1/1 (2007), pp. 93–101

Packer, G., *The Assassins' Gate: America in Iraq* (London, 2006)

Penrose, Edith and E. F. Penrose, *Iraq: international relations and national development* (London, 1978)

Pool, D., 'From Elite to Class: the transformation of Iraqi leadership 1920–1939', *International Journal of Middle East Studies*, 12 (1980), pp. 331–50

Porath, Y., *In Search of Arab Unity 1930–1945* (London, 1986)

al-Qazzaz, Ayad, 'The Iraqi–British War of 1941: a review article', *International Journal of Middle East Studies*, 7 (1976), pp. 591–6

Rathmell, A., 'Planning Post-Conflict Reconstruction in Iraq: What can we learn?', *International Affairs*, 81/5 (2005), pp. 1020–3

Ricks, T. E., *Fiasco: the American military adventure in Iraq* (London, 2006)

Ritter, S., *Endgame* (New York, 1999)

Riverbend, *Baghdad Burning: girl blog from Iraq* (London, 2006)

Baghdad Burning: volume 2: the unfolding story (London, 2006)

Rosen, N., *In the Belly of the Green Bird: the triumph of the martyrs in Iraq* (New York, 2006)

al-Sa'id, Nuri, *Arab Independence and Unity: a note* (Baghdad, 1943)

Salam Pax, *The Baghdad Blog* (London, 2003)

Sands, P., *Lawless World* (London, 2006)

Sassoon, J., *Economic Policy in Iraq 1932–1950* (London, 1987)

Scharf, M. P. and G. S. McNeal, *Saddam on Trial: understanding and debating the Iraqi High Tribunal* (Durham, N. C., 2006)

Schofield, R., *Kuwait and Iraq: historical claims and territorial disputes* (London, 1991)

Shemesh, H., *Soviet–Iraqi Relations, 1968–1988* (Boulder, Colo., 1992)

Shiblak, Abbas, *The Lure of Zion: the case of the Iraqi Jews* (London, 1986)

Shikara, A., *Iraqi Politics 1921–1941: the interaction between domestic politics and foreign policy* (London, 1987)

Shwadran, B., *The Middle East, Oil and the Great Powers* (London, 1955)

Sifry, M. L. and C. Cerf, *The Iraq War Reader: history, documents, opinions* (New York, 2003)

Silverfarb, D., *Britain's Informal Empire in the Middle East: a case study of Iraq 1929–1941* (New York, 1986)

    The Twilight of British Ascendancy in the Middle East: a case study of Iraq 1941–1950 (London, 1994)

Simon, R., *Iraq Between Two World Wars: the creation and implementation of a national ideology* (New York, 1986)

Sluglett, P., *Britain in Iraq 1914–1932* (London, 1976)

Smolansky, O. M. and B. M. Smolansky, *The USSR and Iraq: the Soviet quest for influence* (Durham, N.C., 1991)

Springborg, R., 'Infitah, Agrarian Transformation and Elite Consolidation in Contemporary Iraq', *Middle East Journal*, 40 (Winter, 1986), pp. 33–53

    (ed.), *Oil and Democracy in Iraq* (London, 2007)

Stafford, R. S., *The Tragedy of the Assyrians* (London, 1935)

Stansfield, G. R. V., *Iraqi Kurdistan: political development and emergent democracy* (London, 2004)

Stapleton, B., *The Shias of Iraq* (London, 1993)

Stewart, R., *Occupational Hazards: my time governing in Iraq* (London, 2006)

Tarbush, M., *The Role of the Military in Politics: a case study of Iraq to 1941* (London, 1982)

Tauber, E., *The Arab Movements in World War I* (London, 1993)

    The Formation of Modern Syria and Iraq (London, 1995)

Tibi, B. (ed.), *Arab Nationalism: a critical enquiry* (London, 1990)

Trevan, T., *Saddam's Secrets* (London, 1999)

Tripp, C., 'Iraq', in A. Shlaim and Y. Sayigh (eds.), *The Middle East and the Cold War* (Oxford, 1997), pp. 186–215

    'Iraq in the 1948 War: mirror of Iraq's disorder', in A. Shlaim and E. Rogan (eds.), *Rewriting the Palestine War: 1948 and the history of the Arab–Israeli conflict* (Cambridge, 2000)

    'Symbol and Strategy: Iraq and the war for Kuwait', in W. Danspeckgruber and Tripp (eds.), *The Iraqi Aggression Against Kuwait* (Boulder, Colo., 1996), pp. 21–38 van Bruinnessen, M. M., *Agha, Shaikh and State* (London, 1992)

Vanly, I. C., 'Le Kurdistan d'Irak', in G. Chaliand (ed.), *Les Kurdes et le Kurdistan* (Paris, 1978), pp. 225–305

   Le Kurdistan Irakien (Neuchatel, 1970)

Vinogradov, A., 'The 1920 Revolt in Iraq Reconsidered: the role of the tribes in national politics', *International Journal of Middle East Studies* (1972), pp. 123–39

Visser, R., *Basra, the Failed Gulf State: separatism and nationalism in southern Iraq* (Berlin, 2006)

Warriner, D., *Land Reform and Development in the Middle East* (London, 1957)

Wenner, L. M., 'Arab–Kurdish Rivalries in Iraq', *Middle East Journal*, 17 (1963), pp. 68–82

Wigram, A., *Our Smallest Ally: a brief account of the Assyrian nation in the Great War* (London, 1920)

Wiley, J. N., *The Islamic Movement of Iraqi Shi'as* (Boulder, Colo., 1992)

Wilson, A. T., *Loyalties, Mesopotamia 1914–1917* (London, 1930)

   Mesopotamia 1917–1920: a clash of loyalties (London, 1931)

Winstone, H. V. F., *Gertrude Bell* (London, 1978)

Woodward, B., *State of Denial: Bush at War Part III* (New York, 2006)

Zunes, S., 'The United States in Iraq: the consequences of the occupation', *International Journal of Contemporary Iraqi Studies*, 1/1 (2007), pp. 57–75

Further reading and research

In April 2003, after the American occupation of Baghdad, the building housing the Iraqi National Library (printed books and periodicals) and the Iraqi National Archives (records from the Ottoman period onwards) was looted and burnt twice, on 14 April and on 21 April 2003. The catalogues and inventories were destroyed, as was an unknown number of books and archives. Between the two attacks, library staff managed to save some material from both libraries, depositing it in a mosque in Sadr City and in the building of the ministry of tourism. It is still not known what survives. (Jean-Marie Arnoult, Inspecteur général des bibliothèques, *Assessment of Iraqi Cultural Heritage: libraries and archives 27 June–6 July 2003* (for UNESCO, contract 26 00 00 526A)

Many of the following sources have been used in the writing of this book and constitute useful resources for detailed research.

GENERAL

al-ʿAzzawi, ʿAbbas, *Ta'rikh Asha'ir al-ʿIraq* [History of the tribes of Iraq], 4 vols. (Baghdad, 1937–55)
Basri, Mir, *Aʿlam al-Adab fi al-ʿIraq al-Hadith* [Luminaries of literature in modern Iraq], 2 vols. (London, 1994)
al-Hasani, ʿAbd al-Razzaq, *Ta'rikh al-Wizarat al-ʿIraqiyya* [History of the Iraqi cabinets], vols. I–X (Beirut, 1982)
al-Jawahiri, Muhammad Mahdi, *Dhikriyati* [My memoirs], 2 vols. (Damascus, 1988–91)
Pool, D., 'The Politics of Patronage: elites and social structure in Iraq' (Princeton University Ph.D., 1972)
al-Wardi, ʿAli, *Lamahat Ijtimaʿiyya min Ta'rikh al-ʿIraq al-Hadith* [Aspects of the social history of modern Iraq], 8 vols. (Baghdad, 1969–79)

1 THE OTTOMAN PROVINCES OF BAGHDAD, BASRA AND MOSUL

al-ʿAzzawi, Abbas, *Ta'rikh al-ʿIraq bain al-Ihtilalain* [History of Iraq between two occupations], 8 vols. (Baghdad, 1935–56)
Cetinsaya, G., 'The Ottoman Administration of Iraq 1890–1908' (University of Manchester Ph.D., 1994).

Faidhi, Basil (ed.), *Mudhakkirat Sulaiman Faidhi* [Memoirs of Sulaiman Faidhi] (London, 1998)

2 THE BRITISH MANDATE

The years of British involvement in Iraq, from the occupation of Basra through to the establishment of the Iraqi state and the close supervisory role played by Great Britain in Iraqi affairs up to 1958, are extensively covered in the archives available in London:

India Office Library (for the period 1914–21) at the British Library, Euston Road, London

Colonial Office, Foreign Office and Air Ministry archives (for the period from 1921) at the National Archives, Kew, London; selected documents available online through partnership between the National Archives and Thomson-Gale in 'Iraq 1914–1974 – the Middle East online series 2' www.galeuk.com/iraq/

In addition, the papers of the British Residency and later High Commission in Baghdad (1919–32) are housed at the National Archives of India, New Delhi. Details of these collections can be found in P. Sluglett, *Britain in Iraq 1914–1932* (London, 1976), pp. 332–4.

al-Din, Yusuf Izz, *Poetry and Iraqi Society 1900–1945* (Baghdad, 1962)

Eskander, S. B., 'Britain's Policy Towards the Kurdish Question 1915–1923' (University of London Ph.D., 1999)

Haidar, Rustum, *Mudhakkirat Rustum Haidar* [Memoirs of Rustum Haidar] (Beirut, 1988)

al-Hasani, 'Abd al-Razzaq, *Al-Thawra al-'Iraqiyya al-Kubra Sana 1920* [The Great Iraqi Revolt of 1920] (Beirut, 1978)

al-Husri, Sati', *Mudhakkirati fi al-'Iraq 1921–1941* [My memoirs in Iraq 1921–1941], 2 vols. (Beirut, 1967–8)

Jwaideh, W., 'The Kurdish Nationalist Movement: its origins and development' (Syracuse University Ph.D., 1960)

Nadhmi, W. J. O., 'The Political, Social and Intellectual Roots of the Iraqi Independence Movement of 1920' (University of Durham Ph.D., 1974)

al-Rahimi, 'Abd al-Halim, *Ta'rikh al-Haraka al-Islamiyya fi al-'Iraq 1900–1924* [History of the Islamic Movement in Iraq 1900–1924] (Beirut, 1985)

3 THE HASHEMITE MONARCHY 1932–41

Amin, M., 'Jama'at al-Ahali: its origins, ideology and role in Iraqi politics 1932–1946' (University of Durham Ph.D., 1980)

Dowson, E., *An Inquiry into Land Tenure and Related Questions* (Letchworth, 1931)

Haidar, S., 'Land Problems of Iraq' (University of London Ph.D., 1942)

Hamdi, W., *Rashid Ali al-Gailani: the nationalist movement in Iraq 1939–1941* (London, 1987)

al-Hashimi, Taha, *Mudhakkirat Taha al-Hashimi 1919–1943* [The memoirs of Taha al-Hashimi 1919–1943] (Beirut, 1967) al-Hasso, N. T., 'Administrative Politics in the Middle East: the case of monarchical Iraq 1920–1958' (University of Texas at Austin Ph.D., 1976)

Ibrahim, ʿAbd al-Fattah, *Mutalaʿa fi al-Shaʿbiyya* [A study in populism] (Baghdad, 1935)

Jawdat, ʿAli, *Dhikriyat* [Memoirs] (Beirut, 1967)

al-Nafisi, ʿAbdallah, *Dawr al-Shiʿa fi Tatawwur al-ʿIraq al-Siyasi* [The role of the Shiʿa in the political development of Iraq] (Beirut, 1973)

al-Sabbagh, Salah al-Din, *Mudhakkirati* [My memoirs] (Damascus, 1956)

Shawkat, Sami, *Hadhihi Ahdafuna* [These are our goals] (Baghdad, 1939)

4 THE HASHEMITE MONARCHY 1941–58

Dr Hanna Batatu had the good fortune to have unparalleled access to Iraqi government (Public Security Directorate) archives and to documents of the Iraqi Communist Party covering the period roughly from 1941 to 1968. These are well documented in *The Old Social Classes and the Revolutionary Movements of Iraq* (Princeton, 1978), pp. 1231–40.

al-Chadirchi, Kamil, *Mudhakkirat Kamil al-Chadirchi wa-Taʾrikh Hizb al-Watani al-Dimuqrati* [Memoirs of Kamil al-Chadirchi and the history of the National Democratic Party], 2 vols. (Beirut, 1970)

Ghalib, Sabih ʿAli, *Qissa Thawra al-Rabiʿ ʿAshar min Tammuz wa-l-Dubbat al-Ahrar* [The story of the Revolution of 14 July and the Free Officers] (Beirut, 1968)

Hadid, Muhammad, *Mudhakkirati: al-siraʿ min ajl al-dimuqratiyya fi al-ʿIraq* [My memoirs: the struggle for democracy in Iraq] (ed. Najdat Safwat) (Beirut, 2006)

al-Jaburi, Ibrahim, *Sanawat min Taʾrikh al-ʿIraq 1952–1959* [Years in the history of Iraq] (Baghdad, n.d.)

al-Jamali, Muhammad Fadhil, *Mudhakkirat wa-ʿIbar* [Memoirs and past times] (Beirut, 1964)

Kubba, Muhammad Mahdi, *Mudhakkirati fi Samim al-Ahdath 1918–1958* [My memoirs at the heart of events] (Beirut, 1965)

Salter, Lord James, *The Development of Iraq* (London, 1955)

al-Suwaidi, Tawfiq, *Mudhakkirati* [My memoirs] (Beirut, 1960)

Taqrir Lajnat al-Tahqiq al-Niyabiyya fi Qadhiyya Falastin [Report of the Parliamentary Committee of Inquiry into the Palestine Question] (Baghdad, 1949)

5 THE REPUBLIC 1958–68

Mahkamat al-ʿAskariyya al-ʿUlya al-Khassa (the Special Supreme Military Court) is more generally known as Mahkamat al-Shaʿb (the People's Court); its proceedings provide an invaluable insight into aspects of Iraqi politics and political personalities both before and after 1958: *Muhakamat al-Mahkamat al-ʿAskariyya al-ʿUlya al-Khassa* [Proceedings of the Special Supreme Military Court], 22 vols. (Baghdad, 1958–62).

Caractacus (pseud.), *Revolution in Iraq* (London, 1959)

al-Fakaiki, Hani, *Awkar al-Hazima: tajribati fi Hizb al-Baʿth al-ʿIraqi* [Dens of defeat: my experience in the Iraqi Baʿth Party] (London, 1993)

al-Hajj, ʿAziz, *Dhakirat al-Nakhil* [The memory of the palm tree] (Beirut, 1993)

Handhal, F., *Asrar Maqtal al-ʿAʾila al-Malika fi al-ʿIraq* [Secrets of the murder of the royal family in Iraq] (Beirut, 1971)

Jawad, Saʿd, *Al-ʿIraq wa-l-Masʾalat al-Kurdiyya 1958–1970* [Iraq and the Kurdish question] (London, 1990)

al-Razzaz, Munif, *Al-Tajriba al-Murra* [The bitter experience] (Beirut, 1967)

6 THE BAʿTH AND THE RULE OF SADDAM HUSAIN 1968–2003

The uprising in the Kurdish areas of Iraq in 1991 led to the capture of several tons of Iraqi government and Baʿthist documents. These were removed to the United States where they were given to the Iraq Research and Documentation Project (IRDP) (Director, Kanan Makiya), based at Harvard University. In 2003 the IRDP became part of the Iraq Memory Foundation (IMF) and relocated to Baghdad, where files from the Baʿth Party headquarters were added to the collection. The IMF is sorting this archive, digitising it and gradually making it available on the web at www.iraqmemory.org/en/index.asp

Arab Baʿth Socialist Party Iraq, *The 1968 Revolution in Iraq: experience and prospects – The Political Report of the Eighth Congress of the Arab Baʿth Socialist Party in Iraq, January 1974* (London, 1979)

The Central Report of the Ninth Regional Congress June 1982 (Baghdad, 1983)

Husain, Saddam, *Al-Muʾallafat al-Kamila* [The complete works], 18 vols. (Baghdad, 1987–90)

Talabani, Jalal, *Kurdistan wa-l-Harakat al-Qawmiyya al-Kurdiyya* [Kurdistan and the Kurdish Nationalist Movement] (Beirut, 1971)

United Nations, Office of the United Nations High Commissioner for Human Rights, *Reports on the Situation of Human Rights in Iraq.* Prepared by Mr Max van der Stoel, Special Rapporteur on Human Rights (1991–9), and Mr Andreas Mavrommatis (1999–2004) www.ohchr.org/english/countries/iq/index.htm

7 THE AMERICAN OCCUPATION AND THE PARLIAMENTARY REPUBLIC

Since 2003 a wealth of original sources, unimaginable before, has become available, many of them on the web.

The official record of the Coalition Provisional Authority (2003–4) is maintained at www.cpa-iraq.org/

Most of the major players in Iraqi politics maintain websites, for instance:

Supreme Council for Islamic Revolution in Iraq (SCIRI) www.sciri.org/

Iraqi Islamic Party www.iraqiparty.com/

Kurdistan Democratic Party – Iraq (KDP) www.kdp.se/

Patriotic Union of Kurdistan (PUK) www.puk.org/

Ayatollah ʿAli al-Sistani http://sistani.org/

Kurdistan Regional Government www.krg.org/

Iraqi resistance organisations have also used the web, such as:
The Islamic Front for the Iraqi Resistance http://arabic.jaamiiraq.com
The Army of the Rightly Guided Caliphs www.alrashedeen.net/

Documents and discussion relating to the Iraqi High Tribunal and trial of Saddam
   Husain are available at www.law.case.edu/saddamtrial/

There are many media sites, for example: *Aswat al-Iraq* (voices of Iraq)
   www.aswataliraq.info/index.php (Arabic, Kurdish, English); *Al-Zaman*
   (Arabic, English) www.azzaman.com/; *Al-Sabah* www.alsabaah.com/
   (Arabic, English)

There are also numerous Iraqi blogs, in Arabic, Kurdish and English. For linked
   listings see http://iraqblogcount.blogspot.com/

Index

'Abd al-Hamid, Muhsin 280
'Abd al-Ilah, regent, later crown prince of Iraq
  ambitions in Syria 116, 122–3
  becomes crown prince 128
  death of (1958) 142
  and King Faisal II 128–9, 140
  and Nuri al-Sa'id 109, 116, 124, 128–9, 132
  political views 96, 109, 114
  and Portsmouth Treaty (1948) 117
  in World War II 100–1, 103, 108–9
'Abdallah, amir, later king of Jordan 39, 116,
  119
'Abd al-Nasser, Gamal, president of Egypt
  and 'Abd al-Karim Qasim 147
  and 'Abd al-Salam 'Arif 147, 171–6
  and the Ba'thist regime (1963) 167–8
  and Nuri al-Sa'id 136–7, 140
'Abd al-Rashid, Maher 240
'Abd al-Razzaq, 'Arif 175–6
Abdulhamid II, Ottoman Sultan-Caliph 16,
  19–20, 22
Abdulmecid, Ottoman Sultan-Caliph 14
Abu Ghraib prison 291
Abu al-Timman, Ja'far 52, 69, 77, 83, 89, 90
Afghanistan 271–2, 287
Aflaq, Michel 147, 168, 202
Al-Ahali (newspaper) 82–3, 85, 89
Ahali group, the 82–3, 86–7, 89–90, 94, 111
al-'Ahd 26–9, 33, 36, 65
al-'Ahd al-'Iraqi 36, 39
Ahl al-Thiqa (people of trust) 209, 216
Ahmad, Ibrahim 130, 153–4, 172
Algiers agreement, the (1975) 204, 224
'Ali Rida Pasha 13–14
'Ali bin al-Husain, sharif 280
'Allawi, Ayad 267, 279–80, 286, 292–6, 299,
  302–3
'Ammash, Salih Mahdi 167–8, 184, 187, 190
al-Amn al-'Am (Public Security) 188
al-Anfal (spoils of war) (1987–8) 235–6, 248, 313
Anglo-French Declaration, the (1918) 36

Anglo-Iraqi Treaties, the
  (1924) 51–3, 56
  (1926) 59
  (1927) 62
  (1930) 65, 116, 136
  (1948 – Portsmouth Treaty) 116–18, 129
Ankara Accords, the (1996) 256
al-'Aqrawi, 'Aziz 204
Arab Charter, the (1980) 222
Arab League, the
  Iraq and the founding of 115
  and Iraq's invasion of Kuwait (1990) 244
  and the Kuwait crisis (1961) 160
  Summit, Beirut (2002) 272
Arab Revolt, the (1916–18) 33, 47, 65
Arab Union, the (1958) 140–1
'Arif, 'Abd al-Rahman, president of Iraq 169,
  178–9, 181–4
  and the officer corps 181, 183–4
'Arif, 'Abd al-Salam, president of Iraq
  and 'Abd al-Karim Qasim 147–8, 163
  arrest and trial of (1958) 150
  and the Ba'thist regime (1963) 164, 168–9
  death of (1966) 178
  and the Free Officers 139, 141, 144–5, 147
  and the KDP 172–3, 176
  and the officer corps 168–71, 173–8
  political views 171–5
  and the UAR 147–8
army, the Iraqi 66, 72, 75–6, 127–8, 151–2, 157,
  183–4, 202
  and Arab tribal rebellions 80–1, 85, 90–1
  and the Assyrians (1933) 78
  and the British invasion (1941) 102
  conscription issue 59–61, 81, 84–5
  dissolution of (2003) 282
  foundation of (1921) 45
  and the Gulf war (1990–1) 243–6
  and *al-Intifada* (1991) 246–8
  and the Iran–Iraq war (1980–8) 224, 226–33,
  235

army, the Iraqi (*cont.*)
in Kurdistan 54, 66, 72, 110, 157, 160, 166,173,
180–1, 203–5, 235–6, 248–9, 256
and the Palestine campaign (1948) 119, 122
reconstitution of (after 2003) 293, 295, 307
and US-led invasion (2003) 274–5
and the Yazidis (1935) 84–5
politics of the officer corps
and 'Abd al-Karim Qasim 147, 151–2,160,
163–4
and Ahmad Hasan al-Bakr 187–8, 190–1
and the 'Arif brothers 169–70, 175–7,
179–85
and the Ba'thist regime (1963) 165–9
and the monarchy 76, 86–7, 90–104,
106–7, 128, 139–42
and Saddam Husain 216, 218, 228–9, 231–3,
238–40, 260, 267
Artisans' Society, the (Jam'iyya Ashab al-San'a)
70–2
al-Asad, Hafiz, president of Syria 202, 211, 214
al-'Asil, Naji 89
al-'Askari, Ja'far 27, 36, 46, 56, 59–61, 86, 95
al-'Askariyya shrine (Samarra) 306
Association of Muslim Scholars, the 297
Assyrians, the 31, 72–3, 77–8, 255, 258, 284, 302,
308
al-Awqati, Jalal 163
al-'Ayyubi, 'Ali Jawdat 27
'Aziz, Tariq 221, 245

Baban, Ahmad Mukhtar 141
Baban family, the 9
Badr Brigade, the 238, 246, 287, 298, 307
al-Badri, 'Abd al-'Aziz 195
Baghdad Club, the 83–4, 93
Baghdad Pact, the 135–7, 158
Baghdad Summit, the (1978) 211, 222
Baghdad Summit, the (1979) 222
al-Bakr, Ahmad Hasan, president of Iraq
and the Ba'th Party 187–91
death of (1982) 227
economic policies 197–200
and the KDP 192–4, 203
and the Military Bureau of the Ba'th 164, 167,
183–4
political views 187–8
resignation of 213–14
and Saddam Husain 183, 188, 190–1, 199,
207–8, 214, 227, 240
and the Shi'a 195–7
Banu Lam tribal federation, the 9
Barzani, Shaikh Ahmad 62, 72
Barzani, Idris 203, 219–20
Barzani, Masoud 205, 219–20, 255, 257, 309

Barzani, Masrour 257
Barzani, Mulla Mustafa 184
and the KDP 114, 130, 148, 153–4, 172–3, 176
rebellion (1944–5) 108, 110, 112
rebellion (1961–3) 156–7, 162, 166
rebellion (1964–6) 175–6, 182
rebellion (1968–9) 192–3
rebellion (1974–5) 203–4
death of (1979) 205, 219–20
Barzani, Nechervan 257, 309
Barzani clan, the 234
Barzinji, Shaikh Mahmud 33–5, 53–4, 62, 66
Basra Electricity and Energy Workers Union
298
al-Bassam, Sadiq 119
Ba'th (Renaissance) Party, the (Iraq)
and 'Abd al-Karim Qasim 147–8, 153, 162–4
and 'Abd al-Rahman 'Arif 182–5
and 'Abd al-Salam 'Arif 168–9, 174, 176
and Ahmad Hasan al-Bakr's leadership
183–91, 197, 199–202
dissolution of (2003) 282
and the ICP 156, 162, 165, 168, 182, 189–90,
201, 207, 210
Military Bureau, the 163, 166–8, 183–4, 201
origins 138
7th Regional Congress (1969) 189–90
9th Regional Congress (1982) 228
and Saddam Husain's leadership 208–12,
214–16, 227–8
and al-Sa'di's leadership 156, 163–9
and the Shi'a 138, 195, 208–9, 212–13
Ba'th Party, the (Syria) 168, 189, 202, 211–12
al-Bazzaz, 'Abd al-Rahman 176–7, 179–81, 185
Bell, Gertrude 38–9, 41
Berwari, Nesreen 304
Bint al-Huda 221
Bitar, Salah al-Din 168
Blix, Hans 272
Borujerdi, Ayatollah Murtada 265
Bremer, L. Paul 282–5, 289, 292
British East India Company, the 9, 13
al-Bu Muhammad tribe, the 9, 12
al-Bu Nasir tribe, the 191, 240
Bush, President George W. 270–4, 293, 314–15
'Bush Doctrine' 272

Cairo Conference, the (1921) 45–7
al-Chadirchi, Kamil 83, 89, 90, 111
Chalabi, Ahmad 266–7, 279–80, 293
Chaldeans, the 258
China 253, 268–9
Churchill, Sir Winston 45
Clayton, Sir Gilbert 62–3
Clinton, President Bill 269–70

Coalition Provisional Authority, the (CPA)
    278–93, 304–5
    decree laws of 282, 289–90
Commanders' Council, the 147
Committee for Labour and Social Rights, the
    299
Committee of Union and Progress, the (CUP)
    22–8
Constituent Assembly, the (1924) 55–6
constitution, the Iraqi
    (1924) 48, 56–7
    (1958) 140–1
    (1964) 172
    (2005) 300–1, 304–5
Constitutional Committee, the 300–1
Constitutional Union Party, the (CUP) (Hizb
    al-Ittihad al-Dusturi) 123–5, 131–2
Consumption Tax, the (1931) 69
'Contact Committee', the 126–7
Cox, Sir Percy 36–7, 44, 52–4, 56

al-Dawud, 'Abd al-Rahman 184–5
Dawud Pasha 13
al-Da'wa (the [Islamic] Call) 154–6, 280, 297,
    300–3, 307, 310
    and Muhammad Baqir al-Sadr 154, 196, 212,
    opposition to Ba'thist regime 196, 208, 212,
        221, 237, 246, 263
    and SCIRI 237, 296
death squads (after 2003) 289, 308
Democratic Patriotic Alliance of Kurdistan, the
    296, 302
Development Board, the 125, 133–4, 140
Development Fund for Iraq, the 290
al-Dhari, Hareth 297
Dobbs, Sir Henry 50–1, 56, 62
Dowson, Sir Ernest (Report) 68, 83
Dulaim tribe, the 281
al-Dulaimi, Naziha 152
al-Duri, 'Izzat Ibrahim 190, 214, 245

Egypt
    and Iraq 122–3, 135–7, 140, 160, 167, 171–6,
        211, 245
Electoral Law, the
    (1922) 48, 57
    (1946) 111

al-Fadhila (Islamic Virtue Party) 303, 307, 312
Faili Kurds, the 146, 203
Faisal I, king of Iraq 67, 71, 77
    as amir 33, 36, 39
    and the British authorities 46–9, 52–7
    death of (1933) 78–9
    enthronement as king 47

and Nuri al-Sa'id 62, 64–5, 71
    political views 47–9
    and the Shi'a 48, 56, 77
Faisal II, king of Iraq 96, 128–9, 132
    death of (1958) 142
Falluja, fight for control of (2004) 291, 294–5
Faraj, Muhammad 202
Fatlah tribe 9
al-Faw
    detention camp at 107, 111
    Iranian capture of (1986) 232
    Iraqi recapture of (1988) 238
    oil export terminal at 200, 225, 227
Fawzi, Husain 91, 98
federalism 286, 301
    federalism law (2006) 301
Fidayi Saddam 274
France
    and Iraq 182, 200, 229–31, 252–3, 268–9, 273
Free Officers, the 128, 139–41, 144–7, 150–1, 167,
    181
Futuwa (youth) movement, the 93

Garner, General Jay 279, 282
General elections (January 2005) 295–6, 304
General elections (December 2005) 301–3, 305
General Federation of Iraqi Women, the 218,
    304
General Federation of Iraqi Workers, the
    (GFIW) 299
Germany
    and Iraq during World War II 97–9, 102
Ghaidan, Sa'dun 184–5
al-Gharawi, Ayatollah 'Ali 265
Ghazi, king of Iraq 79–80, 86, 95–6
Golden Square, the 96–103, 107
Government of National Defence, the (1941) 100
Great Britain
    and the foundation of the Iraqi state 36–42,
        44–51, 142
    and Iraq (*see also* Anglo-Iraqi Treaties)
        under the monarchy 73–5, 79, 87, 92,
            95–103, 109, 111, 116–17
        under Saddam Husain 230–1, 253–4, 273
    and the Kurds 33–4, 53–4, 57–8, 65–6, 72
    and Kuwait (1961) 160
    links with Mesopotamia 9, 13, 32
    military occupation of Iraq during World
        War II 102–3, 107
    military occupation of Mesopotamia during
        World War I 28, 30–3
    military occupation of southern Iraq (2003)
        274, 278, 281, 291, 312
    and the Mosul question (1925–6) 54, 57–9
    and Palestine 116

'Green Zone', the 285, 289, 291–2, 306, 313
Grobba, Fritz 96
Gulf war, the (1991)
  air bombardment of Iraq, the (Operation
    Desert Thunder) 245
  cease-fire at Safwan, the 246
  effects on the Iraqi regime, the 244–7
  land campaign to liberate Kuwait, the
    (Operation Desert Storm) 245–6

Haddad, Naʿim 214
Hadid, Muhammad 83, 111
Haidar, Rustum 97–8
al-Hajj, ʿAziz 182, 189
al-Hakim, Sayyid ʿAbd al-ʿAziz 280, 296, 300,
    302, 311
al-Hakim, Ayatollah Sayyid Muhsin 160, 202–3,
    229
al-Hakim, Sayyid Mahdi 195
al-Hakim, Ayatollah Sayyid Muhammad Baqir
    225, 237–8, 246, 285
Halabja, chemical weapons attack against 236, 309
Hammadi, Saʿdun 249
al-Harakiyin (Harakat al-Qawmiyyin al-Arab)
    168, 171
Haras al-Istiqlal (Independence Guard) 40
al-Hashimi, Aqila 305
al-Hashimi, Taha 27, 80–1, 86, 94, 98, 100, 125,
    127
al-Hashimi, Yasin 27, 36, 57–8, 61, 69, 80–1,
    84–6, 90
Hasqail, Sasun 46
hawza 280
Hinnawi, Sami 122
Hiwa (Hope) 108
Hizbullah 307
Husain, Hashimiya 298
Husain, Saddam, president of Iraq 153, 186–7
  and Ahmad Hasan al-Bakr 183, 188, 190–1,
    199, 207–8, 214, 227, 240
  and the Arab world 210–12, 222–3
  and the Baʿth party 183, 189–91, 199, 207–10,
    212, 214–18, 228
  economic policies 197–201, 241–2
  execution of (2006) 314
  and Iran 204–6, 212, 222–5
  and the Kurds 193, 204–6, 234–6, 249, 256
  and the officer corps 228–9, 231–3, 238–40
  organisation of power 215–19, 226–9, 240–1,
    244–5, 259–66
  political views 215–18
  and the Shiʿa 208–9, 212–13, 265
  strategies in Gulf war (1990–1) 244–6
  strategies in Iran–Iraq War (1980–8) 223–5,
    228–33

  strategies under UN sanctions 250–4
  trial of (2005–6) 313–14
Husain, Qusay 263, 285
Husain, ʿUday 241, 262–3, 285
Husain bin ʿAli, sharif of Mecca 33, 36, 39
al-Husaini, Hajj Amin (Mufti of Palestine) 95,
    97, 101, 103
al-Husri, Satiʿ 92–3

Ibn Saʿud, ʿAbd al-ʿAziz, king of Saudi Arabia
    23–4
Ibrahim, ʿAbd al-Fattah 83
Ibrahim, Yusuf ʿIzz al-Din 89
al-Ikha al-Watani (Patriotic Brotherhood) Party
    69–70, 77, 80–1, 83
Iltizam (tax-farming) 9, 16
insurgency, the (after 2003) 278, 285–8, 293,
    305–9, 311–12, 314–15
insurgent organisations 307
Interim Iraqi Government, the (2004–5) 286,
    292–3
International Atomic Energy Authority, the
    (IAEA) 273
International Monetary Fund, the (IMF) 298
al-Intifada (the upheaval) (1952) 127
al-Intifada (Safar) (1977) 208
al-Intifada (1991) 246–7
Iran
  in the Iran–Iraq war 224–7, 229–32, 234,
    236–9
  and Iraq 87–8, 136, 158–9, 192–6, 202–6, 212,
    221–4, 272, 297, 310–2
  and the Kurds 114, 159, 192–3, 203–5, 234–6,
    248, 256, 310
  and the Shiʿa 212, 221, 225, 237–8, 246
Iran–Iraq Frontier Treaty, the (1937) 88, 158
Iran–Iraq War, the (1980–8)
  attacks on Iran's oil installations 230–1
  beginning of 224
  economic costs for Iraq 226–7, 239, 241–2
  effects on the Iraqi armed forces 228–9,
    232–3, 238
  effects on the Iraqi regime 226–9, 238–9
  effects on the Kurds 226, 234–6
  effects on the Shiʿa 225, 237–8
  Iran's acceptance of cease-fire 230, 238
  Iraqi arms purchases 229
  Iraqi casualties 239
  Iraq's use of chemical weapons in 229
Iraq Levies, the 73, 78
Iraq Liberation Act, the (1998) 267, 270
Iraq Petroleum Company, the (IPC) 114, 182,
  1931 Agreement 69
  1952 Agreement 124–5
  1961 Law 80 160–1, 174–5, 200

1965 Agreement 175
1972 nationalisation 200
Iraqi Accord Front, the 302–3
Iraqi Communist Party, the (ICP) 84, 89,
    111–14, 118, 120–1, 126, 130, 132–3, 138,
    144–5, 280
    and ʿAbd al-Karim Qasim 148–9, 151–6, 158,
        163
    and Ahmad Hasan al-Bakr 189–90
    and the Baʿth regime (1963) 165
    and the National Patriotic Front 201–2
    and Saddam Husain 207, 210
Iraqi Communist Party, the (Central
    Command) 182, 189
Iraqi Federation of Trade Unions, the (IFTU)
    298–9
Iraqi Governing Council, the (IGC) 284–6, 293,
    299, 304–5
    IGC Resolution 137 (2004) 305
Iraqi High Tribunal, the 313
Iraqi Islamic Party, the (IIP) 280, 295, 302, 307
Iraqi National Accord, the (INA) 266–7
Iraqi National Congress, the (INC) 266–7, 270
Iraqi National Dialogue Front, the 302
Iraqi National List, the 296, 302–3
Iraqi National Oil Company, the (INOC) 175,
    182, 290
Iraqi Women's Network, the 304
al-Isfahani, Ayatollah Abu al-Hasan 55
Islamic Movement of Kurdistan, the 258
Islamic Party (al-Hizb al-Islami), the 154
Islamic Task Organisation, the 221
Ismaʿil, ʿAbd al-Qadir 89
Israel 137, 189, 195, 211
    1948 war with 119–22
    1967 war with 181–2
    1973 war with 200, 202
    1978 Camp David agreement with Egypt 210
    1981 attack on Osirak reactor 229
    and the Gulf war (1991) 245
Istiqlal (Independence) Party, the 111, 127, 132,
    138
Italy 273

Jabr, Salih 90, 107–8, 114, 117–19, 124–7, 129–30
Jadid, Salah 189, 202
al-Jaʿfari, Ibrahim 280, 297–303
Jalili family, the 9–11, 14
Jamaʿat al-ʿUlama (Society of Religious
    Scholars) 221
Jamaʿat al-ʿUlama al-Mujahidin (Society of
    Struggling Religious Scholars) 225
al-Jamali, Fadhil 92–3, 129–32
Jamʿiyya al-Nahda al-Islamiyya (Society of
    Islamic Revival) 33

al-Jannabi, Muhsin 196
jahsh 157, 226, 248
Jawad, Hazim 168
Jawad, Muhammad ʿAli 91
al-Jawahiri, Muhammad Mahdi 63
Jawdat, ʿAli 80, 100, 122–3, 128, 140
al-Jazrawi, Taha Yasin Ramadan 190, 245
Jewish community of Iraq 11, 44, 119–22, 189
    and the *Farhud* in Baghdad (1941) 103, 120
    and Zionism 120–2
al-Jihaz al-Khass (Special [Security] Apparatus)
    188
Jordan
    and Iraq 115–16, 119, 140–1, 262
al-Jumaila tribe, the 169, 179
Jund al-Imam 221

Kabul 271
al-Kailani family, the 11
al-Kailani, Rashid ʿAli 77, 80, 98–103, 107, 150
al-Kailani, Sayyid ʿAbd al-Rahman 21, 44–6, 52
Kashif al-Ghita, ʿAli 265
Kashif al-Ghita, Ayatollah Muhammad 80–1
Kazzar, Nadhim 188, 201
al-Khafaji, Salama 305
al-Khalisi, Ayatollah Mahdi 54–6
Khazaʾil, Shaikh of Muhammara 23–4
Khazaʾil tribal federation, the 9, 12
al-Khoʾi, Ayatollah Sayyid Abu al-Qasim 196,
    221, 246–7, 265
al-Khoʾi, Sayyid ʿAbd al-Majid 280
al-Khoʾi, Sayyid Muhamad Taqi 265
Khomaini, Ayatollah Sayyid Ruhollah 196, 212,
    227
Khuza, Rajaa 304
Khuzestan 88, 159, 194, 223, 225
Kirkuk events, the (1959) 152
Kirkuk referendum 308
Korea, North 272
Kosygin, Alexei 201
Kubba, Muhammad Mahdi 111
Kurdish Regional Assembly, the 254–5, 296, 309
Kurdish Regional Government, the 255, 268,
    309
Kurdistan
    al-Anfal in (1987–8) 235–6
    autonomy agreement (1974) 204
    creation of 'safe havens' in (1991) 248, 254
    and the Iran–Iraq war (1980–8) 219–21, 226,
        234–6
    KDP–PUK fighting in 255–7
    March 1970 manifesto 193
    reactions to British occupation of 33–5, 43
    reactions to Iraqi independence in 62–3,
        65–6, 72

Kurdistan (*cont.*)
  trade unions 299
  the 'twelve-point plan' for (1966) 181
  war in
    (1961–3) 159, 166
    (1964–6) 172–4, 176, 180
    (1968–9) 192
    (1974–5) 203–5
Kurdistan Democratic Party, the (KDP) 157,162,
  166, 203–5, 219–21, 226, 234–5, 307, 309
  and the Kurdish Regional Government 254–5
  and the Mustafa Barzani–Ibrahim Ahmad
    split 130, 153–4, 157, 172, 174, 176
  and the Mustafa Barzani–Jalal Talabani split
    172, 181, 192, 205
  origins of 114
  and the PUK 205, 234–5, 248, 254–8
Kurdistan Democratic Party-Iran (KDP-I) 220,
  256, 310
Kurdistan Front, the 248–9
Kuwait
  crisis over (1961) 159–60
  in the Iran–Iraq war 230
  Iraqi claims to 96, 159, 243
  Iraqi invasion of (1990) 242–4
  Iraqi recognition of (1994) 253
  the war to liberate (1991) *see* Gulf war

land issues
  landownership
    under 'Abd al-Karim Qasim 149–50
    under the Ba'thist regime 197–9, 241–2,
      260–1
    under the monarchy 50–1, 66–9, 82–3, 94,
      131, 133–4
    under the Ottomans 15–17, 19
  land reform 90, 109–10, 131–2, 149–50, 177–8
  land use 66–7, 113, 133–4, 198
Land Settlement Law, the (1932) 69, 83
Law of Administration for the State of Iraq for the
  Transitional Period, the (TAL) 286, 304
Law Governing the Rights and Duties of the
  Cultivators, the (1933) 83, 89
law of personal status (1959) 305
Law School (Baghdad), the 20, 26
League of Iraqi Youth, the 148, 155
League of Nations, the
  and the Iran–Iraq dispute 88
  Iraqi membership of 58, 61, 66, 72–3
  Mandates 41, 51
  Mosul commission 57–8
Liberal Unionist Party, the (LUP) 26

Mahabad Republic, the 110, 114, 154
al-Mahdawi, Fadil 'Abbas 162

Mahdi Army, the (Jaish al-Mahdi) 280, 287, 291,
  293, 307
Mahmud, Nur al-Din 127
Mahmud II, Ottoman Sultan-Caliph 13
al-Majid, 'Ali Hasan 234–6, 244–5, 261
al-Majid, Husain Kamil 244, 261–2
al-Majid, Saddam Kamil 262
al-Majid clan, the 241, 261
al-Maliki, Nuri 303, 305–6, 308, 311, 315
al-Ma'malchi, Amal 305
mamluk pashas, the rule of the 8–14
marshes, destruction of the 264–5
Mar Shimun, the (Assyrian leader) 78
Ma'ruf, Taha Muhi al-Din 206
al-Mashhadani, Subhi Abdallah 298
al-Mashhadi, 'Abd al-Husain 214
Mehmed Namik Pasha 18
de Mello, Sergio 283, 285
Mesopotamian Expeditionary Force, the (MEF)
  31
al-Midfa'i, Jamil 27, 39, 80–1, 94, 100, 107,
  128–9
Midhat Pasha 15–16, 18
militias (after 2003) 277, 280–1, 287–8, 291,
  293–5, 297–8, 304–8, 311, 314–15
Miri Sirf Law, the (1945) 109
Mirjan, 'Abd al-Wahhab 140
Mithaq al-Sha'b (People's Charter) (1935) 80
Mosul events, the (1959) 151–2
Mousa, Hamid Majid 280
Muhammad, 'Aziz 182, 201
Muhammad, Yanar 304
al-Muhammadawi, 'Abd al-Karim 281
Mukhlis, Mawlud 27
Municipal Fees Law, the (1931) 71
Muntafiq tribal federation, the 9, 12, 18, 53
Muslim Brotherhood (al-Ikhwan al-Muslimun),
  the 154, 184, 280
Mustafa, 'Izzat 208
Mustafa, Majid 108
Muthanna Club, the 93, 120

Nahda (Awakening) Party, the 51–2, 61, 70
al-Na'ini, Ayatollah Muhammad Husain 55
al-Najafi, Ahmad al-Safi 63
al-Naqib, Sayyid Talib 21, 23–7, 28, 41, 48
Naqshabandi (sufi) order, the 10, 154
Nasserists in Iraq, the 171–6, 188
National Action Charter, the (1971) 201
National Assembly, the
  (post-1980) 218, 224, 241
  (post-2005) 277, 290, 295–7, 300–1, 305
National Council of the Revolutionary
  Command, the (NCRC) 164, 167, 169,
  177–8

National De-Ba'thification Commission, the 293
National Defence Bill, the (1934) 80
National Defence Council, the 178
National Democratic Party, the (NDP) (al-Hizb al-Watani al-Dimuqrati) 111, 118, 127, 132–3, 138, 144, 147–8, 151, 153, 162
National Front, the (1954) 132
National Guard (al-Haras al-Qawmi), the 165–8
nationalisation
    the 1964 decrees 173–5, 177–8
    of IPC (1972) 200
National Patriotic Front, the 189, 201, 203–4
National Scientific Club, the (Baghdad) 26
al-Nayif, 'Abd al-Razzaq 184
NGOs 278, 304–5, 309
Nizam-i Cedid (the New Order) 13

Office of Reconstruction and Humanitarian Assistance, the (ORHA) 279–82
oil (*see also* Iraq Petroleum Company and Turkish Petroleum Company)
    concessions 59, 69, 161, 175, 199–200, 290
    discovery of (1927) 69
    pipelines 202, 227, 239, 244, 268
    revenues 69,124–5, 133–4, 161, 174–5, 181, 200, 206–7, 226–7, 239, 242, 252, 268, 289–90
    and UN sanctions 244, 252, 264
Organisation of Petroleum Exporting Countries, the (OPEC) 161, 242
Organisation of Women's Freedom in Iraq 304
Oudh Bequest, the 33

al-Pachachi, Hamdi 22, 27, 109–10
al-Pachachi, Muzahim 26–7, 119–20, 123
Palestine 84, 87, 115
    war of 1948 and Iraq's role in 118–22
Parliamentary Bloc, the 110, 123
Partiya Karkeren Kurdistan (Kurdistan Workers' Party) (PKK) 255, 310
Patriotic Union of Kurdistan, the (PUK) 235, 248, 274, 307, 309
    and the KDP 205, 220, 226, 234–5, 254–8, 266, 296
    and the Kurdish Regional Government 254–5
    origins of 205
Peace Partisans, the 126, 132, 148, 151, 155
peasants' associations, the 145–6
peshmerga 157, 180, 193, 205, 236, 257, 274, 307, 309
Poland 278
Popular Army, the 208, 218
Popular Reform Association (Jam'iyya al-Islah al-Sha'bi), the 89–91

Popular Resistance (al-Muqawama al-Sha'biyya), the 145, 151
Presidential Guard, the 244–5

Qadiri (sufi) order, the 10, 21
al-Qa'ida 270–1, 287
Qasim, 'Abd al-Karim, prime minister of Iraq 163–4, 173, 183, 185
    and 'Abd al-Salam 'Arif 139, 147–8, 173
    death of (1963) 163–4
    and the Free Officers 139, 141, 145
    and the ICP 148–9, 153–5
    and Iran 158–9
    and the Kurds 154, 157, 162
    and Kuwait 159–60
    organisation of power 146–7, 153, 162–3
    political views 146–7, 162
    and the UAR 158, 160
Qassemlou, 'Abd al-Rahman 220
al-Qazzaz, Muhammad Salih 70–1, 83, 89
Qazzaz, Sa'id 130

al-Rabita (the League for the Defence of Women's Rights) 148, 155, 218
al-Radi, Husain 138, 148
Rashidiyya schools, the 20
Reform Society, the (Basra) 24, 27
refugees (post-2003) 294, 308–9, 312
Republican Guard, the 169, 176, 179, 184–5, 232, 245–7, 264
Revolutionary Command Council, the (RCC) (1958) 141
    (1968) 187, 190, 208–9, 214, 227–8, 249
al-Rikabi, Fu'ad 138
Rizgari Kurd (Kurdish Liberation) 112
Royal Air Force, the (RAF)
    action against Arab tribes 71
    action against Kurds 54, 66, 72
    bases 65, 75, 102, 117, 136
    as instrument of British policy 60
Rumsfeld, Donald 272
al-Rusafi, Ma'ruf 63
Russia
    and Iraq 252–3, 273

Saadabad Pact, the (1937) 88
al-Sabah, Shaikh Jabir 243
al-Sabah, Shaikh Mubarak 23
al-Sabah family, the 243, 245
al-Sabbagh, Salah al-Din 91, 96, 98–100
Sadat, Anwar 211
al-Sa'di, 'Ali Salih 156, 163–9, 183
al-Sadr, Ayatollah Sayyid Hasan 40
al-Sadr, Ayatollah Sayyid Muhammad Baqir 154, 196–7, 212–13, 221

al-Sadr, Ayatollah Sayyid Muhammad Sadiq
    265, 280
al-Sadr, Sayyid Muhammad 40, 117–18
al-Sadr, Sayyid Muqtada 280–1, 293–4, 300–3,
    307, 312, 314–15
al-Saʿdun, ʿAbd al-Muhsin 53, 56, 58–9, 62–3
al-Saʿdun family, the 18, 21
Saʿid, Fahmi 91, 96
al-Saʿid, Nuri 66, 69, 71–2, 88, 119, 130–2, 143
    and al-ʿAhd 27, 36
    and the Arab world 115–16, 122–3, 134–6, 140–1
    and the Baghdad Pact (1954) 135–6
    death of (1958) 142
    and King Faisal I 62, 65, 77
    and the Kurds 65–6, 72, 108
    and the officer corps 45, 95–100, 107, 137, 140,
        142
    organisation of power 127–30, 132–4, 137–8,
        142
    and Palestine 94–5, 97, 116, 121–2
    political views 106–8, 126, 135
    and the Regent ʿAbd al-Ilah 103, 109, 116, 119,
        124, 126
Saleh, Hadi 298–9
Salman, Mahmud 91, 96
Salter, Lord (Report) 134
al-Samarrai, ʿAbd al-Khaliq 190, 201, 214
al-Samarrai, Faʾiq 111
San Remo Conference, the (1920) 40
Saudi Arabia
    and Iraq 135, 229, 242, 272
al-Shaʿb (People's) Party 69
Shabib, Kamil 91, 96
Shabib, Talib 167
'shadow state' the 259–67, 304, 308
Shakir, Saʿdun 201
Shammar tribe, the 9, 293
Shanshal, Siddiq 111
Sharaf, Sharif, regent of Iraq (1941) 101
Shatt al-ʿArab waterway 87–8, 158–9, 195, 204,
    223–5, 243
Shawkat, Naji 22, 77, 99, 102
Shiʿa, the
    and ʿAbd al-Karim Qasim 154–5
    and ʿAbd al-Salam ʿArif 173
    and Baʿthist rule 194–7, 208–9, 212–13, 221,
        225, 234, 237–8, 246–7, 264–5
    and the British occupation 33, 44–5
    and community-based political organisations
        33, 51–2, 70, 154–5, 173, 182, 208, 212,
        221, 225, 237–8
    and the 1920 Iraqi revolt 40–4
    and the monarchy 50–3, 54–6, 61, 77, 79–82,
        85, 92–3, 107–8, 117, 125, 131–2, 135, 138
    and the Ottomans 12, 22–3, 32–3

al-Shirazi, Ayatollah Muhammad Taqi 40–1, 43
al-Shirazi, Mirza Muhammad Rida 40, 43
al-Shishakli, ʿAdib 123, 131
Shuʿaiba, the battle of (1915) 31
Shurish (Revolution) 112
Sidqi, Bakr 78, 80–1, 84–6, 88–91, 95
Sirri, Rifʿat al-Hajj 128, 139
al-Sistani, Ayatollah Sayyid ʿAli 265, 280, 283–4,
    286, 296, 300
Slaibi, Saʿid 169, 176, 184
Socialist People's Party (Hizb al-Umma
    al-Ishtiraki), the 125, 127
Sovereignty Council, the 147
Spain 273
Special Supreme Military Court (Mahkamat
    Al-ʿAskariyya al-ʿUlya al-Khassa), the ['the
    People's Court' (Makhamat al-Shaʿb)] 162
strike action 71–2, 83, 90, 112–14
Suez Crisis, the 137–8
Sulaiman, Hikmat 22, 80, 83–4, 86–91, 95
Supreme Council for Islamic Revolution in Iraq,
    the (SCIRI) 237–8, 246, 263, 280, 296–8,
    300–3, 307, 310–12
al-Suwaidi, Naji 63
al-Suwaidi, Tawfiq 22, 62, 111, 113, 124–5, 128
al-Suwaidi family, the 26
Sykes-Picot Agreement, the (1916) 34–5
Syria
    Charter of Joint National Action 211
    and Iraq 115–16, 122–3, 131, 140, 167–8, 202–3,
        210–11, 214, 227, 245, 311–12

al-Takriti, Barzan Ibrahim 201, 244. 314
al-Takriti, Hammad Shihab 185
al-Takriti, Hardan 168, 184, 187, 190
al-Takriti, Husain Rashid 244
al-Takriti, Sibʿawi Ibrahim 244
al-Takriti, Wathban Ibrahim 254, 266
Takritis, the 190, 207, 217
Talabani, Jalal 172, 181, 192–3, 205, 220, 234, 249,
    255, 257, 274
    president of Iraq 297, 303, 311–12
Taleban, the 271
Talib, Naji 181
Tanzimat (Ottoman reforms) 14–19
    Land Law (1858) 15–17
    Vilayet Law (1864) 15
trade unions 70–2, 83, 145–6, 151, 201, 278,
    298–9
Tribal Civil and Criminal Disputes Regulation,
    the 38
tribes and tribalism
    and ʿAbd al-Karim Qasim 149–50
    and the ʿArifs 169, 171, 175–7
    and the British Mandate 38, 42–4, 50–1

and the *mamluks* 8–13
and the monarchy 50, 80–2, 84–5, 90
and the Ottomans 16–22
and Saddam Husain 260–3
Tulfah, 'Adnan Khairallah 209, 240–1, 266
Turkey
    and Iraq 86–8, 115–16, 134–6, 268, 274
    and the Kurds 53–4, 206, 236, 248, 255–6, 310
    and the Mosul question 53–4, 57–8, 88
Turkish Petroleum Company (TPC) [after
1929 Iraq Petroleum Company]
    1925 Agreement 58–9
    and the discovery of oil (1927) 69
Turkmen, the 11, 31, 64, 72, 152, 258, 284, 302, 308

umana' Saddam (Saddam's faithful) 259
al-'Umari, Amin 91
al-'Umari, Arshad 103, 113–14, 132
al-'Umari, Mustafa 126–7
United Arab Emirates, the 253
United Arab Republic, the (UAR) 140–1, 147–8, 158–60, 167, 172
United Iraqi Alliance, the (UIA) 296–7, 299, 301, 315
United Kingdom (*see* Great Britain)
United National Front, the (1957) 138–9
United Nations Monitoring, Verification and Inspection Commission, the (UNMOVIC) 269, 271–4
United Nations Sanctions Committee, the 268
United Nations Security Council, the
    and the Iran–Iraq war 230
    and Iraq's invasion of Kuwait (1990) 244
    and the Kuwait crisis (1961) 160
    and the 'oil for food' resolutions 252–3, 264, 268
    Resolution 688 (1991) 248
    Resolution 986 (1996) 252, 268
    Resolution 1284 (1999) 269
    Resolution 1441 (2002) 272–3
    Resolution 1483 (2003) 283, 290
    Resolution 1546 (2004) 292
    and sanctions against Iraq 244, 249–54, 268–70
    and the US-led invasion of Iraq (2003) 271–3
United Nations Special Commission on Disarmament, the (UNSCOM) 250–4, 269
United Nations Special Rapporteur on Human Rights, the 253

United Popular Front, the (1952) 125, 127
USA
    invasion of Iraq (Operation Iraqi Freedom) 274–6
        military campaign 274
        troop numbers 275
    and Iraq 136, 182, 203, 230–1, 243–6, 248, 253–6, 264, 266, 276
    and the Kurds 203, 205, 256–8
    military casualties in Iraq 275, 295
    military occupation of Iraq 277–92
    US Congress and Iraq 267, 270, 273, 315
USSR 112, 287
    and Iraq 135, 158, 182, 189–90, 194, 200–2, 207, 229–31
    Iraqi–Soviet Treaty of Friendship and Co-operation, the (1972) 200, 203, 207, 224
    and the Kurds 110, 156, 158

al-Wandawi, Mundhir 165, 168
Washington Agreement, the (1998) 256–8
Watani (Patriotic) Party, the 51–2, 69–70
al-Wathba (the leap) (1948) 117–19
weapons of mass destruction (WMD)
    Iraq's development of 229, 250–1, 262
    failure to find evidence of (2003–4) 283
    Iraq's use of 229, 235–6
    suspicions of Iraq's development of 251, 269, 271–3
Wilson, Sir Arnold 36, 38–9, 41
Women's Alliance for Democratic Iraq 304
Workers' Federation of Iraq, the 85

Yahya, Tahir 167–8, 182–3
Yamulki, 'Aziz 91
al-Yawwar, Ghazi 293
Yazdi, Ayatollah Kazim 32, 43
Yazidis, the 10, 31, 72, 84, 302, 308
Young, Sir Hilton (Report) 67–9
Young Ottomans, the 20
Young Turks, the 20–2
Yusuf, Yusuf Salman (Comrade Fahd) 111–12, 114, 120–1

Za'im, Husni 122
Zaki, Amin 100
al-Zarqawi, Abu Mus'ab 287
Al-Zawra' (newspaper) 17–18
Zubaid tribal federation, the 9